DIALECTS OF THE TRIBE
POSTMODERN AMERICAN POETS AND POETRY

Other Books by Lewis Putnam Turco

Nonfiction

The Book of Forms, A Handbook of Poetics, Revised and Expanded Fourth Edition, 2012
La Famiglia / The Family, Memoirs, 2009
Satan's Scourge: A Narrative of the Age of Witchcraft in England and New England 1580-1697, 2009
Fantaseers, A Book of Memories, 2005
The Book of Dialogue, 2004
The Book of Literary Terms, 1999
The Life and Poetry of Manoah Bodman, Bard of the Berkshires, 1999
How to Write a Mi££ion, with Ansen Dibell and Orson Scott Card, 1995
Emily Dickinson, Woman of Letters, 1993
The Public Poet, Five Lectures on the Art and Craft of Poetry, 1993
Il Dialogo, Italian translation by Sylvia Biasi of *Dialogue,* 1992
Visions and Revisions of American Poetry, 1986 won Melville Cane Award for literary criticism Poetry Society of America
The New Book of Forms, 1986
Poetry: An Introduction through Writing, 1973
The Literature of New York, 1970
The Book of Forms, A Handbook of Poetics, 1968

Fiction and Poetry

Epitaphs for the Poets, 2012
The Gathering of the Elders and Other Poems, 2010
The Museum of Ordinary People and Other Stories, 2008
Fearful Pleasures: The Complete Poems, 2007
The Collected Lyrics of Lewis Turco / Wesli Court, 2004
A Book of Fears, Poems, with Italian Translations by Joseph Alessia, 1998
The Shifting Web: New and Selected Poems, 1989
The Compleat Melancholick, 1985
American Still Lifes, 1981
Pocoangelini: A Fantography & Other Poems, 1971
The Inhabitant, 1970
Awaken, Bells Falling: Poems 1959-1967, 1968
First Poems, 1960

DIALECTS OF THE TRIBE

Postmodern American Poets and Poetry

Lewis Putnam Turco

Stephen F. Austin State University Press
Nacogdoches ★ Texas

Copyright © 2012 Lewis Putnam Turco
All rights reserved.

Stephen F. Austin State University Press
P.O. Box 13007, SFA Station
Nacogdoches, TX   75962-3007
sfasu.edu/sfapress
sfapress@sfasu.edu

Cover Imgage: *Tonic Conk*, Scott Runnels
Book Design: Kristi Warren, Laura Davis
Editing: Laura Davis, Brittany O'Sullivan, Lauren Hawkins
Manufactured in the United States of America

LIBRARY OF CONGRESS IN PUBLICATION DATA
Turco, Lewis Putnam
Dialects of the Tribe / Lewis Turco
p. cm.
ISBN: 978-1-936205-30-1
1. Poetry-criticism. 2. Poetics - -20th Century 3. Poetics - 21th Century 4. Poetry - Neoformalism

Except in the United States of America, this book is sold subject to the condition that it shall not, by way of trade or otherwise, be lent, resold, hired out, or otherwise circulated without the publisher's prior consent in any form of binding or cover other than that in which it is published and without a similar condition including this condition being imposed on the subsequent purchaser.

The scanning, uploading and distribution of this book via the Internet or via any other means without the permission of the publisher is illegal and punishable by law. Please purchase only authorized electronic editions, and do not participate in or encourage electronic piracy of copyrighted materials. Your support of the author's rights is appreciated.

The paper used in this book meets the requirements of ANSI/NISO Z39.48-1992 (R1997) (Permanence of Paper)

LINES TO BE ETCHED ON A WINDOW
In memory of Donald Justice

Clearly, you may see clear through me,
As though I were not here.

Acknowledgments

The author owes acknowledgment for original publication of versions of some of these essays, under various titles to these periodicals, books, and collections:

American Poetry for "Delmore Schwartz."

The Cloverdale Review for "Williams' Prosody."

Eclectic Literary Forum for "Howard Nemerov."

The Hollins Critic for "Amiri Baraka," "Donald Justice," "W. D. Snodgrass," "Miller Williams," "R. S. Gwynn," "Weldon Kees," and "Vern Rutsala."

The Mad River Review for "James Dickey."

The *Michigan Quarterly Review* for "Robert Hayden" and "Radcliffe Squires."

Modern Poetry Studies for "Richard Emil Braun."

The New Orleans Review for "John Ashbery."

The New York Quarterly for "Frank O'Hara."

The Poet's Page for "Academic Poets and Postmodern Period Style" and "Richard Wilbur."

American Poets Since World War Two, Third Series, edited by R. S. Gwynn, Detroit: Gale Research, 1992, for "Dana Gioia.

Companion to Contemporary American Literature from the Editors of The Hollins Critic, edited by R. H. W. Dillard and Amanda Cockrell, Farmington Hills: Twayne Publishers, 2002 for "Amiri Baraka," "R. S. Gwynn," "Donald Justice," "W. D. Snodgrass," "and Miller Williams."

John Ciardi: Measure of the Man, edited by Vince Clemente, Fayetteville: University of Arkansas Press, 1987, for "John Ciardi."

Miller Williams and the Poetry of the Particular, edited by Michael Burns, Columbia: University of Missouri Press, 1991, for "Miller Williams."

Robert Hayden: Essays on the Poetry, edited by Laurence Goldstein and Robert Chrisman, Ann Arbor: University of Michigan Press, 2002 and *Robert Hayden* (Bloom's Modern Critical Views), edited by Harold Bloom, Chelsea House Publishers, 2005, for "Robert Hayden."

"Struggling for Wings": The Art of James Dickey, edited by Robert Kirschten, Columbia: University of South Carolina Press, 1997, for "James Dickey."

Short portions of various of these essays have appeared in *American Weave*, *College English*, *The Dictionary of Literary Biography Yearbooks* for the years 1983-1986, *Escarpments*, *Hellas*, *Lake Effect*, *New York Quarterly*, *Poet*, *Poetry*, *Prairie Schooner*, *The Saturday Review of Literature*, *The Sewanee Review*, *Shenandoah*, and *Voices*.

"Lines to be Etched on a Window" is reprinted from *The Gathering of the Elders and Other Poems* by Wesli Court, Scottsdale: Star Cloud Press, 2010.

Contents

Introduction   13

Chapter One. The Academic Poets   19

Delmore Schwartz   23
Richard Eberhart   27
Richard Wilbur   30
Elizabeth Bishop   33
Howard Nemerov   37
Randall Jarrell   43
Theodore Roethke   46
Karl Shapiro   51
Louis O. Coxe   54

Chapter Two. Black Mountain and the Beat Generation   59

Charles Olson   68
Robert Creeley   72
Robert Duncan   75
Joel Oppenheimer   79
David Meltzer   80
Jerome Rothenberg   81
Lawrence Ferlinghetti   82
Allen Ginsberg   86
Gregory Corso   89

Chapter Three. The Confessional Poets.   91

John Ciardi   93
W. D. Snodgrass   98
John Berryman   105
Robert Lowell   110
Anne Sexton   114
Maxine Kumin   117
Sylvia Plath   119

Chapter Four. The Poetry of Protest — 125

Robert Hayden — 129
Gwendolyn Brooks — 135
Amiri Baraka — 138
Denise Levertov — 142
Adrienne Rich — 145
Carolyn Kizer — 149

Chapter Five. Neosurrealism — 151

Weldon Kees — 152
Robert Bly — 156
James Dickey — 160
James Wright — 163
Vern Rutsala — 168
Richard Emil Braun — 173

Chapter Six. American Plainstyle — 177

William Stafford — 179
David Wagoner — 182
Richard Hugo — 184

Chapter Seven. Abstractionism — 187

Radcliffe Squires — 189
Frank O'Hara — 193
John Ashbery — 197

Chapter Eight. Neoformalism — 203

Donald Justice — 204
Miller Williams — 211
Robert Mezey — 221
Dana Gioia — 226
R. S. Gwynn — 235

Appendix 247

The Sullen Art: A Postmodern Radio Interview by David Ossman

Chapter Bibliographies 256

Index 273

"Since our concern was speech, and speech impelled us
To purify the dialect of the tribe
And urge the mind to aftersight and foresight,
Let me disclose the gifts reserved for age
To set a crown upon your lifetime's effort."

— W. H. Auden, from "Little Gidding."

INTRODUCTION

I.

In the history of literature there have always been two major types of poetry, religious and social. In pre-scientific cultures, the "words of power" associated with the gods or God were always controlled by a caste of priests or priestesses who wove them into various ritual religious formats including prayers, liturgies, incantations, curses, oaths, prophecies, and so forth. This is religious or "priest-poetry," and it was of basic importance in every culture. It came to be called Platonic or Romantic, Dionysian or ritual, emotional or "natural" poetry.

Social poetry consists basically of entertainments: songs, word games, stories, plays, puzzles, and so forth. In many ways this type of poetry is as basic as religious poetry, for it is part of the folk life of a culture. It passes on the myths and legends, the lore and the crafts of the people. Without it, there would be no culture. Nevertheless, the class of priests tended to disdain this kind of poetry, which came to be called variously Aristotelian or Classical, Apollonian or secular, intellectual or "artificial." Both types of poetry have always flourished in Europe, and both have always been "formal" there.

In Colonial America religious poetry was paramount, especially in New England. America was a clean slate upon which might be written the Word of God; it was to be the New Jerusalem, dedicated to the establishment of the Kingdom of God on Earth. The land was to be filled with Light, a Light that had been obscured in the corruption of the Old World. The Bible was *The* Book. Art for Art's sake, or for any other than God's sake, was corrupt, like the art of Europe — or, if not corrupt, at best it was frivolous. If language did not serve the purposes of pragmatic communication, it was to serve the purpose of the Church Militant.

However, if America were a clean slate, ought not the literature it produced to be written in a new way? How else to differentiate corrupt literature from purified literature?

As America grew and Puritanism was transformed; as other religions came into America, this attitude toward literature was also changed. But a new element worked itself into the fabric of development: The colonists more and more saw themselves as an autonomous body of people. Pride of country demanded that America be identifiably America, not England-in-America. Americans wanted a unique American national personality, separate from that of the mother country.

A distinction may be made between the "amateur" and the "professional" poet. The former is one who uses poetry as a vehicle for a particular purpose, as Edward Taylor (1642?-1729) did. The latter is simply one who dedicates her life to writing poetry. Thus, Anne Bradstreet (1612?-1672) was America's first "professional poet." Edward Taylor was the first "amateur" and the first poet to evince what would later be seen as Emersonian qualities. There is a third possibility, however, besides the professional and the amateur poet. There is the "agonist," the theoretician of poetry who worries about what poetry is or ought to be, and how one ought to go about writing it, which in America led to Ralph Waldo Emerson in the nineteenth century, during what has been called the "Romantic" movement in England and America, of which Emerson is popularly supposed to be a member. In fact, however, although Emerson when he was a young man had all the tools of a professional poet, apparently what he most wanted to be was a priest-poet. As a result, he became that third type of poet, the agonist, emphasis on *the*; he was America's first and, so far, foremost theoretician of poetry.

When he was young, Emerson could write perfectly acceptable, standard verse in any formal manner he chose, as Hyatt H. Waggoner pointed out in "Chapter II, The Apprentice Years: Composer of Verses" of his book *Emerson As Poet* (Princeton, NJ: Princeton University Press, 1974). In fact, he was a virtuoso performer in the old British formal tradition. He could do anything he wished to do with the English language, but it came too easily to him, apparently, and he felt uneasy about his facility. He agonized over this lack of difficulty he experienced young. As a result, he attempted to roughen up his meters, and his mature writing style is more "amateur"-seeming than his youthful work. Clearly, he *chose* to do what he did in his later work. Emerson began to explore the convergence of prose and verse.

Most of Emerson's later poems develop from prose germs, as if the poems were somehow simply the upper range of ordinary language. Emerson's prose is hardly less full of tropes than his young work was, and often it impresses in the same way the poems do, and yet the question of the frontier between them remains. Emerson wondered what gulf is crossed — if any — in getting from one to the other. It seems that if many of his poems lie closer to the boundary, they compel some awareness of qualities in the performance that point both ways. It's not just a matter of mixing vulgar diction with a certain amount of gorgeousness — but that must be part of it.

For two centuries, until the end of the first decade of the twentieth century, much if not most of American poetry had been derivative and imitative, a sub-branch of British poetry, and this is what fretted Emerson deeply. Only four or five poets had been exceptions to this rule. Ever since William Cullen Bryant, who has been called "the father of

American poetry," though some American literati had been kicking against the traces, most had been unable to break away from traditional accentual-syllabic metrics in practice, including Emerson himself, the agonist for a new poetics. Most of the trouble seemed to be technical — American poets had difficulty in getting personal voices out of the old forms. Emerson prescribed a remedy: invent new forms; cast off the burden of tradition and allow American poems to grow naturally, like plants; operate through intuition in order to attain Vision, which is poetry's core, and the form will follow "organically."

Perhaps, as someone who wished to be a priest-poet, Emerson simply had a theory that poetry ought to be "revealed" to someone who was truly a poet, and that one therefore ought not to have to "think" about what he was doing. Apparently, when he "thought" about metrics, it came very easily to Emerson, and he hated it, so when Walt Whitman came along with his system of grammatic prose-parallels, which Emerson must have recognized as the system used in the Bible, he hailed Whitman as a genius of a "poetic" prose style.

It is true that Emerson's prose sometimes came close to being more "poetic" than his verse, but what he probably wanted was some hybrid system that was neither verse nor prose. Such a system cannot exist, however, because *verse* is "metered language" and *prose* is "unmetered language," and one cannot have unmetered metered language. The Modernists soon came up with a term, however, that covered what Emerson wanted, "free verse," which makes no sense at all.

Emerson's great white whale of American literature Walt Whitman became the exemplar of Emerson's agonisms, the guidon-bearer of the Modernist revolution of the early twentieth century. Because of the old convention that poetry ought to be written in verse, and because people still thought that prose could not be a vehicle for poetry (even Emerson suspected that this might be the case), the twentieth century had to have a new term to apply to prose poems; hence, the confusing term "free verse" was borrowed from the French Symbolists of the nineteenth century who called non-syllabic prosodies *vers libre*. Whitman never used the term; probably, he never heard of it. He knew he was writing prose poems. If Emerson had been born a bit later he would very likely have been writing lineated prose and calling it "free verse," and perhaps he would have been as happy as many ensuing "poets" who hadn't a clue what they were doing and were happy not to have to think about it.

Reacting against the pervasive English conventions of the eighteenth and nineteenth centuries, the "Modernists" who followed from Whitman's prose-poem examples were wildly experimental. The so-called (later on) "Modernist" period, which began about 1912 and lasted through the 1920s, came up with all sorts of prosodies that were called "free verse," though in fact a system is a system, even that of Whitman, and each system can be analyzed, identified, and given a descriptive name. Instead, so many poets wrote to justify prose poetry as a kind of "verse" that "free verse" came to be accepted as a term that actually describes something that exists.

Whitman's influence upon twentieth-century American poetry was not, however, merely prosodic and technical. Like the English Romantics he was the champion of the "common man" and of ordinary speech, and he was the first American poet to speak in prose poetry in what we today would call the "confessional" voice, the subjective first person singular, as Emerson had demanded in his essay "The Poet." Furthermore, he made the egopoetic "I" into a symbol of the New World as a whole — Whitman maintained that he spoke *for* America, not merely for himself.

By the time World War II was over in 1945 the Modernist period was pretty well past, though most of its exemplars were still living: T. S. Eliot, Ezra Pound, Gertrude Stein, E. E. Cummings, Marianne Moore, Conrad Aiken, Amy Lowell, Robinson Jeffers, and Carl Sandburg to name a few. But there was another group of poets also, the late American Romantic formalists including Edwin Arlington Robinson, Robert Frost, Archibald MacLeish, Edna St. Vincent Millay, and the Southern "Fugitives" including John Crowe Ransom and Alan Tate.

The poets who returned to civilian life after having served in the armed forces, like Howard Nemerov, John Ciardi, Karl Shapiro, James Dickey, Allen Ginsberg, and Randall Jarrell, or as conscientious objectors like Robert Lowell and William Stafford, and their female counterparts such as Elizabeth Bishop, Denise Levertov and others, had two literary choices, basically: They could either return to the earlier formalism of the pre-Modernist nineteenth century and become post-Romantics, or they could continue the well-laid-out and well-traveled road of the Modernists and become post-Modernists. The so-called "academic poets" of the 1950s chose the former route, and almost everybody else chose the latter. All of these people, many of them subsequently hopping from one "school" to the other, were dubbed "Post-Modernists."

II.

Perhaps W. H. Auden (1907-1973) was responsible for the post-Modernist period style of post-war America; perhaps he brought it with him from England — or perhaps it was simply a style that was bound to happen and it was being developed by many in his generation because literary forward motion could no longer be envisioned. This became what was known as "academic poetry" in the United States, and it persisted even into the so-called "free verse" (prose) poems of the post-war generations. Some of those poets who were identified as "academic poets" because they taught and were formalists were Theodore Roethke (1908-1963), John Berryman (1914-1972), Delmore Schwartz (1913-1966), Richard Eberhart (1904-2005), Richard Wilbur (1921—), Elizabeth Bishop (1911-1979), Howard Nemerov (1920-1991), Randall Jarrell (1914-1965), and Karl Shapiro (1913-2000). A subdivision of these poets whose vanguard consisted of W. D. Snodgrass (1926-2009), Robert Lowell (1917-1977), and John Berryman, became known, beginning in 1959, as "The Confessional School." Women were prominent among these writers, particularly Anne Sexton (1928-1974), Sylvia Plath (1932-1963), and Maxine Kumin (1925—). Their hallmark was the ex-tremely personal poem. Snodgrass' lyrics regarding marital breakup and divorce, *Heart's Needle*, led the way back up the aisle.

INTRODUCTION

The Black Mountain school originated at the sometime Black Mountain College of Asheville, North Carolina, in the 1950s and gave rise to an anti-academic academy whose "Rector," Charles Olson (1910-1970), was the center of attraction for many of the disaffiliated writers of the period, including some who were known in other contexts as the Beats or "the Beat Generation" and the San Francisco School. Other members of the school were Robert Creeley (1926-2005), Denise Levertov (1923-1997), and Robert Duncan (1919-1988). The "Beats," led by Allen Ginsberg (1926-1997), included Jack Kerouac (1922-1969), Lawrence Ferlinghetti (1919-), and Gregory Corso (1930-2001). Kenneth Rexroth (1905-1982) was the guru of the San Francisco School. All of these writers, often grouped by the public under the rubric "beatnik," stood against the poets of the academy who were seen as rigidly formal and genteelly correct.

Another movement of the period was the poetry of protest, which included the civil rights, anti-war, and feminist movements. Langston Hughes (1902-1967) was the prototypical civil rights poet; others were Gwendolyn Brooks (1917-2001), Robert Hayden (1913-1980), and Amiri Baraka (*ne* Leroi Jones, 1934-). Hughes was a professional writer, not a teacher like Brooks and Hayden. Baraka, a member of the Black Mountain School, became the most militant of the Black poets but wound up in the academy like many members of all the schools. Denise Levertov, also a Black Mountaineer, made her reputation primarily as an anti-war poet, and Adrienne Rich (1929-) became the paradigmatic feminist poet, although the academic Carolyn Kizer (1925-) was perhaps the better writer.

The "deep image surrealism" of the Post-Modernist Robert Bly (1926-), although the term was invented by Baraka, was a late development of Ezra Pound's and Amy Lowell's Modernist Imagism. Identified as a part of the anti-academic movement, it supplanted formal poetry in the academy and burgeoned for years — throughout the 1970's and 1980's — in the graduate writing workshops until it at last gave way before the rise of The New Formalism in the 1990s.

The experimentalism of the 1950s was carried on into the twenty-first century by a school calling themselves, after the periodical they established, The $L=A=N=G=U=A=G=E$ Poets. The modern poet has generally been expected to make leaps of the imagination that surprise the reader, to make associations that others perhaps would not have made. Not everyone is capable of following the poet in these leaps. It is evident that the difficulty readers of post-modernist poetry have with John Ashbery (1927-) and others of the so-called New York School, and of the later "Language poets," is that they jump from one association to another without intervening transitions— it is a Modernist technique, one that Ezra Pound emphasized in the original draft of T. S. Eliot's "The Waste Land" by editing out those transitions and leaving only the narrative and dramatic fragments and the abstract syntax that mirror the fragmentation and technological leaps of the twentieth century. It is a technique from which Wallace Stevens forged a career of writing poetry for himself, not for readers, but that some readers loved anyway (see Lewis Turco, "The Waste Land Reconsidered" in *Visions and Revisions of American Poetry*, Fayetteville, AR: Univ. of Arkansas Press, 1986).

Nevertheless, this new kind of poetry began displacing Robert Bly's "deep imagism" as the "avant garde" movement of the 1980s. It made inroads on the West Coast where most of the L=A=N=G=U=A=G=E poets resided, but in 1986 signs of a further spread became evident, through chapbook publications from the "alternative press" movement, to New England and the South. By 1992 these two schools of "abstract" poetry had spread everywhere, and Ashbery in the 1990's was the most lionized poet in the United States. By century's end the only other school vying with the abstract poets for the literary spotlight was The New Formalists led by Dana Gioia, Marilyn Hacker, R. S. Gwynn and others.

By 1983 there had begun to be widespread rumors of a return to formalism in American poetry. By 1986 those rumors had turned into a full-fledged movement, for that was a considerable year for what critics and readers had begun to call "Neoformalism" or "The New Formalism" in American poetry. The Philip Dacey and David Jauss neoformalist anthology *Strong Measures* appeared during the late winter of 1985-86; it was the first major anthology of formal poetry to be published since the so-called "War of the Anthologies" of the late 1950s and early 1960s between the "Academic Poets" and the "Beat Generation."

Miller Williams' *Patterns of Poetry* was published in August of the same year. It differed from the Dacey-Jauss book in that it was more specifically focused upon the traditional structures of poetry, and it included work by poets ranging back to the Middle Ages. Lewis Turco's *The New Book of Forms* — an updated and enlarged edition of *The Book of Forms: A Handbook of Poetics* (1968), the earliest Neoformalist document, appeared in November.

During the previous score of years before the pivotal year 1986, *The Mississippi Review* had been nearly alone, except for X. J. Kennedy's formalist 1972 magazine *Counter/Measures*, in spotlighting the subject of form in poetry: in 1977 it had published *Freedom and Form: American Poets Respond*. Poets had been asked to submit a poem and then to write a short comment upon its composition and organization. Contributors to that issue included Richard Eberhart, William Stafford, Vern Rutsala, X.J. Kennedy, Lewis Turco and Richard Wilbur. A decade later, in 1987, another formalist book following the same format was published, David Lehman's *Ecstatic Occasions, Expedient Forms*. Contributors included John Ashbery, Robert Creeley, Dana Gioia, Marilyn Hacker, Anthony Hecht, John Hollander, Richard Kenney, Brad Leithauser, Joyce Carol Oates, Molly Peacock, Louis Simpson (who had been one of the three editors of the original showcase of the "Academic Poets," *The New Poets of England and America*, which had been the first shot fired in "the War of the Anthologies" in 1957), Lewis Turco, Mona Van Duyn, and Richard Wilbur— a real potpourri of both the older formalist poets and Neoformalists, plus many antiformalists, young and old.

Lewis Putnam Turco
Dresden, Maine
3 August 2010

CHAPTER ONE
The Academic Poets

Syntax — word order in a sentence — and diction are related, they depend upon one another, but they are not the same thing. Syntax is concerned with the form of the sentence; diction has to do with its tone and style — a "manner of speaking." "Poetic" diction is a manner of speaking designed specifically for writing in the genre of poetry. For instance, in ordinary middle-class speech one might say, "A thought of grief came to me alone." In this sentence the syntax is "normal": the subject comes first, then the predicate. But in Wordsworth's "Ode: Intimations of Immortality..." the syntax is reversed: "To me alone there came a thought of grief." The two sentences say exactly the same thing, but its tone has been "elevated" through syntactical inversion.

Poetic diction has nothing to do with mode — prose or verse. Walt Whitman wrote in prose mode, but his diction was the same elevated poetic diction that William Wordsworth used in verse mode. Opening Whitman's poems at random, one may find examples everywhere: Section 4 of "The Return of the Heroes," for instance, opens with this line: "When late I sang sad was my voice." This passage in normal syntax would be written, "My voice was sad when I sang late[ly]"; or, in middle-class diction, "My voice was sad when I sang recently," or even, "When I recently sang my voice was sad." Much more interesting was the idiosyncratic poetic diction of Emily Dickinson, as in the poem that begins, "Of Course — I prayed — / And did God Care? / He cared as much as on the Air / A Bird had stamped her foot —".

In every era there are always two sorts of poetic diction: that to be found in what David Perkins in the second volume of his *A History of Modern Poetry* called a "period style," as we have here been discussing in terms of the nineteenth century Romantic style, and any number of "idiosyncratic styles" invented by individual poets. Such writers we call "stylists." The 19th-century poet Gerard Manley Hopkins sounded little like his contemporaries; here is the opening of "Hurrahing in Harvest": "Summer ends now; now, barbarous in beauty, the stooks arise / Around; up above, what wind-walks! what lovely behaviours / Of silk-sack clouds! has wilder, wilful-wavier / Meal-drift moulded ever and melted across skies?" Clearly, this is "poetic diction," but in Hopkins' case it has less to do with rearrangements of syntax than with effects on the sonic level of language and with vocabulary.

The English-language Neoclassical period of the eighteenth century also had both its period style and its idiosyncratic styles. Alexander Pope exemplifies (we are told) the best of the period style, as in lines 259-60 of the "Essay on Man": "What if the foot, ordain'd the dust to tread, / Or hand, to toil, aspir'd to be the head?" To flesh this passage out in ordinary prose is to illustrate the difference between ordinary and elevated language: "What if the foot, ordained to tread the dust; or the hand, ordained to toil, aspired to be the head?" Poetic diction is generally intended to intensify the aural experience; perhaps, however, in the hands of most poets what poetic diction actually does is to mask inanity.

Samuel Johnson's contemporary Christopher Smart sometimes wrote in the poetic diction of the Neoclassical period style, as in Section VII of "Hymn to the Supreme Being": "Yet hold, presumption, nor too fondly climb, / And thou too hold, O horrible despair!" Considerably before Whitman he also wrote poems in the prose mode; however, in those poems Smart's poetic diction turned away from the period style and became idiosyncratic, as in "Of the Sun and the Moon": "For the Sun's at work to make me a garment & the Moon is at work for my wife. / For the Wedding Garments of all men are prepared in the Sun against the day of acceptance. / For the Wedding Garments of all women are prepared in the Moon against the day of their purification." Here, the syntax is normal, but the form of his sentences is based upon the schema anaphora (the repetition of an initial word or phrase), and the sensory level of the passage is unusual and arresting.

Another poet of that period who wrote in both prose and verse mode, William Blake, had his own poetic diction, but it was the same or quite similar in both modes. The syntax of this so-called "pre-Romantic" style was more ordinary than that of the succeeding Romantics, as in the beginning of "A Little Girl Lost" from *Songs of Experience*: "Children of the future age, / Reading this indignant page, / Know that in a former time / Love, sweet love, was thought a crime." This was a verse poem, of course, but "Creation" is prose: "I must create a system, or be enslaved by another man's. / I will not reason compare [an inversion: 'compare reason']. My business is to create."

"In the ten years following the Second World War," James E. B. Breslin wrote, "literary modernism, like an aging evangelical religion, had rigidified into orthodoxy. In fact, with the publication of the widely used second edition of *Understanding Poetry* (1950), modernism had been codified into a textbook. The most conspicuous feature of the writing produced by younger poets Robert Lowell, James Merrill, W. S. Merwin, Richard Wilbur, for instance — was their revival of the very traditional forms that modernist poets had sought to dismantle; the predominant mode became the well-made symbolist poem. Yet in the modern era, the very existence of an identifiable mode, much less its perfection, is self-discrediting, so that during the fifties the predominant mode came increasingly to feel limited, excluding, impoverished" (xiv). By the end of the decade it seemed to many readers of contemporary poetry almost as though Modernism had never happened.

The reaction against Modernism had begun as early as the 1930s in the work of the British poet W.H. Auden and his Oxford University contemporaries including Stephen Spender and C. Day Lewis, but the reaction was not a revulsion against the poetry of Eliot, Pound, Yeats, and the other high Modernists so much as it was a feeling of frustration with the apparent impossibility of continuing to explore the outer edges of twentieth-century expression. Auden's first collection *Poems* appeared in 1930, and in it can be perceived the beginnings of the post-Modernist period style.

Auden and his group in the pre-World War II period blended traditionally formal verse structures with an urbane conversational style, as in Auden's "What's the Matter?" — "To lie flat on the back with the knees flexed / And sunshine on the soft receptive belly / Or face-down, the insolent spine relaxed, / No more compelled to cower or to bully, is good; and good to see them passing by / Below on the white side-walk in the heat, / The dog, the lady with parcels, and the boy: / There is the casual life outside the heart." Perkins wrote, "to understand why the poetry of the thirties took the direction it did, we must keep in mind the situation in literary history of these poets born between 1907 and 1917. They were the first generation for whom the development of modern poetry from the 1890s was what it is for us — history, tales of the tribal elders" (v. II, 120).

The "Fugitive" poet and New Critic Allen Tate's complaints about Auden's style in a review of his 1941 book *The Double Man* put it clearly. Tate's assessment is that he "can see in it a great deal that is brilliant and entertaining, and in the sonnets much that is brilliant and moving; but in passage after passage the main poem, 'New Year Letter,' slides off into...parlor magic — or in places it dissolves into the annotations, of which there are 87 pages to 55 of poetic text" (202). Tate ended his review by noting that "Auden has a complex, even a very rich mind; yet his passion for autobiography brings him back always to the question: What does it mean to me? Perhaps he will not be able to tell us fully what it means to him until he no longer asks the question. Or maybe until he asks the question: 'What does it mean?'" (204). That is to say, what does it mean to the human race, not merely to Auden.

Louise Bogan was kind in her description of the prevalent style: "By the middle forties a modern poetic style in English had come into being, broadly workable and capable of a variety of applications. This style was a composite one, derived from many sources. But, since very nearly all of the sources were genuine, the end product was itself authentic. It was a style which tended to veer, it is true, toward verbalism on the one hand, and extreme condensation of meaning and idea, on the other. At its worst, a core of over-compressed thought was surrounded by an envelope of over-inflated words. It was a style rich in allusion, and its tone could vary from conversational flatness to high incantation. Its best practitioners, old and young, had insight into the nature and possibilities of the poetic means, and kept these flexible, according to the nature of the poetic end in view" (98).

This became what was known as "academic poetry" in the United States, and it persisted even into the so-called "free verse" (prose) poems of the post-war generations: here is the contemporary poet William Stafford in "Adults Only": "Animals own a fur world; / people own worlds that are variously, pleasingly, bare."

None of this sounds at all like the poetic diction of Auden's contemporary, the idiosyncratic Dylan Thomas who owed more, perhaps, to Gerard Manley Hopkins than to anyone else, as in "Hold Hard, These Ancient Minutes in the Cuckoo's Month," which is also the first line. The poem continues, "Under the lank, fourth folly on Glamorgan's hill, / As the green blooms ride upward, to the drive of time;.." nor does it sound like Theodore Roethke in Part 2 of "The Visitant": "Slow, slow as a fish she came, / Slow as a fish coming forward, / Swaying in a long wave;.." or John Berryman in "Old Man Goes South Again Alone": "O parakeets & avocets, O immortelles / & ibis, scarlet under that stunning sun / deliciously & tired I come / toward you in orbit, Trinidad!..."

In the latter days of the Modernist Movement preceding World War II, the formal study of poetry written in traditional verse mode, as distinguished from the innovative Modernist "free verse" prose mode, was commonplace in the high schools of the United States. Poetry is a *genre* or "kind" of writing, like fiction or drama; it is *not* a "mode," for any of the genres may be written in either of the modes, prose or verse — *The Oxford English Dictionary* defines *verse* as "metered" or measured language," and *prose* as "unmetered" or unmeasured language. What is measured in language is in most instances syllables, whether stressed or unstressed or both. Poetry written in verse utilizes metrics, but poetry written in both verse and prose use rhyme, figures of speech, and the other techniques and elements of writing to be found on its four levels: the typographical (page layout), the sonic (besides meter and rhyme such techniques as assonance, consonance, alliteration), the sensory (figurative language), and the ideational levels (subject, theme, treatment).

Delmore Schwartz

Despite the experimentalism of the great Modernists, teachers of the Post-Modern period often urged promising students to write rhymed and metered poem-exercises in class and extra-curricularly. The experience of Delmore Schwartz (1913-1966) was in many ways typical, though not every student was as fortunate in his or her mentor. Schwartz was born and went to school in Brooklyn, New York. His high school poetry teacher was Mary J. J. Wrinn, editor of an influential high school textbook on poetry writing, *The Hollow Reed*.

In his biography of Delmore Schwartz, James Atlas mentioned Mary J. J. Wrinn twice. He wrote first, "It was obvious to some of his [high school] teachers that Delmore was a brilliant boy, and in particular to Mary J. J. Wrinn, 'an Irish, red-faced woman with a terrible temper,' as a classmate of Delmore's remembered her, who conducted the school's poetry club and would often argue with Delmore over his poems, which he was reluctant to revise. But she encouraged him in his writing, and was aware of his advanced knowledge of contemporary poetry" (26).

Again Atlas wrote, "One afternoon during the winter of 1933 Delmore pointed out to Maurice Zolotow a girl at a neighboring table in the N. Y. U. student cafeteria and announced that he knew her from Mary J. J. Wrinn's Poetry Club at George Washington High School. Her name was Gertrude Buckman, and a number of her poems had appeared beside Delmore's in *The Poet's Pack*" (63).

"A selection of Delmore's earliest poems can be found," Atlas noted further, "in *The Poet's Pack* of George Washington High School, a voluminous hardcover anthology of poems by 'members of the Poetry Club and Poetry Class 1927-1931.' Of Delmore's four contributions, a sonnet entitled 'The Saxophone' reveals that he had been reading Hart Crane; another, 'Automobile,' was more original in tone, exhibiting a fine dramatic intensity in measured quatrains."

In a "Foreword" Robert Phillips also mentioned *The Poet's Pack* in a note explaining his selections for the *The Last and Lost Poems of Delmore Schwartz*: "Other juvenilia I have not included are the poems 'Automobile,' 'Darkness,' 'E. A. P. — A Portrait,' and 'The Saxophone,' from *The Poet's Pack*...and 'Aubade' from *Mosaic*, I, [1934]." (xix) However, Phillips did not mention Mary Wrinn. Neither he nor Atlas mentioned the fact that Wrinn was, at the time, gathering materials for a high school textbook in poetry writing that would become very well known among the early teachers of creative writing in the schools.

Mary J. J. Wrinn published *The Hollow Reed* in 1935. In it she used quite a number of poems by her high school students, five of them being by Gertrude Buckman, the future Mrs. Delmore Schwartz, and five by Schwartz himself, including, among those mentioned by Phillips, "Automobile," "E. A. P. — A Portrait," and "Saxophone." However, Wrinn used two Schwartz pieces mentioned by neither: "Saturday's Child" and "George Washington Bridge, December 1929." These may be considered two more "lost" poems which have received no attention at all since Wrinn's book appeared, for they have never been collected. Wrinn thus put into hard covers several poems that appeared three years before Schwartz published his own first book of poems and stories, *In Dreams Begin Responsibilities*. All five are formal poems that utilize verse meters rather than "free verse" — prose which has been "line-phrased" or broken into lines at the ends of phrases or clauses.

In Wrinn's anthology "Saturday's Child" faces "Rejuvenation" by Gertrude Joan Buckman on the opposite page. Both appear in Chapter 39, "Miscellaneous," a section Wrinn introduced thus: "In the light of accumulating skill and a habit of observation students of poetry find many subjects for expression. Here are a few that their makers labeled 'optional.' They may suggest other optional poems to their readers" (487).

The subject of "Saturday's Child" is "life." It is written in relatively regular iambic pentameter lines arranged in quatrains. Schwartz did not rhyme the poem regularly; there is only one true-rhyming pair of lines in the three stanzas, and although these form a couplet rhyme, typographically they are not a distich; rather, the rhyme forms a sound bridge across the gap between stanza one and stanza two:

> I think of blue confetti, amusement parks
> And lighted Christmas trees, while carnivals
> Parade like roman candles in my mind...
> How should I dumb this rage? What should I say?
>
> Within the pagan tent of holiday
> Grow memories to brood upon and cherish
> And fling on Monday from the gargoyled church
> Of consciousness into a weary heart
>
> Whose large remorse requires expectation
> Of every joy that Saturday donates
> To taunt that synthesis of monotone
> And toil and firecrackers which is life.

But there are numerous effects other than rhyme on the sonic level, such as apocopated rhyme of the center lines of stanza three: <u>donates-monotone</u>; the consonance — almost the rich rhyme of the center lines of stanza two: cherish-church; the alliterations, (Christmas-carnivals), sonic repetitions (**par**ks-**Par**ade), and internal head rhymes (**par**ks-**car**nivals-**Par**ade). This is precocious work for a high school student.

It is no less precocious on the sensory level. The tropes — "figures of speech" — of "Saturday's Child" are not complex, but they are used in the Symbolist tradition. In particular, the abstract syntax (Donald Davie called it "musical syntax") of the rhetorical question, "How should I dumb this rage?" sounds like a French Symbolist expression, whereas "the gargoyled church / Of consciousness...weary heart" holds a hint of Eliot — it is no wonder that Schwartz's high-school yearbook said, "T. S. Eliot is God, and Delmore

Schwartz is his prophet" (Atlas, 27).

The ideational (thematic) level of the poem is as ambitious as its techniques. Schwartz managed to get into these twelve lines a recapitulation of religion ranging from pre-Christian Paganism and Hebraism through Roman Catholicism, at times blending allusions and extending them metaphorically, as in "Roman candles." This is a meditation on the ambiguity of the Jew, Schwartz himself as "Saturday's Child" (Saturday being the Jewish Sabbath), in the American Diaspora.

"Washington Bridge, December 1929" is to be found in Chapter 13, "Object Poems," of *The Hollow Reed* (Wrinn, 173). The touchstone of this chapter is Keats's "Ode on a Grecian Urn." Of "object poems" in general Wrinn wrote, "things become significant through strange associations. The things on our table at home; a chair that a dear one sits in; our dog's special cushion; a hand bag worn at the corners may almost have the gift of words, so alive is it with significance. There is human interest in many an inanimate object. — the essence of a poem may be found in the history of an object; in its association; in its special physical or spiritual significance.

"Beauty lingers in strange places; her finger has left an impress on many an object, which the unseeing or unknowing may call ugly. —

"Some of the purest poetry has been stimulated through objects." The object Schwartz chose to treat in, again, three stanzas, is the George Washington Bridge linking New York City and New Jersey, but this time there are only two quatrains and a concluding triplet, so the poem is a line shorter than "Saturday's Child."

The meter is again iambic, but variable iambic this time, rather than normative; however, Schwartz did not allow himself much latitude, for the range in line length varies by only one foot, from tetrameter to pentameter. The poem begins with an iambic tetrameter line, but the second line is the longest typographically in the poem, though it is hypercatalectic by only one syllable:

Now in the darkness of the year

When afternoons, grown still, more chill and drifting,
Voyage unseen to dusk and blue loose night,
The wind is voiding our dream of spring.

Schwartz had early such a command of rhythm that the poem, though scansion leaves no doubt as to its meter, is seen to have many variations. Schwartz substituted a trochee for the initial iamb; he inserted a spondee into the central foot of line two, against all the rules of versification, by utilizing compensatory caesura after "afternoons": the pause at that point substitutes for an unstressed syllable which yields three stresses in a row. He has gotten away with it by phrasing, and even extended the effect into the next foot (*more* takes a secondary stress following yet another compensatory caesura after "still," and "chill" is sprung by internal rhyme with "still," so it takes a stress also). In fact, Schwartz put at least one variation into each line of the poem, which reads conversationally:

> But all day long the rivets pulse, and cables
> Crescent a river newly, cradle a word....
> Will the gray sky gather the world to death?
> Over the hush and sleep an iron breath
>
> Tremendously is....No wind nor snow
> Refutes this fleshed geometry, this birth,
> Curving the strength of life over the earth.

This little ode relies more consistently on rhyme as its main sonic effect than did "Saturday's Child," its rhyme scheme being *abcb-deff-ghh*. Although the pattern is not strict, there is rhyme in each stanza, and there is couplet rhyme at the ends of the second and third stanzas. The first stanza is light-rhymed (**drif**t*ing*-**spring**), but it also has internal rhyme, as noted. There is also assonance (bl**ue**-l**oo**se) and considerable consonantal echo (ars and els). The first stanza sets the mood of the poem partly by mellifluous sounds; there is thus a real melding of the sonic and sensory levels, the former supporting the latter.

The second stanza blends images of birth and death. Schwartz was able to take something as hard as steel — the new bridge across the Hudson — and by association, using the word "cradle" connotatively, endow it with fabric, the "fleshed geometry" of the concluding triplet. By the time the poem is ended, the "cables" of the bridge have taken on the coloration of umbilical cords spanning not merely river banks, but birth and death, winter and spring, despair and hope. The ideational level of the poem, then, is as "organic" as the sonic and sensory levels. The fusion is extraordinary in the literary production of an adolescent who had, perhaps, been inspired to write this poem by his reading of Hart Crane's *The Bridge*, which was published early in 1930.

Schwartz's *Summer Knowledge: New and Selected Poems 1938-1958* appeared in 1959. In the last section of this book there appears a series of poems, "Narcissus," the first poem of which is titled "The Mind is an Ancient and Famous Capital." This work exhibits in a developed form many of the aspects of the poet's earliest poems: it is a variable iambic poem utilizing many of the same techniques of metrical variation — substitutions of one kind of verse foot for another.

On the sensory level there is the Symbolist use of tropes; there are literary allusions, as to Shakespeare and to classical mythology; there is the idiosyncratic poetic syntax of "harp o'clock," which is of the same ilk as, "How should I dumb this rage?" Even the tone of the poem is traceable to Schwartz's early work. The poet's development was not apparently harmed by his teacher's emphasis upon formal training in verse-writing.

Richard Eberhart

Richard Eberhart was born in 1904 in Austin, Minnesota, and educated at the University of Minnesota and at Dartmouth, where he took his B.A. in 1926; at St. John's College, Cambridge, England, where he took a second bachelor's degree in 1929; and at Harvard University. He served in the U.S. Naval Reserve as a Commander teaching gunnery from 1942-46. He was a private tutor and a teacher, a businessman, and finally an academic, teaching in a number of institutions including the University of Connecticut, Dartmouth, and the University of Washington. His first book of poems, *A Bravery of Earth*, appeared in 1930, and his fourth book, *Poems, New and Selected*, appeared in 1944, a year before the war ended.

In 1967, at the height of the anti-academic and anti-formalist reaction that began to transform American literature by the late 1950's, Eberhart chose to publish a book of poems he had written when he was a young man. His *Thirty-one Sonnets*, he said in a preface, "were written about thirty-five years ago [that is, about 1932, two years after his first book had appeared]. ...I put them away as being too personal, too youthful, and too imitative...one or two were published in little magazines. The older I grew the more I recognized the uniqueness of their energy and passionate flow.... I wish to publish the sonnets now...work of an early, formative period, a backward glance for those who might be interested to have them in relation to my later work, or to enjoy them for themselves as early poetic realizations." In other words, in the middle of the antiformal decade of the 1960s, a poet of the first post-Modernist generation chose to look back at his formalist youth and to revive it by publishing a book he had written then. In the same year another poet of that generation, John Berryman, did exactly the same thing.

Both Eberhart's and Berryman's sonnet sequences were examples of another kind of split-mindedness common to many members of the post-Modernist generation — the poems themselves were formalist, but their content was personal, and personal poetry had become popular during the years since the publication of Robert Lowell's *Life Studies* and W.D. Snodgrass' *Heart's Needle*, both in 1959. In Eberhart's sonnets, looking back as the poet suggests, the reader can discern, perhaps, the beginnings of that philosophical insight and fresh metaphor that are the hallmark of an important poet.

Eberhart was one of the Academic Poets who may be considered to be precursors of the Confessional Poets of the 1960s. In many of Eberhart's poems — those written in his middle years particularly — the elements of intellect and rationality tended to govern his work through abstractions that undercut the conflict of the flesh and the spirit, of life and death, which were the central concerns of this poet. As Ralph J. Mills wrote in his monograph *Richard Eberhart*, "Eberhart's poems set themselves in a curiously singular relationship to established canons of modern poetic practice, which they seldom heed. These poems treat philosophic themes abstractly; their method is frequently deductive rather than inductive...they rely much of the time on inspiration, in the poet's own words, 'burst into life spontaneously,' during a period in which critical opinion emphasizes careful craftsmanship, the poem as a discovered but also a made object; as a final impertinence they are apt to level undisguised moral judgments while still fighting shy of dogma and firmly insisting on the ultimate mysteriousness of existence, the impenetrable heart of reality" (7).

One of his most famous pieces, "The Fury of Aerial Bombardment," shows clearly this tendency toward over-intellectuality and abstraction, but in this case the poem turns rhetoric into tragedy by means of a simple catalog of names of dead soldiers and concrete detail in the last stanza. As Bernard F. Engel wrote in his introduction to *The Achievement of Richard Eberhart,* "Richard Eberhart is a neo-romantic poet who demonstrates a willingness to assert generalizations and an interest in the exotic, melodic, and *vers d'occasion*. But, being a modern poet, Eberhart stresses...belief in the importance of the experiences and objects of life in the phenomenal world and, perhaps consequently, the need for precision in expression. Although he is confident that moments of illumination can give us knowledge the senses alone cannot reveal, he is always equally aware of the realm of the sensory." (1)

Perhaps not "always," but "The Groundhog" achieves the synthesis of mystery and reality: "In June, amid the golden fields, I saw a groundhog lying dead." This is the personal voice, the egopoetic viewpoint that would shortly dominate American poetry. The poet is shaken, "And mind outshot our naked frailty." The process of decay begins, and the poet returns in Autumn "to see the sap gone out of the groundhog," but the process has not yet been completed. Three years later "There is no sign of the groundhog." The poet is struck at last with the full implications of man's mortality, the fact of eternal mutability, which is the only thing that is unchanging:

> I stood there in the whirling summer,
> My hand capped a withered heart,
> And thought of China and of Greece,
> Of Alexander in his tent;
> Of Montaigne in his tower,
> Of Saint Theresa in her wild lament.

The experience becomes universal, though not in the same way that Nemerov, or even Wilbur, would have managed the feat. Eberhart's technique was generally neither traditional nor experimental, but colloquially elegiac. When he wrote at the peak of his powers his poems confronted powerfully nature and man's dilemma as a conscious creature caught in the toils of mortality, as in "The Cancer Cells,"

> ...a virulent laughing gang.
> They looked like art itself, like the artist's mind,
> Powerful shaker, and the taker of new forms.

If the tendency to over-philosophize was Eberhart's main problem, minor ones were an overuse of large words and sometimes carelessness of detail. As an example of the latter, one might point to "Opposition," the first poem in Eberhart's *Florida Poems* (1981) in which he contrasted Florida with New England (where he lived most of his life). The first stanza talked about Florida; the second and concluding stanza said of New England that the Puritans "thought life could be better, / Prayed to God not to do anything wrong, / Held back their passion, aimed to kill, / Burned as witches free life-loving girls." But no witches were ever burned in North America, they were hanged; and it was not the girls who were accused of witchcraft in Salem Village (now Danvers, Massachusetts) in 1692, it was the girls, the famous "witch-bitches of Salem," who were the accusers of the "witches," most of whom were older women. Anyone who knows these historical facts must realize that the poem self-destructed through erroneous detail.

Richard Wilbur

Through all the social turmoil and fashionable change of the period since the end of World War II there were those who continued to ply their traditional craft quietly and well — Richard Wilbur, born in New York City in 1921, was one of those. Wilbur was educated at Amherst College, taking his B.A. in 1942. He served in the U.S. Army from 1943 to 1945; upon his discharge he attended Harvard University where he took an M.A. in 1947. He became an assistant professor there in 1950, moved on to Wellesley College in 1955, and settled into Wesleyan University two years later, remaining there except for academic excursions until his retirement.

Among his contemporaries, Richard Wilbur most consistently developed and maintained much of what was best in the post-Modernist academic style. He continued to be, through the 1960-80s, that rare phenomenon of contemporary literature, a man of letters. To many critics Wilbur appeared to be a poetic throw-back to the original mainstream of American poets deriving from the British tradition, representatives of which include Longfellow, Whittier, Poe, Robinson, and Frost — that is to say, the formal traditionalists. That this line of descent is still viable has been often disputed since 1960, yet Wilbur's reputation steadily rose over the years despite attacks on his formalism, the elegance of his diction and style, and the equanimity of his vision.

Wilbur's books include *Ceremony* (1950), *Things of This World* (1956) which received both the Pulitzer Prize and the National Book Award; *Poems 1943-1956* (1957); *Advice to a Prophet* (1961); *The Poems of Richard* Wilbur (1963); *Walking to Sleep* (1969); *Seed Leaves* (1974), and *New and Collected Poems* (1988). Essentially a poet of ideas, and therefore in one sense at least a classical rather than a romantic poet, Wilbur wrote poems constructed in such a way that his themes stood out clearly before they were transformed into, anchored by, the images of the poem "Love Calls Us to the Things of This World":

> And the heaviest nuns walk in a pure floating
> Of dark habits,
> Keeping their difficult balance.

Another example of this method is his poem "The Aspen and the Stream" which is a dialogue between an idealist, the aspen (whose conversation is cast in stately heroic couplets) and a cynic, the stream (who speaks in quick iambic trimeter quatrains rhyming *abab*) (205). The tree addresses the stream,

> Beholding element, in whose pure eye
> My boughs upon a ground of heaven lie —

and the stream responds,

> Why should the water drink,

> Blithering little tree?
> Think what you choose to think,
> But lisp no more at me.

The verse forms themselves help to characterize the "persons" engaged in this argument, the optimism of the aspen showing forth in the stately measures of the long line, and the stream's pessimism in the quicker, livelier lines running through the debate.

Donald L. Hill wrote in his book *Richard Wilbur* that there were four overlapping qualities in Wilbur's work, "a speculative and logical temper, sharp and true observation, technical virtuosity, and a kind of amused good humor." (19) Each and all of these are clearly characteristics not merely of the poems, but of the poet who wrote them. A consummate craftsman and therefore, assumedly, almost totally a conscious writer, Wilbur nevertheless held to a neo-romantic notion that took possession of the poetry of the 1960s that "the poem chooses its own form," as though it were a living organism rather than an artifice of language whose development is controlled by the writer. In no contemporary poet did this split-minded position appear to be so anomalous; in none was the contradiction between theory and practice so obvious as in Wilbur who, in his best work, gave as much pleasure through skill and contemplation as through vision and "inspiration," for of all his peers Wilbur was consistently the most overtly formal poet.

Wilbur, like Auden, used many of the standard verse forms of the English tradition, ranging from alliterative, strong-stress Anglo-Saxon prosody in such poems as "The Lilacs" and "Junk" (pp. 118 & 185) —

> An axe angles
> from my neighbor's ashcan
> It is hell's handiwork, ;
> the wood not hickory,
> The flow of the grain
> not faithfully followed.

— to the "Sonnet," as in the poem so titled (235). In this formalism Wilbur defied the movement of most American poets since the 1950s toward so-called "organic" poetry, an extension of the undeveloped British tradition of lineated prose — that is to say so-called "free verse" — begun by Christopher Smart and William Blake in the 18th and early 19th centuries, and by Martin Farquhar Tupper who influenced the American Walt Whitman in the later 19th century.

The origin of English prose poetry lies in the 17th-century translation of the King James version of the *Bible*. It was developed to a degree in the mystical and prophetic books of William Blake, beginning with *The Book of Thel* (1789) and ranging through *Milton* and *Jerusalem*, (both published in 1804); in the posthumous *Rejoice in the Lamb* (1839), written from 1759-1763 by Christopher Smart; popularized in both Great Britain and the early United States by the English poet Martin Farquhar Tupper whose *Proverbial*

Philosophy (1838) sold a million copies in this country, ten years before America's first major prose poem, Edgar Allan Poe's *Eureka* (1848), and seventeen years before Whitman's influential book of prose poems, *Leaves of Grass* (1855). Many of the Modernists claimed Whitman as a precedent unique to the New World. A century after Whitman, however, few of the Academic Poets, including Wilbur, were using his mode, though it would experience a resurgence beginning in the 1950s at the hands of other schools of poetry.

Elizabeth Bishop

Elizabeth Bishop (1911-1979) was born in Worcester, Massachusetts, an almost exact contemporary — within two months — of her fellow citizen Charles Olson who would be the cornerstone of the Black Mountain School of poetry during the 1950s and 1960s. The early death of her father and the mental problems of her mother caused Bishop to be brought up by aunts in Nova Scotia and in Boston. She took her bachelor's degree from Vassar College in 1934 and began to travel shortly thereafter; beginning in 1951, Bishop spent sixteen years of foreign residence in Brazil.

These peregrinations, however, did not prevent her at last from sharing the situation of the Academic Poets. In 1966 and 1973 she was Poet-in-Residence at the University of Washington in Seattle, and from 1970 she was a lecturer in English at Harvard University. Bishop's first book, published in 1946, was *North and South*; her second, *Poems: North and South — A Cold Spring*, was published in 1955 and won the Pulitzer Prize for 1956. *The Complete Poems*, which appeared in 1969, received the National Book Award the following year.

Elizabeth Bishop's poems were a study in contrasts, as the titles of her two early books would indicate. A traditionally formal poet in much of her work, Bishop nevertheless wrote lineated prose poems when the mood suited her. Often her subjects were austere, as in "At the Fishhouses," set in the Atlantic Northeast, but equally often they were exotic, as in "Song for the Rainy Season." She wrote about nature and nature's indifference to man in many pieces, such as "Florida," but she also wrote about the city and its blank visage, as in "Letter to New York."

Similarly, Bishop's work can be as objective as that of her good friend and fellow poet Marianne Moore, as in "A Cold Spring," but in other poems the realism of the poem is undercut by pure fantasy — Bishop's most-anthologized poem of this sort is "The Man-Moth." Karl Malkoff, writing in his *Crowell's Guide to Contemporary American Poetry*, said that Bishop created "imaginative worlds that exist parallel to our own." (69) He continued, "Seeing a misprint for the word 'mammoth' in the newspaper, she conjures up an image from the lost nightmare regions of the mind, a queer Man-Moth, climbing the facades of buildings at night, hoping to reach and investigate that small hole at the top of the sky, the moon." Bishop selected "The Man-Moth" for inclusion in the Engle-Langland anthology *Poet's Choice*. In commenting on it she wrote, "This poem was written in 1935 when I first lived in New York City.

"I've forgotten what it was that was supposed to be 'mammoth.' But the misprint seemed meant for me. An oracle spoke from the page of the *New York Times*, kindly explaining New York City to me, at least for a moment."

The juxtaposition of opposites gave Bishop's work what Anne Stevenson in her book *Elizabeth Bishop* called "Precision and Resonance." (77) "Resonance" is "overtone" or, in existential terms, "ambiguity," a typically twentieth century perception of the quality of modern life. Elizabeth Bishop, like others of her fellow formalists, considered it her job to give detailed ambiguity a voice and an eye.

The Man-Moth scales buildings by night in futile attempts to reach the moon, a small silver hole in the black sky, but "he fails, of course, and falls back scared but quite unhurt."

> Then he returns
> to the pale subways of cement he calls his home. He flits,
> he flutters, and cannot get aboard the silent trains
> fast enough to suit him. The doors close swiftly.
> The Man-Moth always seats himself facing the wrong way
> and the train starts at once at its full, terrible speed,
> without a shift in gears or a gradation of any sort.
> He cannot tell the rate at which he travels backwards.

"Returning to the ground, and beneath, the Man-Moth rides the subways," Malkoff continued, "riding always backwards at a rate 'he cannot tell.' Finally, the poem builds to its climax. If you can get hold of him, the poet suggests, hold a flashlight to his eye.

> "...Then from the lids
> one tear, his only possession, like the bee's sting, slips.
> Slyly he palms it, and if you're not paying attention
> he'll swallow it. However, if you watch, he'll hand it over,
> cool as from the underground springs and pure enough to drink."

Thus, Bishop invents an urban myth. Her method here is Symbolist, for the French Symbolists of the 19th century, and the 20th-century Symbolists like Eliot and Yeats, believed with the psychologist Karl Jung that the inchoate forces and urges that drive mankind are represented in art by "archetypes," or embodiments of the emotional fantasies of the unconscious mind, so that they may be rendered apprehensible to the conscious mind as well. The Man-Moth is the personification of city life, a timid, sly, underground kind of life that "must / be carried through artificial tunnels and dream recurrent dreams." He must avert his gaze from the hidden poisons running beneath the train.

> If you catch him,
> hold up a flashlight to his eye. It's all dark pupil,
> an entire night itself, whose haired horizon tightens
> as he stares back, and closes up the eye.

"The influence of the surrealists is surely present in the poem," Malkoff continued, "but modified by Bishop's clarity of vision, giving many of her poems the feeling of a fantastic dream that, while it lasts, seems more real than the waking world."

Randall Jarrell, discussing the poet's early work in his *Poetry and the Age* said, "Instead of crying, with justice, 'This is a world in which no one can get along,' Miss Bishop's poems show that it is barely but perfectly possible — has been, that is, for her. Her work is unusually personal and honest in its wit, perception, and sensitivity — and in its restrictions too; all her poems have written underneath, I have seen it." (210) The things she has "seen," then, are external and internal, objective and subjective, real and imaginary. One must call her an "eclectic formalist," for she would choose from a large range of technique and experience those elements which made the poem in hand work, both for her and for her readers.

To illustrate something of Bishop's meticulous craftsmanship, her ability to work within the most stringent poetic contexts and still not preach but suggest vast and perhaps unspeakable truths, one might turn to her poem titled "Sestina." Antistrophe repeats a single word throughout a poem, particularly an end-word or teleuton, as in the French sestina, of which this is an example: The six end-words of the first stanza reappear in a pre-set particular order required by the form, as the end-words of the following stanzas, and as both end-words and buried words in a particular order in the final stanza, which is called the envoy (*envoi*) in all French forms. An envoy is a coda half-stanza: either a climactic tail appended to the body of a poem, or an address to the poem itself to go to whomever or wherever the author directs it to serve its function as an envoy — "Go, little poem, to my lover 's place / And tell her what I can't say to her face."

SESTINA

September rain falls on the house.
In the failing light, the old grandmother
sits in the kitchen with the child
beside the Little Marvel Stove,
reading the jokes from the almanac,
laughing and talking to hide her tears.

She thinks that her equinoctial tears
and the rain that beats on the roof of the house
were both foretold by the almanac,
but only known to a grandmother.
The iron kettle sings on the stove.
She cuts some bread and says to the child,

It's time for tea now; but the child
is watching the teakettle's small hard tears
dance like mad on the hot black stove,
the way the rain must dance on the house.
Tidying up, the old grandmother
hangs up the clever almanac

>   on its string. Birdlike, the almanac
>   hovers half open above the child,
>   hovers above the old grandmother
>   and her teacup full of dark brown tears.
>   She shivers and says she thinks the house
>   feels chilly, and puts more wood in the stove.
>
>   It was to be, says the Marvel Stove.
>   I know what I know, says the almanac.
>   With crayons the child draws a rigid house
>   and a winding pathway. Then the child
>   puts in a man with buttons like tears
>   and shows it proudly to the grandmother.
>
>   But secretly, while the grandmother
>   busies herself about the stove,
>   the little moons fall down like tears
>   from between the pages of the almanac
>   into the flower bed the child
>   has carefully placed in the front of the house.
>
>   Time to plant tears, says the almanac.
>   The grandmother sings to the marvelous stove
>   and the child draws another inscrutable house.

Where is the missing father? Where, in fact, is the mother? Why is the grandmother weeping and trying to hide her tears from the child at the same time that she is reading jokes and laughing? What does the almanac tell us about the seasons, about spring and planting and the seeds that are planted? Writing in John Ciardi's *Mid-Century American Poets*, Bishop did not find the contrasts inherent in her work to be something to wonder about. "It all depends on the particular poem one happens to be trying to write," she said, "and the range of possibilities is, one trusts, infinite. After all, the poet's concern is not consistency" (267).

Howard Nemerov

Howard Nemerov was born in New York City on Leap Year Day in 1920, the older brother of the woman who became known later as the photographer Diane Arbus. He was educated privately in the Fieldston School and attended Harvard University where he took his bachelor's degree in 1940. During World War II he served as a pilot in the Royal Canadian Air Force and then in the U. S. Army Air Corps. In 1944 he married, and after the war returned to New York where he published his first book, *The Image of the Law,* in 1947. His next book, *The Salt Garden*, did not appear for eight years, but it was followed in 1958 by *Mirrors and Windows* and seven other collections including *The Collected Poems* in 1977. He published books of fiction and other prose as well. Examples of all these genres were included in *A Howard Nemerov Reader* which was published in 1991, the year of his death from esophageal cancer. He taught at several institutions during his lifetime, including Hamilton College, Bennington, Brandeis, and finally at Washington University in Saint Louis, along the way winning numerous prizes and awards.

Howard Nemerov had all the talents of the bards, but they were disguised, for his poems can at first appear to the occasional reader to be as unprepossessing as ordinary conversation. His surfaces are casual, colloquial, often overtly witty, and it is possible to overlook the fact that the poems are usually written in tight, traditionally formal constructions, as for instance his "A Primer of the Daily Round."

One is unlikely to remark on first reading that the poem is an English sonnet, for it does not carry the burden of tradition of the sonnet — it sounds nothing like something by Shakespeare or Milton, or by Wordsworth or Mrs. Browning or Millay, or anyone else conventionally associated with the sonnet form. Other than the rhyme scheme, which is scarcely noticeable, the only clue that this is a sonnet is the fact that, typographically, the concluding heroic couplet is indented. The whole poem is otherwise a solid block of print, and unless one is alert, the quatrains will go unrecognized for a while, especially inasmuch as Nemerov has enjambed them — the entire poem is syntactically a single sentence.

The meters also are hardly detectable, especially early in the poem, which sounds rather more like straight prose than any sort of verse. Even if one scans the first few lines, one will hardly identify them as being written in iambic pentameter measures. But counting the syllables will gain the suspicious metrist the knowledge that every single line of the poem contains ten syllables exactly.

Something else one is unlikely to notice is how much of the world is included in the poem. Even those readers who do not know what a primer is will catch the "abeceness" of the poem, but they may not be aware that in such didactic poems "A" often stands for "Adam" or "apple," as it does here — to the latter overtly, to the former inferentially by allusion:

> A peels an apple, while B kneels to God,
> C telephones to D, who has a hand
> On E's knee, F coughs, G turns up the sod
> For H's grave,...

By the time the reader has gotten this far in the poem he or she understands that the era of the poem is the modern period, not that of the Garden of Eden. Nemerov's voice is operating on the level of gossip. People are carrying on affairs, being brutalized by the police, entertaining themselves, working, burying each other, carrying on affairs, eating, traveling, dying, gossiping, carrying on affairs. Meanwhile, somewhere far off and long ago, "A" peels the forbidden fruit to get the whole thing going. How much of the world and human history is in this poem? All of it. This was Nemerov's greatest ability — to take everything, absolutely everything, and squeeze it down into something apprehensible not only to the mind, but to the senses as well.

To a degree seldom equaled by any of his contemporaries, Nemerov was capable of anchoring his cosmic abstractions by linking them with unusually appropriate images based in reality. That the reader is not startled by these tropes is owing to the deceptive plainness of his diction and syntax. Thus, he might equate the loneliness of Being with an electrical noise, as in "The Dial Tone," and thereby make palpable and familiar the existential sadness of the human condition.

> Suppose that in God a black bumblebee
> Or colorless hummingbird buzzed all night,
> Dividing the abyss up equally;
> And carried its neither sweetness nor its light
> Across impossible eternity.
>
> Now take this hummingbird, this bee, away;
> And like the Cheshire smile without its cat
> The remnant hum continues on its way,...

That last onomatopoeic line takes the visual images into its heart and makes them all into the sound of eternity.

In none of his contemporaries were the elements of craft and reflection, sensation, sound, wit and sense more completely integrated in a poetry of balance. That this equilibrium expresses the ambivalence and ambiguity of modern man's position in the natural and intellectual worlds rather than affirmations or denials of faith is no criticism, but a compliment of the highest order, for post-Modernist literary theory insists that the classical methods of Nemerov are not relevant to a period, beginning around the later 1950s, when many writers were caught in the toils of the self — self-consciousness and self-expression.

Nemerov's quiet poems reconnected the self with the world in which it found itself held hostage to time, to fate, and to the universal consciousness. "The May Day Dancing" is an example. In this poem a Maypole ritual brings forth the various school classes, beginning with kindergartners, dressed in costumes of various periods and traditions: "They braid the Maypole with a double thread; \ Keep time, keep faith, is what the music says." As the parents watch "...they see \ Not seven classes of children, but only one, \\ One class of children seven times again \ that ever enters on the dancing floor...." All generations are but one generation repeated forever. At last, the ritual expands to mythic proportions and becomes a representation of the universal life process as each child dances

> Around the brilliant morning with the sun,
> The dance that leads him home,
> The May Day dance that tramples down the grass
> And raises dust, that braids a double thread
> Around the pole, in the great room of the sun.

It is tempting to call Nemerov a religious poet, but to do so might be to frighten off the odd wary reader. Nevertheless, his concerns were, indeed, "religious," or at least metaphysical. If he was an agnostic, his agnosticism was of the kind typified by the "Creation Myth on a Moebius Strip":

> This world's just mad enough to have been made
> By the Being His beings into Being prayed.

A Moebius strip is a narrow length of paper which is given a single twist before its two ends are brought together. If one runs a finger along its surface now, one discovers that it has only one side — it has become a paradox: a single-sided object in a three-dimensional world. In this case Nemerov took an actually physical thing and put an idea to it that is exactly equivalent to the thought he wanted to express. There can be no clearer example of a metaphor, of an anchored abstraction. Which came first, the Creator or his creatures? If the latter, then it is a mad possibility that the creatures created the Creator who then created them. It is an improvement on the classical image of the self-generating, self-consuming universe represented by the Hermetic Worm in a Circle, Ouroboros, the snake that devours its own tail.

Or perhaps Nemerov was an atheist, not an agnostic. If so, his atheism was as droll as that of "A Memory of My Friend,"

> A Jewish atheist stubborn as Freud
> (the only Father he left undestroyed),
> Who when you left his house at night would nod
> And say, instead of "Good Night," "Go with God."

How many angels can fit upon the head of a pin? How can one even conceive of such a thing? How many worlds are there in a world? In "Angel and Stone" Nemerov undertook to bring such immense calculations down to size, for "In the world are millions and millions of men, and each man, / With few exceptions, believes himself to be at the center, / A small number of his more or less necessary planets careering / Around him in an orderly manner,..." It is possible not only to understand the image, but to agree with it, and with the further observation also that, "Since this is true not of one man or of two, / But of ever so many, it is hard to imagine what life must be like." Yet it was not beyond the power of Nemerov to imagine it for us, for "...if you drop a stone into a pool, and observe the ripples / Moving in circles successively out to the edges of the pool and then / Reflecting back and passing through the ones which continue to come / Out of the center over the sunken stone, you observe it is pleasing." How much more pleasing to drop two stones, but "...if you throw a handful of sand into the water, it is confusion, / Not because the same laws have ceased to obtain, but only because / The limits of your vision in time and number forbid you to discriminate / Such fine, quick, myriad events as the angels and archangels, thrones / And dominations, principalities and powers, are delegated to witness / And declare the glory of before the Lord of everything that is."

The reader is suddenly deep in the firmament of the Jewish and Christian faiths, but not so deep that he or she cannot see a way clear now that Nemerov has shown us the path. The poem at this point becomes a treatise on archangelic bookkeeping, a catalogue of the physical and mathematical universes, of genetics and chemistry. And then, at the end, back to the simplicities, to the individual items being counted by the heavenly accountants: "...the pyramids stand still / In the desert and the deermouse huddles in his hole and the rain falls / Piercing the skin of the pool with water in water and making a million / And a million designs to be pleasingly latticed and laced and interfused / And mirrored to the Lord of everything that is by one and one and one."

What was it like to be a part of all this once, when one was young and everything was alive, even inert and inanimate things? There used to be gods in everything, and now they've gone. Can we recollect it? Does this world continue to exist in the house of recall? If it does, Nemerov's poem "The Companions" is still able to conjure it again to surround us as it used to do when we walked out into the bright dawn of childhood, for a small god

> I remember, in a green-gray stone,
> Would watch me go by with his still eyes of a toad,
> And in the branch of an elm that hung across the road
> Another was; he creaked at me on windless days.
>
> Where have these familiars gone? Why have they deserted us?
> Now that he's gone I think he might have wanted praise
> For trying to speak my language and getting that far at least
> Along on the imitation of a speaking beast.

Perhaps, however, the little gods did not fail us so much as we failed them.

> Maybe he wanted help, maybe they all cried out
> As they could, or stared helpless to enter into thought
> With "read me," "answer me," or "teach me how to be

> Whatever I am, and in return for teaching me
> I'll tell you what I was in you, how greater far
> Than I are seeking you in fountain, sun, and star."

This poem is Frostian: "That's but interpretation, the deep folly of man / To think that things can squeak at him more than things can." Still, we can all remember the voices. We can remember when they spoke to us, and when we replied. And then we grew up and "turned away."

> I must have done, I guess, to have grown so abstract
> That all the lonely summer night's become but fact,
> That when the cricket signals I no longer listen,
> Nor read the glowworms' constellations when they glisten.

Nemerov's perspective was "The View from an Attic Window." In part "2" of this poem the poet said, "I cried because life is hopeless and beautiful." That is also why he wrote. The house below the boy dreaming in the garret is a great inventory of the ordinary, of which lifetimes are composed: "Down in the cellar, furnace and washing machine, / Pump, fuse-box, water heater, work their hearts / Out at my life, which narrowly runs between / Them and this cemetery of spare parts / For discontinued men, whose hats and canes / Are my rich remains." These things are still alive for the adult looking back. They are inhabited by the past, by all the generations gone and still to be born. As he looks out of the window at his neighborhood beneath the falling flakes of winter storm, of which there are

> As many as the sands of all the seas,
> As all the men who died or who will die,
> As stars in heaven, as leaves of all the trees;
> As Abraham was promised of his seed;
> Generations bleed,
>
> Till I, high in the tower of my time
> Among familiar ruins, began to cry
> For accident, sickness, justice, war and crime,
> Because all died, because I had to die.

Although Nemerov's poems are models of bardic craft, their true value lies in the help they give his readers; help in getting through the ordinary day, through depression and crisis — getting through life a little easier, with a little more insight into human frailty, the conditions of our conditional existences, sometimes with a touch of humor, a wry twist of the lips, or a bit of rue misting the eyelids. Few poets can take a common situation and add to it incrementally as Nemerov did until, suddenly, we are spinning around the sun, as in "The May-Day Dancing," or listening in to the power of eternity, as in "The Dial Tone," or facing the fact of our self-delusion without illusion, as in "The Goose Fish" —

> There in the China light he lay,
> Most ancient and corrupt and grey.
> They hesitated at his smile,
> Wondering what it seemed to say
> To lovers who a little while
> Before had thought to understand,
> By violence upon the sand,
> The only way that could be known
> To make a world their own.

Nemerov was a poet of large thought and, at the same time, of the physical, not merely the metaphysical world. Not even Wallace Stevens made the existential condition more palpable.

Randall Jarrell

Randall Jarrell, a poet, critic, and novelist, was born in Nashville, Tennessee in 1914. He attended Vanderbilt University where he was influenced by the New Critics and The Fugitives — these formed his aesthetic and informed his practice throughout his life. During the war he served in the Army Air Corps from 1942-1946; however, Jarrell's time was spent in the U.S. where he served on a B-29 bomber base in Arizona. His first book of poems, *Blood for a Stranger*, appeared in 1942 during the war, and it was as conventional as most books of the period. His second, *Little Friend, Little Friend*, was published in 1945 as the war came to a close. His first real success, however, was with his third book, *Losses*, which appeared in 1948.

As a professional Jarrell, like his mentors at Vanderbilt, taught at various institutions of higher learning including Sarah Lawrence, Kenyon College (where the New Critic John Crowe Ransom had gone to teach and found *The Kenyon Review*), Princeton, and the University of North Carolina at Greensboro. Like some of his mentors, he published a great deal of formalist criticism in periodicals such *as The Nation, Partisan Review*, and *The Yale Review*. His last book of poems, *The Lost World*, appeared in 1965, the year of his untimely and apparently accidental death.

Stephen Stepanchev, in his *American Poetry Since 1945*, noted the vigor of Jarrell's second and third volumes (42). It appeared to him that Jarrell had found his animating subject: war and the military — everything to do with regimentation, routine, and combat, though he had no experience of the latter. Jarrell's imagination was enlivened by these; they enabled him to find powerful symbols and archetypes to make the suffering of all the victims of brutality, including the combatants, solid and real to the minds of his readers. On the other hand, sometimes his symbolism could be too distancing, the narration of his stories too objective. These strengths and weaknesses of Jarrell's work were often the strengths and weaknesses of his contemporaries as well.

J. A. Bryant, Jr., writing in his *Understanding Randall Jarrell*, said, "Jarrell never saw combat during World War II and never served overseas. Having failed to qualify for ferry-pilot training, he enlisted in the army air [corps] as a private and served for a time as a link trainer instructor. When the need for that duty diminished, he qualified as a celestial-navigation tower operator. Nevertheless, the poems that Jarrell wrote during this period in his life have enabled him to stand with [the British World War I poets] Siegfried Sassoon and Wilfred Owen as a war poet of distinction and with the popular correspondent Ernie Pyle, whose work he respected and even admired as one of the significant voices of World War II. Today there are those who know nothing else Jarrell wrote but can quote phrases and lines from 'The Death of the Ball Turret Gunner'." (48-9)

Frederic J. Hoffman noted in his *The Achievement of Randall Jarrell* that the poet's first book, which was dedicated to his mentor the Fugitive poet Allen Tate, was full of poems that were written in the style admired by the New Critics: they were formal and ironic, but many of them also had a certain dreamlike quality; in fact, they could border upon the surreal. The dreamer would awaken and be unable to tell which was reality, his wakening or the dream. Jarrell would find archetypal symbols that would objectify such things as death and birth, fear, nurture, guilt. These subjects continued in his *Little Friend, Little Friend* (1945) which ended with "The Death of the Ball Turret Gunner," one of the most-anthologized poems to come out of World War II and still Jarrell's best-known single piece. (1)

In this surreal, loosely iambic-pentameter quintet poem with only two lines rhyming — the second and fifth — the voice of the speaker comes from beyond the grave. The dramatic narrator is an animal as well as a human being. His "mother" likewise has a double identity — she is a bomber and a woman; her womb is the Plexiglas bubble on the fuselage of that warplane, perhaps a Mitchell Liberator or a Flying Fortress. When she gives birth, she gives up a terrified animal to society, which is supposed to make a person out of it.

Life, however, is unreal, more unreal than the preconscious womb. Those who have not experienced it can only attempt, with Jarrell's help, to imagine what it must have been like to be suspended under the belly of an airplane in a transparent ball, firing a machine gun at the fighter planes rising out of the clouds and smoke, their own guns blazing: When he dies "they" wash him out of the turret with a hose. The nightmare ought to be over, but it is not — the gunner is still conscious, even in death. The final line of the poem is a damnation. Although it appears to be a flat statement, it still has a compound nature: sleep is an awakening to a dream of life, to a nightmare of death, but death is not sleep; rather, it is a terrible awareness of the nature of reality.

Jarrell's poetry continued to reflect not only the precepts of the New Criticism — its objectivity, its concern with ambiguities, with Jungian archetypal imagery and Freudian sexual energy, its attention to craft and intelligence — but also the dramatic structure that is evident in "The Death of the Ball Turret Gunner." Jarrell brought to his work a deep sense of concern about the nature of the human animal, and a commitment to use words in order to educate his readers. In the "Introduction" to her study *The Poetry of Randall Jarrell* Suzanne Ferguson took note of Jarrell's drive to dig deeply into the psychological complexities of mankind but at the same time to objectify those knots of consciousness through narrative and dramatic techniques rather than burrow inward toward the core of the self. (3) This approach would be unusual in the 1960s when most of Jarrell's contemporaries would turn away from public utterance to personal statement — but Jarrell would not survive the decade of the 'sixties; his last book was the posthumous *Selected Poems* (1966).

Ferguson further pointed out that, of the poets of his generation, only the reputations of Theodore Roethke and Robert Lowell loom larger than that of Jarrell in the contemporary period. (3-4) Further, only Roethke and Lowell are more deeply "personal" in approach and subject matter; nevertheless, Jarrell was capable of writing extremely powerfully using his dramatic voices.

Jarrell felt, according to his own words in *Poet's Choice*, edited by Paul Engle and Joseph Langland in 1962, that "'Eighth Air Force' expresses better than any of the other poems I wrote about the war what I felt about the war." But one of the dead children in the dialogue poem "Protocols" who says that the gas in the strange room in the Nazi camp "smelled like hay," not realizing that the scent is that of poison gas, of death, can make the reader feel powerfully, in this case through dramatic irony, what an unbearable experience can be like.

Theodore Roethke

Theodore Roethke (1908-1963) did not serve in the military forces during the War. In his livelihood, however, he fitted the general pattern of the Academic Poets, for he was by reputation not only a considerable poet but a great teacher. Born in Saginaw, Michigan, where his father was a nurseryman, he attended the University of Michigan and, for a short time, Harvard University. He taught in various institutions, but he was most closely associated in his later years with the Pacific Northwest where he was a member of the faculty of the University of Washington in Seattle.

Roethke's first book, *Open House* (1941), was the typical formalist debut volume, but beginning with *The Lost Son and Other Poems* (1948) he began to receive considerable critical attention. According to David Perkins Roethke's education was "almost entirely literary." (367-8) In mid-life, however, he read the works of some of the foremost modern religious thinkers including Tillich, Buber, and Kierkegaard. He was as interested as Randall Jarrell in psychology, but his experience was more responsible for the information about it that he absorbed, for his manic-depressive condition caused him to undergo numerous nervous and mental crises.

According to William Heyen in his Profile of *Theodore Roethke* there is evidence that Roethke courted this state, or at least that he attempted to exercise some sort of "control" over it. (100) Roethke thus was playing the role of the Platonic poet, the divine madman of the romantic tradition. Willard J. Martz in his *The Achievement of Theodore Roethke*, quotes the poet: "'I proclaim once more a condition of joy,' he announces" in "I Cry Love!" "O to be delivered from the rational into the realm of pure song," he exclaims in "What Can I Tell My Bones?" (1)

Roethke, then, at least in his own view, was not the craftsman of the classical Aristotelian tradition at all; he took the idea of the "organic" poem, the poem that chooses its own form. The poet is the shaman through whom the gods speak when they take possession of him. As Hyatt H. Waggoner wrote in his *American Poets from the Puritans to the Present*, this practice made Roethke a follower of Ralph Waldo Emerson and Walt Whitman, not merely an academic man of letters. (pp. 564-5)

These ideas, which had been lying dormant in American literature since the nineteenth century, would during the 1960s explode in contemporary poetry and dominate the scene, in various forms, for a quarter-century. Roethke's mind and practice, however, were after all as split on this subject as were those of some of his contemporaries, most notably Richard Wilbur. Roethke attempted to write a poetry, in the middle period of his life — from *The Lost Son and Other Poems* of 1948 to *Words for the Wind* a decade later — that was poetry of the unconscious mind, as in part 2, "The Pit," of the title poem of the former volume:

> Where do the roots go?
> Look down under the leaves.
> Who put the moss there?

> These stones have been here too long.
> Who stunned the dirt into noise?
> Ask the mole, he knows.
> I feel the slime of a wet nest.
> Beware, Mother Mildew.
> Nibble again, fish nerves.

Yet the last poems in *Collected Poems*, aside from the final section, "Previously Uncollected Poems," were as formal as those of his first volume, rhyming and metering just as he had done when he'd been young.

The great example of this split-mindedness is Roethke's use of an extremely tight verse form, the medieval Provençal villanelle, to enunciate Emerson's central thesis about "organic" poetry. "The Waking" is one of Roethke's most famous works, one of the most anthologized poems in contemporary literature. It appeared in his 1951 collection *Praise to the End*! The form is nineteen lines long, and it is made up of five triplets and a concluding quatrain; all lines turn on only two rhymes. The first stanza contains two refrains, lines one and three:

> I wake to sleep, and take my waking slow.
> I feel my fate in what I cannot fear.
> I learn by going where I have to go.

Line one ends stanzas two and four; line three ends stanzas three and five, with slight variations:

> We think by feeling. What is there to know?
> I hear my being dance from ear to ear.
> I wake to sleep, and take my waking slow.

"We think by feeling. What is there to know?" Roethke wrote, but certainly it was impossible for him to have written that line without thinking, and it would not have been necessary to write it at all if, indeed, we "think" by "feeling." The poem is a closed-circuit paradox which the New Critics would argue makes it a good poem, for it expresses the ambiguity that comprises the existential experience of human beings:

> Of those so close beside me, which are you?
> God bless the Ground! I shall walk softly there,
> And learn by going where I have to go.

The New Critics would also have approved of the symbolism of the poem, both religious and archetypal:

> Light takes the Tree, but who can tell us how?
> The lowly worm climbs up a winding stair;
> I wake to sleep, and take my waking slow.

Another feature of the poem, besides the sensory level of imagery, is the sonic level. Aside from the meters, the rhymes, and the repetitions, Roethke also used such devices as alliteration and assonance as in the sequence of stanza five, "lively...lovely, learn":

> Great Nature has another thing to do
> To you and me; so take the lively air,
> And, lovely, learn by going where to go.

Lines one and three of the first stanza reappear as the penultimate and last lines of the concluding quatrain, and it is not merely a climactic stanza, but one that obviously deliberately compounds the central paradox of the poem:

> This shaking keeps me steady. I should know.
> What falls away is always. And is near.
> I wake to sleep, and take my waking slow.
> I learn by going where I have to go.

An examination of "The Waking" makes it clear that the sonic and sensory levels of the poem were a good deal more important to Roethke than the ideational. In *Conversations on the Craft of Poetry*, a tape recording and transcript edited by Cleanth Brooks and Robert Penn Warren, Roethke had said, "What do I like? Listen.

> "Hinx, minx, the old witch winks,
> The fat begins to fry,
> There's nobody home but Jumping Joan,
> And Father, and Mother, and I.

"Now what makes that catchy, to use Mr. [Robert] Frost's phrase?" Roethke continued. "For one thing, the rhythm. Five stresses out of a possible six in the first line." (48) Walter D. Kalaidjian discussed Roethke's usage of such "folk rhythms" in his *Understanding Theodore Roethke*, and some other techniques Roethke used to avoid the traditional iambic line that he had been trained in. (39 *ff*.) Roethke's prosody is called "podics," or strong-stress verse. It is a derivation of the alliterative-accentual system called Anglo-Saxon prosody, the ancient, original English-language method for composing poetry which counts only overstressed syllables in a line of verse, not all syllables and stresses, as in the accentual-syllabic verse of most of the Academic poets, though among the Modernists John Crowe Ransom of the Fugitives also used podics as a vehicle for his poems.

The dipodic line, like the hemistich of Anglo-Saxon prosody, contains two accented syllables. These are all that are counted—the unaccented syllables are ignored. The first accent is often a secondary stress (.); the second is a primary (heavy) stress (´). Sometimes there are variations in this pattern. Normally, two dipodic lines (one stich) are needed to complete the unit, which is a rhymed couplet often with falling endings (ending on the unstressed syllable as distinguished from masculine, which end on the stressed syllable). An example is part two of Roethke's "The Shape of the Fire":

     . ˘ ´
Where's the eye?

  ˘ ´ ˘ ˘ ´
The eye's in the sty.

  ˘ ´ ˘ ´
The ear's not here

  ˘ ´ ˘ ´
Beneath the hair.

  ˘ ˘ ´ ´ ˘ ´
When I took off my clothes

  ˘ ´ ˘ ´
To find a nose,

  ˘ ˘ . ˘ ´ ´
There was only one shoe

  ˘ ˘ ´ ˘ ´
For the waltz of To,

  ˘ ´ ˘ ´
The pinch of Where.

The scansion of this stanza shows that there is no running foot, as in accentual-syllabic prosody. Furthermore, the numbers of syllables in the lines vary widely, from three in line one to six in lines five and seven. The only thing that remains relatively stable is the stress count — two strong stresses per line except where there is an extra secondary stress as a variation.

To put it simply, a dipodic unit is nothing more than a couplet made of two rhyming stichs of Anglo-Saxon prosody: the caesura between hemistichs became the ends of lines 1 and 3, so that the couplet appears on the page as a quatrain. Here are the first four lines of Roethke's "Once More, The Round" laid out as two stichs of Anglo-Saxon prosody with the requisite caesura in the center of each line:

  .   ´   ´   ´
What's greater, • Pebble or Pond?

  .   ´   ´ .
What can be known? • The Unknown.

  ´ . ´   . ´
My true self runs • toward a Hill

 ´ . ´   ´ .
More! O More! • visible.

  Roethke's critical viewpoint was derived from the 19th-century precepts of the Transcendentalist poet and critic Ralph Waldo Emerson; Hyatt H. Waggoner referred to Roethke's criticism in a section of his book *American Poets from the Puritans to the Present* titled "Anti-Modernist Ideas" where the first two poets considered are Roethke and James Dickey. In a review Waggoner quoted from the January 1946 issue of the magazine *Poetry* where Roethke attacked the poetry of his contemporaries, "whole schools of verbalizers, nerveless, slick and often macabre; squeezers of the obvious, vulgar jostlers with words; cerebral gibberers and wild-eyed affirmers; helter-skelter impressionists and frantic improvisers; pip-squeak euphuists who expand a tiny emotion far beyond its proper size, who make grandiloquent pronouncements on large issues long before they have mastered the smallest of private worlds." And he continued, "The trouble probably lies in the age itself, in the unwillingness of poets to face their ultimate inner responsibilities, in their willingness to seek refuge in words rather than transcending them." Waggoner commented, "The terms of his abuse imply that the poet uses words but that poems are not 'about' words." (606 *ff.*)

Karl Shapiro

A native Baltimorean, Karl Shapiro was educated at the University of Virginia, Johns Hopkins, and the Enoch Pratt Library School in Baltimore before America entered the war. He served in the U.S. Army from 1941 to 1945. Shapiro's first book, *Poems*, was published in 1935. During the next ten years Shapiro wrote four other books, two of which were particularly well-received: *V-Letter and Other Poems* (1944) and *Essay on Rime* (1945), both formalist volumes.

Like other members of his poetic generation, Shapiro was of two minds, literarily speaking — he grew up during the Modernist revolution reading and admiring the great experimental poets of his day, but in the high school and college classrooms he read the traditional British and American poets and was trained in their methods. Shapiro was a stranger neither to formal craft nor prosodic experiment. Shapiro's *Essay on Rime*, in fact, was a study and consideration of the traditional approaches to poetry, the entire volume itself being written in verse rather than in prose mode. Not until 1958 and his *Poems of a Jew* did Shapiro write another book that achieved an equal success.

During the 1960s some of the formalist poets were persuaded to the new view of the "Beats" and the Black Mountain poets that formalism was no longer relevant to the times, which were becoming oriented to social activism and reform. Karl Shapiro was one of the first of the formalists to adopt the new stance. He gave a lecture in the early 1960s at various universities, including the Fenn College (now Cleveland State University) Poetry Center, that resurrected the theories of the 19th-century British satirical novelist Thomas Love Peacock to the effect that mankind ought to have outgrown poetry which was no more than the nursery rhymes of an infant society. Shapiro said that if poetry was that which was "lost in translation," then he wanted his work to sound as much like translations as possible, for he wanted no part of rhymes and meters and such linguistic tinkle-toys any longer.

Shapiro joined the Beats, also, in making the connection between formal poetry and the "military-industrial complex" when he wrote in *College English*, the issue of October 1964, "An overnight collapse of the stanza might be as dangerous as the abolition of the Army. Poets still need close-order drill and the barracks mentality. It's too bad that they do. Novelists don't nor does any other kind of artist I know of. But poets are still the hostages of convention." Kenneth Rexroth, a founder of the San Francisco School of poetry had been saying exactly the same thing for years.

This was not the same Shapiro to be found in *An Essay on Rime* nor even in *Trial of a Poet*. In his volume of prose poems *The Bourgeois Poet* (1964), Shapiro tried to out-Beat Allen Ginsberg. By the time *White-Haired Lover* appeared in 1968, however, Shapiro had done another about-face and was writing sonnets again, at least part-time, just as Peacock — despite his haranguing on the subject of formal poetry — had sneaked sonnets into his novels.

To read through Karl Shapiro's *Collected Poems 1940-1978* is to ride a roller-coaster through the literary fashions of the times, during all of which Shapiro was an academic teaching at various universities — in particular the University of Nebraska from 1956 to 1966 and, beginning in 1968, the University of California at Davis — and editing periodicals mainly of an academic stripe, including the long-lived magazine Harriet Monroe founded in Chicago, *Poetry*, originally the showcase of Modernist work but, during the decade of the 1960s, one of the last bastions of formalist practice. Thus one of the earliest of the post-Modernist generation of poets, one of the first contemporary formalists, led the parade to anti-formalism in the academy, and then was the earliest of the converted to backslide again to formalism, long before the Neoformalist movement got its foothold in the 1980s.

"The Fly," which appeared in Shapiro's first book, became one of his most famous and most anthologized exercises. It can stand as well as any of his poems as an example of the poet's formal style. Here is the first stanza:

> O hideous little bat, the size of snot,
> With polyhedral eye and shabby clothes,
> To populate the stinking cat you walk
> The promontory of the dead man's nose,
> Climb with the fine leg of a Duncan-Phyfe
> The smoking mountains of my food
> And in a comic mood
> In mid-air take to bed a wife.

By the mid-sixties, Shapiro had moved to straight, "unlineated" prose as a vehicle, as his "Death of a Student" shows:

> Down the funeral aisle ("my" student in coffin, car wreck, youngish death, eyeglasses polished, suit pressed as if for class, except that he's dead) come the grandparents, farmers, barely walking. Followed by yet another generation — over the arm of a younging man a girl about three asleep—drugged?—her golden pony tail flopping, asleep.
>
> Tie tied, suit without lint, the curt sadistic sermon. Love stiffens her back. The child evades the question, as if tossing her hair. Nihilo lies sleeping.

By the standards of the time, and compared with the output of such people as Allen Ginsberg, this prose poetry was quite tame and unrevolutionary. Nevertheless, by the time *The Bourgeois Poet* was published, many of the Academic poets were abandoning not only formal verse, but the teaching of the elements of formal verse writing. They were stepping down from their hard-won positions of leadership and joining, as foot soldiers in the war against the "Military-Industrial Complex," the legions of their anti-intellectual students who were crying "Make Love, Not War" and "You Can't Trust Anyone Over Thirty." As a sign of their good earnest, the former Academic Poets tried to act as though they didn't know as much as they did, but only enough to get by. Teachers began to hear their students say in class that learning the techniques that had been used to write poetry in English for centuries was too "constricting." They had to be "free." Arguments to the effect that ignorance was not freedom and that the more one knew how to do, the more one could do, fell upon deaf ears.

As the 'sixties turned into the 'seventies, a generation of student writers could hardly imagine how Shakespeare could have written those sonnets. By the time the late 'seventies had arrived, many of these student writers became teachers themselves in the proliferating writing arts programs and workshops around the nation. By the 'eighties, so much competence and lore had been lost, it was hard to imagine how it could ever be regained.

Louis O. Coxe

Louis O. Coxe was Born in 1918 in Manchester, New Hampshire and was educated in the same state at St. Paul's School in Concord. He took his A. B. from Princeton University in 1940 and subsequently served during World War II in the Naval Reserve. The year of his discharge, 1946, he was married and began his teaching career at his *Alma Mater*. He was Briggs-Copeland Fellow at Harvard from 1948-49 and from 1949-55 he taught at the University of Minnesota. Coxe went to Bowdoin College in Brunswick, Maine, in 1956 where he remained except for excursions to Trinity College, Dublin, Ireland, and the University of Aix-Marseilles, France, until his death in 1993, a victim of Alzheimer's disease.

Coxe, always a formal poet, published his first book, *The Sea Faring and Other poems* in 1947. This publication was followed by *The Second Man and Other Poems* eight years later, in 1955; *The Wilderness and Other Poems* (1958); *The Middle Passage* (1960); *The Last Hero and Other Poems* (1965); *Nikal Seyn, Decoration Day: A Poem and a Play* (1966), *Passage Selected Poems 1943-1978*, and *The North Well* (1985). Coxe was the author also of three other plays and four nonfiction books.

"Winter Night" first appeared in *The New Yorker*, and it was collected in *The Second Man*, but its anthologization in *The New Yorker Book of Poems* was what brought this poem to the attention of a wide and appreciative audience. Written in verse mode, "Winter Night" consists of six quatrain stanzas. Its prosody is normative accentual-syllabics, and its meter is iambic tetrameter. The rhyme scheme is *abab*, *cdcd*, etc.; its stanzas therefore belong to the group called "common measure"; they are, in fact, long hymnal stanza — there is nothing fancy about them:

> The circuit closes. House and heart
> Must cut and save the heat they use.
> A circuit closed by sleep shall start
> The nightlong quarrel life must lose.

Nor did Coxe do many clever things by way of counterpoint; he substituted verse feet now and then. The substitution of a trochee in the first and third feet of the second stanza produces a rocking rhythm in the line — iambs thus do not predominate in it. In the second line of the same stanza a spondee is substituted in the first foot, and a trochee in the same spot in line three. In the first foot of line four there is a demotion in the first syllable of the first foot, which otherwise would have been a spondee:

Ticking like deathwatches, my house

Stands up this night to ice once more,

Knowing at last it cannot rouse

That strength and sap it knew before.

Coxe did the same thing in the first foot of stanza three, line two. In the first line a promotion occurs in the sixth syllable. In the next line an anapest follows a spondee for considerable counterpoint, and in the fourth line a demotion takes place in the fifth syllable:

The seasoned timbers of the stair

Creak to my weight; a dog outside

Howls windily. How should hearts prepare

To front a cold few beasts abide?

Stanza four is very interesting sonically. In the first foot of the first line there is a trochee, and a demotion occurs in the fifth syllable again — there is a promotion in the fourth syllable of the second line. Lines two and four are hypercatalectic because of the double (falling) rhymes. In line three a trochee is substituted in the third foot, and the fourth line begins with a trochee:

Padding the hall I pause by doors

And listen to my children's breathing,

While cold of night-fear and remorse

        ′ ⌣ | ⌣   ′ | ⌣   ′ | ⌣   ′ ⌣
Puddles and curds for all the sheathing,

All the revetment I had tiered
To insulate from northern breath:
My house, for all the worst I feared
And bargained for, shall catch a death.

The same sorts of variations occur in the rest of the poem, until the last line, which again sets up the rocking rhythm of the first line of stanza two:

And lusts that spread today in sun,
Flattered in pride of life grown tall,
Shall clot by gradual ice to one

      ′ ⌣ | ⌣   ′ | ′   ⌣ | ⌣   ′
Standing with held . breath in the hall.

Between these two "rocking feet" a natural caesura occurs; thus, the meter of the line exactly illustrates rhythmically the sense of the line. The odd rhythm does not come as a shock to the reader because the poet set the premise for its possibility earlier in the poem, where the caesura could not exist because it would then have occurred in the center of the word "deathwatches" — though a hint of it does occur anyway, like the pause between the ticks of a watch. The caesura is suspended until just before the final iamb of that line, so that the basic iambic beat is emphasized. Still, the precedent is there for the poet to utilize in his climactic ending.

    Coxe was not unaware of other sorts of devices to be used on the sonic level — consonantal echo (cir**c**uit **c**loses. Hou**s**e); alliteration (**h**ouse and **h**eart); repetition (cir**cuit** - **cut**); vocalic echo (must cut, closes - closed). Esses in particular are used onomatopoeically throughout, but particularly in stanzas one and six.

    On the sensory level the primary trope used is extended metaphor. The word "circuit" is used to mean both an electrical circuit — the thermostat — and a cycle. The reader picks this up with the next phrase, a parallel construction: "House and heart" must "cut" [the heat] and "save" [energy]. The house, then, is the tenor of the metaphor, and the heart is the vehicle. Coxe immediately begins to extend the figure: the "circuit closed by sleep shall start / The nightlong quarrel life must lose." It becomes clear, on the symbolic level, that sleep is to be equated with death. This extension is reinforced with the next line overtly: "Ticking like deathwatches, my house...." A simile and a pun, the overtone of "deathwatches" is evident. Sleep closes the circuit of consciousness in the "nightlong quarrel" to regain consciousness, a struggle that "life must lose" at last.

    The house "stands up...to ice once more," but it is a fragile shell, like the body, like the original trees from which it was made. But houses cannot "know," only human beings can do that, so we know the poet is speaking of the human body when he says the house knows "it cannot rouse / That strength and sap it knew before." "How should hearts prepare to [con]front" the impending cold of death? Worse, how does one protect one's loved ones? The wakeful man pads the hall, listens at doors for the sounds of his children's breath in the cold seeping through the house, the "cold of night-fear and remorse." This last word is enigmatic. What is the nature of this remorse? Is it chagrin and sorrow for having brought into this world creatures, like the narrator himself, who may in their own time walk the houses of night?

Nothing can withstand the cold, not shingles nor clapboards. No matter what, "My house, for all the worst I feared / And bargained for, shall catch a death." The colloquialism, "catch a death of cold" is an ironic pun only partially stated, its punch implied. All that one pridefully believes and puffs himself up about in the light of day freezes, clots "by gradual ice to one / Standing with held breath in the hall."

The usage of tropes is in the metaphysical tradition; these six stanzas are one conceit. The emotional thrust of the poem is of dread and sorrow. The poet has appealed mainly to the senses of feeling (heat, cold), and hearing (tickings, creakings, howls).

On the ideational level, the subject of the poem is death. The general form of the poem, then, is the elegy. The schemas used are primarily inclusive and constructional, in particular parallelism, dualities of house and heart. The viewpoint is egopoetic; the narrator is the author, and the syntax used is subjective, though the passage, "While cold of night-fear and remorse / Puddles and curds for all the sheathing, // All the revetment I had tiered / To insulate from northern breath" borders on abstract syntax, at least in part (puddles and curds — what does that mean?). However, the pun on "tiered" is clear. The level of diction is meditative, traditional for an elegy; the style is literary. The theme is that death can be warded off for only so long.

Fusionally, the poem is an occasional lyric. All three levels are important, the ideational being supported at all points by the sonic and the sensory. The poem is at once typical of the work of this contemporary New England poet, and an outstanding example of it.

Coxe's last collection, *The North Well*, contained less formally traditional lyrics than most of his books had done. His vision had changed little, however; it was still dark and darkly stoical. These are the finely wrought poems of a survivor, whose survival has perhaps been made possible by the writing of such laments as "Aphasia":

> It never came on time
> to reach me, the late news:
> my dates were wrong, the beam
> swept out but didn't scan.
>
> Out there blip and beep
> came on ticking the time

to others. Caught in the sweep
I turned them out of tune

into shapes of plot and pattern
that leapt on the scope and died
telling me "No matter."
Whatever I did, they lied

to me alone. This sickness
fingered and fed with dark
stands as sole witness
to a long night's work.

CHAPTER TWO
Black Mountain and the Beat Generation

It has been convenient for more than a hundred years to distinguish between "classical" and "romantic" poetry, or between the Aristotelian and the Platonic. The former is "professional" or art poetry, and it derives from the social practices of mankind — storytelling, word-games, lullabies, worksongs and suchlike activities. The latter is "amateur" or, to use Hyatt H. Waggoner's term, "vatic poetry"; its derivation is from the system of "Sympathetic Magic" which obtained in the world at large before the age of science. The object of vatic poetry is to control the environment of mankind through "words of power": incantations, prayers, charms, blessings and so forth.

Professional poets tend to define poetry as "language art," but amateur poets, depending on their particular religious or philosophical set of mind, define poetry in more circumscribed ways, as "vision" or "prophecy" or "revelation" or "ecstasy," as Waggoner has discussed. Such poets consider language not as their primary focus, not as the substance of their product, poetry, but rather as the vehicle for their religious experience, whatever it may be.

A third sort of poet, however, besides the professional and the amateur, is the "agonist" — a professional who is as committed to language art as any other poet, but who is more interested in theories than in performance. Sometimes such poets — as for instance Wallace Stevens — will embody their theories in poetry rather than in essays. Although William Carlos Williams was a member of the great Modernist generation of the 20th century, he remained a poetry activist until his death in 1963 and was always, in his own way, a propagandist who made great claims for a liberal America in his poetry. Williams was not, however, a Stevens-style agonist, for it was not in his poetry that he did most of his theorizing; rather, it was in his letters to young poets, and in the comparatively little prose he published — sometimes in his long pastiche poem, *Paterson*, in *In the American Grain*, and in *Something to Say* which, according to its editor, "collects all of Williams' known writings — reviews, essays, introductions, and letters to the editor — on the two generations of poets that followed him, from Kenneth Rexroth and Louis Zukofsky to Robert Lowell and Allen Ginsberg." None of the great Modernists, not even Ezra Pound, was more generous and welcoming to new talent, more encouraging of the development of new voices and styles, or more insistent that these be recognizably *American*.

Despite William Carlos Williams' charter membership in the school of Modernist poets originally called "Des Imagistes" by its founder, Ezra Pound, and his public adherence to the slogan, "No ideas but in things," which he coined, Williams was in fact very much interested in the dance of language. Imagism gave rise subsequently to Robert Bly's "deep image surrealism," among other movements including Charles Olson's Black Mountain school and Charles Reznikoff's cadre of "Objectivists," both of which split their loyalties between Williams and Pound. Yet it was Williams' interest in prosodic theory and his invention of a variably accentual three-line unit that gave rise to Olson's opaque theories of "projective verse" — often reprinted but never adequately interpreted — and to many later attempts to justify lineated prose-mode poetry as some sort of "free verse," as Stephen Cushman did in an essay titled "Forms of Poetry." "What we have wanted," Cushman quoted Williams as saying, "is a line that will allow us room in which to develop the opportunities of a new language, a line loose as Whitman's, but *measured* [my emphasis] as his was not."

Some critics consider that Williams was a proselytizer for a certain kind of amateur poetry; he was a sort of American prophet following Whitman and, many have argued, the Whitman line, for American "poetry" isn't about language, it isn't about art, it's about patriotism, in a peculiar way. Stephen Tapscott wrote, "Williams chose Whitman as an appropriate model because Williams needed to invent a tradition to join," for, as Williams remarked to his son, "I have wanted to link myself up with traditional art."

George S. Lensing, discussing the Tapscott book in his essay, "Williams after the First Quarter-Century," wrote, "Whitman was American, vernacular, committed to place, experimental in form, consciously rebellious — all qualities extolled by Williams. Whitman's transcendentalism, however, was regarded with suspicion; and many of the formal experiments, according to Williams, failed." In other words, Williams did not see himself as a prose-mode vatic poet like Whitman.

American poetry, when it was defined by Emerson and Whitman, was defined specifically as vatic poetry, but a particular kind, in order to distinguish it from European amateur poetry. American poetry was to be anti-formal, intuitive, "organic." Whitman, as the prime poet-prophet of America, was concerned with mythologizing American experience in this "new" way. It is itself a myth, however, that Williams was essentially a follower of Whitman.

Waggoner claimed that Williams "really knew very little about Whitman." (377) Williams was interested in only part of Whitman's program. Waggoner talked about the mainstream of American poetry deriving from Whitman and Emerson, but then he made distinctions among those poets who derive directly from Emerson's Transcendentalist credo, those who derive directly from Whitman's prose-poetry practice, and those who derive from a combination of the two.

Williams derives primarily from Whitman's practice, not from Emerson's agonism. That is to say, Williams was interested in Whitman's attempt to write in prose, thus getting away from traditional British practice. Rather than write prose poems, however, Williams wanted to write in a "measured" line. For many years he experimented, and finally Williams invented a verse prosody — variable accentuals — that looks, acts, and sounds like prose most of the time. In this way he was like Whitman superficially.

Williams was also interested in the "common man," as Whitman professed to be, but in Williams' poetry the reader will find real people whereas in Whitman's work one may find laborers mentioned and over-mentioned in catalogs of people, but the only person one will find is Whitman himself, or at least the image of himself that he projected. Williams was interested in Everyman; Whitman was interested in himself as the icon of Everyman, but it is a tossup which of these two poets was more responsible for the proliferation of "democratic" poetic schools and canons in mid-century American poetry.

To say that Ezra Pound and the Imagist poets were influenced not only by Whitman's practice but also by Japanese poetry — especially the haiku — is to utter a truism, but the argument can be made that Williams deliberately invented an American accentual stanza in his "triversen" that is the equivalent of the Japanese haiku — or, more exactly, the three-line katauta, as I have discussed in chapter 12, "Of Imagery," in *Poetry: An Introduction Through Writing*. (161-172) In effect, in his earliest poems — those to be found in the first volume of his *Collected Poems*, from which all the illustrations used here have been taken — Williams adapted to American poetry the syllabic prosody of the haiku and katauta by transmuting it: syllables became stresses; the seventeen syllables of the haiku and the nineteen syllables of the katauta, arranged in three lines of 5-7-5 or 5-7-7 syllables, became a "variable foot," to use Williams' terminology, also arranged in three lines.

Besides the "variable foot," Williams talked about the "breath pause," an accentual prosody version of the katauta which is, according to Robert H. Brower and Earl Miner, "A fragmentary form of three lines of 5, 7, 7 syllables. Sometimes used in pairs for dialogue; suggests incompleteness when alone." (507) There are actually two forms that are called "katautas"; both are formal, but only one is a stanza form *per se*, and both are based upon spontaneous "utterances" which, in the Japanese tradition, are sudden, emotive words as in the first line of Williams' poem "Mujer":

> Oh, black Persian cat!

The first form of the katauta is an emotive question or its answer, as in lines two and three of the same poem:

> Was not your life already/ cursed with offsprings?
> (*Collected Poems*, Vol. I, 78).

A pair of such katautas is a mondo as in Williams' poem "The Hunter," stanzas two and three:

> Where will a shoulder split or
> a forehead open and victory be?
>
> Nowhere.
> Both sides grow older (*CP* I, 164).

Mondos may look like the Western syllogism and appear in similar parallel constructions, as for instance in stanza one of Williams' "The Fool's Song":

> I tried to put a bird in a cage.
>   O fool that I am!
> For the bird was Truth.
>   Sing merrily, Truth: I tried to put
>   Truth in a cage! (*CP* I, 5-6).

But the katauta answer is not derived logically; it is intuited, as in the Zen koan or "unanswerable question," for Zen Buddhism is at the root of the haiku. As Yoel Hoffman noted in *Japanese Death Poems*, "Zen literature eventually came to serve as a means to enlightenment in Zen monasteries. Several times a week, every monk would meet alone with the master. The latter would tell an anecdote or present a koan, a sort of problem or riddle from Zen literature. The monk's response would not necessarily be verbal, and it is often difficult to see the connection between the answer and the anecdote." (73) An example of such intuition is to be found in lines two through four of Williams' "Fire Spirit":

> I am old.
> You warm yourselves at these fires?
> In the center of these flames
> I sit, my teeth chatter!
> Where shall I turn for comfort? (*CP* I, p. 58).

The last line in this strophe is a rhetorical question, not a katauta question, and the first line is merely a statement, not an emotive utterance. One can see the difference between the two sets of lines if lines one and five are juxtaposed —

> I am old.
> Where shall I turn for comfort?

or, in reverse order,

> Where shall I turn for comfort?
> I am old.

— and then set against the three middle lines:

> You warm yourself at these fires?
> In the center of these flames
> I sit, my teeth chatter!

This cannot be said to be a logical consequence of a rational action.

The second kind of katauta is a stanza or poem form. It is made up of three parts arranged in lines of 5-7-7 syllables, these lengths being approximately breath-length, or the appropriate lengths in which to ask a sudden, emotive question and respond to it, also emotively. Seventeen syllables — as in the haiku, or nineteen — as in the katauta, are as many as can normally be uttered in one short breath; five to seven syllables are approximately equal to the utterance of an emotive question or its answer. The Japanese poet Igarashi wrote of this basic and organic unit of Japanese poetry, "Katauta is a poem of three lines in which the first two lines consist of one short and one long one; and the last line is the same length as the second line, which is added as a prop to help harmonize the rhythm. This is the unit of Japanese poetry." (Turco, 163)

In Williams' "variable foot" accentual prosody version of this unit, two to four stresses are approximately equal to the utterance of an emotive question or its answer, and six to twelve stresses are the outer limits of the utterance of a question and its intuitive "answer." Arranging these stresses and emotive utterances into lines not exceeding four stresses each, one will have a stanza or poem three lines in length, each line being equal to one phrase. In fact, this system in grammatical prosodies is called "lineating" (by Cushman and others) or "line-phrasing," and there is such a grammatical element in some Japanese forms as well, particularly in the tanka which, like the katauta, takes two forms (Brower, 511; Y. Hoffman, 19-22).

Both forms of the tanka are externally alike in that they are quintet poems with lines, in this order, of 5-7-5-7-7 syllables. In the first tanka form, called the waka, one subject is treated in the first two lines, another in the next two, and the last line is a refrain or paraphrase or restatement: 5-7, 5-7, 5. The first two lines are a dependent clause or a phrase, the last three an independent clause. Grammatically, Williams often did similar things with his stanzas: note the stanza from "The Fool's Song" above.

The second type of tanka consists of two parts. The first three lines are an independent unit ending in a noun or verb after which a turn takes place: 5-7-5, 7-7. The triplet is an observation, the couplet is a comment on the observation. Returning to Williams' "Fire Spirit," and dropping the first line to last position, we have the form — disregarding syllabification — of this kind of tanka:

> You warm yourself at these fires?
> In the center of these flames
> I sit, my teeth chatter.
>
> Where shall I turn for comfort?
> I am old.

In his poem "Epitaph" Williams used this same division though, again, not the syllabification:

> An old willow with hollow branches
> slowly swayed his few high bright tendrils
> and sang:
>
> Love is a young green willow
> shimmering at the bare wood's edge (*CP* I, 160).

The second line of this poem is unusually long for Williams, and it does not fit the "variable foot" pattern in that it is a line of more than four stresses. Williams wanted to avoid the English iambic pentameter line, and his development of the triversen stanza allowed him to do so. The stress pattern of "Epitaph" is as follows, (where the breve [˘] stands for an unstressed syllable, the accent [ʹ] stands for a primary stressed syllable, and the dot [.] stands for a secondary stressed syllable):

1. ˘ ʹ ʹ ˘ ˘ ʹ ˘ ʹ ˘
2. ʹ ˘ ʹ ˘ ʹ . ʹ ʹ ˘
3. ˘ ʹ
4. ʹ ˘ ˘ ʹ . ʹ ˘
5. ʹ ˘ . ˘ ʹ . ʹ (r-glide elision in shim*mering*.)

Line two is heavily overstressed, or "sprung," with alliteration and assonance so that, though it has too many stresses to fit the triversen pattern, it nevertheless avoids the five-stress regularity of iambic pentameter, accentual-syllabic verse. Line five is exactly five stresses long, but the elision of "shim'ring" and the springing of the last three syllables avoid pentameter as well.

A renga, according to Brower, is "Linked verses. Historically two different forms, both involving more than one author. The earlier form, called tanrenga, or 'short renga,' is a tanka whose first three lines were composed by one poet, and last two lines by another;..." (509) This final couplet response is the hanka. A renga chain or "long renga" is a poem made of a sequence of rengas and composed by two or more authors. The first triplet sets the subject, the succeeding couplet and all ensuing triplets and couplets amplify, gloss, or comment upon the first triplet. Various other changes might also be rung upon the long renga, but what is important to this discussion is the development of the haiku from the tanka and the renga.

The tanka developed from an older form, the choka, which was a poem written in alternating 5-7-syllable lines. (Brower, 504) The conclusion of the choka would be, often, an envoy that doubled the last 7-syllable line: 5-7-7 — the katauta — or that consisted of two choka couplets with a doubled last line: 5-7-5-7-7 — the tanka. One can see the katauta is the base of the tanka, and one can see the haiku growing out of the first three lines of the tanka. But it was from the renga chain that the hokku developed. (Y. Hoffman, 15-16) The word is Chinese in origin, and it came to specify in Japanese poetry the first triplet of a renga chain. This first verse set the theme of the chain and was the most important part of the poem, the rest of which, beginning with the succeeding 7-7-syllable hanka couplet, served to elaborate upon or gloss the hokku. (Brower, 505) The hokku of a renga chain ended with a full stop — it was complete by itself.

The term haikai no renga applies to the humorous renga chain, and it means, specifically, "renga of humor." (Hoffman, 16) By various stages the term haiku — a corruption and blending of the dissimilar words "hokku" and "haikai" — came to denote an independent tercet of 5-7-5 syllables. The haiku dropped all hankas, glosses, comments, and elaborations. It became a poem which had as its basis emotive utterance, an image, and certain other characteristics as well, including spareness, condensation, spontaneity, ellipsis, and a seasonal element.

Ideally the haiku, though complete in itself, would be open-ended in that its statement would "reverberate" beyond itself into overtone. Williams' "The Soughing Wind" is a good example of what the haiku poet tries to accomplish by way of suggestion:

> Some leaves hang late, some fall
> before the first frost — so goes
> the tale of winter branches and old bones (*CP* I, 158).

The haiku has perhaps been best described as a moment of intense perception. A distinction is sometimes made between the senryu and the haiku, though both have the same syllabic form. The senryu was originally a parodic haiku, but in its serious aspect it has been characterized as an inquiry into the nature of man; the haiku, an inquiry into the nature of the universe. There seems to be a number of dualities in the Japanese tradition: two kinds of katautas, two kinds of tankas, and two kinds of haiku.

Williams was particularly successful in adapting to American poetics not only Japanese prosodic theory, but also the spirit of the haiku to the American sensibility. Many other Western poets have been notably unsuccessful in writing good haiku or haiku-style poetry, and this failure has to do with their attempting what Williams did not attempt to do: naturalize Zen Buddhism, of which the haiku is a relatively recent outgrowth.

Haiku translated into English often appear to members of Occidental cultures to be overly sentimental. The Zen poet attempts to put the self into the thing perceived, to do more than empathize with it and "become one" with the thing; thus, by extension, with all things. (Brower, 361) In Western traditions empathizing with objects is sentimental; there is even a term, "the pathetic fallacy," to describe the state of excessive personification or over-empathy. If American poets try to become one with the object of their perception, their work will appear to be self-indulgent and egocentric. Williams doubtless understood his danger, for, as has been noted above, it was he who gave Des Imagistes their slogan, "No ideas but in things." It was T. S. Eliot, though, who produced the theory that Williams put into practice, the theory of "the objective correlative": the poet must choose that object which will be the idea, not merely the symbol of the idea, which was the theory of another Modernist school, the Symbolists. Another Williams poem, "Spring," will illustrate:

> O my grey hairs!
> You are truly white as plum blossoms (*CP* I, 158).

The "objective correlative" is nothing more than the "vehicle" of the metaphor of the poem, the figure of speech that carries the weight of the identification of one object with another, dissimilar, object. In this Williams couplet mote the "grey hairs" is the tenor or subject of the metaphor, and "plum blossoms" — a traditional Japanese symbol for spring, incidentally — is the vehicle or object; that is, the "objective correlative": that object which is relative to the idea of the tenor. In the context of the poem the objective correlative allows the implication or overtone that something old can paradoxically be young. The hairs are at once white and wintry, white and spring-like. Williams' "idea-in-the-thing" substitutes for Zen Buddhist "thing-empathy," but much of the effect of the Zen identification with an object is preserved, though the observer of the poem is emotionally severed from the perceived article. It is through this objectivity or aesthetic distance, finally, that the poet in English — at least a poet like Williams — achieves empathy, which is only a way of saying that there is no such thing as pure objectivity where human beings are concerned.

As a final support for the thesis that the Japanese forms are analogous to Imagist poetry in English, and specifically that the Japanese 5-7-5-syllable count is analogous to Williams' phrasal-accentual prosody, here is Williams 1916 poem "Marriage":

> So different, this man
> And this woman:
> A stream flowing
> In a field (*CP* I, 56).

The original version of poem is a sentence that has been line- phrased; that is to say, the sentence has been broken into phrases and each phrase has become a line. This is the stressing pattern:

1. ´´ ˘ ´´

2. ˘ ´´ ˘

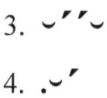

The first syllable of line four is promoted because, in the sentence, it is the middle syllable in a series of three unstressed syllables. Thus, in this early poem there are no more than four, and no fewer than two strong stresses in any line, as in the triversen stanza, but there are four lines here, not three. However, if the lines of this poem are rearranged in syllabic lengths of 5-7-5, the poem becomes a perfect three-line senryu:

> So different, this
> man and this woman: a stream
> flowing in a field (Turco, 170).

The senryu itself first showed up unmistakably in Williams' poetry only three pages farther along in the *Collected Poems*, on page 59, as the 1917 poem titled "Chinese Nightingale":

> Long before dawn your light
> Shone in the window, Sam Wu;
> You were at your trade.

Its syllabification is off by only one syllable in the first line, but the poem is a lineated compound sentence.

The prosody Williams developed from Japanese sources has become widely dispersed among American poets since its early appearances in short, haiku-like poems written by the Imagists. Williams himself soon used it as a stanza pattern, developing out of the haiku a triplet, each line of which equals one phrase, the whole triplet equal to one independent clause, each line containing no more than four stressed syllables and generally no fewer than two.

In Williams' work there are literally dozens of poems that fit this description. The triversen stanza first showed up in section VII of the 1923 *Spring and All*, and thereafter it occurred with increasing frequency in his work, though it cannot be claimed that it became his mainstay strophe.

To list examples of the triversen stanza and of pseudo-haiku in the work of other poets would be an endless task, but one other poet who did fine things in the Japanese tradition — once only, and atypically — was Wallace Stevens in "Thirteen Ways of Looking at a Black Bird," his only truly Imagist, as distinguished from Symbolist, poem. (Stevens *C.P.*, 92-5) But in "Not Ideas about the Thing but the Thing Itself" Stevens not only wrote a poem in triversen stanza, he glossed Williams' Imagist credo as well. (534)

Charles Olson

In 1983 a massive work was published, *The Maximus Poems of Charles Olson*, edited by Olson's younger disciple, George F. Butterick of the University of Connecticut. The books brought together in the volume were *The Maximus Poems* (1960); *Maximus Poems IV, V, VI* (1968), and the posthumous *Maximus Poems: Volume Three* (1975), all long out of print. Twenty-nine new poems, previously uncollected, were added, errors in the previous editions were corrected, and the sequence of the final poems was modified through research. Olson thus received the kind of treatment that is usually allotted a poet only after he has been gone from the scene for a century at least.

Charles Olson, like his fellow townsman and close contemporary Elizabeth Bishop, was born in Worcester, Massachusetts, in 1910. He died at the age of sixty in 1970. Olson was educated at Wesleyan University, at Yale, and at Harvard where he took his B.A. in 1932 and an M.A. in 1933. He began teaching as an instructor at Clark University and at Harvard from 1936-9, but the peak of his academic career came when he was "Instructor and Rector" of the experimental Black Mountain College from 1951 to 1956. As Kenneth Rexroth pointed out, the school drew to itself many members of the generation that called itself "Beat" in other contexts, and a folklore, a mythology grew up around it that has grown more archetypal over the years.

Robert von Hallberg wrote in his *Charles Olson: The Scholar's Art* that the poet, after the dissolution of Black Mountain College in 1956, could no longer rely on having a captive audience for his work, but when Donald Allen's anthology appeared Olson instead began to build a nation-wide audience and following both in the U. S. and Canada, his work appearing particularly in the experimental little magazines of the period. (41) Although it was larger, this audience was less well-defined than it had been when his colleagues and disciples contributed their work to Cid Corman's little magazine *Origin* and its sibling *The Black Mountain Review*. However, once "avant gardist" poets had appeared in these pages they were thereafter identified as members of the group even though they may not have attended the school itself, and they constituted the advance shock troops of Olson's advance toward literary acceptance.

Thus, when the College failed and its residents scattered, Black Mountain's presence continued to be felt in the literature of the 1950s and 1960s. The members of the movement kept in touch with one-another, published each other, followed each-other about until Olson landed, finally, at the State University of New York at Buffalo where his colleague and friend Robert Creeley continued to teach through the 1980s. Though Olson died at the end of the decade of the 1960s, the so-called "Black Mountain College II" continued as a sort of academic unit at the Buffalo university, and it sent out rhizomes to various other schools including the Universities of Connecticut and Maine, S.U.N.Y. at Albany, and various other places in the eastern and western United States, not to mention Canada where the movement eventually practically took over poetic practice by the 1990s.

If Olson was the post-Modernist guru of Black Mountain, as Kenneth Rexroth and others pointed out, it was Ezra Pound and William Carlos Williams among the Modernists who were his idols to the extent that Olson has been characterized by some critics as "the poor man's Pound." His theories of composition were widely circulated, but they were derived — to the degree that they can be comprehended — from the theories of Williams. The chief essay exposing his "composition by field" theory was titled "Projective Verse" (1950). In it Olson repostulated Ralph Waldo Emerson's "organic poetry" opinions regarding form as an extension of content and fleshed them out with remarks about the association of syllables with "breath."

Prosodics and poetics were never the chief selling points of Black Mountain, however, for in fact the poets associated with it were a heterogeneous group and the school was nothing if it was not a "cult of personality." Olson was a huge man physically — well over six feet tall, and built on a massive scale. His mere presence was overwhelming. His "lectures" were famous — interminable, rambling peregrinations over masses of territory — Von Hallberg has characterized a good deal of his production as "rhetorical" and "didactic." They were filled with oracular pronouncements, sighs and rumblings in the style of the great 18th-century scholar-poet Samuel Johnson, incoherences, references and jests for the initiates; yet for those who were apostles they remain some of the most memorable moments of a lifetime. For the unconvinced and uninitiated, they might be characterized, to quote another word Von Hallberg used to describe some of the poetry, "pompous."

Don Byrd, the State University of New York at Albany representative of the second-generation of Black Mountain poets, averred in his *Charles Olson's Maximus* that "Maximus is the noun-magician." Byrd claimed that "He is not simply the namer" (Ralph Waldo Emerson had written in his essay "The Poet" that the true poet was "The Namer, the Sayer"); Maximus is "'the man in the word,' the flesh made Logos," Byrd said, falling back upon another Emerson-derived priest-poet concept. (55) "Although there are important secondary resonances," Byrd continued, "Maximus's name means, most simply, large. By implication, he is also the Neo-platonic philosopher and magician, Maximus of Tyre, as well as homo maximus, the redeemed man of alchemy, but above all, he is a big man, as large as his name, and, at the beginning of the poem, largely unknown. He is located in Gloucester, Massachusetts, a little fishing village on Cape Ann, which daily fills his eyes and ears, so it is his most common concern, but much passes there which has reference to other places and other times, frequently far away or long ago."

Olson's main model for his work was *The Cantos* of Ezra Pound. Olson's *The Maximus Poems* were often imitations, as in "Maximus, to Gloucester, Letter 15," part III:

And for the water-shed, the economics & poetics thereafter?

Three men,

coincide:

>   you will find Villon
> in Fra Diavolo,
> Elberthubbardsville,
> N.Y.
>
>   and the prose
> is Raymond's, boston, or
>
> Brer Fox,
> Rapallo,
> Quattrocento-by-the-Beach,#
> 429
>   the American epos, 19-
> 02 (or when did Barton Barton Barton Barton and Barton?
>
>   To celebrate
>
> how it can be, it is
>
> padded or uncomforted, your lost, you
>
> found your
> sneakers
>
>   (o Statue,
> o Republic, o
> Tell-A-Vision, the best
> is soap. The true troubadours
> are CBS. Melopoeia
> is for Cokes by Cokes out of
>   Pause.

The reference to "Brer Fox" is to Ezra Pound; "Rapallo" is the city in Italy to which Pound was exiled after his long post-war incarceration in St. Elizabeth's Hospital in Washington, D.C., where he was sent after he was deemed insane by the American courts instead of being tried for treasonous activities in behalf of Italian Fascism during World War II. The level of diction is that of a hip wiseguy; the syntax is not much different from that to be found in the Auden style — it is ordinary speech jazzed up in "lineated" prose lines rather than slickly crafted in traditional verse forms. The poem is aimed at a particular audience — the in-jokes, arcane references, and micterismal sarcasms are set like land mines and tank traps to keep at bay the bourgeois uninitiated.

Sherman Paul wrote, "...Olson's push, to use his own emphatic and often self-characterizing word, is important. This may be gauged by the fact that anyone wishing to understand recent poetry and writing — postmodernism, literature since World War II — has sooner or later to come to him. He is a central figure, a 'vortex,' rightly compared with Ezra Pound, one of his masters in a preceding generation. As Paul Blackburn, a poet of Olson's generation, puts it [in his poem titled 'Shop Talk']:

> "We have had our gene-
> ration of innovators, 19
> 15 & the rest.
> What Pound and Williams & Moore have done
> is in the air, is, perhaps, the air.
> Let the species now give rise to a few
>   masters
>   (since the fields are open
>   and the air cleared)

"Blackburn — his own poem is an instance of what it asserts — refers to the generation of 1915, the generation of modernists that included not only Pound, [W. C.] Williams, and Moore, but Eliot, [James] Joyce, [D. E.] Lawrence, and Yeats. And he refers to his own generation, the postmodernists, whose advent may be marked by the publication in 1950 of Olson's 'Projective Verse,' an essay comparable in importance to Pound's early essays and notes on poetry ('A Retrospect') and Eliot's 'Tradition and the Individual Talent'." (xv)

Or, to approach the question from a slightly different perspective, David Perkins noted Olson's self-assessment: "In a 1965 reading at Berkeley, Olson remarked, according to the tape recorder, 'I mean, I wrote a — a flagrant autobiography of myself imitating Ezra Pound...but every imitation stinks...I'd be proud to have been the in-man in this century and, like, here I am dragging my ass after Ezra'." (v. II, 499)

Robert Creeley

The Maximus Poems was dedicated to Robert Creeley who was born in Arlington, Massachusetts, in 1926. He entered Harvard in 1943 but left school to serve in the American Field Service in Burma and India during World War II, 1944-5. He returned to Harvard in 1946 but took his B.A. from Black Mountain College in 1955. An M.A. from the University of New Mexico followed in 1960. He began his academic career by teaching two semesters at Black Mountain, wandered about a bit, and then settled into the English faculty of "Black Mountain II" at the State University of New York at Buffalo in 1967.

According to Arthur L. Ford in his book *Robert Creeley,* "Creeley has long been aware that he is part of a definable tradition in the American poetry of this century, — so long as 'tradition' is thought of in general terms and so long as it recognizes crucial distinctions among its members. The tradition most visible to the general public has been the Eliot-Stevens tradition supported by the intellectual probings of the New Critics in the 1940s and early 1950s. Parallel to that tradition has been the tradition Creeley identifies with, the Pound-Olson-Zukofsky-Black Mountain tradition — what M. L. Rosenthal [in his book *The New Poets: American and British Poetry Since World War II* (1967)] calls 'The Projectivist Movement'." (25) This "movement" Rosenthal derives from Olson's essay on "Projective Verse," mentioned earlier.

Le Fou, Creeley's first book, was published in 1952, and since then, according to his publisher, barely a year has passed without a new collection of poems. The 1983 entry, titled *Mirrors*, had some tendencies toward concrete imagery, but Creeley's greatest weakness was always vagueness and abstraction. It was hard for many readers and critics to understand Creeley's reputation as an innovative poet; even harder for some to imagine that his work lived up to the Black Mountain tenet — which he is supposed to have articulated — that "form is never more than an extension of content," for his poems were often written in couplet, triplet, and quatrain stanzas that break into and out of random rhyme as happenstance appears to dictate. An example is "The Hero," from *Collected Poems*, also published in 1982 and covering the span of years from 1945 to 1975.

"The Hero" is written in variable isoverbal ("word-count") prosody; the number of words per line varies from three to seven, but the norm is four to six. Another technique to be found in this piece is variable rhyme — there is no set rhyme scheme, but some of the lines rhyme and the poem concludes with a rhymed couplet. All of the stanzas are quatrains, as in the first two:

> Each voice which was asked
> spoke its words, and heard
> more than that, the fair question,
> the onerous burden of the asking.

> And so the hero, the
> hero! stepped that gracefully
> into his redemption, losing
> or gaining life thereby.

Despite these obviously formal elements various critics continue to insist that Creeley wrote in lineated prose or so-called "free verse," but most of his forms were strict enough so that it is a question whether it can even be maintained that he wrote in forms of prose. This particular poem is without doubt verse-mode, not prose-mode. M. L. Rosenthal in his *The New Poets* quoted Creeley's "'preoccupation with a personal rhythm in the sense that the discovery of an external equivalent of the speaking self is felt to be the true object of poetry,'" and went on to say that this speaking self serves both as the center of the poem's universe and the private life of the poet. "Despite his mask of humble, confused comedian, loving and lovable, he therefore stands in his own work's way, too seldom letting his poems free themselves of his blocking presence." (148) When he used imagery, Creeley could be interesting and effective on the sensory level.

In an essay titled "Poetry: Schools of Dissidents," the Academic poet Daniel G. Hoffman wrote in *The Harvard Guide to Contemporary American Writing*, which he edited, that as he grew older Creeley's work tended to become increasingly fragmentary in nature, even the titles subsequent to *For Love: Poems 1950-1960* hinting at the fragmentation of experience in Creeley's work: *Words, Pieces, A Day Book*. In Hoffman's opinion, "Creeley has never included ideas, or commitments to social issues, in the repertoire of his work; his stripped-down poems have been, as it were, a proving of Pound's belief in 'technique as the test of a man's sincerity'." (533)

But perhaps Hoffman and Rosenthal both were being too kind, for here is a late entry, from *Mirrors* — the appropriately titled "Greeting Card," the six central couplets of which read,

> Know love's surety
> either in you or me.
>
> Believe you are always
> all that human is
> in loyalty, in generosity,
> in wise, good-natured clarity.
>
> No one more than you
> would be love's truth —
> nor less
> deserve ever unhappiness.
>
> Therefore wonder's delight
> will make the way.

The poem is filled with clichés; its lofty diction is tied to inverted syntax which has made much 19th-century verse unpopular in the twentieth century. This sort of writing would be anathema to the avant-garde if it were not the product of a member in good standing of the Black Mountain group. Not even the title saves it from banality. Such verses of Creeley are formally disconcerting, and their "content," which their "form" is supposed to follow, can descend as low as the mundane and may rise only as high as the obscure.

Robert Duncan

Robert Duncan's work appeared in the anti-establishment anthologies of the 1950s and 1960s, and he was an important influence on the West Coast poetry scene during the early days of the Beat movement, largely through his involvement with the San Francisco Poetry Center. Duncan was born in Oakland, California, in 1919; he died there in 1988. He attended the University of California at Berkeley from 1936-38, and again from 1948-50. He lived in Majorca during 1955-6, then taught at the do-it-yourself, communal Black Mountain College of Charles Olson in North Carolina in 1956. Despite his otherwise militantly anti-academic stance, Duncan — like many others of the Beat Generation — was closely identified with various other institutions of higher education during his life, including San Francisco State College — later San Francisco State University when it absorbed the Poetry Center, and the University of British Columbia in Vancouver, Canada.

One of the original members of the "San Francisco School" of American poetry which, for all practical purposes, was a subdivision of, and indistinguishable from, the so-called "Beat Generation," Duncan issued his first book, *Heavenly City, Earthly City*, in 1947. In the section of "Biographical Notes" in the Donald Allen anthology Duncan wrote, "With Jack Spicer I learned that the poem that might be fantastic life, that might be insight into the real, was a rite. The poem was a ritual referring to divine orders." (433) With this remark Duncan clearly aligned himself with the Emersonian "priest-poet" tradition of American literature; that is to say, poetry was not primarily an art — the art of language — but a vehicle for revelation or prophecy.

The immigrant Yugoslavian-American poet Stephen Stepanchev (b. 1915) in his *American Poetry Since 1945* called Duncan "a poet of cosmic consciousness whose mystical raptures transport him into areas of spirit where the Many are One, where all forms have their Original Being, and where eternal Love encompasses all reality, both Good and Evil. As a visionary, he has a bridge-building, time-binding, and space-binding imagination. He speaks of a meadow which is like

> a scene made-up by the mind
> that is not mine, but is a made place,
> that is mine, it is so near to the heart,
> an eternal pasture folded in all thought
> so that there is a hall therein
>
> that is a made place, created by light
> wherefrom the shadows that are forms fall.

"It is this 'light' from which all forms fall that is at the center of his universe, his God, and it is there that all life returns, as the 'Pasture' section of 'Four Pictures of the Real Universe' makes clear:

> The Great Sun Himself comes
> to eat at my heart, asks
> that I return myself into Him.
>
> And the white body, a Moon,
> in the precincts of the Earth revolves.
> How the Dead draw the Sea after them!
>
> But the Living, the immortal corpuscles
> sail without shadow
> toward the pyres of the Sun."

In 1984 Duncan published a collection titled *Ground Work*, a reference, evidently, to a haiku by the classic Japanese poet Bashō: "Will it soon be spring? / They lay the groundwork for it, / the plum tree and moon." (160) Duncan had changed his poetics little over the years. In his introduction to *Ground Work* Duncan wrote again the sort of essay that had become a requisite of "underground" poetry since the 1960s. It was a hortatory exposition of neo-Transcendentalist "poetics" which was incomprehensible to most ordinary readers, and deliberately so, for poets who identify with a group or school often feel that outsiders need to be kept outside, ostracized through language that contains elements of ritual understandable only to initiates of the group. The primary thing to be communicated to non-members is that orthodoxy is with the group, not with the outsiders.

Duncan wrote in his introduction, "In Passages verses may be articulated into phrases or tesserae of utterances and silences leading to a series of possible sentences. As 'Passages' themselves are but passages of a poem that calls itself Passages and that is manifest only in the course of the books in which it appears, even so phrases have both their own meaning and yet belong to the unfolding revelation of a Sentence beyond the work." Often Duncan's poems were more comprehensible than his essays, as for instance "The Gate," section one of "Four Pictures of the Real Universe" from his 1960 collection, *The Opening of the Field*:

> O Lords of Intensity, initiates of catastrophe:
> the star observed by Tycho Brahe in 1572
> visible in bright daylight, the star
> recorded by Chinese astronomers in the year
> 1054, the Star of our Lord...
> into the holocausts of helium
> the ravenous spirit sends out its hunters.
>
> The Queen that dwells in the dark
> feeds on the death of stars, devours
> emanations out of light perishing.

Section two, "The Wall," shows the deliberate misspellings of various common words that give the clue to initiates that here is one of the rebel writers of the period and that, in the 1960s, was simultaneously an annoyance to pedants and pedagogues of the literary establishment; this practice was standard among all of the Beat Generation, though not in every poem. It was an imitation — to a degree — of the practice of Ezra Pound in some of his Cantos:

> Crownd Beast of Pure Thriving!
> You pass thru the wall of thot,
> thru the stone wall, thru the walls of the body,
> gathering all into your strength,
> altering nothing.
>
> From your roar, legions fly thru the universe
> ringing the suns, sounding flames of immediate victory
> that we see as white flowers
> lost in the waves of morning green.

"We have poets writing now whose language can attain to the power of prophecy but whose vision cannot," wrote Robert B. Shaw in his essay, "The Poetry of Protest," in *American Poetry Since 1960: Some Critical Perspectives*, edited by himself. "The first lines of Duncan's 'Up Rising' are an example:

> 'Now Johnson would go up to join the great simulacra of men,
> Hitler and Stalin, to work his fame
> with planes roaring out from Guam over Asia,
> all America become a sea of trifling men
> stirred at his will, which would be a bloated thing,
> drawing from the underbelly of the nation
> such blood and dreams as swell the idiot psyche
> out of its courses into an elemental thing
> until his name stinks with burning meat and heapt honors
>
> And men wake to see that they are used like things
> spent in a great potlatch, this Texas barbecue
> of Asia, Africa, and all the Americas...'

"'Up Rising' in its entirety reaches unusual rhetorical heights. And yet there is something off-putting about a poem which straightway insists on an equation of [President Lyndon Baines] Johnson with Hitler. Many of us, while holding no brief for Johnson, may still not think of him as being quite in Hitler's league. It is too bad that this should be one of Duncan's major premises, for it means that the poem will fade as its occasions do; it is less likely to escape the mid-'sixties in the way that [Allen Ginsberg's] *Howl* does the mid-'fifties. I am aware that it is not the business of a prophet to make nice political distinctions. And yet his message ought to strike us as informed with the abiding clarity of revelation, not the myopia of a past moment of passion."

Shaw felt that zeal can be blinding. Duncan here went overboard, carried away in the waves of his rhetoric. Further, the poem is "occasional," written for a particular time and place and event. Unless it has something more to offer than vitriol, it will disappear as the years pass; has, in fact, already disappeared for all intents and purposes, its occasion fading into the generations.

Joel Oppenheimer

Another member of the Black Mountain school, Joel Oppenheimer, was born in 1930. He began his college career by attending Cornell University for two semesters, 1947-8, transferring in his sophomore year to the University of Chicago. He made his third hop to Black Mountain College, staying there from 1950 to 1953, studying with Charles Olson and the other members of the group.

The Jargon Society of Highlands, North Carolina, was a publisher of several of the alumni of Black Mountain. The press, founded by Jonathan Williams, Oppenheimer's classmate, issued his first collection, *The Dancer*, in 1952, and in 1957 it brought out his second collection, *The Dutiful Son*. *The Love Bit and Other Poems* appeared in 1962, *In Time: Poems, 1962-1968* was the first of his books to be brought out by a first-line publisher.

"Grown Alba" from this latter collection is typical of his approach and style. First, his idiosyncrasies were few, and they were primarily on the typographical level — using a small "I," for example, for the personal pronoun, and forgoing punctuation and initial capitalization as often as not, like E. E. Cummings. For the rest of it, his diction is ordinary. His observations are of the commonplace, and his epiphanies are of the common variety. He delineates concrete situations, and his characters have body — they strike the reader as being real. His mode is prose, and his prosody is simply line-phrasing his sentences. Oppenheimer was capable of writing in parallel structures when he felt it was necessary, as in strophe three of the same poem.

The difficulties with this kind of writing are surface difficulties. The most complicated aspect of this poem is that it gives the semi-impression that it is written in stream-of-consciousness style, but that is mainly a function of its sparing use of punctuation — it is not hard to read what Oppenheimer has written or to understand what he was saying.

As ever, Oppenheimer in his last collection, *New Spaces: Poems 1975-1983*, was the democratic poet, speaking to the American Everyman from the perspective of the guy next to him at the bar. His subjects were what happened that day at work, or in the park, or sitting in the kitchen waiting for the coffee to be done. The poems were readable and objectifying: readers were able to see themselves from a little distance, as though they were the stars in a drama of the commonplace, and they might even laugh a little at themselves now and again.

Oppenheimer was a member of the brown-bag labor force for years before he succumbed to the blandishments of the academic life and left New York City, where he was born and usually lived, for the rustic pleasures of Henniker, New Hampshire, and New England College. He was a member of the faculty of that school when he died in 1988.

David Meltzer

David Meltzer, one of those mentioned by Rexroth as a charter member of the San Francisco group, was born in 1937, and his first collection, *Poems*, with Donald Schenker, was privately printed in 1957 in San Francisco. Like Robert Duncan, he believed that poets are instruments of the gods, by which he means that poems write themselves.

In her essay titled "American-Jewish Poetry: An Overview," included as an entry in Lewis Fried's *Handbook of American-Jewish Literature*, R. Barbara Gitenstein identified Meltzer as the author of both poetry and prose books and translator of "Jewish esoteric texts." She claimed as well that he was a follower of Whitman in his writing techniques, of which the primary one was grammatical parallelism, but his primary affinity with Whitman is his stance as mystic and prophet: a major subject of his 1969 poem titled "Abulafia" and of the longer 1973 "Tohu" is personal and traditional "inspiration" as the initiator and substance of poetry. "In the shorter reference to Abulafia," Gitenstein wrote, "the American poet recognizes his identity with the medieval kabbalist who thought of himself as a messianic aspirant. For both Abulafia and Meltzer, the sound of words and the manipulations of the language form the poetics of a mystical art." (135-6)

This is the first paragraph of Meltzer's Introduction to *The Name Selected Poetry 1973 1983*:

> "I wrote my first poem at eleven. It came through me and out of me, a combination of vision and transmission. Maybe 'trance-mission' would be more accurate. I was in the center of its energy like a glass or lens where words not light come through."

The reader might reasonably expect that the products of such a visionary experience would be ineffable rather than prosaic, profound rather than clever like the pun, apocalyptic rather than cryptic. Most of these poems are in series.

Jerome Rothenberg

R. Barbara Gitenstein published a book that traced this sort of writing to and through a tradition of American poetry that stems from different sources than Emerson and Whitman. Her study, *Apocalyptic Messianism and Contemporary Jewish-American Poetry* (1986), located the beginnings of the tradition in 19th-century Sephardic-American literature, and then in later Ashkenazic, Eastern European immigrant work. Gitenstein examined the effect that Jewish mystical traditions have had on recent and current poetry in the United States.

Jerome Rothenberg and John Hollander were two poets whom Gitenstein examined in depth. Rothenberg was born in New York City in 1931. He took his B.A. from City College in 1952 and his M.A. from the University of Michigan in 1953. Subsequently, the year after the Korean War ended, he entered the U.S. Army for two years. He founded the Hawk's Well Press and published his own first book, *White Sun, Black Sun*, in 1960. Though Rothenberg has been an academic, his poetry has always been associated with "experimental" schools — Diane Wakoski, an influential poet, critic, and apologist for the avant-garde schools of the 1950s, has written appreciatively of his work.

Hollander was also born in New York City, two years earlier than Rothenberg; there the likenesses end. Hollander took his A.B. (Phi Beta Kappa) from Columbia in 1950 and his M.A. in 1952. His Ph.D. was from the University of Indiana, 1959. His rise in the world of academe was swift and steady until he settled into the faculty of Yale University. He was from the beginning associated with formalist poetry.

Of the two, Rothenberg must be seen as more the "apocalyptic" poet than Hollander, though Hollander used his ethnic and religious background no less zealously. The paradox is that Hollander, who was an art poet and a formalist, has been accused by both the old and the new antiformalists, including Diane Wakoski, of being elitist and undemocratic, whereas Rothenberg and Meltzer considered themselves to be William Carlos Williams-style democratic poets. Yet it is art poetry, not priest poetry, that is accessible to most readers, because it is written for all of the literate, not merely a caste of shamans and priests. It uses inclusive, not exclusive techniques.

Lawrence Ferlinghetti

Like his contemporary and (ultimately) fellow San Franciscan Robert Duncan, Ferlinghetti was born in 1919 but on the opposite coast of the country in Yonkers, New York. Between them Duncan and Ferlinghetti described the outer limits of geography within which the Beat Generation moved and flourished. In a way, the two poets also described the limits of Beat ideology, for Duncan was the Priest-poet, the visionary, whereas Ferlinghetti is the folk poet, the jongleur.

Ferlinghetti took his bachelor's degree from the University of North Carolina and served in the Naval Reserve from 1941 to 1945. He worked for *Time* magazine in New York City, earned an M. A. from Columbia University in 1948, and a Doctorat de l'Universite from the Sorbonne in 1951. Ferlinghetti's first book was *Pictures of the Gone World*, self-published from City Lights Books, the press he founded in 1955 in association with the bookstore he had bought; it has ever since remained a major publisher of the literature of the Beat movement.

At first Ferlinghetti had a true lyric ear. He might have used it to become a fine traditional poet. Instead, he chose to write prose poems like those of his friend Allen Ginsberg. Ferlinghetti's ear manifested itself most lyrically in *A Coney Island of the Mind*, not insignificantly his most popular book. Karl Malkoff wrote of Lawrence Ferlinghetti in *Crowell's Handbook of Contemporary American Poetry*, "His most widely known book is still *A Coney Island of the Mind* (1958), which included selected poems from *Pictures of the Gone World*," the poet's first book, published three years earlier. (121) Malkoff continued, "The characteristic method of that book, which Ferlinghetti handles with great skill, is the use of literary or cultural allusions to develop images of the modern world. The technique must be distinguished from the allusiveness of Ezra Pound or T. S. Eliot." But the book is to be distinguished in other ways as well.

Here is No. "20," usually titled in anthologies from its first line — one of the most popular selections from that popular collection:

                        ˘ ´ | ˘ ´ | ˘ ´ | ˘ ´ | ˘ ´
The pennycandystore beyond the El
is where I first
fell in love
with unreality
Jellybeans glowed in the semi-gloom
of that september afternoon
A cat upon the counter moved among
the licorice sticks
and tootsie rolls
and Oh Boy Gum

> Outside the leaves were falling as they died
> A wind had blown away the sun
>
> A girl ran in
> Her hair was rainy
> Her breasts were breathless in the little room
>
> Outside the leaves were falling
> and they cried
> Too soon! Too soon!

Although there is no punctuation in this line-phrased poem, Ferlinghetti indicates the beginnings of sentences with capital letters. At first glance it would appear that this is a prose poem, but if it is scanned one may see it is variable iambic verse: the first line is perfect iambic pentameter, despite the running together, in the manner of E. E. Cummings, of three words. The second and third lines are iambic dimeter; the third, trimeter. Line four is a tetrameter line, but the first foot is a trochee followed by an iamb, an anapest, and a final iamb. Line six following is perfect iambic tetrameter verse, and the next, line seven, is perfect iambic pentameter again. "the licorice sticks" is iambic dimeter (licorice is an elision, "lic'rice"), and so is "and tootsie rolls." The next line is dimeter as well — "Boy" is demoted because it is the central syllable in a series of three stressed syllables.

"Outside the leaves were falling as they died" is iambic pentameter once more, with the substitution of a spondee in the first foot. The next line is perfect iambic tetrameter, followed by a perfect dimeter line, then another with the substitution of an amphibrach for the second iamb. The next line is iambic pentameter again; the next, iambic trimeter (beginning with a spondee), but it is part of a refrain, (line 11 incrementally repeated), so it must be taken together with the next line, which is dimeter — thus, the two lines make up another pentameter line. The climactic "Too soon! Too soon!" is a dimeter line made up — depending on how much rhetorical stress one puts on too — either of two spondees (unlikely) or two iambs.

Sonics used in the poem include rhyme (gloom/room, afternoon/soon, El / fell / Jellybeans, licorice / sticks); consonance (gloom / afternoon Gum / among, sun / soon, ran in / rainy — actually, all of these words consonate or have sonic relationships with one another, including the rhyme words, giving the effect of analyzed rhyme; alliteration (first / fell, cat / counter), assonance, vocalic and consonantal echo — no need to go through them all, as they are apparent everywhere — although it is disguised, this is clearly a formal lyric.

Between 1958 and 1986, in *Over All the Obscene Boundaries*, Ferlinghetti wrote didactic harangues and speeches that often made their points by the rhetoric of sarcasm and parody, or attempted to get a reaction through the use of cue-words, like "obscene" in the latter title. However, in this book Ferlinghetti returned to the scenes of his youth, in Paris and elsewhere. In reminiscing, his good ear reasserted itself briefly, with only occasional lapses of judgment.

Thomas Parkinson, in *Essays on the Beat*, quoted Ferlinghetti as saying, in a "Note on Poetry in San Francisco," "There are all kinds of poets here, writing very dissimilar types of poetry.... But I should say that the kind of poetry which has been making the most noise here is quite different from the 'poetry about poetry,' the poetry of technique, the poetry for poets and professors which has dominated the quarterlies and anthologies in this country for some time and which of course is also written in San Francisco. The poetry which has been making itself heard here of late is what should be called street poetry. For it amounts to getting the poet out of the inner esthetic sanctum where he has too long been contemplating his complicated navel. It amounts to getting poetry back into the street where it once was, out of the classroom, out of the speech department, and — in fact — off the printed page." (124)

Although readers may wonder that a person with an academic doctorate would make this sort of statement, it is nevertheless typical of the rhetoric of the Beats, who made statements of personal opinion that sounded as though they might be true, but which in fact may never have been; at least, there had not been a "poetry of the streets" since the days when there were wandering jongleurs and minstrels in the European nations and no such things as printing presses. Even then, the minstrels and the scribes who wrote the poetry were part of the educated segment of society, not of the masses who could not even read. Surely Ferlinghetti was aware of these facts. Under those circumstances, of course, poetry had to be performed orally for such audiences.

"Because of Lawrence Ferlinghetti's early association with the Beat Generation," Malkoff wrote later on, "we often find ourselves searching his poetry for traces of the Beatific Vision, for some flirtation with Eastern mysticism, or perhaps some new doctrine of his own. And the traces are indeed there. But the title of one of his later books, *The Secret Meaning of Things* (1969), promises us more than a taste. As a matter of fact, the mystical vision is once again not there...." (123) Nor is the poet's sense of language music. Early and late, Robert Duncan was much more the vatic, and the more virulent anti-metrist as well.

Perhaps Ferlinghetti was more interested in taking poetry back to the days of the jongleurs who were performers as well as poets. During a panel presentation in Portland, Oregon, in late March of 1980, when it came time for Lawrence Ferlinghetti to make his preliminary remarks, he instead began to chant "Light!" from his seat. He grew louder and louder, arose, and began to dance about. One of the other participants, having anticipated such a scene, pulled a handful of balloons out of his pocket, then began blowing them up and jetting them about over the heads of the audience. Another panelist, the surrealist poet Vern Rutsala, donned his sun-glasses, flicked on his cigarette lighter, and began to peer about the room as though he, too, were looking for the light. At a break in the panel Ferlinghetti approached the panelists and said, "I hope you didn't think I was arrogant by doing what I did instead of discussing things as you were doing, but I felt that there was a stance that I was expected to take, and so I did." And so he continued to do, in his poems as in person.

"There are limits to Lawrence Ferlinghetti's poetic powers," Malkoff said. (124) "To what extent his poems are the direct communication of a reality rather than simply a commentary on that reality (a readily paraphrasable commentary at that) is a question often raised by critics. But at his best he possesses an unquestionable power. And he seems one of the finer examples of a man in whom the poet and the human being are not separated." (124)

It is when he is singing a song that Ferlinghetti is at his best. Unfortunately, over the years he has delivered many speeches, given many performances, but he has sung few songs.

Allen Ginsberg

Allen Ginsberg was seven years younger than his friend and fellow "Beat poet" Lawrence Ferlinghetti, having been born in 1926, but his *Howl and Other Poems* was published in 1956 from City Lights, only a year after Ferlinghetti's own first book. When it arrived on the scene "Howl" was hailed by the Beat Generation as the greatest American opus since Walt Whitman's *Leaves of Grass*. The Modernist William Carlos Williams wrote an introduction for it, which Ginsberg reprinted in his *Collected Poems 1947-1980*:

"When he was younger, and I was younger, I used to know Allen Ginsberg, a young poet living in Paterson, New Jersey, where he, son of a well-known poet [Louis Ginsberg], had been born and grew up. He was physically slight of build and mentally much disturbed by the life which he had encountered about him during those first years after the first world war as it was exhibited to him in and about New York City." (811) However, Ginsberg was no more a product of the unwashed masses than Walt Whitman was, no more a poet of the streets than Ferlinghetti or most of the other "Beatniks," as the Establishment liked to call them, using a linguistic back-formation from "Sputnik," the first satellite to orbit the earth, launched by the USSR in 1957. The term was meant to have the overtone of being subversive or Communist.

However, Allen Ginsberg served in the Military Sea Transport Service during the World War II, subsequently taking his B.A. from Columbia University in 1948, the same year that Ferlinghetti took his first graduate degree there. Ginsberg's father, Louis, as Williams noted, was known as a minor traditionally formal poet, and one must assume that it was at least partially against this background that Allen originally rebelled. This is what the father was writing in *The Grub Street Book of Verse*, edited by its publisher, Henry Harrison, in 1927 — it is from a poem titled "To My Two Sons":

> My little sons, because I know
> That Love perpetuates only woe,
> I write these lines so you may read
> Some night upon your hour of need.

"Howl" is a straight prose poem built in grammatical parallel structures — catalogues of clauses in the manner of Whitman and of the British poets Martin Farquhar Tupper in the nineteenth century, and William Blake and Christopher Smart in the eighteenth. But Ginsberg was more than influenced by the poetry — both the verse and the prose poetry — of the visionary William Blake, for in 1948 he heard Blake speak to him "across the vault of time," as Paul Portuges wrote in *The Visionary Poetics of Allen Ginsberg*:

> "As Ginsberg experienced the auditory apparition, an overwhelming emotion arose in his soul in response to it. The emotion produced a sudden visual realization that helped him comprehend the

> meaning of this awesome phenomenon. He was, at the moment of the visual sensation, looking out through the window at the sky; suddenly, he felt, with Blake's voice guiding him, that he could penetrate the essence of the universe. He felt himself floating out of his body and thinking that heaven was on earth. He had a great realization that 'This existence was it.' His sense of hopelessness vanished. He felt he had been chosen to experience a vast cosmic consciousness. Looking out of his window, the sky seemed very ancient. It was the 'ancient place that he [Blake] was talking about, that sweet golden clime."

It was a "priest-poet" experience of the first order. Ginsberg "swore never to get lost," Portuges wrote a bit further on, "in the endless maze of superficial distraction, such as the mundane jobs and middle-class pursue its American life offers. Instead, he must, as a poet, always pursue the visionary calling, for 'the spirit of the universe was what I was born to realize,'" in the opinion of the poet. (11-12)

"'I would call that man a poet,'" John Tytell in his essay, "Allen Ginsberg and the Messianic Tradition" — from his book *Naked Angels: The Lives and Literature of the Beat Generation* — quoted Henry Miller as having written, "'who is capable of profoundly altering the world': "Howl" and "Kaddish" are two examples of a body of poetry that has had a tremendous impact on the values of a generation. Ginsberg has focused his vision on the forces depleting the life spirit of the West. While his inspiration has been apocalyptic, he offers us compelling alternatives to the general disaster he sees."

"Howl" had a tremendous impact on Ginsberg's generation, and on the period of the 1960s as well. In the anthology titled *New Naked Poetry*, edited by Stephen Berg and Robert Mezey in 1976, contributors were asked to make their donations to the poetics of organic form or "open poetry," and Allen Ginsberg attempted to explain something about the composition of his poem: "Part one uses repeated base who, as a sort of kithera BLANG, homeric (in my imagination) to work off each statement, with rhythmic unit."

Actually, the poem is divided into three sections, the first of which, after an introduction, has parallel clauses beginning with the word "who":

> I saw the best minds of my generation destroyed by madness,
>   starving hysterical naked,
> dragging themselves through the negro streets at dawn looking for
>   an angry fix,
> Angelheaded hipsters burning for the ancient heavenly connection
>   to the starry dynamo in the machinery of night,
> who poverty and tatters and hollow-eyed and high sat up smoking in
>   the supernatural darkness of cold-water flats floating across
>   the tops of cities contemplating jazz,
> who bared their brains to Heaven under the El and saw Mohammedan
>   angels staggering on tenement roofs illuminated,

and so on for six pages, all of it just one sentence. The next section is made up largely of clauses beginning with the word "Moloch." Part three is addressed to Carl Solomon, to whom the entire work is dedicated — it is the "I'm with you in Rockland" section.

M. L. Rosenthal wrote in his *The New Poets* that "The initial excitement over Allen Ginsberg's *Howl and Other Poems* when it appeared in 1956 was perhaps mainly the result of its vocabulary. For the first time in the history of serious American poetry with a relatively popular appeal, Ginsberg and some of his 'Beat' associates were writing lines" that used words like "copulated" and related four-letter words. (89-92)

It was a replowing of the ground that Whitman had broken out of the American forest primeval in the 19th century, but something happened to Ginsberg between the 'fifties and the 'eighties, for he began to sound in some poems not only like his early self again, but like his father. According to Allen Ginsberg's *Collected Poems 1947-1980* (1984), this is what the son was writing in his 1948 pre-Beat days — from a poem titled "A very Dove":

>   A very Dove will have her love
>   ere the dove has died;
>   the spirit, vanity approve,
>   will even love in pride.

And this is Allen Ginsberg returning to his roots in verses titled "Love Forgiven," written in 1979:

>   Straight and slender
>   Youthful tender
>   Love shows the way
>   And never says nay

There is even a 1980 poem with a Greek title written in classical Sapphic stanzas:

>   Red cheeked boyfriends tenderly kiss me sweet mouthed
>   under Boulder coverlets winter springtime
>   hug me naked laughing & telling girl friends
>   gossip till autumn

In between are all the prose "poems" for which Ginsberg became celebrated. The return to formalism that got under way around the nation during the 1980s may thus be perceived by some critics as not an unmixed blessing.

Gregory Corso

If Joel Oppenheimer be excepted, perhaps, Gregory Corso was the first genuine "man of the people" among this host of anti-academic academics. Born in New York City in 1930, he never attended college and he held various laborer's, merchantmen's, and detentive positions until he somehow became a member from 1965 to 1970 of the English faculty at the State University of New York at Buffalo.

His first book, *The Vestal Lady on Brattle and Other Poems* was published in Cambridge, Massachusetts, in 1955. When *Long Live Man* (1962) was published it showed some development over his earlier work, and many of the prose poems were genuinely funny, a unique quality among the caste of "visionaries" and "prophets" that made up most of the Beat Generation, but it was technically and intellectually impoverished. Between 1975 and the year of his death, 2001, little was heard of Gregory Corso, the true poet of the streets that Ferlinghetti had called for.

CHAPTER THREE
The Confessional Poets

    W. D. Snodgrass has been credited with being the founder of the so-called "Confessional School" of contemporary American poetry, which began at the University of Iowa where Snodgrass was a student from 1949 to 1955, but if there was a messiah of the school it was John Holmes who was born in Somerville, Massachusetts, in 1904. He was educated there and at Tufts University, from which he took his bachelor's degree in 1929. While spending a year at Harvard he studied briefly under Robert Hillyer, then he began his teaching career as an instructor of English at Lafayette College. Subsequently he moved back to Tufts and Medford, Massachusetts, where he remained until his death.

    Of Holmes' first book, *Address to the Living*, published in 1937 by Robert Frost's own publisher, the older poet said in the only jacket copy he ever wrote for any other poet, "Here are poems again, and it is gratifying to find that they hold their own, even gain, thus assembled from the magazines. They certainly put together into a new and attractive poet." If Frost appeared to be less than enthusiastic, there was good reason, for the poems were largely a mere gathering of the 'prentice-pieces of a novice.

    Holmes' next book, *Map of My Country*, appeared in 1943, and seven years passed before his third, *The Double Root*, was published in 1950. *The Symbols* appeared in 1955. Holmes wrote personal poems in formal structures, and he taught this approach to John Ciardi and his other pupils at Tufts. From him Ciardi learned to write the autobiographical poem that told a story or sang a song — Ciardi was never a breast-beater. Nor was Holmes who, during his lifetime, was largely ignored, although a few people paid him the compliment of remarking upon his classical New England control over his egopoetic subject matter.

    The poems of *Map of My Country* had much more weight and solidity than Holmes' first poems, and a recognizable voice began to emerge, but it was in The *Double Root* that the poet's voice was fully developed. That development, however, appeared to stagnate with many of the poems in *The Symbols*, which seemed, as Ciardi put it, an eddy between freshets.

Holmes wore neither his heart nor his introspection on his sleeve; rather, he worked his emotions, built them into ideas and attitudes, then pulled these elements together into an honest appraisal of himself and the human situation. Holmes' fifth book, *The Fortune Teller*, had resonance and overtone, fidelity and presence as well as brilliance and range. In that collection might be found not merely the craftsman but the man as well; not only the composer of inward vision, but the musician, as the title poem of the book indicated.

Holmes' *Selected Poems* was published posthumously, with an introduction titled "A Man's Voice" by John Ciardi, in 1965. In it Ciardi wrote, "Certainly it is a freshet that carries forward the poems of *The Fortune Teller*...despite what I feel to be the willful intensity of the title poem. It is still fact that speaks. The instant this voice finds fact to say, it says more than fact. 'Order Clearly Asking' might serve as that voice's description of itself and of its purpose: 'It is not style. The design is in the materials'." (ix)

Holmes was known as a remarkable teacher, but despite his devotion to craft, he too, like Richard Wilbur and the Beats, held the creative process in mystic awe and didn't want to scrutinize it too closely. In Ciardi's *Mid-Century American Poets* Holmes wrote,

> "The fact is that I do not really want to know how and why I write, and I had rather keep my ways and means to myself. A miner, a carpenter knows what he has to work with, and what he can do. Poets don't know; at any rate, I don't. As an additional handicap to my deliberate ignorance, I teach college students how to write poetry. This year-in-year-out gamble is sometimes good for them, sometimes for me. They get the thrill, which I deprecate, of studying poetry with me, an actually published poet, and they get a certain amount of useful suggestion, and not very much severity. I always mean to be severe, and never am. I get from them a depressing realization of what it means to begin from the bottom of September; but they do it once, and I do it every year. All this doesn't help. One has too many strands of life to rope and handle anyway, without teaching the writing of poetry, which is being a kind of stand-in for one's self. But it happens that I like to teach, and I think that by this time I know all the risks and penalties of being a writer who teaches writing, and I know the rewards and privileges." (203)

In his 1960 textbook *Writing Poetry* Holmes said — in some ways paraphrasing Emerson's observations in his essay "The Poet" — "The poet knows that he is. The poet knows who he is. The poet knows where he is. He is alive in time and space, the newest member of earth's miraculous voyage. He is acutely aware of the precarious exact crossing of his native latitude and longitude, and of where to lay his hand upon the subtle knot that makes him man. He stands there open to the four seasons and the twelve winds; his eyes are wide, his ears are keen, he feels earth hard under the heel, and the blood rich in his body, and he writes his poetry." (247)

John Ciardi

John Ciardi was born in 1916 and educated before World War II first at Bates College which he entered in 1933, and then at Tufts, to which institution he transferred eighteen months later. Edward Krickel, writing in his book *John Ciardi*, said that at Tufts Ciardi "found in John Holmes, 'just the teacher one insane adolescent had been starved for'" (19). Krickel further observed, "It is a turning point in the development of every budding young intellectual or artist when he finds his first real master. And he is lucky if in his full maturity he can recall the experience with gratitude. Holmes was the first such experience for Ciardi, as Roy W. Cowden of Michigan was to be the second."

Subsequent to finishing his graduate work at the University of Michigan Ciardi began his academic career in 1940 as an instructor at the University of Kansas City, the same year in which his first book, *Homeward to America*, appeared. The years from 1942 to 1945 he spent in the Army Air Corps and returned to teaching at Harvard as Briggs Copeland Instructor of English after his discharge. *Other Skies* was published in 1947, and *Live Another Day: Poems* appeared in 1949. He ended his teaching career early, as a professor of English at Rutgers, in 1973, but he continued his contact with the academic world through his directorship for many years of the Bread Loaf Writers' Conference at Middlebury College.

Ciardi was always a formal poet, and he encouraged formal writing in many ways over the years, not least as poetry editor of *The Saturday Review*. Ciardi was a master of the art of the narrative as well. Reading his work could be both an entertainment and an education, as a reading of "A Knothole in Spent Time" will show. This poem, from one of Ciardi's most neglected books, *The Lives of X*, is an example of Ciardi's ability to catch and hold the attention of the reader in the same way that a novelist or short fictioneer does. Like all Ciardi's work, this is a verse-mode, not a prose-mode piece. It begins with two thirteen-line stanzas in which the poet reminisces about his wedding — the poem is typical in this regard, too, for much of his work was autobiographical and nostalgic. Ciardi often reached back into his past to pull out of the shadows moments dappled by the sunlight of recall, to consider them in the leisure of time, and to take out of them lessons learned, epiphanies achieved.

Ciardi began by talking about his bride-to-be showing him where her school once stood in the southern woods, how they picked blackberries there and Judith got poison ivy. Then, the trip to Chicago and an itchy honeymoon, Ciardi sneezing through the cold he caught — the tone of humorous recollection is set, as is the prosody, normative accentual-syllabics, for Ciardi was always a formal poet, if one could catch him at it. His meter was going to be iambic pentameter blank verse in this poem, but he would allow himself enough freedom to give the impression that he was writing prose: one finds, if one scans a few lines, that there are hexameters among the five-foot lines, and even in the normative lines there are reversals and substitutions of feet.

A third "stanza" appears to continue the story of his wedding and its aftermath; instead, however, Ciardi launches into a series of rhetorical tropes as he asks how Wordsworth or Tennyson might have reacted had they gone back to their childhood haunts: "All change unghosts / something we change in leaving." What would they have done had they discovered "Super Mkts, / cloverleaf ramps, and ten Drive-In Self-Service / Omnimats —?" The "stanza" extends itself for an extra line and three-fourths, then it drops down to the next space and turns itself into a strophe instead, a strophe and a verse paragraph that begins with "Craddock School" — and Ciardi has dropped with it into the farther past, to his small-boyhood in Boston.

It is Ciardi's first day in kindergarten; although "it's out of focus now," he remembers the elms synesthetically, "a whispering sky that spattered sunlight through" like rain. The roof of this world is closer, yet it is still high above his head. Indoors are "walls like the sides of a ship," an "ark" full of small creatures that need to be tamed and civilized. Indoors the hallway ceilings appear to be as high as the trees outdoors, "lost in their own dusk." Ciardi piled similes upon descriptions — the hallway "smelled of chalk, / the furnace room, and sneakers. It creaked and breathed / as if there were giants sleeping in its attics."

The poet has done what a good storyteller does: introduced his protagonist — himself, set the scene, and pulled the reader into the story, for we remember these things as well, even though we have not lived through them ourselves. The reader experiences the school as the small boy does. The senses of smell, sight, hearing have been brought to bear upon these evocations, but literacy itself is not ignored, for the poet springs an allusion on us, an allusion out of school:

> If heaven needed a barn for better beasts
> than any of us were, the Craddock School
> would have done for Apollo's cattle.

The poet-to-be sits down. We are ready to be introduced to our first antagonist in the shape of a woman characterized by nomenclature and simile: "Miss Matron-Column" who "stood pillared / over our heads like a corseted caryatid / spilling out of her corsets on a scale / of two of anyone's mother...." The second antagonist is not far off:

> Ma meant the day to be ritual, and had made me
> a jumper-something called a Buster Brown,
> and bought me new school shoes, and long white stockings
> that buttoned, or tabbed, into my underwear.
> I wasn't exactly comfortable but I took it
> until a pug-nosed Irish snot behind me —
> Tom something-or-other — got his needle in
> to let me know white stockings were for girls
> and that I was not only a Dago but a sissy.

This foreshadowed the inevitable after-school fight, which did not occur, however, until the poet's teacher called him "John Sea-YARD-I," a foreign sound which was to stick until he was old enough and far enough away to assert the correct pronunciation of his name.

Ciardi was very good with textures, characterizations, imaging, but he could go deeper. After the fight he must go home to his widowed mother who will likely be waiting with a strap to discipline the reprobate who has not lived up to her expectations. The boy spends time worrying about it:

> Ma would be waiting with that strap. My tail
> would come away from it ridged. Then she'd cry,
> and I would have to stop bawling to comfort her.
> I'd never thought far enough back — not for trying —

[he says, thinking back,]

> to understand how we came to that arrangement.
> I know it had something to do with my being ghosted
> into her husband and he into her son.
> Sometimes I think she was beating him for dying,
> and me for not being enough of what she'd lost.

That is complicated psychological analysis stated in simple terms. When Ciardi wanted to paint a scene into the reader's memory or to drive home a point, he could do so with more than imagery or rhetoric, he could do it with sound. Though there are no end-rhymes in this verse tale, there is plenty of music. When he is promoted to the next grade, our Hero meets Miss Absolute Void whom he cannot remember at all except as an absence in his personal history. What he does remember is the sound of emptiness:

> I droned fly-drowsy sun its leafy day
> down through the elm's own daydream into mine.

The image has its tunes as well as its associations — alliteration (droned-drowsy-day-down-daydream), internal rhyme (I-fly), repetition (day-daydream), consonantal and vocalic echoes (ars, els, eys and wys), consonance (droned-sun-down-own). The meaning of this passage resides in how it sounds as much as in "what" it says — it's no coincidence that Ciardi once edited a textbook titled *How Does a Poem Mean?* Ciardi's mastery of the sonic and sensory levels of a poem would be enough for many poets, but he wanted his stories and confessions to have point as well. In all of them, he was going somewhere. This is where he had been heading all the while with "A Knothole of Spent Time," for the poem is a voyage into the land of epiphany, of self-discovery:

The boy has been daydreaming. Suddenly, the teacher calls on him to pick up the oral reading in the book before him: "The book was on my desk but I'd lost the page. / I got to my feet. Somewhere in a separate haze / I remembered a girl reading and her last words / still floating in the elmtops. I held the book / and said from memory whatever Blind Mice / or Chicken-Little came next, pretending to read...." And he pulled it off! Elation! He had fooled his teacher, who was made of clay after all. What an amazing victory!

>Then hit on a truth as if I'd cracked my skull —
>they wouldn't believe me! Ma wouldn't understand.
>My sisters wouldn't care. Miss Absolute Void —
>well, how could I tell her? I was alone
>my first time into the world, at an edge of light
>that dizzied like a dark; my gloat, half fear,
>my eye at its first peephole into heavens
>where Teachers were only people and could be wrong,
>and all Ma's stations and candles could be rounded
>by a truth I'd caught and held, and couldn't tell!

Yet here he is telling it after all, and we believe it! Not only that, it isn't, in context, at all a trivial incident, though perhaps it would have been had Ciardi told it in any other way.

The poem was not quite over — there is a denouement in which the author, like the professional raconteur he was in person or in his role as poet, winds up the loose ends and ties them into a neat knot, but that is the climax and the point of the performance, for that is what it is, the performance of a work of language as relevant to our world as it is to the teller's. "This is the room. / The first place in the world where I was alone / with more than I could tell of what was true."

On this level of the ideational Ciardi took his subject, growing up, and cast it in the form of an autobiographical narrative. He mixed his viewpoints to correspond — egopoetic and narrative — so well and subtly that one may have a difficult time telling opinion from description, narrative from discourse. His syntax, likewise, has been a blend of the subjective and the objective. The level of diction he chose was the conversational, and his style was literate but not overly literary. The major genre of the poem is clearly the narrative, but there is an undercurrent of the didactic as well, as in all good stories that are but illustrations of lessons learned about life.

In the two years preceding his unexpected death in the spring of 1986 John Ciardi published two books of his poetry. *The Selected Poems* appeared in 1984, Ciardi's first showcase collection since the 1955 *As If: Poems New and Selected*, and it contained work from that volume as well. The following year, 1985, Ciardi published a book mainly made up of lyrics. He didn't find it necessary to invent new prosodies or forms in order to speak colloquially yet musically — the old forms did very well in *The Birds of Pompeii*, just as they had done for Ciardi's Bread Loaf colleague of many years, Robert Frost.

When Ciardi wanted to be subjective he understood that he had to sing in order to keep the reader's attention, as in "At Least with Good Whiskey":

> She gave me a drink and told me she had tried
> to read my book but had had to put it down
> because it depressed her. Why, she wanted to know,
> couldn't I turn my talent (I raised my glass)
> to happier things? Did I suppose it was smart
> to be forever dying? Not forever,
> I told her, sipping; by actuarial tables
> ten years should about do it. See what I mean?
> she hurried to say — always that terrible sadness.
> Well, maybe, I said. (This is good whiskey, I said.)
> But ten years, plus or minus, is not much time
> for getting it said — do you see what I mean? — which leaves me
> too busy to make a hobby of being sad.

W. D. Snodgrass

Born in Wilkinsburg, Pennsylvania, in 1926, W. D. Snodgrass began his undergraduate career at Geneva College in 1943-44. After his freshman year he entered the U. S. Navy and served until 1946 when he returned to college and married Lila Jean Hank. He stayed in school only briefly, then, in 1949, he entered the University of Iowa where he took his B.A. in 1949, his M.A.in 1951, and his M.F.A. in 1953, the same year in which he was divorced from his first wife. It was the breakup of this marriage that he chronicled in a sequence of poems titled "Heart's Needle," which became the title series of his first book, *Heart's Needle*. The collection appeared in 1959 and won both the first award in poetry of the Ingram Merrill Foundation and the Pulitzer prize in 1960.

While he was at Iowa Snodgrass began to write a very personal, very lyrical kind of poetry. Snodgrass' subjects were those which were closest to him and to most readers — family, environment, the everyday happenings behind which there often exist something so meaningful that the average person is unable or unwilling to confront it, let alone write about it. Snodgrass felt that it is the poet's job to write about these things. His poetry is a continual stripping away of the surfaces of our world, and a simultaneous exposure of the mental and emotional reasons behind our actions and reactions. Most of the poems in *Heart's Needle* struck a balance between feeling and sense, as in the first stanza of "Song":

> Observe the cautious toadstools
> still on the lawn today
> though they grow over-evening;
> sun shrinks them away.
> Pale and proper and rootless,
> they righteously extort
> their living from the living.

The poet said what he had to say boldly and lyrically. His verse was polished without seeming slick, like stone tiles worn by the passage of the living. For the most part Snodgrass worked within strict metrical nonce-forms, but he found considerable freedom within their limits; the current of his thought ran swiftly and strongly beneath the surface of his lines, no matter what subject motivated him: divorce, marriage, loss, love, return. His work had personality and craftsmanship; often he touched a responsive chord in the reader. As in "A Cardinal," one could hardly gainsay him when he ended,

> We whistle in the dark
> of a region in doubt
> where unknown powers work,
> as watchmen in the night
> ring bells to say, Watch out,
> I am here; I have the right.

In various of his early poems the narrative first-person "I" was not merely the poet speaking of himself, but the persona of the poet speaking for Everyman in the real and terrifying world, out of despair and into human joy. Here, in this first book of poems, was a man's life shown to the bone, and one knew it was not made of whole cloth. Many readers were deeply moved by *Heart's Needle*.

Not the least of Snodgrass' qualities was his sense of humor, almost unique among the members of the Confessional School, if one does not count John Berryman's bitter clowning. In the poem titled "These Trees Stand..." Snodgrass acknowledged the humor of his last name in the refrain, "Snodgrass is walking through the universe." Readers will not appreciate the full import of this line unless they know the etymology of the poet's name, but will respond merely to its sound. It is, in fact, two words compounded: *grass* and the past participle of the archaic English verb, "*to snid*" or mow; thus, "Snodgrass" means "mown lawn" or "cut grass." The third and final stanza of this poem begins, "Your name's absurd, miraculous as sperm / And as decisive."

Not a prolific poet, Snodgrass has since published few other collections of his own poems (excluding translations). *After Experience* appeared in 1968, and *Remains* in 1970. This latter collection was published in a new edition in 1985 because the first edition was a very limited issuance of those poems the poet published under the anagram pseudonym "S. S. Gardons" — the poet still fooling around with his surname. The chapbook is made of those pieces Snodgrass originally felt were too personal and familial even for the original confessional poet to publish.

The Fuehrer Bunker: A Cycle of Poems in Progress appeared in 1977, but *The Complete Cycle* did not appear until 1995; it was a departure from the poet's earlier lyrical approach. Snodgrass wrote in an "Afterword," to the original volume, "All the figures in this cycle were actually in the places, doing and saying pretty much the things these poems show." The poems are dramatic, not lyric or narrative. Each character speaks in his or her own voice; there is thus a strong documentary element in these poems about Nazi Germany during World War II. There is a much greater range of approach as well. Some poems are written in prose mode, or prose intermixed with verse prosodies

"April Inventory" from *Heart's Needle*, like many lyrics before it, sang its confession, and no distinction would have been made between Snodgrass' work and traditional lyric poetry if it hadn't been for two things: the new subject matter of broken marriage together with the problems attendant upon divorce, the everyday frictions of home life in conflict with infidelities of the mind and of the heart; and the fact that John Berryman and Robert Lowell were influenced by his work and began writing their own confessional poetry. "April Inventory" became a standard anthology piece of rueful good humor as it examined the position of the aging teacher-poet among the coed flowers of the campus. It was and is wistful, nostalgic, and funny, yet it made the necessary observation and comment as well, even as it sang: one of the traditional ways in which the best egopoets capture and hold the attention of the reader is through lyricism. It is in many ways typical of Snodgrass' early production.

One notices immediately on the typographical level, simply by the layout of its lines, that this is a verse mode, not a prose mode poem, and it is stanzaic rather than strophic — there are ten sestet stanzas; therefore, the poem is sixty lines long. It is soon clear to the reader that the sonic level is strong. Scansion shows that the poem's general prosody is accentual-syllabics; specifically, normative accentual-syllabics. All lines are the same length; the meter is iambic tetrameter. The rhyme scheme is *ababcc*, but there is linked rhyme between stanzas 1 & 2, 5 & 6, and 7 & 8, so that the complete rhyme scheme is *ababcc, cdcdee, fcfcgg, hihij¹j¹, k¹k²k¹k²ll, lmlmnn, opopqq, qrqrss, j¹j²j¹j²j³j³, tutuvv*. Some of these are falling rhymes, specifically the l rhymes in stanza 5 (where they first show up) and in the following stanza 6, where the em rhymes also fall; the pee rhymes in stanza 7, the ar rhymes in stanza eight, and the vee rhymes in stanza ten, closing the poem (the rhymes with superscripts are consonances)..

Snodgrass utilizes metrical variations in a craftsmanly way to provide sonic interest:

> The green catalpa tree has turned
> All white; the cherry blooms once more.
> In one whole year I haven't learned
> A blessed thing they pay you for.
> The blossoms snow down in my hair;
> The trees and I will soon be bare.   - 6

The first line of the poem is acatalectic — that is, perfect iambic tetrameter (˘ ´ ˘ ´ ˘ ´ ˘ ´), but the second line opens with a spondee (´ ´) substituted for the first foot (all white). The next two lines are acatalectic, but a trochee (´ ˘) is substituted for the third iamb in line five (down in). The last line of the first sestet is perfect again.

Thereafter substitutions occur relatively frequently, often of spondees or trochees for the prevailing iambs, as in the first foot of stanza two, line three (whole line 9), where a trochee substitution occurs. In the first foot of the next line (10), a demotion occurs in the first syllable of the first foot. This line also contains a w-glide elision ("gradually") and a caesura which compensates for a missing unstressed syllable just after the elision:

> The trees have more than I to spare.
> The sleek, expensive girls I teach,
> Younger and pinker every year,
> Bloom gradually . out of reach.
> The pear tree lets its petals drop
> Like dandruff on the table top.   -12

In the first line (13) of stanza three there is a promotion — by means of rhetorical emphasis — of a syllable, "so," to the level of a secondary stress in foot three, and there is another spondee substitution in foot one, line three (15). The English language hates three unstressed syllables in a row, and as a result "with" in line sixteen takes a promotion to secondary stress, thus giving it rhetorical emphasis — both teeth and hair are falling:

> The girls have grown so young by now
> I have to nudge myself to stare.
> This year they smile and mind me how
> My teeth are falling with my hair.
> In thirty years I may not get
> Younger or shrewder or out of debt.   -18

The last line of this stanza substitutes two trochees in the first two feet ("younger, shrewder").

    Stanza four is acatalectic throughout:

> The tenth time, just a year ago,
> I made myself a little list
> Of all the things I'd ought to know,
> Then told my parents, analyst,
> And everyone who's trusted me,
> I'd be substantial, presently.   -24

The first line (25) of stanza five puts rhetorical stress on the word "one," but its position in the line, between two strong stresses, counteracts the emphasis; the result is a promotion only to secondary stress: (⏑́⏑́ . ́⏑́). This promotion tends to make the reader aware that the last word of the line, "about," is likewise rhetorically emphasized: "I haven't read one book **about** a book." In the last line (30) a trochee is again substituted in the first foot (**Get** the de**grees**):

> I haven't read one book about
> A book or memorized one plot.
> Or found a mind I did not doubt.
> I learned one date. And then forgot.
> And one by one the solid scholars
> Get the degrees, the jobs, the dollars.   -30

There are other substitutions in stanza six: a spondee in the first foot of the third line (33), "one lovely girl"; a trochee in the first foot of the next line (34), "Lacking," and a trochee in the third foot, "a source-book or." In the next line (35) there is a promotion in the first syllable of the second iamb ("I showed one child"), and in the last syllable a secondary stress is forced upon the preposition "of" at the end of the line (syllable 8) by means of its position where a strong stress ought to occur in the meter, and because it rhymes with "love" in the next line (31) which, though the previous line (30) was end-stopped with a period, is nevertheless an enjambment. The effect of this construction is to invoke sarcasm and thus emphasize the stereotype being set up:

> And smile above their starchy collars.
> I taught my classes Whitehead's notions;
> One lovely girl, a song of Mahler's.
> Lacking a source-book or promotions,
> I showed one child the colors of
> A luna moth and how to love.   -36

In the next sestet another promotion is forced by overstressing through alliteration in the second line (38), syllable one, foot two: "to bark back, loosen love and crying"; notice that "loosen love" is also an alliteration:

> I taught myself to name my name,
> To bark back, loosen love and crying;
> To ease my woman so she came,
> To ease an old man who was dying.
> I have not learned how often I
> Can win, can love, but choose to die.   -42

In the fourth line (40) of this stanza there is another substitution of a trochee for an iamb in the third foot ("Man who"), and in the next line (41) a rhetorical emphasis promotes the unstressed syllable in the second iamb ("I have not learned") — had the poet written "haven't," there would have been no promotion, no deviation from the norm.

Stanza eight repeats this phrase in the first line (43): "I have not learned there is a lie," and alliteration with the rhyme-word in the first syllable of the next line (44), "Love shall be," forces the substitution of a trochee in the first foot. "Loves" in the fourth line

(46) of the stanza is both a repetition and a continuation of the alliteration; thus, the first foot of this line is a spondee, "Loves only...":

> I have not learned there is a lie
> Love shall be blonder, slimmer, younger;
> That my equivocating eye
> Loves only by my body's hunger;
> That I have forces, true to feel,
> Or that the lovely world is real.   -48

By this time in the poem the falling rhymes have become prominent, and the effect of the spondee and trochee substitutions, together with the repetitions and the promotions, is giving the poem a considerable feeling of metrical variation and a concomitant sense of acceleration, both metrical and rhetorical. The return to acatalexis in the last two lines (47 & 48) of this stanza merely emphasizes this sense, for it causes the poem to pause suddenly. To use a metaphor from boxing, Snodgrass has been jabbing faster and faster, peppering the reader with softening-up and setting-up blows. Now he has used a combination and stepped back before he delivers the haymaker.

Stanza nine returns to the metrical norm, including rising rhyme, except for a rhetorical promotion of the first syllable of line three (51), "my," and another of the second syllable in the first foot of the fifth line (53): "There is a value underneath." In the second syllable of foot three of the following line (54), a preposition is promoted because of its position in the line: "The gold and silver in my teeth," which has a rhetorical effect:

> While scholars speak authority
> And wear their ulcers on their sleeves,
> My eyes in spectacles shall see
> These trees procure and spend their leaves.
> There is a value underneath
> The gold and silver in my teeth.   -54

Another rhetorical promotion takes place in the second syllable of the second line (56) of the last stanza: "We shall afford," and in the same spot in the next tree lines as well, (57): "There is a gentleness"; (58): "That will outspeak," and (59): "There is a loveliness exists," so that the four middle lines of the last stanza are a series of grammatical parallels that serve the rhetorical function of delivering the climactic knockout blows:

> Though trees turn bare and girls turn wives,
> We shall afford our costly seasons;
> There is a gentleness survives
> That will outspeak and has its reasons.
> There is a loveliness exists,
> Preserves us, not for specialists.   -60

Fusionally, the major genre of "April Inventory" is that of the lyric. The minor genre is that of the "confessional" poem, or perhaps it would be more accurate to say that it is a humorous lament with a didactic point. In any event, it is a poem with its levels in balance, and this equilibrium is mirrored in the qualities of character that show through the poet's lines. He is complex — funny and intelligent, suffering and indignant, disdainful and confused, logical and sympathetic.

Although in his later work Snodgrass began to move away from traditionally rhyming and metering poems this balance of the levels of poetry continued to be characteristic of Snodgrass' work in all his books of lyrics including *After Experience*, *Remains* (1970 & 1985), *If Birds Build with Your Hair* (1979), and *A Locked House* (1986), though not in *The Fuehrer Bunker* which moved away from the lyric and into the dramatic. A tour through *Selected Poems* (1987) will prove the point:

Even when Snodgrass appears to be writing lineated prose poems he is in fact maintaining this same balance of the levels of poetry. One good example is "Old Apple Trees" which is an extended metaphor that begins immediately with a pair of similes: "Like battered old millhands, they stand in the orchard — / Like drunk legionnaires, heaving themselves up,..." The conceit is carried forward over the whole poem as the narrator imagines a night on the town among real people like the old trees which, when he returns home, he sees as now historical and universal, both as trees and people, "...the rough trunks holding their formations / Like elders of Colonus, the old men of Thebes / Tossing their white hair, almost whispering,..." In fiction this would be called a circle-back ending, but here it is a return to the origins of the poem both literally and figuratively, with a greatly amplified power of allusion and overtone.

Some people might call these lines "free verse" or line-phrased prose, but it is in fact a form of blank verse: variable, unrhymed iambic pentameter lines. Merely to look at the poem laid out is to see that most lines are nearly of a length, except toward the end of the poem where they narrow to approximately tetrameter length. Such lines as, "No man should come here except on a working pass" or "Till even the belly dancer leaves,

Robert Lowell's *Life Studies* appeared in the same year as *Heart's Needle*. Inasmuch as Snodgrass was a student of Robert Lowell and John Berryman at the University of Iowa, it was perhaps a foregone conclusion that the three poets would be seen as forming a "school" of personal poetry. One of the earliest people, if not the very first person to use the expression "Confessional Poets" was Donald Justice, a student in the Iowa Workshop himself at the time, and later a teacher there. Donald J. Greiner said that "Snodgrass acknowledges the debt to Lowell, but he mentions several times a remark of Randall Jarrell's: 'Snodgrass, do you know you're writing the very best second-rate Lowell in the whole country?'" (267-8). At the time of his death in January of 2009 Snodgrass, though he set aside the narrative and dramatic genres of the academic formalists, was nevertheless still utilizing some of the favorite New Critical techniques and approaches of that school.

John Berryman

A Native Oklahoman, John Berryman was educated at Columbia University where he took his A.B. in 1936, and at Clare College, University of Cambridge, where he took a second bachelor's degree in 1938. Thereafter he spent his life in academe, teaching at Wayne State, Harvard, and Princeton universities, and the Universities of Washington, Cincinnati, Iowa, and Minnesota. (60)

Berryman was an early adherent of the Confessional School while he was on the faculty of the University of Iowa Writers' Workshop where W. D. Snodgrass, the original confessional poet, was one of the members of his class. "I have been very fortunate twice in my career as a student of poetry," William Dickey wrote in Ed Dinger's *Seems Like Old Times*, "first to have been at Reed College as an undergraduate with Gary Snyder, Philip Whalen and Lew Welch, second to have been in John Berryman's extraordinary and intense poetry workshop with W. D. Snodgrass, Donald Justice, Philip Levine, Paul Petrie, Robert Dana, Constance Urdang, Jane Cooper, Donald Finkel, Henri Coulette — the list continues beyond the capacity of my memory, but it was a course I approached with rapture and fear, owing in part to Berryman's sometimes jagged abruptness, as when, having warned me beforehand that he was going to exhibit the profound mortality of one of my works, he held it out at arm's length in the class, looked at it with loathing, and said, 'Now, what are we to say about this ridiculous poem?'" (Dinger, 23)

"I remember a day in the old tin barracks that served as our classroom down by the river, when John Berryman scribbled some lines of mine on the blackboard," Robert Dana added. "'Dana!' he shouted across two rows of chairs, 'Do you know what that is?' He rapidly marked the scansion. 'Metrical chaos! that's what that is! Metrical chaos!'" But chaos was a large and natural part of Berryman's own life, including his poetry:

"It was that kind of blow-torch approach that cut Berryman's class, in two weeks, from about 40 to thirteen." Dana continued. "I like to think of us now as 'The Lucky Thirteen,' but we were crazy too. Crazy with the kind of toughness it took to hang in there against John's special mix of crankiness, brilliance, and cruelty. And we were brash in our own ways.

"Phil Levine punched Berryman in the eye one night, breaking a pair of glasses and establishing a life-long friendship." These kinds of personal relationships were always of great importance to Berryman. It is a question whether he influenced his students more than they influenced him.

On the other hand, the British poet and contemporary of W. H. Auden, Stephen Spender, did not believe that this sort of hot-house atmosphere was necessarily good for poets. Spender has written, "The bad — or perhaps I should say the tragic — result of campus patronage [in the U. S.] is the depressing effect it sometimes has on major talents. I think that the tragic and near-suicidal deaths of Randall Jarrell, Theodore Roethke and John Berryman are not unconnected with their being in positions where, although they were admired, they were very isolated." (Spender, 286)

Berryman's first book was *Poems*, published in 1942 during the Second World War, and his second was *The Dispossessed*, which appeared six years later. In 1956 a long and cranky work, *Homage to Mistress Bradstreet*, earned him his first real critical acclaim; the 1964 *77 Dream Songs* received the Pulitzer Prize, and the 1968 *His Toy, His Dream, His Rest*, were published in 1969 in one volume as *The Dream Songs*. By that time Berryman, though not a "popular" poet, was well established as an important force in the literary world of poetry, and he was widely read among his contemporaries.

In 1967, in the heart of the restless decade, like his elder contemporary Richard Eberhart Berryman published a book of near-juvenilia, *Berryman's Sonnets*, of which the author wrote in a verse preface, speaking of himself in the third person, "He made, a thousand years ago, a-many songs / for an Excellent Lady, wif whom he was in wuv, / shall he now publish them?" Perhaps he should. "So free them to the winds that play, / let boys & girls with these old songs have holiday / if they feel like it" (ix)

Berryman's archness notwithstanding, the collection was interesting because it shows that his distinctive poetic diction had roots well back in his creative life. This is what "Sonnet 102" sounded like:

> A penny, pity, for the runaway ass!
> A nickel for the killer's twenty-six-mile ride!
> Ice for the root rut-smouldering inside!
> Eight hundred weeks I have not run to Mass. —
> Toss Jack a jawful of good August grass!
> 'Soul awful,' pray for a soul sometimes has cried!
> Wire reasons he seasons should still abide!
> Hide all your arms where he is bound to pass. —
>
> Who drew me first aside? her I forgive,
> Or him, as I would be forgotten by
> O be forgiven for salt bites I took.
> Who drew me off last, willy-nilly, live
> On (darling) free. If we meet, know me by
> Your own exempt (I pray) and earthly look.

In Berryman's early pieces the neo-Elizabethan imagination and metaphysical wit of *Homage to Mistress Bradstreet* and the other books mentioned, plus the posthumous *Delusions, Etc.*, which was published in 1972, the year of his death by suicide, are linked with the passion of youth, causing some readers, perhaps, to wish that the later Berryman had retained some of the charm and commitment to blood found in the *Sonnets*, instead of going far down the road toward arch confession and idiosyncratic style, as he did in his later work.

The poet and critic Robert Phillips wrote that the poet's second collection "is filled with accounts of friends' deaths and suicides, events which took their toll on Berryman's psyche: Randall Jarrell, Sylvia Plath, R. P. Blackmur, Yvor Winters, William Carlos Williams, and above all, Delmore Schwartz, to whose memory Berryman dedicated the book and penned *Dream Songs* 146-157 and also number 344. These personal losses were experienced during a time of great public loss as well: John Kennedy, Robert Kennedy, Martin Luther King, Ernest Hemingway, William Faulkner. Yet none of these personal or public deaths figure so importantly in the volume as the suicide of Berryman's father which is, in one sense, the sole subject of the latter collection." (93) Berryman's own suicide was not the first among the Confessional poets.

As he developed, Berryman went in the opposite direction from that which Lowell took; he got more elaborate and obscure. "Berryman is a poet so preoccupied with poetic effects as to be totally in their thrall," James Dickey wrote. "His inversions, his personal and often irritatingly cute colloquialisms and deliberate misspellings, his odd references, his basing of lines and whole poems on private allusions, create what must surely be the densest verbal thickets since [the Modernist English poet and critic William] Empson's ." (Dickey, 198)

In his 366th "Dream Song" Berryman himself wrote, "These Songs are not meant to be understood, you understand. / They are only meant to terrify & comfort." "And understood many have not been," Phillips wrote. "Packed with private jokes, topical and literary allusions (Berryman's reading and personal library are legendary), they boggle many minds. When the first *77 Dream Songs*...were published, Robert Lowell admitted," Phillips wrote, "'At first the brain aches and freezes at so much darkness, disorder and oddness. After a while, the repeated situations and their racy jabber become more and more enjoyable, although even now I wouldn't trust myself to paraphrase accurately at least half the sections.'" Phillips continued, "The situation was considerably beclouded when four years later, Berryman dumped on the world a truckful of 308 additional *Dream Songs*, under the title *His Toy, His Dream, His Rest*." (Phillips, 92)

As his career progressed, unlike Robert Lowell and most other members of the school except for Snodgrass, Berryman remained a formalist, inventing for his work not only a poetic diction and a style of writing that is clearly recognizable as his own and no one else's, but a specific poem-form as well in *The Dream Songs*. The form consisted of three sestet stanzas rhyming *abaaba*. The rhymes changed in subsequent stanzas; the third and sixth lines in each stanza were shorter than the rest.

This is only an approximate description of the form, however, as Berryman left himself considerable leeway. Another feature of the poems had to do with their narrative voices. These were not, strictly speaking, egopoems, for they were often dialogues among characters named "Henry," "Mr. Bones," and the poet himself.

There was, then, a distinct dramatic element in the Dream Songs, as in no. 80, "Op. posth. no. 3," from *His toy, His Dream, His Rest*:

> It's buried at a distance, on my insistence, buried.
> Weather's severe there, which it will not mind.
> I miss it.

> O happies before & during & between the times it got
>   married
> I hate the love of leaving it behind,
> deteriorating & hopeless that.
>
> The great Uh climbed above me, far above me,
> doing the north face, or behind it. Does He love me?
> over, & flout.
> Goodness is bits of outer God. The house-guest
> (slimmed down) with one eye open & one breast
>   out.
>
> Slimmed-down from by-blow; adoptive-up; was white.
> A daughter of a friend. His soul is a sight.
> Mr Bones, what's all about?
> Girl have a little: what be wrong with that?
> You free? — Down some many did descend
> from the abominable & semi-mortal Cat.

    This is one of the few poems in *The Dream Songs* that has a title, and from it the reader can infer a subject: the speaker's death. Since the speaker of the poem is dead and the poem itself is not only published, but composed, after the speaker's demise, then one may also infer that it is a dramatic poem, the speaker imagining himself both as dead and alive and writing what amounts to an elegy for himself. The "it" of the first three lines is the speaker's corpse, which the "I" misses. "It" was happy at times in its life. The "I" must leave "it" behind — an odd twist, since usually it is the person dying who leaves the living "behind." The "I" will probably be assumed by most readers to be the soul of the "it."

    Where is the "I" going, then? He has followed "the great Uh" which "climbed above" the "I," upon the "north face" — this is mountaineering talk. "Uh" has climbed beyond "I." Does "Uh" love "I"? "over, & flout." What is over? Who is flouting whom?

    "The house-guest" is obscure until one recalls that the coffin has in English literary traditions been called "the narrow house." The "it" is "slimmed down" to a skeleton "with one eye open" and its "breast out."

    The third stanza explains that before "it" was buried "it" began to be "slimmed down" before death as a result of a "by-blow," another seemingly obscure word which is cleared up by reference to the OED: The third definition of "by-blow" is "One who comes into the world by a side-stroke; an illegitimate child, a bastard." The rest of the line thus clears up: "adoptive-up; was white." The next line is a bit cloudier, "A daughter of a friend. His soul is a sight." But we can be a bit easier in our assumption that "I" is the soul of "it."

    Who is the speaker? is it "Mr. Bones," for a new voice in minstrel dialect appears to ask him, "what's all about? / Girl have a little: what be wrong with that? You free? —" It's the most natural thing in the world that a girl should want to have sex, become pregnant, and give birth to a child. No, it isn't Mr. Bones, for previous poems will show us that the "hero" of most of the Dream Songs is someone named "Henry." The "— Mr. Bones" is a dramatic tip-off that the poser of the question is Mr. Bones asking "Henry," the "soul" a question.

It has been presumed that both "Henry" and "Mr. Bones" are aspects of Berryman himself; if Mr. Bones is not, then perhaps — some critics say, taking their cue from the word "bones" — he is Death who stalks the poet. One can maintain with good circumstantial backing, however, that Henry is at least "Mr. Interloc'tor," the master of ceremonies of the traditional minstrel show that is Berryman's life, and that Mr. Bones is the blackface end-man who is the thorn in the side of the emcee.

Henry's reply to Mr. Bones in this case is cryptic. Many if not most of Berryman's *Dream Songs* will probably remain as unsatisfactorily explicated and obscure as many of Ezra Pound's *Cantos*.

Robert Lowell

Robert Lowell began as an arch-formalist deeply indebted to his teacher John Crowe Ransom and his mentor-friend Alan Tate, both members of the so-called Modernist "Fugitive" poets of Vanderbilt University in Tennessee. Ransom was himself a leading member of the New Critics, and the precepts he held close to his heart were those of the English Renaissance and the 17th-century. Certainly, Stephen Spender's observations about the isolation of American poets in academe are not borne out by the life of Lowell; quite the opposite — much of Lowell's early success appears to have been owing to his connections. It may even be that, when Lowell came to distrust his "accomplishments," the root of his unease may have been his inability to distinguish between his individual talent and his social prominence.

Lowell was born in 1917 into the family of Boston Brahmins that included the 19th-century Household Poet James Russell Lowell and the Imagist Amy Lowell of the Modernist period. One of the things that set the younger Lowell apart from his New England Puritan background was his conversion to Roman Catholicism. The prep school he attended was St. Mark's, where his older contemporary poet Richard Eberhart came to take a place on the faculty and an influential part in the life of his student who, for the first time, began to think seriously about himself becoming a poet. Lowell continued to correspond with Eberhart after he went on to attend Harvard from 1935-37 and then transferred to Kenyon College where he studied under Ransom and took his A.B. in 1940. It was while he was at Kenyon that Lowell fell out with Eberhart, whom he regarded by that time as an easy-going "popular" poet.

During the ensuing World War II Lowell became a conscientious objector. Rather than serve in the armed forces, he spent a term in prison from 1943 to 1944. His first marriage, to the writer Jean Stafford, ended in divorce in 1948. He spent only one year at the University of Iowa as an instructor in the Writers' Workshop, 1949-50. Although it was a seminal year, he disparaged the writing program after he had left it. On November 24, 1964, the director Paul Engle wrote a letter to Lewis Turco, a former student, that included this comment: "As for Lowell, I feel he is not quite fair. We saved him, in a sense, by being the first place in the USA to give him a job, to help him develop confidence after the shattering sequence of psychopathic hospital and federal prison. Only Iowa would take a chance on him; others did, after we made the initial risk. It gave Cal security and a hope; both the Dept. Head and the President took a hard look at the risks involved, and decided to hire him because I said he was the best poet." (Turco, *A Sheaf of Leaves*, 119) Subsequently Lowell taught at various places in the U.S. and at Kent University in England before his death in 1977.

Lowell's first four books, from *The Land of Unlikeness* (1944) through *The Mills of the Cavanaughs* (1951) were extremely formalist in the tradition of the Metaphysical poets of the 17th century. Allen Tate wrote of Lowell's first book, in his *The Poetry Reviews, 1924-1944*, "There is no other poetry today quite like this. T. S. Eliot's recent prediction that we should soon see a return to formal and even intricate metres and stanzas was coming

THE CONFESSIONAL POETS

true, before he made it, in the verse of Robert Lowell. Every poem in this book has a formal pattern, either the poet's own or one borrowed, as the stanza of 'Satan's Confession' is borrowed from [the English Renaissance poet Michael] Drayton's 'The Virginian Voyage,' and adapted to a personal rhythm of the poet's own.

"But this is not, I think," Tate continued, "a mere love of external form. Lowell is consciously a Catholic poet, and it is possible to see a close connection between his style and the formal pattern. The style is bold and powerful, and the symbolic language often has the effect of being willed; for it is an intellectual style compounded of brilliant puns and shifts of tone; and the willed effect is strengthened by the formal stanzas, to which the language is forced to conform." Sometimes that language — the images, meters, rhymes and syntax — could be extremely convoluted, even crabbed, as in the first stanza of one of his most famous poems, "Mr. Edwards and the Spider":

> I saw the spiders marching through the air,
> Swimming from tree to tree that mildewed day
> In latter August when the hay
> Came creaking to the barn. But where
> The wind is westerly,
> Where gnarled November makes the spiders fly
> Into the apparitions of the sky,
> They purpose nothing but their ease and die
> Urgently beating east to sunrise and the sea;...

There is considerable difference between this style and that of Lowell's first "Confessional" book, *Life Studies*, as exemplified by another of his well-known poems, "Memories of West Street and Lepke"; here are the first two stanzas:

> Only teaching on Tuesdays, book-worming
> in pajamas fresh from the washer each morning,
> I hog a whole house on Boston's
> "hardly passionate Marlborough Street,"
> where even the man
> scavenging filth in the back alley trash cans,
> has two children, a beach wagon, a helpmate,
> and is a "young Republican."
> I have a nine months' daughter,
> young enough to be my granddaughter.
> Like the sun she rises in her flame-flamingo infants' wear.
>
> These are the tranquilized Fifties,
> and I am forty. Ought I to regret my seedtime?
> I was a fire-breathing Catholic C. O.,

> and made my manic statement,
> telling off the state and president, and then
> sat waiting sentence in the bull pen
> beside a Negro boy with curlicues
> of marijuana in his hair.

"The poetry which Lowell wrote and published before *Life Studies* recorded an able, sometimes precocious poet in search of materials for an art as well as a style to manage that art," Arthur Oberg wrote in his *Modern American Lyric*, "If Lowell later rejected much of what he felt this earlier work represented to him as art and in a life, he also [went] back to parts of it in successive volumes, reworking some of the poems, including others in new contexts, and showing the same respect for craft and language and intelligence which marked his work from the very beginning." (7) It was this later much-simplified style that was to influence the academic poetry of the 1960s, not those of Berryman or Snodgrass.

As his books were issued Lowell's work got emotionally sloppier and sloppier, though formally it tightened up a bit, until it sounded like this in "Dear Sorrow 2" in *For Lizzie and Harriet* (1973):

> Each day more poignantly resolved on love,
> though the stars in their courses war against us...
> I have climbed to the last step of the stairs to look:
> an open window roughs the central heat,
> my lackluster pictures, Holbein's Sir Thomas More
> and Audubon's Blue Jays, shine in the January air —
> more cries of the city than that woodsman could name....
> If we have loved, it's not returnable;
> this room will dim and die as we dim and die,
> its many secrets change to others' things.
> Can I be forgiven the life-waste of my lifework?
> Was the thing worth doing worth doing badly?
> Man in the world, a whirlpool in a river —
> soul cannot be saved outside the role of God.

Hyatt H. Waggoner wrote in the revised edition of his *American Poets from the Puritans to the Present*," Lowell's later volumes...show a falling-off of power. More and more he turned to translations, imitations, adaptations — for instance to dramatizing versions of stories by Hawthorne and Melville in *The Old Glory* (1965), in which the verbal brilliance he had long before demonstrated could not compensate for the impoverishment of meaning as 'Endecott and the Red Cross,' 'My Kinsman, Major Molineux,' and 'Benito Cereno' were adapted for the stage, in the process being reduced to political tracts on such conscientious issues of the decade as racism. Reading them today, we can approve the ethical messages they carry even as we miss the subtleties of Hawthorne's and Melville's classics." (585)

The moment he was dead, Robert Lowell became the subject of instant reappraisals, even vicious attacks, in journals ranging from *The New York Times Book Review* to the little magazines and literary quarterlies. His socio-historical position was no longer sufficient to protect him.

Anne Sexton

Anne Sexton was the paradigmatic Confessional Poet. Her life, at least from her own point of view — which was the only viewpoint of any value so far as she was concerned — was quintessentially unhappy, and it can be read in her naked poetry, to borrow Robert Mezey's phrase and apply it in an appropriate context. Robert Phillips says that "with Anne Sexton the poetry of misfortune reaches some sort of apogee. So many are her afflictions, we recognize in the poet a female Job. One is able to reconstruct a hellishly unhappy life from her nakedly autobiographical poems: Birth into the well-to-do Harvey family in Newton, Massachusetts, in 1928; her mother's materialism and father's alcoholism; apparently an accident at the age of six, in which the young girl nearly lost an arm in a clothes wringer; the arrival to live with the Harveys of a great-aunt, who later suffered deafness and lapsed into madness; summers on Cape Cod; marriage to an unimaginative man; the deaths of two poet friends, John Holmes and Sylvia Plath; the birth of two daughters, Linda and Joy; the death of both parents within three months of one another, in 1959; her confinements in mental institutions; the temporary loss of a daughter; her search for release through religion, drugs, lovers, art." (73)

Anne Sexton's educational background was atypical of most of the poets of these years, for she attended Garland Junior College and Radcliffe Institute (not College) from 1961-63. The "unimaginative man" she married was Alfred M. Sexton in 1948. She was a Boston fashion model for a year, 1950-51. She met Sylvia Plath at Boston University in 1958 while both women were attending a course in poetry writing taught by Robert Lowell. Sexton taught high school in the late 1960s for one year, then began teaching writing arts classes herself at Boston University in 1970. In 1972 she was made Crawshaw Professor of Literature at Colgate University. Two years later, in 1974, she was divorced and died by suicide.

Sexton objected — as Lowell did as well — to being classified as a "Confessional" poet. In an interview published posthumously in William Heyen's *American Poets in 1976* Sexton said, "Well, for a while, oh for a long while, perhaps even now, I was called a 'confessional poet.' And for quite a while I resented it. You know, I thought 'Why am I in this bag?' And then I kind of looked around and I thought 'Look, Anne, you're the only confessional poet around.'" (309) She said further, however, that she preferred to think of herself as an imagist who dealt with reality and its hard facts, writing what she thought of as stories about life. She never became a straight prose poet, preferring to work sometimes, like Snodgrass, in strict forms, and at others to shake things out with what she termed "loose poems." Her themes, she said, had to do with "life and death, insanity, daughterhood, motherhood and love." Particularly, perhaps, with insanity, for she is said to have begun writing poetry as therapy while under treatment.

Heyen asked her whether the madsongs of her first book, *To Bedlam and Part Way Back* (1960), and her second collection, *All My Pretty Ones*, (1962) were "real poems about madness? Or were they poems about real madness?" "I don't think I was ever really mad," Sexton replied. "I mean...but then again, of course, perhaps I was, but it depends on the clinical evaluation, really. 'Mad' is an open term. But they were about my...they were confession, let us put it that way. I mean they were my experiences, some of my experiences, about feelings, disorientation, mental hospitals, whatever, and I got that label very early, the 'mad poet' and all that. And at one point just a short while ago I said 'I shall never again write about a psychiatrist, a madhouse, or anything to do with those themes.' But, you know, of course, you can't really predict, you just make these little predictions." (309)

Nevertheless, her tenth and last collection, published posthumously in 1978, was titled *Words for Doctor Y,* and the main feature of the book, a sequence of twenty-three poems titled "Letters to Dr. Y," is addressed to a fictive psychiatrist "who is seen," according to the jacket copy, "as father-confessor, conscience, corrector and comforter."

Like Snodgrass, Berryman, Lowell, and Sylvia Plath, Anne Sexton was a formalist originally, but as early as 1960, when "Letters to Dr. Y." was begun, she was writing more loosely:

> Dr. Y.
> I need a thin hot wire,
> your Rescue Inc. voice
> to stretch me out,
> to keep me from going underfoot
> and growing stiff
> as a yardstick.
>
> Death,
> I need your hot breath,
> my index finger in the flame,
> two cretins standing at my ears,
> listening for the cop car.
>
> Death,
> I need a little cradle
> to carry me out,
> a boxcar for my books,
> a nickel in my palm,
> and no kiss
> on my kiss.
>
> Death,
> I need my little addiction to you.
> I need that tiny voice who,
> even as I rise from the sea,
> all woman, all there,

> says kill me, kill me.
> My manic eye
> sees only the trapeze artist
> who flies without a net.
> Bravo, I cry,
> swallowing the pills,
> the do die pills.
> Listen ducky,
> death is as close to pleasure
> as a toothpick.
> To die whole,
> riddled with nothing
> but desire for it,
> is like breakfast
> after love.

The poet's daughter, Linda Gray Sexton, in an "Editor's Note" said that "The first section of this book, 'Letters to Dr. Y.,' written from 1960 to 1970, was originally a series of poems Anne wanted to include in her sixth volume, *The Book of Folly* [1972]." But her advisors evidently felt that Sexton's death wish was too explicit in it, and they "convinced her it did not belong there," so the series was "specifically reserved...for publication after her death," the "only time she ever set work aside for such a purpose." (v.)

Writing in *From Babel to Byzantium* about Sexton's first book James Dickey said, "Anne Sexton's poems so obviously come out of deep, painful sections of the author's life that one's literary opinions scarcely seem to matter; one feels tempted to drop them furtively into the nearest ashcan, rather than be caught with them in the presence of so much naked suffering. The experiences she recounts are among the most harrowing that human beings can undergo: those of madness and near-madness, of the pathetic, well-meaning, necessarily tentative and perilous attempts at cure, and of the patient's slow coming back into the human associations and responsibilities which the old, previous self still demands. In addition to being an extremely painful subject, this is perhaps a major one for poetry, with a sickeningly frightening appropriateness to our time. But...the poems fail to do their subject...justice.... Perhaps no poems could." (133)

At any rate, upon her suicide in 1974 a reaction set in similar to that detonated by the death of Robert Lowell. Critics stopped mentioning her, including the Boston critic Helen Vendler who, in her 1980 book *Part of Nature, Part of Us*, did not mention Sexton in the table of contents or discuss any of her books, though John Berryman, Robert Lowell, and Sylvia Plath were given whole chapters.

Maxine Kumin

Although she was born Jewish in Philadelphia in 1925, Maxine Kumin went to Catholic schools and Radcliffe College in Boston from which she received a B. A. in 1946 and an M. A. in 1948. She married an engineer, Victor Kumin, and raised a family of two daughters and a son. She studied poetry writing with John Holmes at the Boston Center for Adult Education where one of her classmates was Anne Sexton who became her friend and with whom she lunched the day before Sexton committed suicide. She became a colleague of Holmes at Tufts University in the late 'fifties and the 'sixties. Like Sexton and Holmes both, Kumin originally wrote in the standard academic formalist forms and style.

Maxine Kumin's subject matter in her first book, *Halfway* (1961), was the same as that of the other Confessional Poets, that is, life as it must, not ought to be lived, but somehow this insight often got lost in the observation, even in a poem titled "The Moment Clearly" after the first simply described opening quatrain:

> The pipes thump in the still house.
> A mouse scratches behind the stair.
> I hear the rise-and-fall of sleeping children
> Calibrating the quiet and the night.
>
> Write, saying this much clearly:
> Nearly all, this is nearly all,
> The small sounds of growing, the impress
> Of unarrested time raising
> The prized moment.
>   And this is ours.
> Love moves about, opening the doors.

One of the things Kumin never forgot how to do, however, is to tell a story in this and subsequent books. *The Privilege* appeared in 1965 and was followed five years later by *The Nightmare Factory*. Some critics compared Kumin with Elizabeth Bishop rather than with Sexton because often her poems, as in *The Long Approach* (1985), were exceptions to the egopoetic rule-of-thumb. Although they logged the subjective voyages of the heart, they never excluded the reader from their narratives through excessive privacy, for the reader was always shown the compass, the latitude and the longitude of those voyages, and immersed in particulars. If the poems in this book that made the strongest impression were those that were longer-lined, those that approached, and sometimes achieved, the condition of verse, and the weaker poems were line-phrased prose, nevertheless this was a strong collection, one that gave sustained pleasure to the reader. This condition remained a characteristic of Kumin's poems throughout her career as was shown clearly in her *Selected Poems 1960-1990*.

Over the years Maxine Kumin continued to write some of the best poetry of her school, and she branched out into fiction and nonfiction as well. She was honored with a volume edited by Emily Grosholz, *Telling the Barn Swallow: Poets on the Poetry of Maxine Kumin*, in 1997.

Sylvia Plath

Sylvia Plath was born in Boston, Massachusetts, in 1932. She was educated at Smith College and at Newnham College, Cambridge, England, which she attended on a Fulbright fellowship. It was in England that she met her husband-to-be, the English poet Ted Hughes, and settled into her marriage as well as it could be managed, which was not very well. Plath had a history of mental disturbances which were semi-autobiographically chronicled in her autobiographical novel *The Bell Jar*. Her attachment to her father was broken by his early death, from which she never recovered. She attempted suicide at intervals throughout her brief life; the third attempt was successful.

Plath's *Ariel* (1966) was a book of manic postpartum poems that appeared posthumously, after her death by suicide on February 11, 1963. The pieces in this book were so emotionally stunning, the images so astonishing, that for a time the literary world was dazzled and mortified by the loss of such a poet. People forgot Plath's background and training as a formalist, but she remained throughout her life as much in control of her material as she had been in her first book, *The Colossus* (1960), appearances to the contrary notwithstanding. *Winter Trees*, a book of poems that were written contemporaneously with *Ariel*, was published in 1972.

In her discussion of Plath's *Crossing the Water* (1971) Helen Vendler wrote in *Part of Nature, Part of Us*, "Sylvia Plath's ruthlessness toward her own work is clear in her relentless advance, in *Ariel* and other posthumously published poems, toward a purer selfhood. To criticize the poems in *Crossing the Water* is to share in her own evident self-criticism of them: she went on to do better. But even here there are some poems which justify themselves without apology, and the fact that they are among the most clinical and harsh shows the direction, never fully traveled, in which her verse was going." (275)

Since her death, however, it has been fashionable to perceive Plath not as the stickler for exactitude and rigorous craft but, to quote the jacket of *The Collected Poems* (1981) edited by her widower, as "a tormented, visionary young woman, to whom the world's anguish and her own are implacably intertwined." *Ariel* was published with a "Foreword" by Robert Lowell who wrote, "Everything in these poems is personal, confessional, felt, but the manner of feeling is controlled hallucination, the autobiography of a fever." (ix)

It is not true that everything is "personal, confessional," though one may be convinced that everything is "felt." One of the things the critic must look at is the narrative voice of these poems. The first-person, egopoetic "I" — not the narrative or the dramatic "I," nor the second- or third-person — is the viewpoint of choice for personal statement. Yet the very first poem of *Ariel*, "Morning Song," has a second-person "you" narrator. This is obviously narrative viewpoint, not egopoetic, even if one considers that the "you" is the impersonal *you* substituted for the more formal *one*. "The Applicant" later on is also a second-person narrator, as is "The Rival."

Enough of these poems have an "I" narrator, certainly, to back the thesis that they are "hallucinatory" and "confessional," but Lowell also wrote, "What is most heroic in her, though, is not her force, but the desperate practicality of her control, her hand of metal with its modest, womanish touch." (ix) Judith Kroll in *Chapters in a Mythology* discussed some of the sources of Plath's psychic disorder. She wrote, "Plath's father's death both caused and came to represent the fundamental division in her sense of herself: at least, this is how the 'story' of her poetry expresses it. The self that she had defined through her deep attachment to her father continued to press its claims without possibility of satisfaction or development. If her relation to her father was of central importance in her life, then life without him had the character of absence, of unreality and stagnation; and life with him, in the suspended time of childhood, was impossible of fulfillment. This is the basis of the sense of suspended time and stasis that pervades her later poetry. (When she separates from her husband, she experiences his absence in a similar manner.)" (9)

Winter Trees reinforced the manic effect of *Ariel*, but when *Collected Poems* appeared readers were able to see whence it was that Plath had come as a craftsman. A glance through the traditional verse forms she used in her juvenilia, gathered in an appendix of the *Collected Poems*, shows that she was a trained formalist, and like Snodgrass she never forgot how to form and build her work, even in her deepest depressions. She had early experimented with villanelles, terza rima, sonnets, and a kind of terza rima rondeau-redoubled without refrains, her own invention, in "The Princess and the Goblins." But more important than these exercises were such poems as "Mirror," written in 1961. Here again is the dramatic voice, but this time it is a looking-glass speaking. The mirror reflects upon what it sees — a bedroom and a woman who, over the years, grows slowly older — until, in a quietly shattering last two lines it confronts the woman with herself:

> I am silver and exact. I have no preconceptions.
> Whatever I see I swallow immediately
> Just as it is, unmisted by love or dislike.
> I am not cruel, only truthful —
> The eye of a little god, four-cornered.
> Most of the time I meditate on the opposite wall.
> It is pink, with speckles. I have looked at it so long
> I think it is a part of my heart. But it flickers.
> Faces and darkness separate us over and over.
>
> Now I am a lake. A woman bends over me,
> Searching my reaches for what she really is.
> Then she turns to those liars, the candles or the moon.
> I see her back, and reflect it faithfully.
> She rewards me with tears and an agitation of hands.
> I am important to her. She comes and goes.
> Each morning it is her face that replaces the darkness.
> In me she has drowned a young girl, and in me an old woman
> Rises toward her day after day, like a terrible fish.

The Confessional Poets

Alicia Suskin Ostriker wrote in *Stealing the Language: The Emergence of Women's Poetry in America* that "The modern masters had taught the superiority of art to the absurdity of life, and Plath in the 1950s was a good student. Her early verse employs tight formal structures, bookish diction, an armory of allusions to sanctioned works of art and literature, and a consistently ironic impersonality of tone, which has everything to do with controlling experience, little to do with dwelling in it. The looser, less traditional forms of her late work intensify rather than relax our sense of the poet's control. She manipulates rhyme and off-rhyme [consonance], regular and irregular meter, with the casualness of a juggler tossing knives, and her mature mastery of colloquial idiom illustrates her contempt for the vulgar and cruel social relations which generate such idiom. She becomes a mocker of the vernacular, using language against itself." (101)

"Amnesiac" was written on 21 October 1962. It originally appeared in *The New Yorker* and it was reprinted in *The New Yorker Book of Poems* (1968). According to Hughes' "Notes on Poems," "Sylvia Plath's own prepared collection of poems, titled *Ariel*," was to include "Amnesiac" (which Hughes numbered 189), but it did not appear in the published version of *The Collected Poems* (275-296). It was first collected in *Winter Trees*, although it had been widely circulated for several years, and it became at least as well known as the other *Ariel* poems, with the possible exception of "Daddy."

Two things strike the reader on the typographical level of the poem; first, that it is written in triplet stanzas, then that its mode — judging from the lengths of the lines — is prose rather than verse. A scansion of the first few stanzas confirms that Plath did not meter the poem. Reading through it, however, causes one to hesitate at the last triplet which feels relatively regular. Adding to this feeling is the fact that, alone among the nine stanzas of the poem, the last one contains rhymes. Perhaps one will look back through the poem at this point to see what else Plath did on the sonic level, and it will be noted that, though the only other rhyme appears to be in the last line of the next-to-last stanza, which rhymes with the last line of the poem, there are many other sorts of sound, including in particular consonance as in the first triplet —

> No use, no use, now, begging Recognize!
> There is nothing to do with such a beautiful blank but smooth it.
> Name, house, car keys,

where lines one and three consonate. In the second triplet there is assonance between the end words of lines four and five:

> The little toy wife —
> Erased, sigh, sigh.
> Four babies and a cocker

The falling rhythm of the ending of line six is mirrored in the first line of the third triplet, line seven —

> Nurses the size of worms and a minute doctor
> Tuck him in.
> Old happenings

with consonantal (k and r) echo. Thus, although the poem doesn't rhyme, it sets the precedent for heavy emphasis on the sonic level; when rhyme eventually shows up it will not come as a great surprise.

Reading the poem through, however, has raised other problems on the sensory and ideational levels. The first of these has to do with viewpoint. What is the poem's orientation and its person? A cursory reading might have left the impression that this is a confessional poem, but closer attention shows that it is an author-oriented narrative, not a personal statement. Scrutiny of line one will discover that the narration is implied second-person you: the author-narrator is addressing another person present with him/her in the hospital room of the amnesiac of the title. The clue given is the capitalization of the last word of the first line, "Recognize!" The narrator is saying to his or her companion, ["There is n]o use, no use, now, [in your] begging [him, ']Recognize [me!']".

Plath did not include quotation marks, although she capitalized the beginning of the quotation, because she wished to disguise the last stanza, which is also a quotation — it is the author putting words into the amnesiac's mouth. The lack of quotation marks in the final triplet is the main argument used by those who believe that this piece is an egopoem, but it cannot be so. Lethe is the river of forgetfulness in the Greek underworld of Hades, and it is the male amnesiac who has forgotten his past, including his wife. Still, Plath did invent the words for the amnesiac to say, words he cannot possibly say for himself — the victim of forgetfulness cannot recall the people of his past to speak of them — so the words have a double edge: they are both the amnesiac's and the author's words. Plath got the effect of egopoesy into what is one of the two examples in the poem of dramatic viewpoint and she set this effect up in the first line with "Recognize!"

Plath managed to put herself into the mind of the amnesiac, so the narrative exhibits subjective access as a feature of its viewpoint. The poet further imitated the hallucinatory nature of the amnesiac's thought processes by her use of stream-of-consciousness surrealism, for the "Old happenings" in the fourth triplet

> Peel from his skin.
> Down the drain with all of it!
>
> [like hair, like the outer layer of skin in the bath or shower]
> Hugging his pillow
>
> Like the red-haired sister he never dared to touch,
> He dreams of a new one —
> Barren, the lot are barren!

Although this passage is, of course, matter for Freudian analysis, on the sensory level the reader can see that Plath was introducing hues and tones now to her narrative:

> And of another color.
> How they'll travel, travel, travel, scenery
> Sparking off their brother-sister rears
>
> A comet tail!
> And money the sperm fluid of it all.

Parenthetically one may note that Plath had introduced another sonic effect earlier, and that it is emphasized here — repetition. The poem begins with "No use, no use," and in stanza two the device reappeared in "sigh, sigh." Now the "travel, travel, travel" reasserts the childishness of the state of the amnesiac.

> One nurse brings in
>
> A green drink, one a blue.
> They rise on either side of him like stars.
> The two drinks flame and foam.

The last line of this eighth triplet, the reader is to discover, will rhyme with the last line of the poem. It is at this point that Plath began the ploy that would transform the poem from a narrative cast in the form of prose triplets into a dramatic nursery rhyme written in the accentual prosody podics which is traditional to nursery rhymes: "The two drinks flame and foam," line twenty-four, is a bridge from triplets to a final quatrain effect. If one scans it, one sees it is accentually regular; it is a tetrapodic (four-stress) line, but this meter went unnoticed during first reading because Plath allowed herself such variety of lengths in the prose of the earlier lines — the shortest is line eight, "Tuck him in." All of the final triplet scans:

> O sister, mother, wife,
> Sweet Lethe is my life.
> I am never, never, never coming home!

The first of these lines is, like the preceding line, tetrapodic, as is the next, line twenty-six. The climactic last line extends the meter — it is hexapodic (six-stress). This is the nursery rhyme quatrain effect of the last four lines of the poem:

        ´   .   ´   ´
The two drinks flame and foam.

    ´ ´   ´   ´
["]O sister, mother, wife,

     ´ ´   .   ´
Sweet Lethe is my life.

    ´   ´   ´   ´   ´
I am never, never, never coming home!["]

One should note in passing that "Lethe is" and "I am" are y-glide elisions. "Drinks" and "is" are demoted to secondary stresses because they are the central syllables in sequences of three stressed syllables, the other two of which are long syllable sounds. "My" takes no stress because its vowel is suppressed in ordinary speech: "m' life."

    An analysis of the viewpoint of "Amnesiac" shows that it is an author-oriented, second-person, subjective access, single-angle (only what happens in the neighborhood of the amnesiac himself is shown) narrative poem of mixed mode (prose and verse). This poem is not perfectly typical, perhaps, of the *Ariel* poems, but it does illustrate Plath's dedication to craftsmanship, even in the midst of her overwhelming melancholy. She was never the unthinking confessional, the totally feeling egopoet. In her worst moments she was, as a writer, in command of her medium.

    Plath's reputation bloomed for a while during the early years of the Feminist movement of the 1970s, and then — at least in the literary world — it began to diminish in overreaction to the sensation Plath had caused.

CHAPTER FOUR
The Poetry of Protest

During the 1960s there was great ferment in the land, and all of that ferment was reflected in the poetry the nation's poets were writing. Martin Luther King, Jr.'s Civil Rights Movement had poets of all political shades not merely marching but publishing as well, from the newly militant such as Gwendolyn Brooks to the radicalized, like Le Roi Jones who, when he became a Black Muslim, changed his name to Amiri Baraka. The undeclared "War in Vietnam" began to draw poets to the podium of protest as early as 1962 when the first "Poets for Peace" reading took place in Cleveland, Ohio, at University Circle in front of the art museum with Mac Hammond, P. K. Saha, Leonard Silver, Lewis Turco and others reading poems written for the occasion. Anthologies of antiwar protest and "ban the bomb" poetry began to be issued by 1967 when Gary Youree edited *Poets for Peace*, an anthology of poems that came out of a fast conducted in New York City but participated in by others elsewhere as well. The Black Mountain-affiliated poet Denise Levertov edited *Out of the War Shadow* for the War Resisters League in the same year.

In 1963 President John F. Kennedy's assassination drew an enormous outpouring of elegiac poetry. A year later *Poetry* ran a special issue of Kennedy memorials, as did Sunday supplements all over the country, and a major anthology edited by Erwin A. Glikes and Paul Schwaber, *Of Poetry and Power*, appeared. The Robert Kennedy and Martin Luther King assassinations, the Democratic National Convention of 1968 — the poets were involved in all of these at least as reporters and odists, if not as active participants. There was the capping national student strike of 1970, after Ohio National Guardsmen opened fire at students of Kent State University — *60 on the 60s*, edited by Robert McGovern and Richard Snyder, gave a retrospective view of the whole scene when it was issued in that same year. It seemed to many that such turbulent times called for turbulent poetry. Looking back, it was difficult to find precedents, but there was one, at least.

Langston Hughes (1902-67) was a native of Joplin, Missouri, but he grew up in various places in the American Midwest and in Mexico where he taught and was a ranch-hand for his father. He moved on to manual labor in New York City, France, and

Washington, D. C.; however, Hughes was also one of the earliest American Black writers to make a living as a writer. He began as a poet, but his literary output was enormous and covered the field: drama, fiction, autobiography, libretti for musicals, opera, and a cantata.

Although he was associated with the Modernist "Harlem Renaissance" of the 1920s and '30s, he lived into the Decade of Protest and stood as a model for post-Modernist Blacks such as Robert Hayden, Gwendolyn Brooks, Amiri Baraka, and Russell Atkins. Notwithstanding that Hughes was accused by some critics of being the next thing to a member of the literary establishment and of not writing enough consciousness-raising material, he was in fact the first to write civil rights poetry of protest that was identifiable as such, and he did it when it was quite dangerous to do so, long before it was fashionable. Furthermore, Hughes wrote in a variety of styles and techniques: he was as capable of penning a traditionally formal poem as a prose poem in the style of Whitman, such as "A Negro Dreams of Rivers." Even when he wrote a more or less "normal" poem, Langston Hughes was not above experiment. Here is "Go Slow":

> Go slow, they say —
> While the bite
> Of the dog is fast.
> Go Slow, I hear —
> While they tell me
> You can't eat here!
> You can't live here!
> Don't demonstrate! Wait! —
> While they lock the gate.
>
> Am I supposed to be God,
> Or an angel with wings
> And a halo on my head
> While jobless I starve dead?
> Am I supposed to forgive
> And meekly live
> Going slow, slow, slow,
> Slow, slow, slow,
> Slow, slow
> Slow
> Slow,
> Slow?
> ????
> ???
> ??
> ?

Everything is "normal" in this polemical piece until toward the end of the poem. There, the repetition of the word "slow" comes slowing down until it turns into a question in the fifth-to-last line — a rhetorical and sarcastic question: The answer is obvious. At this point the spatial element, at the climactic moment of the poem, becomes paramount: the tail of question marks descends visibly, carrying on the slowing-down process, but at the same time it ascends climactically to the final question mark, which emphasizes the great question being asked. At the end of the poem meaning resides primarily in how the poem looks on the page — "The medium becomes the message," to paraphrase one of the media gurus of the 1960s, Marshall McLuhan: it was during the sixties that the spatial "concrete" poem began to come into its own as an art form.

Hughes is given credit for making the "blues" as much a part of American literature as it was of American music, for as artistic expression, the blues is a phenomenon of Black American musical tradition rather than Black literature specifically. A sub-genre of jazz, blues is equally a form of lamentation or complaint with roots in the Bible, in particular the Old Testament which, more than the New Testament, has guided and solaced generations of American Blacks. Blues first appeared as a consciously literary form in Langston Hughes' poem, "The Weary Blues," which won *Opportunity* magazine's poetry prize in 1925 and, in the following year, was the title poem of his first book, *The Weary Blues*.

The poems of this volume settled into no particular stanza form, however, and it was not until the 1970s that the blues stanza came to be recognized as an identifiable literary form. At that time Stephen Henderson, in the introduction to his 1973 anthology *Understanding the New Black Poetry* (a title which was intended to be a reply of sorts to the New Critical Brooks and Warren "Bible" of the Caucasian academy, *Understanding Poetry*) wrote about the "'classic' twelve-bar, three line form" of the blues, as in Eddie 'Son' House's 'Dry Spell Blues'":

> The dry spell blues have fallen, drove me from door to door.
> Dry spell blues have fallen, drove me from door to door.
> The dry spell blues have put everybody on the killing floor.
>
> Now the people down south sure won't have no home.
> Now the people down south sure won't have no home.
> 'Cause the dry spell have parched all this cotton and corn.

These rhythms are to be found in earlier English poetry as well, however, specifically in Robert Browning's "A Toccata of Galuppi's."

House's line is identifiable as loosely iambic hexameter and Browning's as a loose fourteener (i.e., a "fifteener," each line containing fifteen syllables), but the blues line may vary in length from tetrameter to heptameter; thus, both examples are within the metrical boundaries of the tradition. The triplet stanza and its rhyme scheme are as important to the blues as its meters. Browning's stanza rhymes *aaa* but in the strict form of blues stanza the rhyme scheme is *AAa*. The second line is an incremental refrain, a repetition of the first line; the third line is a synthetic parallel which gives a consequence of the repeated lines.

To many young Black poets, however, Langston Hughes was — to use a catch-term of the times — "irrelevant," despite everything he had done to make it possible for minority poets and writers to function as professionals in the world of publishing and public performance. Young Blacks wanted not only to identify with "role models" that were closer to their age, but that were also clearly militant. Although they were interested in the subject of music, especially jazz and rock — a development from rhythm and blues of the 1950s — they, no less than the rest of their generation, wanted to appear to be "free," and in their poems they chose various prose-mode tactics to use rather than the old literary or musical forms, whether they be identified as "white" or "Black."

Robert Hayden

Although Robert Hayden did not write specifically in blues forms, nevertheless for many years he wrote an individual, seminal, and protean poetry, and many of his poems were derived from Black musical forms and traditions. Born in Detroit in 1913, his health — in particular his eyesight — prevented Hayden from serving in the armed forces during the Second World War. He was educated at Wayne State University and at the University of Michigan where he won Hopwood Awards in writing and took his M.A. in 1944. He began teaching at Fisk University, a black college, in 1946, and he ended his career back at Michigan.

Hayden was always a formal poet, but his formalism was not — except in his earliest work — of a traditional nature. He experimented with language approaches; however, unlike some of his ethnic contemporaries, such as Gwendolyn Brooks, he was not politicized by the Civil Rights Movement of the 1960s to the point where he deliberately set about writing identifiably "Black" poetry as — following the example of Langston Hughes — Brooks did. Hayden did not want literature to be ghettoized because he wanted to be judged by universal standards, not specialized, "Negro only" criteria. That way, he felt, was playing into the hands of academic racists who could then compartmentalize minority work in such courses as "Black Studies" or "Women's Studies" apart from the standard curriculum. And what he feared came to pass. On the other hand, Hayden did not shrink from utilizing his heritage and his family background.

Heart-Shape in the Dust appeared in 1940, and *The Lion and the Archer*, with Myron O'Higgins, was published eight years later, in 1948. Langston Hughes and Arna Bontemps included eight Hayden poems in their anthology, *Poetry of the Negro, 1746-1949* (1949), "but Hayden generally found recognition and time for writing both equally rare commodities," Fred M. Fetrow wrote in his study *Robert Hayden*. "Finally, he won a Ford Foundation Grant, which allowed him relief from classroom duties at Fisk and the opportunity for travel and writing in Mexico during 1954-1955." (1984, 19)

Fetrow wrote further, "During the era in which Hayden was developing..., the distance from *Heart-Shape* to *The Lion and the Archer* also spans his changing practices in the technical aspects of his craft. Virtually every element of prosody reflects a shift, suggests a trend. His habits in prosody during those early years move from sometimes almost slavish adherence to traditional modes of rhyme and meter, through patterns imitative of contemporaries, to a more original, organic freedom to correlate subjects, themes, and prosody." (p. 59)

Only one collection appeared during the next decade, *Figures of Time* in 1955. Two collections were issued during the 1960s — *A Ballad of Remembrance* (1962), published in England, and *Selected Poems* (1966). *Words in the Mourning Time: Poems* appeared in 1970, and *The Night-Blooming Cereus*, again from London, in 1972. Hayden died in 1980, but *American Journal: Poems* appeared posthumously in 1982.

According to the jacket copy of *Angle of Ascent* (1975), "When Robert Hayden's... *Words in the Mourning Time* was published, Julius Lester, writing in *The New York Times*

Book Review, said that Hayden was 'one of the most underrated and unrecognized poets in America.'" This was true. Various reasons might be given to account for this fact, among them foreign publication of two volumes and small press publication of others, with the attendant problems of limited distribution.

However, Hayden himself had better insight into the situation. In a videotaped interview that he made for the "Writers' Forum" series at the S.U.N.Y. College at Brockport, Hayden was asked about "Black poetry." His response was that such a term, which had the approval of many militant black poets, was useful primarily to white academics who wish to ignore poetry written by blacks. The inference to be drawn therefrom, Hayden said, is that somehow poetry written by black Americans is not good enough, or not universal enough to be included in the Anglo-Saxon literary canon.

In a letter dated February 24, 1976, Radcliffe Squires, in his capacity as editor of *The Michigan Quarterly Review*, published by the University of Michigan where Hayden was teaching at the time, wrote to one of his regular reviewers who happened to be a white academic, "to ask you if you could review Robert Hayden's *Angle of Ascent*.... He feels bad that every place seems to feel it must have him reviewed by another black. I agree that is both silly and intolerable. Anyway, I hope you will be willing to undertake this...."

Hayden always wanted to be judged merely as a poet among poets, not one to whom special rules of criticism had to be applied in order to make his work acceptable in more than a sociological sense. His stance, reiterated in the Brockport interview, was well known for a long time both to militant blacks and to "liberal" whites. Thus, if the latter relegated Hayden to the literary ghetto along with the other Black poets, the former have seen him, if not as an "Uncle Tom," at least as a reluctant resident. Perhaps this situation best explains why Hayden was ignored during his lifetime. Yet Hayden wrote as much out of his ethnicity as anyone else. He was a paradigmatic poet of the English language who was also true to his roots and history, though not circumscribed by what is merely racial, ethnic, or personal.

There are, of course, such things as "Black" styles of writing, Black themes, Black allusions — what Stephen Henderson called "saturation" (116-132). There are no such things, however, as Black "techniques" of the English language, as Henderson also claimed. Hayden used many such themes, but writers of other ethnic groups could, if they wished, write on those topics as well, and many have done so, just as Hayden himself wrote on topics not associated with his race only. Hayden also wrote some poems that were "saturated" with Black ethnic referents, though nearly always in such a way that the general reader of whatever background might understand — Hayden was not above providing a context for his ethnicity rather than building barriers to understanding, as many poets of the 1960s did, following the lead of the militant Amiri Baraka, born Le Roi Jones.

Hayden had at his disposal all the techniques the language allows, including cataloguing in the manner of Whitman, though not nearly at Whitman's prolix length. Hayden began *Angle of Ascent* with a set of poems titled "Beginnings," the first section of which reads,

> Plowdens, Finns,
> Sheffeys, Haydens,
> Westerfields.
>
> Pennsylvania gothic,
> Kentucky homespun,
> Virginia baroque

Hayden used cataloguing to particularly beautiful effect in "Theme and Variation," a poem of two parts and four stanzas, the first of which reads, "Fossil, fuschia, mantis, man, / fir and water, earth and air — / all things alter even as I behold, / all things alter, the stranger said."

If prose arranged as "free verse" is America's folk mode, Hayden was not unfamiliar with a folk prosody of the British, for he could handle the accentual system called podics very well, as he showed in Part V of "Beginnings," "(The Crystal Cave Elegy)" where he modulated into podic rhythms much as Sylvia Plath did in her poem "Amnesiac": "Floyd Collins oh / I guess he's a goner, / Pa Hayden sighed, / the Extra trembling / in his hands." If the rhythms are jazzy, they are also as old as the English language.

Hayden was not in any way scatological, in the manner and tradition of the Black "dozens" literature, nor even as the early English podic poet John Skelton (1460-1529) could be, but that is not necessarily a criticism. Neither was he much interested in rhyming, particularly obvious rhyming. The closest Hayden came, perhaps, is in "Incense of the Lucky Virgin" where some consonance is used instead of rhyme, and each stanza uses an incremental refrain as a sort of substitute for rhyme.

The brag, an English tradition as old as *Beowulf*, was adopted by 19th-century America and transformed into what folklorists call "the backwoods boast." Hayden was acquainted with the tradition and used it in "Witch Doctor" — "'He's / God's dictaphone of all-redeeming truth. / Oh he's the holyweight champeen who's come / to give the knockout lick to your bad luck; / I say he's the holyweight champeen who's here / to deal a knockout punch to your hard luck.'"

Hayden wrote one of the most touching contemporary poems utilizing litotes, "Those Winter Sundays," one of his best-known poems also:

> Sundays too my father got up early
> and put his clothes on in the blueblack cold,
> then with cracked hands that ached
> from labor in the weekday weather made
> banked fires blaze. No one ever thanked him.
>
> I'd wake and hear the cold splintering, breaking.
> When the rooms were warm, he'd call,
> and slowly I would rise and dress,
> feeling the chronic angers of that house,

> speaking indifferently to him,
> who had driven out the cold
> and polished my good shoes as well.
> What did I know, what did I know
> of love's austere and lonely offices?

If this is lovely in its simplicity, Hayden could be as obscure as any poet of any race, on occasion; he has been called by some a "Symbolist," and a few of his poems, such as "Stars," Part II, which appears to have a relation to Hayden's Baha'i theology, can be baffling:

> Betelgeuse Aldebaran
>
> Abstract as future yesterdays
> the starlight
> crosses eons of meta-space
> to us.
>
> Algol Arcturus Almaak
>
> How shall the mind keep warm
> save at spectral
> fires — how thrive but by the light
> of paradox?
>
> Altair Vega Polaris Maia

Some of Hayden's favorite techniques were such things as parallelism, incremental repetition, and orthographical schemas, elision and apocopation primarily, as in the ending of "Runagate Runagate" which uncharacteristically utilizes some true rhyme as well:

> Armed and known to be Dangerous
>
> Wanted Reward Dead or Alive
>
> Tell me, Ezekiel, oh tell me do you see
> mailed Jehovah coming to deliver me?
> Hoot-owl calling in the ghosted air,
> five times calling to the hants in the air.
> Shadow of a face in the scary leaves
> shadow of a voice in the talking leaves:
>
> Come ride-a my train

> Oh that train, ghost-story train
> through swamp and savanna movering movering
> over trestles of dew, through caves of the wish,
> Midnight Special on a sabre track movering movering,
> first stop Mercy and the last Hallelujah.
>
> Come ride-a my train
>
> Mean mean mean to be free.

Curiously enough, though Hayden used parallelism often, there does not appear to be a single poem in *Angle of Ascent*, except possibly "Witch Doctor," that imitates the style of the Negro sermon, though there are references to preachers, as to the murdered Martin Luther King, Jr., in "Words in the Mourning Time." This poem, though, is about the assassinated Kennedy brothers as well, and Hayden wrote not only about Christianity, but also about Judaism, Baha'i, and Mohammedanism.

Henderson said in his Introduction, "There are...important ways in which music, Black music, lies at the basis of much Black poetry, either consciously or covertly." Like many other poets of all nations, languages, and times, Hayden used such allusions to music in many poems including "A Ballad of Remembrance," "The Dream," and "Beginnings," Part IV.

That Hayden was influenced by such "song forms" as "blues, ballads, hymns, children's song," to which Henderson referred, comes as no great surprise, but Hayden was not usually content merely to be influenced by a form; rather, he transformed it into something uniquely his. Though "The Ballad of Nat Turner," for instance, looks typographically like a traditional ballad, and might even fool the casual reader into thinking it is one, in fact it does not rhyme, as most ballads do, it consonates; and, though repetition is sometimes used as a substitute for rhyme, there is no ballad refrain. Some stanzas do not even consonate or contain repetition, yet the whole poem has the effect of a unified narrative song. This is a masterful wedding of tradition with personal style.

Hayden used all sorts of other musical "techniques" in his language, heavy with Black referents but not unavailable to members of other races, as in such poems as "Soledad" and "Homage to the Empress of the Blues":

> Because there was a man somewhere in a candystripe silk shirt
> gracile and dangerous as a jaguar and because a woman moaned
> for him in sixty-watt gloom and mourned him Faithless Love
> Twotiming Love Oh Love Oh Careless Aggravating Love,

and so forth. Hayden's intent here, however, was not to appeal to one ethnic minority above another, but to build a context for such allusions — in this case a pop song — which enables any reader to understand the situation and emotion of the narrator.

One of Hayden's finest poems is full of 19th-century Negro southern dialect: "The Dream" alternates narration regarding a character named Sinda with Black letters from the Civil War front. It is the most effective dialect poem one could hope to read, though Hayden claimed that many people have misinterpreted it. The only reason for such a misunderstanding is perhaps that the unexpected character dies.

In "O Daedalus, Fly Away Home" Robert Hayden used such ethnically saturated words as "juba" and "conjo" in a musical context, building a beautiful and, simultaneously, sad song of loss beginning,

> Drifting night in the Georgia pines,
> coonskin drum and jubilee banjo.
> Pretty Malinda, dance with me.
>
> Night is juba, night is conjo.
> Pretty Malinda, dance with me.

The poem turns to the thought of "home" — Africa, and of death as a release from longing for rest, ending with

> Night is a mourning juju man
> weaving a wish and a weariness together
> to make two wings.
>
> O fly away home fly away

No other poet was more capable of couching the totality of the American Black's experience and situation, emotion and ambience in language that is beautiful and allusive for everyone. Hayden built contexts for his ethnic vocabulary that provided the reader who is alien to the culture with points of reference that allow him or her to understand some of the overtones with which the cues are laden — Hayden built landmarks in the landscape of his mind, road maps to his heritage. He did so in poem after poem — he cared about the reader, whoever he or she might be.

Gwendolyn Brooks

No less may be said of Gwendolyn Brooks who was three years younger than Robert Hayden. For many years, despite her early involvement with the NAACP, Brooks wrote a formal poetry; during the 1960s, however, influenced by the militancy of her old friend Langston Hughes and by the aggressive posture of the young Blacks, such as Amiri Baraka, she found she could no longer afford to appear as though she remained on the sidelines. She therefore began to write a more militant kind of poem. In the lead essay of *A Life Distilled* edited by Gary Smith and herself, Maria K. Mootry, in her essay titled "'Down the Whirlwind of Good Rage': An Introduction to Gwendolyn Brooks," said that "at the nexus of Brooks's art lies a fundamental commitment to both the modernist aesthetics of art and the common ideal of social justice." (1)

Brooks was born in 1917 in Topeka, Kansas, and educated at Wilson Junior College in Chicago, from which she was graduated in 1936. She married three years later and became the mother of two. During the Depression she worked as publicist for the NAACP Youth Council in Chicago, and subsequently she taught at various institutions of higher education in and around that city including Northeastern Illinois State College, Columbia College, and Elmhurst College.

"Nowhere is this dual commitment more apparent," Mootry continued, "than in the multiplicity of voices in her works. If the reader finds echoes of T.S. Eliot and Countee Cullen in her poetry, there are also equally strong folk vernacular voices punctuating her forty-year literary career. Her three early works, *A Street in Bronzeville* (1945), *Annie Allen* (1949), and *The Bean Eaters* (1960), present a wide range of poetic forms, including blues poems, ballads, experimental free verse, quatrains, Petrarchan sonnets and Chaucerian stanzas. Her subsequent publications, *In the Mecca* (1968), *Riot* (1969), *Family Pictures* (1971), *Beckonings* (1975), and *To Disembark* (1981), are written primarily in free verse and show her increasing concern with social issues, yet the variety of speakers continues."

Brooks' *Selected Poems* was published in 1963. In the "Foreword" to *New Negro Poets U.S.A.*, edited by Langston Hughes, Gwendolyn Brooks wrote, "At the present time, poets who happen also to be Negroes are twice-tried. They have to write poetry, and they have to remember that they are Negroes. Often they wish that they could solve the Negro question once and for all, and go on from such success to the composition of textured sonnets or buoyant villanelles without the transience of a raindrop, or the gold-stuff of the sun. They are likely to find significances in those subjects not instantly obvious to their fairer fellows.

"The raindrop may seem to them to represent racial tears — and those might seem, indeed, other than transient. The golden sun might remind them that they are burning." (13)

One of Brooks' simplest and most-anthologized poems exemplifies both her innovative approach to traditional verse forms and her social commitment:

WE REAL COOL
The Pool Players.
Seven at the Golden Shovel

"We real cool. We
Left school. We
Lurk late. We
Strike straight. We

Sing sin. We
Thin gin. We
Jazz June. We
Die soon."

First, on the typographical level, it is clear that this is a poem written in couplet stanzas. The second immediately noticeable point is that it is a parallel series, for each line except the last ends with the word "we." Next, the eye is caught by the fact that immediately preceding the last word of each line, except the final one, there is a period — the series is made up of short independent clauses, a set of assertions.

When we read the poem, though, we wonder at first, perhaps, why *we* ends the lines; it ought to appear at the head of each line, for it is the subject of the parallel clauses: "We real cool. We left school. We lurk late. We strike straight. We sing sin. We thin gin. We jazz June. We die soon." But when we read it in its "correct" parallel arrangement we realize why Brooks wrote it otherwise: it is not syncopated. Read "normally," another thing happens to its rhythms: Some of the strong stresses are demoted. Written as Brooks has written them, each line except the first and last consists of three strong stresses. The prosody is accentual verse. Line one has four beats, the last has two.

The rhymes of the poem from lines two through seven thus appear medially — they run right down the center of the poem. All the verbs — the strongest words — from line two on, are pushed to first place; they are drum beats. The rhyming words are also drum beats sprung by their sounds, and each is followed by a full stop, a rest. Then another drum stroke, we: ´ ´ [] ´, and the line is enjambed into the next stress. The poem is jazz; it is a dirge played in the streets, like those of the black bands that march in slow time through New Orleans alleys to the graveyard. The dirge begins slowly with four beats, and it ends abruptly with two. The entire little poem is an exercise in linguistic counterpoint.

The level of diction of the poem is idiomatic, the tropes mainly rhetorical — it is heavy with macho braggadocio. And it ends with the assertion of a truth that brings the reader up short with a jolt. The major genre of the poem is, plainly, the lyric, but it is also almost equally a didactic poem with a clear social message.

Brooks' second book, *Annie Allen*, received the Pulitzer Prize in 1950. "Then, as now," Bernard W. Bell wrote in the introduction to his anthology *Modern and Contemporary*

Afro-American Poetry, "Miss Brooks' race consciousness was low-keyed, yet keenly felt in every line. And her lyrics pulsate with the joys and sorrows of life. (9-10)

"Stylistically, *Annie Allen* is a masterpiece. Tracing the path of a black child's movement from innocence to experience, Miss Brooks skillfully employs adaptations of many of the major metrical patterns and stanzaic forms in the English tradition, from couplets and blank verse to sonnet sequences and free verse. In this and subsequent volumes, she maintains a remarkable balance between being a poet's poet and a poet of the people."

Writing in *Women Poets of the World*, edited by Joanna Bankier and Deirdre Lashgari, Barbara Christian, in her essay titled "Cultural Influences: African American" said, "Gwendolyn Brooks wrote much of her poetry during the 1940s and 1950s when Blacks were striving to achieve integration into the American social structure. By the 1960s, the Civil Rights movement gave way to the Black Power movement. Brooks' later work, published in the late 1960s and early 1970s, reflects that shift. The dominant literary movement of that period, Cultural Nationalism, focused on the development of Black selfhood and nationhood. There was a renewed interest in African and Afro-American history and culture. Poets saw themselves as revolutionaries in the service of their people" (337-8). Gwendolyn Brooks died in 2007 as one of America's most highly respected literary figures.

Amiri Baraka

60 on the 60's (1969), the anthology of poetry edited by Robert McGovern and Richard Snyder, covered the issues of that decade of civil protest and public war. There was cause during those years for anguish on the part of many, including those to be found inhabiting the American academy. The editors, in their "Introduction," wrote, "This book, then, is a celebration of the dignity of human sensibility in the face of war, assassination, poverty, alienation, exploitation of nature, fear of extinction, and other shocks of our evolution. It is a collection of song, which should make it an optimistic record of history. Where there is song, however painful or even despairing, there is hope for human salvation. The themes developed in this volume have not been devised by the editors; rather, the unity of feeling about our world derives from the nature of poetry and poets. While the writers in this book demonstrate a spread of generation, a distinction of race, religion, and sex, there is little gap in sensibility." (5)

Poets represented in the volume included Gwendolyn Brooks who wrote on "Martin Luther King, Jr.," Daniel Berrigan, S. J., who in future years would serve time for his non-violent civil protests against the military draft and the Vietnam conflict; Robert Bly on the "March in Washington Against the Vietnam War"; Denise Levertov who two years earlier, in 1967, had edited an anti-war anthology, *Out of the War Shadow*, for the War Resisters League; Richard Wilbur, who contributed "A Miltonic Sonnet for Mr. Johnson" — that is, Lyndon Johnson, President of the United States of America; Robert Lowell on "R. F. K." — the assassinated brother of President Kennedy, and many others. Not represented in the book was LeRoi Jones — or Amiri Baraka, as he was by then known

Everett LeRoi Jones was born in 1934, a native of Newark, New Jersey, where he attended school and began college at the Newark branch of Rutgers University. He transferred to Howard University subsequently and took his B. A. there in 1954. He was a member of the U.S. Air Force after the Korean War, from 1954 to 1956. He married a white Jewish woman in 1958, was divorced in 1965, and married again the following year. His teaching career included holding academic positions at the New School for Social Research in New York City from 1961 to 1964 and shorter stints at the State University of New York at Buffalo, Columbia University, and San Francisco State University.

His first book of poems, *Preface to a Twenty Volume Suicide Note* appeared in 1960, and *The Dead Lecturer*, Jones' second book, appeared in 1964; *Black Art* in 1966, *Black Magic: Poetry 1961-1967* in 1969, and *It's Nation Time* in 1970. By the publication in 1972 of *Spirit Reach*, Jones was "Amiri Baraka" and well-established as the premier black militant of the world of poetry, but he was also establishing himself as a playwright; he had written two books of fiction — a novel and a collection of short stories, and he had edited or written many other titles, most of them on social issues. His *Selected Poetry* was published in 1979.

Baraka has inspired more scholarship since 1973 than any other black poet in America. "If Baraka is a villain in the eyes of whites," Theodore Hudson wrote in *From LeRoi Jones to Amiri Baraka: The Literary Works* (1973), the first study to appear, "he is a hero in the eyes of the current generation of black nationalists and their sympathizers. No one so captures the cultural sensibilities of young black cultural revolutionists. He has great drawing power on predominantly black campuses. There is no doubt that among young black readers he is the most consistently read of all the current black writers." (37)

Baraka never wrote formalist poetry like that of Robert Hayden or Gwendolyn Brooks. His earliest work was line-phrased prose, and it remained so, though as his work matured Jones sometimes treated prose in the manner of Walt Whitman and Allen Ginsberg, as in the "A New Reality Is Better Than a New Movie!" the first part of which is quoted:

> "How will it go, crumbling earthquake, towering inferno, juggernaut, volcano, smashup, in reality, other than the feverish nearreal fantasy of the capitalist flunky film hacks tho they sense its reality breathing a quake inferno scar on their throat even snorts of 100% pure cocaine cant cancel the cold cut of impending death to this society. On all the screens of america, the joint blows up every hour and a half for two dollars an [sic] fifty cents. They have taken the niggers out to lunch, for a minute, made us partners (nigger charlie)
> or
> surrogates (boss nigger) for their horror."

But it was the proposition of William J. Harris, in his book *The Poetry and Poetics of Amiri Baraka: The Jazz Aesthetic* (1985), that it is difficult to pin the poet down because of his Protean transformations "of avant-garde poetics into ethnic poetics, of white liberal politics into black nationalist and Marxist politics, of jazz forms into literary forms. Baraka's entire career is characterized by such transformations.... Because it emulates a transformation process typical of jazz revision, I call Baraka's method of transformation the jazz aesthetic, a procedure that uses jazz variations as paradigms for the conversion of white poetic and social ideas into black ones." (37)

Particularly Black Mountain ones. Harris pointed out that Baraka was "influenced by the Projectivist School; no one, however, has made it clear how profound and lasting this influence has been. The main source of influence is the great white whale of American literature, Charles Olson." (35) This insight explains Jones' sojourn for a summer in the Little Black Mountain of S.U.N.Y. at Buffalo in 1964. "From the Projectivists," Harris continued, "and from Olson in particular, Baraka absorbed his sense of the poem as open form, his sense of line, his sense of the poem as a recorder of process, and his conception of the poem as definition and exploration. For instance, speaking of form, Baraka...said [in Donald Allen's *The New American Poetry, 1945-1960*, p. 425]: 'There must not be any preconceived notion or design for what a poem ought to be. "who knows what a poem ought to sound like? Until it's thar" says Charles Olson...& I follow closely with that. I'm not interested in writing sonnets, sestina[s] or anything...only poems'."

In this respect, then, Baraka's primary literary influences were those of a renegade white academy rather than those of Hughes, Hayden, or Brooks, who worked out of a tradition of black formalism deriving from, on the one hand, mainstream English literature and, on the other, black musical forms. But at this point Baraka's practice approached those of his older black contemporaries. Harris maintained that "Baraka...blackens the white avant-garde poem with scatting — a jazz singing technique that substitutes nonsense syllables for traditional lyrics — and by creating poems more suited to oral than written presentation. Scatting occurs when singers imitate musical instruments. Baraka uses scatting both to incorporate black rhythms into his poems — to make them familiar — and to break down conceptions of what the elements in a poem should be to radicalize poetic form." (107) The example Harris uses is

> these
> dribble
> dee
> bibble
> dees
> these warm street shoobies
> my soul gets off behind

from *Black Magic*. (144) Another that also shows the Olson influence is the first strophe of "Like, This Is What I Meant!" from *Selected Poetry*:

> Poetry makes a statement
> like everything
> like everything poetry
> makes a statement
>
> Poetry is a being of words
> a being of language flicks
> produced by the life
> of (DAH da da Dah!)
> "ThE pOeT"
> But here is where we differ
> from Funk & Wagnalls, Empson
> Thaddeus Dustface
> & the rest of assorted bourgeois functionaries
> of the inherited
> decaying
> superstructure
> "Take Class Struggle
> as the Key Link", sd Mao, "Act according
> to the past principles" (294)

Here is much that is frustrating to many readers about the 1960s: the in-group jargon, including shorthand words ("sd" for said), imitation Ezra Poundisms-via-Olson of a low order, such as allusions to "Funk & Wagnalls," "[William] Empson," the British New Critic; "Thaddeus Dustface," who may or may not be an "Academic Poet," and Chairman "Mao" Tse-Tung; the idiosyncratic arrangement of phrases on the page, which Harris and others would excuse as "jazz," and the "scat" syllables that Stephen Henderson made much of before Harris did. A comparison of Baraka's early work with his late will not show, in the opinion of some critics at least, an improvement or, indeed, much of a "transformation" from early to late. Unfortunately, he did not transform Olson's prosodic peculiarities into his own style as successfully as Hayden and Brooks combined black ethnic traditions with English language formal techniques to make a poetry as effective as any written during the period of protest.

Denise Levertov

Another Black Mountain-affiliated poet, Denise Levertov, was associated in the minds of many readers of the decade with the anti-war movement primarily. Levertov was born in Ilford, Essex, England in 1923 and educated privately. She was a nurse during World War II, and her first book of poems, *The Double Image*, was published in London in 1946, the year after the war ended. She married in 1947 and immigrated to the United States the following year, becoming a naturalized citizen in 1955. Two years later Lawrence Ferlinghetti's San Francisco City Lights Press published her second book, *Here and Now* — during the eleven years between her first and second publications she had become a card-carrying member of the extended Black Mountain community.

Jargon, the official Black Mountain press, issued her third book, *Overland to the Islands*, in 1958, and she has published many books since, including *With Eyes at the Back of Our Heads* (1959), *The Jacob's Ladder* (1961), *O Taste and See* (1964), *A Marigold from North Vietnam* (1968), and *Footprints* (1972). As has been noted, she edited a major anti-war anthology, *Out of the War Shadow: An Anthology of Current Poetry*, for the War Resisters League in 1967.

Hyatt H. Waggoner, in the revised edition of his book *American Poets from the Puritans to the Present* (1984) wrote, "In Denise Levertov's long, distinguished, and prolific career we find two strains at work fighting it out for dominance, that of the musing dreamer nostalgic for her Judeo-Christian heritage as the daughter of a Jewish convert who became an Anglican priest, and that of the intensely committed political activist who would make of her poems instruments for public good." (605)

M. L. Rosenthal in *The New Poets* (1967) wrote, "Her characteristic expression had been, earlier, the indirect formulation of an abstract thought, perhaps set off by a literary allusion, and then its resolution in some concrete piece of narration or image. The obtrusive tendency of the whole Black Mountain group to call attention in their poems to the fact that they are writing poems, or to offer some nugget of aesthetic wisdom as the cream of a poem on a quite different subject, is present in Miss Levertov's work as well." (185)

Levertov's involvement in anti-war activity during the 1960s and 1970s came close to obscuring everything else about her work. Waggoner wrote, "Beginning with the Vietnam war the poet's effort 'to make / of my song a chalice / of Time, / a Communion Wine' is interrupted by the poems of social protest. Righteous anger often seems the dominant emotion in these poems, as it does especially in 'A Poem at Christmas, 1972, during the Terror-Bombing of North Vietnam,' which begins 'Now I have lain awake imagining murder,' goes on to recount a dream of the poet's throwing napalm into President Nixon's face, and concludes with the wish 'O, to kill / the killers!'." (605-6)

Her book *Footprints* focused largely upon the war in Vietnam, and it raised a greater number of moral issues than perhaps the poet had intended. One of these had to do with the commitment of the antiwar "artist." It had become obligatory during the war for artists of all sorts to comment, and take stands, on many issues, not all of them clearly related. The example of "Hanoi Jane," as the movie actress Jane Fonda was called by her enemies, is perhaps the most memorable of the period. Like other poets before her, including John Greenleaf Whittier, Walt Whitman, and even Herman Melville, Levertov became famous for her activism rather than for her art.

One question troubled some students of the period: Where does one draw the line between activism and careerism? What is true of most protest poetry of any period was true of Levertov's work and of much of the work by others that she promoted — it was more protest than poetry. Most of the work that appeared in the various ban-the-bomb, anti-war, civil rights, and other activist anthologies of the period could not be called art, for they tended to be harangues which called attention to the self-righteous stances of the poets rather than the atrocities at which the occasional pieces were ostensibly directed.

One of Levertov's pieces from *Footprints* was "Overheard over S. E. Asia," a dialogue written from the dramatic rather than the subjective viewpoint — something quite unusual in Levertov's work which is largely egopoetic. What often happens when the poet steps out of the self to observe the world objectively and become either a narrator or a dramatic persona, is that the barrier of the writer's ego is removed and the reader can empathize with one or more of the characters in the poem. But Levertov was still too emotionally involved with her subject, and she fell into the trap of what has been called "the pathetic fallacy" — putting too much emotional weight upon the inanimate objects of a metaphor and not enough weight upon the subjects — the human beings — of her personifications:

> 'White phosphorous, white phosphorus,
> mechanical snow,
> where are you falling?'
>
> 'I am falling impartially on roads and roofs,
> on bamboo thickets, on people.
> My name recalls rich seas on rainy nights,
> each drop that hits the surface eliciting
> luminous response from a million algae.
> My name is a whisper of sequins. Ha!
> Each of them is a disk of fire,
> I am the snow that burns.
> I fall
> wherever men send me to fall —
> but I prefer flesh, so smooth, so dense:
> I decorate it in black, and seek
> the bone.'

Nevertheless, this is one of the more effective poems in the collection having to do with war and its evils. "But with Vietnam over at last," Waggoner wrote, "the occasional poems tend to give way to poems like "Human Being," which opens *Life in the Forest*

(1978).... "Still," Waggoner continued, "even the most recent volumes contain many 'political' poems, with the nuclear 'Age of Terror' replacing Vietnam as focus." (606)

When the Vietnam War was over at last her eye wandered to other social issues including the threat of nuclear war, Feminist concerns, prejudice, but not all of Levertov's work could be characterized as "anti"; at least one critic, Alicia Suskind Ostriker, in her book *Stealing the Language* (1986), felt that Levertov is "perhaps the sweetest and most life-celebratory of poets writing today.

"Nevertheless," Ostriker continued, she "writes of a 'coldness to life,' an inner-directedness which seems 'unwomanly' because it is insufficiently nurturing of others." (78-79) This may be another way of saying that Levertov liked people best in the abstract, but that she also hated them in the abstract and had difficulty either relating to or writing about others concretely. If one is writing primarily for the subjective audience, the audience of the first person, oneself, perhaps art is irrelevant. Certainly, artlessness was always Levertov's long suit — not the strongest suit for an artist to hold. She died in 1997.

Adrienne Rich

It was the poetry of genteel academic gamesmanship against which Adrienne Rich reacted when she was radicalized and became an early member of the Feminist Movement. Like Karl Shapiro a native Baltimorean, she was born in 1929 and took her A.B. from Radcliffe College in 1951. She earned no other academic degrees but began teaching college at Swarthmore as Visiting Poet in 1966. After that she taught in a variety of faculties in the eastern states. Her first book. *A Change of World*, won the Yale Series of Younger Poets Award and was published in 1951.

The poetry of this volume was clearly formal, but it had authority as well as traditional structure. One of her best-known and still most highly regarded poems, "Aunt Jennifer's Tigers," was included in her first collection; it is a poem that showed her incipient involvement with the problems of women in a paternalistic society:

> Aunt Jennifer's tigers prance across a screen,
> Bright topaz denizens of a world of green.
> They do not fear the men beneath the tree;
> They pace in sleek chivalric certainty.
>
> Aunt Jennifer's fingers fluttering through her wool
> Find even the ivory needle hard to pull.
> The massive weight of Uncle's wedding band
> Sits heavily upon Aunt Jennifer's hand.
>
> When Aunt is dead, her terrified hands will lie
> Still ringed with ordeals she was mastered by.
> The tigers in the panel that she made
> Will go on prancing, proud and unafraid.

In her book *Inspiring Women* (1986), Mary K. DeShazer wrote, "Rich has commented on the problems she confronted in coming as an outsider to the masculine world of poetry. Because her models for 'serious' poetry were mostly male and because, as Auden's words suggest," — in his introduction to Rich's first book, which Auden had chosen to appear in The Yale Series — "only rigorous objectivity was likely to command critical praise, she turned to formal craftsmanship in order to establish herself as an artist." (142)

Not many years later, however, Rich forsook "masculine" formal poetry to write programmatic Feminist poems in "open" prose forms imitated — with a certain amount of irony — from such male models as Walt Whitman and Robert Lowell. "It is not surprising to find Adrienne Rich drawn to both Walt Whitman and Emily Dickinson," Barbara Charlesworth Gelpi and Albert Gelpi wrote in their "Introduction" to *Adrienne Rich's Poetry* (1975), "Whitman projecting an ideal America beyond divisive polarities, including the sexual; Dickinson keeping a polar privacy in her bedroom under her father's roof and yet 'having it out at last,' as Adrienne Rich wrote of her, 'on her own premises.' From the beginning Rich's theme, personal and collective, has been woman in the patriarchy: her own identity, the identity of woman on man's established terms; and, more urgently, the possibility of identity on her own, on woman's own terms." (xi)

It is difficult to see the literary influence of Emily Dickinson in Rich's work. It is perhaps theoretically and inspirationally that Emily Dickinson affected Rich, not practically. Dickinson never wrote political manifestoes such as those in which Rich has indulged, at first in behalf of the cause of feminism, but later on in behalf of other causes. A clearer influence upon Rich's work was the 17th-century Puritan Anne Bradstreet, not merely the first woman poet of significance in America, but the first significant poet of either sex.

Rich wrote the "Foreword" to *The Works of Anne Bradstreet* edited by Jeannine Hensley (1967), ending it with these remarks, which indicated her admiration for a role model with whom she could empathize and whom perhaps she might attempt to emulate:

> "Still, with all stoic recognition of the common problem in each succeeding century including the last half-hour, it is worth observing that Anne Bradstreet happened to be one of the first American women, inhabiting a time and place in which heroism was a necessity of life, and men and women were fighting for survival both as individuals and as a community. To find room in that life for any mental activity which did not directly serve certain spiritual ends, was an act of great self-assertion and vitality. To have written poems, the first good poems in America, while rearing eight children, lying frequently sick, keeping house at the edge of wilderness, was to have managed a poet's range and extension within confines as severe as any American poet has confronted. If the severity of these confines left its mark on the poetry of Anne Bradstreet, it also forced into concentration and permanence a gifted energy that might, in another context, have spent itself in other, less enduring directions." (xx)

Wendy Martin, writing in *An American Triptych* (1984) said, "Married at twenty-four, with three children by the time she was thirty, Adrienne Rich discovered that cooking, cleaning, shopping, caring for the children, and entertaining her husband's colleagues left her little time to write. Overwhelmed by frustration and anger about the disparity between her professional accomplishments and aspirations and the reality of traditional domestic life, she feared that she would be deprived of selfhood altogether." (167) But she was widowed young and never remarried — she seems to have drawn as much bitterness from the death of her husband as her contemporary Sylvia Plath did from the death of her father.

Rich's development took a considerable turn during the 1970s. Martin wrote further "In an essay, 'Compulsory Heterosexuality and Lesbian Existence,' published in 1980, Rich issues a radical challenge to the cultural definition of lesbianism as deviant or perverse." Furthermore, Rich "emphasizes the fact that the nature of female sexuality is

The Poetry of Protest

defined by men, who use shame and guilt as a means of controlling women's behavior...." (211-12) But of course there are homosexual men as well, including both Whitman and Auden, who have been defined as "deviant," not merely by other men but by society as a whole.

Rich expressed her new militancy in the "Foreword" to her *Poems Selected and New, 1950-1974*: "As I type these words we are confronted with the naked and unabashed failure of patriarchal politics and patriarchal civilization. To be a woman at this time is to know extraordinary forms of anger, joy, impatience, love, and hope. Poetry, words on paper, are necessary but not enough; we need to touch the living who share our animal passion for existence, our determination that the sexual myths underlying the human condition can and shall be recognized and changed. My friends — above all, my sisters, the women I love — have given me the heat and friction of their lives, along with needed clarity, criticism, tenderness, and the daring of their examples. Midway in my own life, I know that we have only begun."

Rich wrote in 1986 in the jacket copy of *Your Native Land, Your Life* (1986), "In these poems I have been trying to speak from, and of, and to, my country. To speak a different claim from those staked by the patriots of the sword; to speak of the land itself, the cities, and of the imaginations that have dwelt here, at risk, unfree, assaulted, erased. I believe more than ever that the search for justice and compassion is the great wellspring for poetry in our time, throughout the world, though the theme of despair has been canonized in this century. I draw strength from the traditions of all those who, with every reason to despair, have refused to do so." In other words, she switched her focus slightly in her poems, away from strictly Feminist concerns, but she continued writing confessional orations out of the 1960s, as in No. V of "Sources":

> All during World War II
> I told myself I had some special destiny:
> there had to be a reason
> I was not living in a bombed-out house
> or cellar   hiding out with rats
>
> there had to be a reason
> I was growing up safe, American
> with sugar rationed in a Mason jar
>
> split at the root   white-skinned social christian
> neither gentile nor Jew
>
> through the immense silence
> of the Holocaust
>
> I had no idea of what I had been spared
> still less of the women and men my kin

>   the Jews of Vicksburg or Birmingham
>   whose lives must have been strategies no less
>   than the vixen's on Route 5

By the twenty-first century this sort of hortatory expression had become dated, to say the very least.

Carolyn Kizer

Unlike Adrienne Rich, Carolyn Kizer never forgot how to keep an eye on the language and make it dance and go deep simultaneously. Born in Spokane, Washington, in 1925, she was educated at Sarah Lawrence College. She held a number of positions both in and out of academics; her academic career included teaching stints in the Writers' Workshop of the University of Iowa, Ohio University, University of North Carolina, Barnard College, Columbia University, and the University of Washington in Seattle.

Kizer's first book, *The Ungrateful Garden*, was published in 1961. Her long poem "Pro Femina," from *Knock Upon Silence* (1965), was an early feminist work which, in the opinion of some, has never been excelled by any other poem on the same subject before or since. She speaks in this poem "about women of letters, for I'm in the racket," and it's a man's world in which she must make her way and find her place. Her third collection, *Midnight Was My Cry: New and Selected Poems*, appeared in 1971, *Mermaids in the Basement* and *Yin* in were published in 1984, and *The Nearness of You* came out in 1986. In each of these books her wide range of emotion appeared packaged in all sorts of formal bottles — she has been accused by critics of using her technical skills to "distance herself from pain." However, Kizer was well aware that humor is a weapon with a sharp edge, keener even than a sharp tongue.

Another element of Kizer's success is that she never forgot how to tell a story, and no one told a story quite the way she did, as a slow passage down the pages of *Yin* demonstrated. Though her material was topical, it was also timeless, and Kizer remembered how to get and keep the reader's attention without resorting to the sensational or the hortatory. In "Semele Recycled," for instance, the poet told a narrative out of Greek myth, but she made it so near, familiar, and compelling; loaded it with so much resonance, that the reader wanted to keep going and going.

Semele was the mother of Dionysus — god of wine and fertility — by Zeus, the supreme father-god. Semele asked Zeus to appear to her in all his majesty, but the apparition was so terrifying that she died. Semele's various body parts were scattered and had undergone transformations and sundry adventures, but then her lover returned, and the body parts, hearing the rumor, "leapt up" and as many as could do so reunited themselves.

"This empty body danced on the river bank. / Hollow, it called and searched among the fields / for those parts that steamed and simmered in the sun, / and never would have found them." Then Semele and Zeus were reunited; their "two bodies met like a thunderclap / in mid-day — right at the corner of that wretched field / with its broken fenceposts and startled, skinny cattle. / We fell in a heap on the compost heap / and all our loving parts made love at once,...."

When the poem ended, the reader might have wished to read it again immediately to savor its richly concrete language, its psychological complexity, the narrative embodiment of the war between the sexes, and the eternal truce that is struck again and again. Then the reader may have turned the pages to find another poem as good — and one would be found, over and over.

Although *Mermaids in the Basement* was subtitled *Poems for Women*, for many years Kizer wrote with real power for an audience that was wider than the special interest audiences that so many Post-Modern American poets tried to reach during the period following the Second World War: Kizer kept her balance with *The Nearness of You* which was subtitled *Poems for Men*.

CHAPTER FIVE
Neosurrealism

Surrealism succeeded the Swiss Modernist movement called Dadaism which viewed modern life as meaningless and absurd. The term "surrealism" means literally "over-real" or "beyond-real," but as a 20th-century literary term it meant an approach to reality that is distorting, as in a nightmare, as distinguished from "existential" — approaching reality as though it were composed of meaningless phenomena, a chaos to be organized by each individual mind if it is going to be negotiated "successfully." Nightmares cannot be negotiated at all, only endured without thinking, for to think about them is to be driven insane.

Franz Kafka was perhaps the most famous practitioner of early literary surrealism. In his story "Metamorphosis" a man, Gregor Samsa, wakes up to discover he is no longer a man, he is a beetle. His life in his ordinary home, with his ordinary parents, from that point is a perfect nightmare. Seen from Gregor's perspective, reality has been transformed and totally distorted, although he can see the world he used to know — indeed, continues to inhabit, and it is perfectly ordinary. At last his desiccated carcass is swept out with the trash. Federico Garcia Lorca (1898-1936) in his plays approached the surreal in much the same way, for his Spanish personae did not speak in a distorted manner.

The most significant early American precedent for surrealism in poetry would probably be Edgar Allan Poe who often envisioned a world that was distorted in strange ways, as for instance in the poem titled "Ulalume" in which the speaker discusses in a weird landscape somber subjects with an abstraction, "Psyche," or in "The Raven," in which the narrator has a conversation with a bird who, though it can speak only one word, nevertheless dominates the conversation and the mood of the poem.

Weldon Kees

Weldon Kees was a poet not thought of as a surrealist during his lifetime, yet he was one certainly. But in his poems Weldon Kees does not imagine himself or anyone else as a beetle; he imagines himself as something much worse — a human being. Here is the first poem Donald Justice included in his edition of Kees' *Collected Poems*, "Subtitle," published in 1936 when Kees, who was born in 1914, was twenty-two years of age:

> We present for you this evening
> A movie of death: observe
> These scenes chipped celluloid
> Reveals unsponsored and tax-free.
> We request these things only:
> All gum must be placed beneath the seats
> Or swallowed quickly, all popcorn sacks
> Must be left in the foyer. The doors
> Will remain closed throughout
> The performance. Kindly consult
> Your programs: observe that
> There are no exits. This is
> A necessary precaution.
>
> Look for no dialogue, or for the
> Sound of any human voice: we have seen fit
> To synchronize this play with
> Squealings of pigs, slow sound of guns,
> The sharp dead click
> Of empty chocolatebar machines.
> We say again: there are
> No exits here, no guards to bribe,
> No washroom windows.
>
> No finis to the film unless
> The ending is your own.
> Turn off the lights, remind
> The operator of his union card:
> Sit forward, let the screen reveal
> Your heritage, the logic of your destiny.

Here is Kees' mature style, developed already in his early manhood, when Kees was twenty-two. It is a "plainstyle," what Justice said in his Preface to Kees' poems answered to "the classical definition of a good prose style: natural words in a natural order. His work, in fact, belongs to what might be called the Prose Tradition in poetry." It changed very little for the rest of his life. Nor did his vision change.

Kees was born in 1914 in Beatrice, Nebraska. He began to publish short stories in Midwestern periodicals before he graduated from the University of Nebraska in 1935, and poems two years later. His literary interests from that point were primarily in poetry. He was a strict formalist, often experimenting with villanelles and sestinas and other traditional forms, bending them to his own strange uses. Sometimes his style could be prosaic and baroque at the same time, as in "Variations on a Theme by Joyce" from his first book, *The Last Man*, published in 1943.

This poem is written in the form of a stave — a six-line stanza enclosed by a refrain line: *AbccbA*. Some of the rhymes are true, others are consonances. The meters are loose, tetrameters, but they approximate prose because they are a combination of anapests and iambs, which is the composition of prose in English; however, the anapests sometimes outnumber the iambs, which is not usual in prose. Here is the first stanza:

>   ˘ ′ | ˘ ˘ ′ | ˘ ˘   ′ | ˘ ˘ ′
> The war is in words and the wood is the world
> That turns beneath our rootless feet;
> The vines that reach, alive and snarled,
> Across the path where the sand is swirled,
> Twist in the night. The light lies flat.
> The war is in words and the wood is the world.

This poem is atypical of Kees in that its music is overt; it is full of sound — alliteration and echo, assonance, and its organization over-all is by grammatical parallelism. Another unusual feature of the poem is its sensory level — the images are less concrete than in most of Kees' poems, but they are vivid nevertheless. In the two succeeding stanzas the structures, both external and internal, remain the same, but the rhymes change.

Kees began his professional career as an editor for the Federal Writers' Project in Lincoln, Nebraska, but by 1943 he was on the staff of *Time* magazine in New York City. His interests began to broaden into film-making and painting — in everything he tried he was professionally successful if not affluent. When he went to San Francisco in 1951 he continued his work in films and added music and photography to his bag of talents — Kees became a jazz pianist and composer, and he illustrated with photographs a book on communication with photographs, *Non-Verbal Communication*, with an academic collaborator, though Kees himself was never an academic of any kind.

The Fall of the Magicians appeared in 1947, and in it were "Five Villanelles," a series of poems that are quintessentially Keesian. "One," is a nightmare in a tight form that returns the reader to the world of "Subtitle":

> The crack is moving down the wall.
> Defective plaster isn't all the cause.
> We must remain until the roof falls in.

Nothing could be more prosaic than its opening, which describes a bleak and vacant domestic scene. Kees made no attempt to keep line lengths uniform — the first is perfect iambic tetrameter, the second is perfect pentameter, the third is pentameter with the substitution of a trochee in the first foot and an inversion — the demotion of *falls* — in the fifth foot. The last word of the third line, *in*, is not normally stressed, but here it stands in the place of a stress, and it gives a peculiar feeling to the line; it is almost onomatopoeic — the line nearly collapses as the roof threatens to do.

> It's mildly cheering to recall
> That every building has its little flaws.
> The crack is moving down the wall.

Why is it "mildly cheering," in the second stanza, to recall that "every building has its flaws"? Is it because the end is in sight? Is it because everyone is in the same boat, wherever one happens to be? Is this Everyman's nightmare?

> Here in the kitchen, drinking gin,
> We can accept the damnedest laws.
> We must remain until the roof falls in.

And why must "we" remain until the roof falls in? It is because there is still no exit. But who are we, anyway? Are these all of us?

> And though there's no one here at all,
> One searches every room because
> The crack is moving down the wall.

"We" are alone, each of us singly, though we search the house for each other. We can make no contact with any other human being. The only thing of significance that is happening is that the crack is moving down the wall toward the foundation — this is a surreal rather than a romantic House of Usher where we are trapped.

> Repairs? But how can one begin?
> The lease has warnings buried in each clause.
> We must remain until the roof falls in.

Remain and listen, now and again hearing something, yet knowing in the end that it is nothing that is going to change anything either for the better or for the worse:

> These nights one hears a creaking in the hall,
> The sort of thing that gives one pause.
> The crack is moving down the wall.
> We must remain until the roof falls in.

Kees' *Poems 1947-1954* appeared the year before Kees himself disappeared. "It was on July 18, 1955," Justice relates, "that *The New Republic* printed a review by Kees entitled 'How to Be Happy: Installment 1053,' in which the following passage appears: 'In our present atmosphere of distrust, violence, and irrationality, with so many human beings murdering themselves — either literally or symbolically....' On that day his car was found abandoned on the approach to the Golden Gate Bridge. He had spoken to friends of suicide; he had also spoken of going away to start a new life, perhaps in Mexico." (vi) But no one has ever seen his dead body, and reports that he has been sighted in Mexico and elsewhere are apocryphal. Nevertheless, his influence has grown over the years among his younger contemporaries including the surrealist Vern Rutsala and the New Formalist poet Dana Gioia.

Robert Bly

Robert Bly first saw the light of day in Madison, Minnesota, in 1926. After high school he served in the U. S. Navy from 1944 to 1946 and, after the war, attended St. Olaf College for a year. He transferred to Harvard where he took his B.A. in 1950, then went to the University of Iowa where he studied in the Writers' Workshop and took an M.A. in 1956. He has not held a regular academic position, but he earns his living "giving readings at American colleges and universities, and translating," in his own words. In 1958 he founded the extremely influential little magazine originally titled *The Fifties*, then *The Sixties*, and, briefly, *The Seventies*, together with the press of the same names.

Bly's first book of poems was *Silence in the Snowy Fields* (1962), and it remained his best known and perhaps most highly regarded work, although his second collection, *The Light Around the Body* (1967) also achieved a considerable reputation and won the National Book Award in 1968 — at the award ceremony Bly made the grand gesture of turning over his prize check to an anti-draft organization.

In his periodical and in the books that he issued from his press, no less than in his own work, Bly began to press two ideas. The first was that, in order to write quintessentially "American" poetry one had, quixotically and paradoxically, to study the work of the Chilean Marxist poet Pablo Neruda and the Scandinavians, including Gunnar Ekelof and Thomas Tranströmer, all of whom Bly was translating.

In an essay titled "The Need for Poetics: Some Thoughts on Robert Bly," published in *Of Solitude and Silence: Writings on Robert Bly* (1981), edited by Richard Jones and Kate Daniels, Gregory Orr wrote (p. 149), "When, in conjunction with his translating, Bly affirmed what he called 'the image' (and which has since acquired the critical label, 'deep image'), he was attempting to reunite American poetry with the mainstream developments of Romantic poetry as it had evolved on the European mainland: a poetry structured by symbolic imagination and making extensive (Neruda, surrealism) or intensive (Rilke, Tranströmer) use of symbols."

Bly's second idea was that poets needed to get in touch with their basic natures somehow, needed to reach down into their ids to pull up and bring to light the primal urges of the brute and somehow reconcile them with their conscious existence. The way to do this was to utilize what has come to be called called the "underground" or "deep image," a term coined by LeRoi Jones, but an idea Bly derived from Theodore Roethke whose method it was to walk the edge of madness, not falling over into insanity nor, on the other hand, giving in to the logical mind. It was the poet's job to bring from the side of the unconscious those images that would enable humankind to face and understand itself. These images would, of course, be distortions of "reality" as the conscious mind perceived it; therefore, "deep imagism" was a type of literary surrealism.

According to neural physiologists, however, there was a major flaw in the second of Bly's notions: As Arthur Koestler explained it in his Chapter XVI, "The Three Brains" in his book *The Ghost in the Machine* (1968), neither the lowest ("reptilian") brain, nor the central ("mammalian") brain can think. Only the upper ("human") brain can do so, and it thinks through the manipulation of abstractions, including language symbols — words. It is the homo sapiens-specific neo-cortex, the so-called "thinking cap" that writes poems; the lower brains have no ability to understand concepts, only feelings and urges.

While perhaps images might filter up from the unconscious in dreams and so forth, and poets may write poems utilizing them —making them palpable, as it were, to the rational mind — the movement of these images is in an "upward" direction only, for, once put into words, those images and thoughts cannot proceed downward into the unconscious mind. As Koestler pointed out, it may be possible for the lower brain to control the man, but it is unlikely that the man can control the lower brain, or even "understand" it. Dream analysis is thus little more than literary criticism, for the analyst cannot analyze the dream, but only the narrative of the dream as it is recalled and consciously organized and related by the patient lying on the couch.

Nevertheless, Bly pressed ahead with his theories, and soon he had a great many converts. One of the most beautifully lyric academic poets of the period, James Wright, joined the ranks of the Deep Imagists, as did a lesser light, Donald Hall. Wright went on to gather an excellent reputation as a poet for, though much was lost in his switch to the ranks of Bly, his talent was large enough to bridge the gap. Hall was not so lucky. Bly's major conversion, however, was perhaps that of James Dickey, although the association between him and Bly was short-lived. Soon the "pink fog" (to use the term of the Upstate New York poet Dugan Gilman) of Deep Imagism began to envelop the college graduate writing workshops, of which there began to be a great many throughout America during the late 1960s and the 1970s.

Unlike every other art taught in the academy, poetry became the step-child of "intuition." If anyone wanted to find out what he or she was actually doing with pen, muse, and paper, it had to be learned privately, on one's own in the silent hours. To judge by the Neoformalist movement of the late 1980s, that is just what some of the young poets did.

In 1966, four years after the first "Poets for Peace" reading by Cleveland poets, Robert Bly became active in the anti-Vietnam War movement. Deborah Baker, in her essay "Making a Farm: A Literary Biography" in the previously cited Jones / Daniel book on Bly, wrote (on p. 61) that "Because Bly was still active as an editor, he felt he had a responsibility to outline a new approach to poetry that would incorporate a concern with political issues.

"In doing that he challenged many poets and critics who feel that poetry dealing with political subjects is propagandistic by nature. The relationship between the challenge of political content and the earlier challenge of the New Imagination is noteworthy because Bly now formulates a critical theory to support both concerns in poetry. This was to be the beginning of his comprehensive aesthetic and would later be articulated fully in his books *Leaping Poetry* [1973] and *News of the Universe* [: *Poems of Two-Fold Consciousness* (1980)]. On the surface, surrealist poetry and the subjective poetry of the 'deep image' appear to be at odds with political content. Yet Bly's most treasured poets of South America and Spain — Lorca, Vallejo, and Neruda — wrote excellent political poetry that does not abandon the surrealist vision; and their example convinced Bly that political poetry is indeed possible, and even a natural responsibility of the poet."

It was during this phase of his development as poet, editor, activist, and proselytizer for various causes both literary and political that Bly fell out with his friend and early convert James Dickey over Dickey's poem "The Firebombing." It was Bly's opinion that Dickey's attitude toward the total destruction by air-raid firebombing of Dresden during World War II — Dickey had been serving in the Army Air Corps then — was anti-human and politically retrogressive.

Over the years Bly published many books of various sorts, traveled widely across the country giving readings and other programs, and becoming the hero of neo-Imagists, activists, and anti-academics of all stripes and colors. The style he espoused became almost universal in the graduate writing workshops. By 1983 and the publication of *Four Ramages of Robert Bly*, however, the "deep image" had been shown to be one of the most sentimental programs for poetry writing ever conceived, although it had been Bly's intention to achieve an opposite effect, for he hated and inveighed against confessional poetry, in particular that of Robert Lowell and Anne Sexton.

In his book *Robert Bly* (1986, p. 23), Richard P. Sugg attempted to make a distinction between the "I" speaker of the poems of Lowell and his school, and the "I" speaker of *Silence in the Snowy Fields*: "Instead of the anguished 'I' of the confessional poets, spoken from behind a persona-mask, Bly's poetry in *Silence* is spoken by an 'I' who is virtually identical with the poet himself. Bly often attacked the intellectual style that used a persona to achieve an ironic distance between a poet and his voice, and even accused poets of evading moral responsibility by hiding behind a persona. Bly argued that the persona technique made poetic language a separate, privileged language, and kept the reader so distanced from the poem that he could never discover himself within it nor feel truly moved by it."

Nevertheless, Bly used the same "I" speaker in his poems, the same egopoetic viewpoint. Ingegerd Friberg, in her *Moving Inward: A Study of Robert Bly's Poetry* (1977, p. 16) writing about "Three Kinds of Pleasures," the introductory poem in *Silence in the Snowy Fields*, said that "The 'I' used here, as well as in many other poems, seems really to refer to the poet, to Bly himself. In his prose writings he mentions with contempt the poet who hides behind a persona...." But who was to judge whether a poet was using a "persona" or was speaking in his own sincere and ungarnished voice? Evidently it was Robert Bly who was to make this judgment.

Many years later in his *Ramages*, even in poems that were purported to be neo-imagistic, the inherent sentimentality of Bly's personality and technique had overwhelmed and smothered his poems. Through four pages of unprepossessing, philosophical prose, the world of literature was given this sort of observation: "There is a gladness in the not-caring / of the bear's cabin; and in the gravity / that makes the stone laugh down the mountain." "Grackles stroll about on the black floor of sorrow." But bears do not have cabins, nor do cabins either care or not-care, and they are not "glad" under any circumstances whatever; stones do not laugh down mountains, except insofar as the sound of stone against stone sounds like laughter, perhaps, to give Bly as much leeway as possible with his image;

and grackles do not stroll on the black floor of sorrow — at least they don't without some context beyond non-sequitur: Bly hated to explain his images, perhaps assuming that the reader's unconscious mind would understand his deep images if the thinking cap did not.

In 1985 Bly published more of the same in *Loving a Woman in Two Worlds*. As usual, his voice-of-choice was the egopoetic I, just as Lowell and Sexton had chosen; unlike their ruminations, however, Bly jumped about from one random noun to another, and the reader was left in the topography of the poet's mind without landmarks or guideposts. Here is "Such Different Wants":

> The board floats on the river.
> The board wants nothing
> but is pulled from beneath
> on into deeper waters.
>
> And the elephant dwelling
> on the mountains wants
> a trumpet so its dying cry
> can be heard by the stars.
>
> The wakeful heron striding
> through reeds at dawn wants
> the god of sun and moon
> to see his long skinny neck.
>
> You must say what you want.
> I want to be the man
> and I am who will love you
> when your hair is white.

Perhaps it ought to go without saying that of course "The board wants nothing," since it is inanimate, but "the elephant dwelling on the mountains" certainly does not want "a trumpet so its dying cry can be heard by the stars," nor does a heron want "the god of sun and moon to see his long skinny neck" under any circumstances, for only mankind understands abstractions like the concept of godhood. The only lines that make "sense" — any kind of sense at all, including poetic sense, which is not the same as logic — are the last two, and they are the least interesting, the most trite.

James Dickey

James Dickey did not begin as an academic, nor was his literary practice as linear as those of some of his contemporaries. Dickey was born in Atlanta, Georgia, in 1923. He attended Clemson College briefly in 1942 before he served in the U.S. Army Air Corps during World War II and, later, during the Korean "Police Action." Dickey took his bachelor's and master's degrees from Vanderbilt University, that institution which had bred the school of literature called "The Fugitives" during the Modernist era, though their heyday was over by the time Dickey matriculated there.

The Fugitives were largely responsible for the post-war hegemony of formalism in American academic institutions. Not only did the Vanderbilt ensemble make writers respectable and acceptable as teachers, it also linked teaching and writing with literary criticism by helping to develop what became known as "the New Criticism" and publishing both creative writing and criticism in a series of important literary magazines, several of which were founded and edited by its members. The first of these periodicals was Vanderbilt's own *The Fugitive*, from which the group had taken its name. Later on, members scattered far and wide to publish such influential journals as *The Kenyon Review*, *The Sewanee Review*, and *The Southern Review*. Robert Penn Warren became co-author and editor, with the critic Cleanth Brooks, of the most important introductory college text-anthology of the period, *Understanding Poetry*, (1938), which went through many editions and dominated the college classrooms of the nation for a generation with its formalist, objectively analytical New Critical approach. It is still an important book.

James Dickey could not but be influenced under the circumstances, but he never accepted the New Critical stance without reservation. After his graduation Dickey became an executive in an advertising firm, subsequently accepting his first teaching position at Rice University in 1950. Thereafter he taught at various schools until 1968 when he accepted his professorship at the University of South Carolina. Dickey became not only an important poet and teacher, but also an influential anti-formalist critic and the author of a best-selling novel, *Deliverance* (1970), for which he wrote the equally successful screenplay.

James Dickey's first collection of poems was *Into the Stone* (1960), published in volume VII of the Poets of Today series edited by John Hall Wheelock. The poems in it were unusual because of Dickey's habit of stating and restating the major and minor themes in each poem. In between these demi-refrains the language was controlled, the ideas were concise, and the emotion was implicit rather than explicit — it was stylized, as Roethke's poems were, though the resemblance was not obvious. Still, Wheelock in his introduction wrote, "The influence of Theodore Roethke makes itself felt in a frequent use of the single end-stopped line containing a simple declarative sentence, whereby what is said gains force and emphasis from its compression, and there the repetition of such lines, one after the other, gives a curiously incisive, staccato effect, not unlike that of much contemporary music." (23-4) The poems could also remind a knowledgeable reader of Theodore Roethke cerebralized, made less basic — the images of *Into the Stone* were not so startling and sensual as those of Roethke. Poems such as "Sleeping Out at Easter" and "The Call" did not take the chances that Roethke's poems took. If the similarities between the two poets were not evident to many critics, Dickey settled the question when he acknowledged his debt to Roethke in a eulogy he wrote for *Poetry* magazine in 1963 following Roethke's death.

By 1967 and James Dickey's *Poems 1957-1967* it became clearer that he had not completely understood Roethke's metrical prosody, which was often podics. Dickey had wanted to get away from the traditional accentual-syllabic prosody used by the academic poets, but he had not understood strong-stress verse as Roethke did; instead, he had substituted for Roethke's podic verses the accentual-syllabic verse foot called the dactyl, a stressed syllable followed by two unstressed syllables ($'\smile\smile$) with its "falling rhythms," or the reverse of the dactyl, the anapest ($\smile\smile'$). An example from *Into the Stone* is the first few lines of "The Underground Stream." Though there are variations, the running anapest of this poem is clear.

In his second book of criticism, *Babel to Byzantium*, Dickey made even clearer what it was he had been trying to do metrically. "Although I didn't care for rhyme and the 'packaged' quality which it gives even the best poems," he wrote, "I did care very much for meter, or at least rhythm.... Most of the material I read on metrics concluded that the systematic use of anapests and dactyls tends to monotony, and I accepted this judgment on faith and continued to try to work with the customary English iambic line." The iamb worked no better for him than rhyme, and as a result Dickey went on experimenting until he developed what he called the "split line," thereby approaching the original Anglo-Saxon prosody from which podic prosody was derived in the fifteenth century. Dickey appeared to be reinventing the roots of English versification (282 *ff.*).

This was an unusual thing for a poet in the Platonic tradition to be concerned with, for elsewhere in *Babel to Byzantium* Dickey objected to poets having a concern with form in poetry composition. Criticizing the work of the poet Lewis Turco who, he felt, displayed too much art in his *First Poems* (1960) and not enough soul, Dickey wrote, "The important thing is not to say something with wit and skill, but to say the right, the unheard of, the necessary thing: necessary because the subject is what it is, and because the writing man, including his relationship to the subject, is what he is. Without this kind of live conjunction nothing else really matters...." (141) Yet six years later Dickey wrote in the dust-jacket copy of Turco's *The New Book of Forms: A Handbook of Poetics* (1986), "Belongs in the hands of every poet, student, and teacher, for the greater good of the art." He had been using *The Book of Forms* as a required text in all his classes since it had first been published in 1968.

Hyatt H. Waggoner wrote, "Nearly twenty years after Roethke's review [which has been quoted above] what he had said there still seemed to need saying. In 1964 James Dickey gathered together his poetry reviews; added an introduction, a middle section, and a conclusion; and called the whole *The Suspect in Poetry*." (607) In both of Dickey's books of criticism, Waggoner wrote, "Dickey is restating in contemporary language some of Emerson's leading ideas about poetry." (609) Richard J. Calhoun and Robert W. Hill, writing in their study *James Dickey*, said that Dickey believed in the instinct and in intuition, just as Emerson and Roethke claimed to do, and that at times it is necessary for the poet who would be seer and prophet as well "momentarily to put away reason, to withdraw from traditional social communion, to be alone to tap the sensual imagination. Even in so civilized an activity as poetry, rational modes must sometimes be prevented...." (9)

By the end of the decade of the 1960s Dickey, inheriting the mantle of Randall Jarrell, had become a pervasive influence on American poetry through his criticism as well as his poetry. However, whereas Jarrell had been a New Critic, Dickey was, as Calhoun and Hill pointed out, a "neo-romantic," and as Waggoner showed, not merely that, but an American variety, a neo-Emersonian, at least in his criticism if not always in his poetry.

For most of the decade Dickey was also influenced by Robert Bly, but by the 1970s they had fallen out with one another and gone their separate ways. Bly continued with his so-called "deep imagism," a form of surrealism which also derived, at least in part, from the poetry of Theodore Roethke, but from the sensory level, not the sonic. Bly had jettisoned meters of all kinds, gone to the long prose line, kept Roethke's images of the "unconscious" mind, and himself become a pervasive influence among the poets of the college workshops which had proliferated after the War.

By the time of his death in 1997 Dickey had grown away from the "instinctual lyricism" of Roethke and developed into the contemporary equivalent of a Byron, becoming interested in a poetry of narrative, just as he was also interested in prose narrative. He was prolific — in 1983 alone *Night Hurdling* — subtitled "Poems, Essays, Conversations, Commencements, and Afterwords" — and *The Central Motion: Poems 1968-1979* were published. In the former there were only four poems, all written in "split-line" prosody; the second book contained a much fuller survey of his work, for it was a gathering together and reprinting of three previous collections, to which was added a selection of his more recent work. Dickey's hallmark came to be the lurid story told in "split-line prosody": a stewardess falling from an airplane and, on the way down, experiencing mythic fantasies ("Falling"); the bottled fetus of an inter-species union between a sheep and a human being delivering itself of a philosophical monologue ("The Sheep Child"). "The Shark's Parlor" broke out of anapestic rhythms and into prose written out in "split" lines:

> The shark flopped on the porch, grating with salt-sand   driving back in
> The nails he had pulled out   coughing chunks of his formless   blood.
> The screen door banged and tore off   he scrambled on his tail   slid
> Curved   did a thing from another world   and was out of his element and in
> Our vacation paradise   cutting all four legs from under the dinner table
> With one deep-water move   he unwove the rugs in a moment throwing pints
> Of blood over everything we owned   knocked the buck teeth out of my picture
> His head full of crushed jelly-glass splinters and radio tubes thrashing
> Among the pages of fan magazines   all the movie stars drenched in sea-blood.

James Dickey exhibited more than merely a split line in his later work; throughout his life he also had a split mind about how one ought to go about composing poetry, whether it should be "instinctive" or craftsmanly.

James Wright

James Wright, Bly's major convert after James Dickey, was born in Ohio in 1927. He attended Kenyon College in his native state, where he took his bachelor's degree. Subsequently he took an M. A. and a Ph. D. at the University of Washington in Seattle. He later held academic positions at the University of Minnesota, Macalaster College, and finally at Hunter College in New York City where he died of cancer in 1980.

Wright's first book, *The Green Wall*, was published in the Yale Series of Younger Poets in 1957. It contained poems that identified their writer as having one of the purest lyrical ears among the academic poets of the period. "A Song for the Middle of the Night" is an example — it began with an epigraph: "By way of explaining to my son the following curse by Eustace Deschamps: 'Happy is he who has no children; for babies bring nothing but crying and stench.'"

> Now first of all he means the night
> You beat the crib and cried
> And brought me spinning out of bed
> To powder your backside.
> I rolled your buttocks over
> And I could not complain:
> Legs up, la la, legs down, la la,
> Back to sleep again.

The prosody of this octet stanza is accentual-syllabic verse, the meter is iambic tetrameter in the odd-lines, trimeter in the even; the rhyme scheme is, in the first stanza, *abcbDeFE* — the odd lines do not rhyme, and the capital letters here indicate lines that will be repeated in the second stanza. In effect, then, the eight lines are made up of two quatrains of common measure, but because three of the last four lines are refrains, Wright really had invented a nonce form. In the second stanza the rhymes of the first half change, but the second half do not *hijiDeFE*:

> Now second of all he means the day
> You dabbled out of doors
> And dragged a dead cat Billy-be-damned
> Across the kitchen floors.
> I rolled your buttocks over
> And made you sing for pain:
> Legs up, la la, legs down, la la,
> Back to sleep again.

In the third stanza Wright abandoned the refrain line that had appeared as line five in the preceding two stanzas, but the reader will not perhaps catch it, because the new line ends with *shoulder*, which consonates with "over" — *klmldeFE*:

> But third of all my father once
> Laid me across his knee
> And solved the trouble when he beat
> The yowling out of me.
> He rocked me on his shoulder
> When razor straps were vain:
> Legs up, la la, legs down, la la,
> Back to sleep again.

The last stanza abandons even the consonance of line five, so that there are as many unrhymed as rhymed lines, yet little of the lyricism of the poem has been lost:

> So roll upon your belly, boy,
> And bother being cursed.
> You turn the household upside down,
> But you are not the first.
> Deschamps the poet blubbered too,
> For all his fool disdain:
> Legs up, la la, legs down, la la,
> Back to sleep again.

The poem partakes of the nursery rhyme and the drinking song, at the same time that it is a didactic poem with an argument and a point. It retains the reader's interest with its sound at the same time that it builds a parallel series of narrative incidents with which one can empathize. Is the poem "sincere"? Perhaps one may provide an answer by asking another question: Can the reader recognize himself or herself in the poem?

No great change had taken place by the time Wright's second book, *Saint Judas*, was published two years later, in 1959. Most of the poems were still those of a formalist, though there was perhaps a bit of loosening detectable. In *The Pure Clear Word: Essays on the Poetry of James Wright*, edited by Dave Smith, Henry Taylor wrote that "Wright's well-known shift in style was a necessity, a survival tactic. *Saint Judas* is a splendid book, but it contains considerable evidence of Wright's growing impatience with the style in which most of it is written. Moreover, the shift seems to have been more stylistic than thematic. I do not deny the new subtlety of perception, the new sensitivity, in Wright's later work, but I am suspicious of claims that the shift was a cataclysmic transformation of the whole man." (49-50)

Dave Smith asked Wright about his old teacher at Kenyon College, John Crowe Ransom: "How do you now value Ransom's poetry?" Wright replied, "His poetry, as the years go by, seems to me to be finer than I had realized. I always liked it. Ransom is in slightly bad odor right now, partly because he writes the so-called square poem: you can glance at his poems on the page and see that they scan. If you look a little closer, unless you happen to be as tone-deaf as some of our reviewers apparently are — I don't say that in malice, I say it as a kind of curiosity, you can hear that his poems rhyme.

Furthermore, Ransom plainly shows in his poems that he is willing to let his conscious intelligence operate in the poems and this is very much out of fashion. It's ridiculous that it should be out of fashion. It is part of the terribly self-flattering, self-indulging anarchic spirit of our times, the spirit of confusion." (11-12)

Five years earlier than the interview Norman Friedman wrote in *Contemporary Poets*, "James Wright's *Collected Poems* [1971] contains most of *The Green Wall*, and all of *Saint Judas, The Branch Will Not Break* [1963], and *Shall We Gather at the River* [1968], plus some translations and 33 new poems. This impressive volume, although it covers a poetic career of only 14 years, reveals a genuine experimenter, a poet who can, like Yeats, consciously transform himself. Thus we can speak already of Wright's rich and formal poems of the first two books; the spare and 'deep image' work of *Branch*; and the loose and pain-filled later poems. For these stages also reveal a strange and tragic curve of emotional development: Wright's concern for human suffering, which was never absent from his earlier work, and which seemed to have been temporarily balanced by the bright joy of so much of *Branch* now reappears as an obsession without let or hindrance or (often) control in an avalanche of anguish and despair in *River* and *'New Poems.'*"

Smith also asked Wright about the one course in poetry writing he had taken with Theodore Roethke at the University of Washington. Wright said that "A course with Roethke was a course in very, very detailed and strenuous critical reading. Here was an assignment: he wanted us to go to the library and find ten or maybe even twenty iambic trimeter lines that had a caesura after the first syllable. He made us do that." A bit later Wright said, "So, we knew Roethke was a very fine man, an intelligent and learned man, and when he asked us to do something we would do it. He was not trying to violate our psyches or something."

A book that Friedman didn't mention was one titled *The Lion's Tail and Eyes: Poems Written Out of Laziness and Silence* (1962), a committee effort by Wright, William Duffy and Robert Bly, but Wright denied that Bly had exercised any undue influence upon him. Smith asked Wright, "How do you feel about your early poems?" to which Wright replied, "I haven't read them for a while. About three years ago I sat down and read my whole *Collected Poems*. Some of them I couldn't remember having written and some of them I didn't understand. It is true that I wrote to my publisher after *Saint Judas* and said I don't know what I am going to do after this but it will be completely different. This comment, and also Robert Bly's essay on my work, has given rise to some sort of assumption that I calculated that I was going to be born again or something, that I would become a completely different person. I think that this is nonsense. There was a good essay by Mark Strand regarding changes in poetry. He used my work as an example and he said the only difference, really, was that I don't rhyme so often now. I don't think that a person can change very quickly or easily." (18)

Wright's demurrer to the contrary notwithstanding, there was a great difference in style between the poet's second solo book and his third, *The Branch Will Not Break*, which was clearly "deep image" poetry, though not nearly as self-conscious and sentimental as the work of Bly. It was more sinewy as well, leaner and clearer. Wright emphasized the shift in his style by publishing as the opening pair in *Collected Poems*, first, "The Quest" (3), written in the earlier lyrical style, and then (4), "Sitting in a Small Screenhouse on a Summer Morning." It is interesting to compare the opening stanzas of the two poems. Here is the opening of the first:

> In pasture where the leaf and wood
> Were lorn of all delicious apple,
> And underfoot a long and supple
> Bough leaned down to dip in mud,
> I came before the dark to stare
> At a gray nest blown in a swirl,
> As in the arm of a dead girl
> Crippled and torn and laid out bare.

And here is the opening of the second poem:

> Ten more miles, it is South Dakota.
> Somehow, the roads there turn blue,
> When no one walks down them.
> One more night of walking, and I could have become
> A horse, a blue horse, dancing
> Down a road alone.

The second poem is quite different from the first in tone, in style, in level of diction. The tone is cool and objectifying, not elegiac; the style is the new "plainstyle" which was being developed by poets in the Northwest including William Stafford and David Wagoner; the level of diction is colloquial rather than literary. The second poem relies on the sensory level primarily, not upon the sonic. The first poem develops an idea in formal, logical order, makes its point; the second abandons the denotations of words and makes the most of connotations and associations, leaping from one image to another, in the manner of the haiku. Both poems are well written, beautifully paced, clearly the work of a wordsmith. The second poem's images are the type of the "deep" image, the effect surreal: "It is so still now, I hear the horse / Clear his nostrils. / He has crept out of the green places behind me. / Patient and affectionate, he reads over my shoulder / These words I have written." The poem shows that, no matter what the theory, no matter how far out or unfounded it may be, in the hands of someone who can truly write, it will work.

After his third solo book Wright's style continued to change, becoming more jagged and expressive of personal suffering; this is the third phase of Wright's career that Friedman identified. "The emotional — and sometimes artistic — descent, however, is dizzying as we come to *Shall We Gather at the River* and the 'New Poems'" section of *Collected Poems*," Friedman wrote. (1719) "For unrelieved wretchedness, these pieces must be unmatched in contemporary poetry, and suggest that Wright is returning, after the brief high of *Branch*, to some old and fundamental unresolved despair. Whether these poems were premonitory or only an expression of a mid-life crisis it is impossible to say, but some of them, such as 'At the Grave,' from the 1974 *Two Citizens*, were maelstroms of despair."

"I believe the grave James referred to," the poet's widow Anne wrote Lewis Turco in a letter dated July 29, 1989, "was that of his English teacher at Kenyon [College], Philip Timberlake. He has several poems dedicated, in this manner, to Mr. Timberlake. Needless to say, it has many other meanings too, but James loved Philip Timberlake, who took such a great interest in James when he was a student and was so supportive and such an intellectual force in James' life."

> All I am doing is walking here alone.
> I am not among the English poets.
> I am not even going to be among
> The English poets after my death.
> You loved them the best.
> And you liked me, fine. It is still raining
> This morning, this November morning.
> And I am not even standing at your grave.
> I am fiddling with a notebook in New York,
> Wondering about Ohio where now at this moment
> A leaf hangs on a locust thorn shredding
> Its form into the rain.
> John Keats, coughing his lungs out,
> John Clare, crazy,
> And Geoffrey Chaucer the only one.
> And Edward Thomas, who got killed, the only
> Soldier in this century who was sane.
> If these lines get published, I will hear
> From some God damned deaf moron who knows
> Everything. The dead are nothing.
> And he will be right.
> The living giggle in the dark all night,
> And the dead are nothing.

This is confessional poetry as melancholy as that of Anne Sexton, as manic as that of Sylvia Plath. "I agree," Anne Wright wrote, "that 'At the Grave' is both melancholy and manic." James Wright's last book, *To a Blossoming Pear Tree*, was published in 1978; he died of cancer of the esophagus two years later.

Vern Rutsala

Vern Rutsala was born in McCall, Idaho, in 1934 of Finnish stock and educated at Reed College in Portland, Oregon, where he took his B. A. in 1956. Subsequently, he served as an enlisted man in the U. S. Army for two years, then attended the Writers' Workshop of the University of Iowa where he earned an M. F. A. in 1960. Rutsala spent his entire academic career at Lewis and Clark College in Portland except for visiting appointments at the University of Minnesota in Minneapolis and Bowling Green State University in Ohio.

In Rutsala's first book, *The Window*, published in 1964, there were poems that remain immediately recognizable as Rutsala's and no one else's, for he had already developed a surrealist style that has continued to run through all his books, even the 1978 book of absolutely prose, but not prosaic, poems titled *Paragraphs*. Some of the elements of that style, evident throughout *Selected Poems*, were and are these: Sentences that are statements laid out in apparently prose lines broken by phrasing; images that might best be described as "a surrealism of the everyday"; a vision of existential stolidity in the face of the inevitable incursions of time and the world upon our minds and bodies; a sense of the idiocy of it all, of self-satire. All these elements are to be found in "Marriage Contract" from his first book:

> No one spells out the unwritten agreement,
> the fine unphrased concessions made
> between the two parties.
>
> She, party of the first part,
> protects him from seeing his own face
> on mirrored walls. She covers the glass
> with delicate pictures, subtle drawings
> which equal his imagined self as he
> lumbers through halls breaking china,
> shattering delicate glass and smiling
> a ludicrous grin at dreams of himself.
>
> He, party of the second part, accepts
> his role and plays the crude but sensitive man.
> In the night he practices his gait,
> lumbering through dreams of flowers,
> breaking the stems of trees, hiding
> his own soft face like mollusc flesh
> within the grinning shell
> he's sworn by secret law to wear.

Rutsala continued to sneer at life while he enjoyed it in *Small Songs* (1969), a chapbook sequence of epigrammatic poems:

> All our books used to say
> read us see our fine paper
> we have margins and chapters and stanzas
> our white space is rich as cream
> read us
> we have footnotes in italics
> and paragraphs
> all of different sizes

The Harmful State (1971), was also a chapbook. *Laments* (1975) appeared next, then the chapbook *The New Life* (1978). *The Harmful State* held twelve "Paragraphs" which were reprinted in *Paragraphs* (1978), the first entry of which, "On Paragraphs," is a foreword or prologue which discusses some things about what a "paragraph" is supposed to be:

> The Paragraph is a prose poem, but it is also related to the fable, the aphorism, the maxim, the character, and the joke, and may draw energy from the ghosts of those forms in the way free verse is said to rely on the hint of traditional meter." [I wish to call the reader's attention particularly to this remark, about which I will have more to say later on.]
>
> Occasionally a Paragraph will read like a parody of an aphorism. This is purposely done. They are supposed to be poems rather than chips of wisdom, but they do play with expectations the appetites that exist for the 'inspirational,' 'living thoughts,' box-of chocolates kind of knowledge that so many people secretly admire.

And here is a "Paragraph" itself:

> We sense a criticism, possibly overhearing it as we walk, and immediately we begin rearranging our past to fit the crime we suspect we are suspected of. By the time we reach home we have altered our history, discredited all alibis, documented and labeled evidence, and, opening the door, we begin to serve our sentence.

In *The Journey Begins* (1976), and *Walking Home from the Icehouse* (1981), Rutsala kept showing us ourselves darkly in the pane of his mirror, but his sadistic good humor took the edge off sometimes, as in "Words":

> We had more than
> we could use.
> They embarrassed us,
> our talk fuller than our
> rooms. They named
> nothing we could see —
> dining room, study,
> mantel piece, lobster
> thermidor. They named
> things you only saw in movies —
> the thin flicker Friday
> nights that made us
> feel empty in the cold
> as we walked home
> through our only great
> abundance, snow.

In 1985 Rutsala published two collections, a book, *Backtracking*, and a chapbook, *The Mystery of Lost Shoes*. Each was filled with poems that were unmistakably Rutsala; in them things lay in wait to trip the reader out of his ordinary walks of life, to take the reader down where surfaces close overhead and one breathes an air of dread and fascination as in "The Empty House," which sits in the midst of poverty in the empty western reaches of our nation and imagination, a place Rutsala remembers from his childhood:

> Again I answer the cold phone, again
> I hold my breath between each
> word, again I fly
> over snow-dusted plains.
> I give up each possession. I turn off
> the last light. Like a hobo I travel.
> (Nameless all the lights go out.)
> A bat weaves an arc like an eyelash
> on the sky and all the roads
> roll up. When I sleep I sleep
> under bridges. When I sleep
>
> I dream this dream.

Although these poems look like "free verse" or line-phrased prose; although Rutsala has never written in overtly metrical lines, and although he has in the past maintained that he is incapable of doing so, nevertheless this passage, like much of his work, is basically iambic. The first line in this passage contains two iambs, ˘ ´ ˘ ´, a "double iamb," ˘ ˘ ´ ´, and a final iamb, $\smile'$. The whole line scans like this: $\smile'|\smile'|\smile\smile''|\smile'$, which is iambic pentameter. If the next line is not broken after "each" but is allowed to run to the next "again," like the first line, then we have another iambic pentameter line, perfect this time: $\smile'|\smile'|\smile'|\smile'|\smile'$. If the third line is broken after "give," then we have a line that looks metrically like this: $\smile'|'\smile|''|\smile'|\smile'$, which is iambic pentameter with two variations, a trochee substitution in the second foot and a spondee substitution in the third. Let the next line run to "last," and we are back to nearly perfect iambic pentameter again, the only variation being a demotion (of "up") in the first foot: $.\,'|\smile'|\smile'|\smile'|\smile'$. The line-endings as they are printed serve as a sort of rhythmic counterpoint to the basic iambic measures. Here is what these lines would look like laid out as we have scanned them:

> Again I answer the cold phone, again
> I hold my breath between each word, again
> I fly over snow-dusted plains. I give
> up each possession. I turn off the last
> light.

If it wasn't obvious before, it is now clear that Rutsala is using many traditional sonic devices such as repetitions (*Again, again, again*), assonance (**co**ld, ph**o**ne, h**o**ld, **o**ver, sn**o**w, p**o**ssession), internal rhyme (*cold/hold*), alliteration (**l**ast, **l**ight) and consonantal echo (**b**rea**t**h, **b**e**t**ween). This combination of colloquial diction, conversational syntax, hidden traditional rhythms and sonic patterns, and a "surrealism of the ordinary" — in prose fiction it might be called "magical realism" — is Rutsala's hallmark.

The last segment of *Selected Poems* (1991) was taken from Rutsala's 1987 *Ruined Cities*; there is no section of new poems. When the reader has reached this far he realizes, looking back over the earlier books, that there has been considerable variety along the way, of line-lengths, strophes, stanzas, even prose paragraphs; of imagery and subject matter, yet through it all the voice has been steady, at once reassuring and unsettling. Every poem feels solid, and every one is filled with ambiguity, with the double-vision of someone who sits on the edge and observes calmly the depths of the abyss beneath his feet. The reader must take to heart the "Prospectus for Visitors":

> Here are some things
> you should know: First
> if you come here
> be ready to spend long
> days in thought, long days
> indoors, deeper indoors
> than you've ever been.
> In the steady sweet
> rain you'll get beyond
> the anterooms of thought,
> you'll explore rooms
> you've never seen.

Although he has been appreciated by readers over the years, Vern Rutsala has not yet been acknowledged to be the master craftsman he is, a major representative of the neglected generation of poets who came of age in the 1960s. Writing of *The Window* Norman Friedman said, "Vern Rutsala seems to me to have one of the keenest poetic responses to contemporary middle class society that I can remember since Cummings, Auden, the earlier Karl Shapiro, and some of Louis Simpson. His special achievement in *The Window* is to have made the furniture of everyday bourgeois life in America available to the uses of serious poetry."

Friedman wrote further, "But there is here not merely a familiar world of skate keys, wagons, bicycles ('Sunday'); there is also a commanding vision which governs the shaping of that world. He hears the glacier knocking in the cupboard and the rumble of violence and despair hidden within our domestic walls. Rutsala deals card after card, building up unbearably to a remorseless climax, until not a corner is left for us to hide in, nothing is spared — not a toothbrush, family album, mantelpiece clock, visit from relatives, souvenir ashtray, flushing of the toilet, garden hose — nothing escapes his illumination of things so ordinary that we have forgotten them, so close we haven't seen them, revealing what we thought we already knew but never quite understood."

Friedman's insights are as accurate today as they were yesterday, and they will be accurate tomorrow as well. One day readers will open their eyes and discover that Vern Rutsala's work had entered their minds when they weren't looking, and they will realize that he is there to stay. By then they will know who wrote "X's Poems":

> These are the poems which steal,
> which siphon gas, which
> break in at night. These poems
> are cat burglars, cold-eyed
> prowlers. These poems shoplift
> your cart empty at the store.
> When you've read these poems
> you're picked clean, you're naked
> and alone, you're bankrupt
> without hope or gender. It's then
> these poems bring
> a freezing wind, foul and piercing,
> from the arctic dump.
> These poems take everything
> but ice and bone. Each one writes
> each reader's elegy in cold blood.

Of all the many poets who followed Bly's lead into surrealism in the 'sixties, not many found themselves able to grope their way out of the pink fog and to invent distortions of reality that were totally original stylistically, owing nothing to the Modernist Spanish poet Federico Garcia Lorca, to Pablo Neruda or Tranströmer or even to Robert Bly. One was Rutsala, and another was Richard Emil Braun.

Richard Emil Braun

Born in Detroit on St. Cecilia's Day in 1934, Richard Emil Braun took his master's degree in Latin from the University of Michigan in 1957 and a Ph.D. in Latin and Greek from the University of Austin in 1969. For many years he was a classics professor at the University of Alberta in Edmonton, Alberta, Canada. His poem "Goose" first appeared in Richard Ashman's strange little magazine of the 1950s, *A Huoyhnhnm's Scrapbook*. It was the first of the odd pieces that began to mark the advent of a new poet with an arresting surrealist style and an idiosyncratic point of view. Other work soon followed, also published by Ashman — "Flirt" and "Harland's Hobby." Since that time Braun has published several collections of poetry. The first, *Companions to Your Doom*, began the Fresco Chapbook Series in 1961. It was followed by *Children Passing* (1962), *Bad Land* (1971), and *The Foreclosure* (1972), in which his original chapbook appears as part two of the three-part collection. Braun died on September 29, 2001.

An American poet who lived and taught classics in Canada, Braun was neither fish nor fowl in either country. He is, in addition, a difficult poet in offbeat, even macabre ways. He is often a narrative poet, but the stories he tells are enigmatic. The interests of his lyrics are similarly unconventional. The surfaces are extraordinarily clear. The reader seems to be skating on a transparent blue ice; he or she has the sense that one is able to see to the bottom of a frozen pond; there are no impediments either to progress or to vision. Then — one is not sure just when or how — there is a thickening of texture or of color within the water, the suggestion of a shadow, but the reader is moving too fast to make it out. Suddenly, however, one is sure: In the water there is the form of a monster swimming — but blink, and it is gone. The day has been fundamentally altered. The pond is no longer merely frozen water. It is a sinister lens that focuses deeply; unnamable menaces lurk on the peripheries but do not show themselves clearly.

And what is it that Braun seems to say in his telling? There is some sort of point being made, some kind of theme being discussed, some overtly philosophical statement being asserted. Terror inhabits the poem, but it is an embarrassing terror. Things on the surface seem to remain normal, and the reader suspects he is being foolish to be aware suddenly, in such ordinary circumstances, of his mortality. Everything is so very clear — and baffling. Yet one knows Braun has made his point. One can feel it, even if one cannot pin the point down in so many words, as the poet has done. Which is to say that Braun has said what he had to say in the only way it could be said — a reasonable definition of poetry.

These characteristics are major elements of that early poem, "Goose," which is a narrative of ordinary events that coagulate to terror, and a thematic discussion that refuses to settle into blunt statement. The two elements have remained as a constant in Braun's poetry and explain in part why it was not as dangerous for him as for most poets to include early poems in a collection published ten years later, especially a collection not labeled a selected or collected poems. The elements have allowed Braun a consistent excellence throughout his career. It is difficult to see a "development" in his style other than refinements of his original vision. It is as though he sprang full-blown from the forehead of his haunted Muse and set immediately to work developing a microcosm of interrelated poems.

In "Goose" and many other poems these two elements are so closely fused that they are inseparable, but there is one poem in which the fusion never takes place. In "Flirt," reprinted, in *Children Passing*, unchanged from its periodical appearance, the narrative takes place in four stanzas and the theme is appended in an additional stanza. It is instructive to study this poem for, good as it is, it is not typical of Braun's procedure and effect, his blending of elements. Rather, it is to a degree typical of poems written by other poets of the 1950s.

Had Braun continued like this to write obviously good poems — one means "obviously" in both its major senses — he might have been perceived as merely a somewhat strange academic poet, but it was his intention to imitate the order of existence more closely. It may be, sometimes, that we experience something and then, afterwards, in an epiphany, learn something from the experience, but more likely what we learn is the experience itself. To tack meaning to the tail of experience is to moralize, and Braun appears to believe that there is not merely one essential truth latent in a particular experience. If our responses to experience are complex, then the poet must develop a mode of expression that is equal to its task. "Island Lore" from *Children Passing* is precisely this. It suffices as an example — easily followed, if not easily understood — of the fusion of the two elements:

>After a downpour sometimes you can hear
>trumpeting and hoots from deep in the bush.
>The winos at the station
>tell you it's elephants,
>but you know that's a lie.
>Ask a native and he'll claim a tree has
>gone mad. Even the placid breadfruit may
>become a man-eater,
>and if you pass too near
>the branches sweep at you.
>
>These natives marry with peculiar freedom.
>One lad I knew lived with a bag of stones,
>and I was present at
>the wedding of twin girls
>to abalone shells.
>If you inquire how despite this practice
>their race has avoided decimation
>they laugh and wink and quickly
>bring up some general topic
>as though you were a child.

There it is, the strange, clear narration, the ordinary language, the commonplace nightmare, the offhand tone, the large and ominous theme enigmatically stated. The reader does feel foolish, "like a child," because he suspects that perhaps he is being had by the natives unless, of course, they know something he does not, in which case he's a fool anyway. Another poem from the same book, "Are There Any Questions," illustrates the same fusion of simple narration and large, complex theme:

> I think we need no longer spot naiads
> or detect poltergeists
> to realize our intimate
> reverberations.
>
> This morning, I found something lodged in dust
> beside the bed. To all
> appearances it was my missing
> bicuspid or
>
> a piece of ginger root. But actually
> it was a thing, radically
> unidentifiable. I must
> confess: I've been
>
> inhospitable. I bit one appendage
> off; then, attempting to crush
> the whole thing, beat it; then quit, fearful
> of grief, or the noise,
>
> or of finding pain for pain somehow. I tried
> to move it out of sight,
> to cover it, but didn't manage.
> Now, I don't care.

This is a species of surrealism in which the ordinary — though it remains ordinary — is so transformed that the effect is extraordinary. Details are crystalline, hard-edged, yet the peripheries of vision loom forebodingly into existential terror. In his subsequent work Braun modified the nightmare, modulated it to a point where it is not so overtly surreal, and the effects are considerably more subtle and capable of handling layer upon layer of sensation and thought.

Richard Emil Braun and Vern Rutsala invented brands of surrealism that are quintessentially American and have almost nothing in common with the various pop brands of "deep image," Latinate surrealism that were imported wholesale into the common stock of the creative writing workshops during the 1970s. Braun is in the tradition of the foremost narrators of the enigma of existence. His forebears are writers like Nathaniel Hawthorne, Herman Melville, and Edgar Allen Poe who live next door to "An Unknown Friend" in *The Foreclosure*; they feed the headless goose.

Braun went his own way to become an inimitable American stylist hiding in Canada, outside the eddies and backwashes of American poetic fashion, while Rutsala sat quietly on the West Coast, among poets who received more and better press than he did, and dissected the American middle classes to greater effect than the Black Mountaineers, the Beat Generation, or the Deep Imagists were able to achieve. Few of the "middle generation" of poets can claim to have done as much, or to have developed styles so capable of large statement and nuance.

CHAPTER SIX
American Plainstyle

Another style of writing that developed during the 1950s and had exactly the opposite effect of surrealism was "plainstyle," and the person who was most responsible for it was Rutsala's elder stablemate at Lewis and Clark College, William Stafford. In his book *Style and Authenticity in Postmodern Poetry* Jonathan Holden said that in the Postmodern period poets have not turned away from a concern with form, only that they have in effect substituted genres for specific forms. "Deprived by the modernist revolution of any sure sense of what poetic form should be," Holden wrote, "poets have increasingly turned to nonliterary analogues such as conversation, confession, dream, and other kinds of discourse as substitutes for the ousted 'fixed forms,' substitutes which in many cases carry with them assumptions about rhetoric that are distinctly antimodernist. Indeed, it is through deployment of such relatively 'personal' analogues as conversation and confession that a substantial number of our poets are attempting to recover some of the favorable conditions for poetry which had seemed to obtain before the triumph of modernism." (11)

Thus, Modernism outmoded the ancient traditional forms, and to substitute for them poets, in effect, substituted genre and voice; that is to say, instead of choosing a specific lyric form like the sonnet, a poet might now choose to write in the genre of confession using lineated prose, and as a substitute for the thick sonic level of the lyric, invent and display a personal "voice" that perhaps pretended to be speaking confidentially to the reader, as in the case of Robert Bly. This is the theory behind what is being discussed here under the term "plainstyle."

"To talk sensibly about postmodern poetic form, instead of resorting to vague, 'organic' mystifications," Holden wrote, "we might better (1) recognize that postmodern poetic form is predominantly analogical; (2) extend the range of categories by which we refer to poems, using the analogues to name these categories. In fact, if an analogical poem is any good, the name of its formal 'category' will tell us far more about the poem than even a term like 'sonnet' or 'villanelle.'"

Although this is a good talking point, "analogical" form is not different from traditional genres and subgenres of poetry, as for instance the lyric, the narrative, the dialogue, to name the major genres, and such traditional minor genres as bucolics (pastoral poems), didactics (teaching poems), liturgics (poems of religious ritual, such as the prayer or the "sutra"; satirics, and so forth. Poetry has always had both fixed forms and general forms: the two major general forms of occasional poetry, for instance, are the ode and the elegy, but one may write specific fixed-form odes such as the Pindaric, homostrophic, or English odes, and one may write an elegy in set forms also, including the classical line called elegiacs. One learns different things from discussing "analogical" and "fixed" forms, as we may see in considering the work of William Stafford, among many others here.

William Stafford

Born in Hutchinson, Kansas, in 1914, Stafford took his B.A. from the University of Kansas in 1936. During World War II he was a conscientious objector active in pacifist organizations. His first book, *Down in My Heart* (1947), was not poetry; rather, it was a nonfiction chronicle of his pacifist experiences. After the war he returned to the University of Kansas and took an M.A. there the same year his book was published. The following year Stafford joined the faculty of Lewis and Clark College. He returned to graduate school again and took a Ph.D. from the University of Iowa in 1954, visited some schools for a few years, then went back to Lewis and Clark and remained there for the rest of his academic career except for excursions into other groves of academe and poesy.

Stafford's first published collection of poems was *West of Your City* which appeared in 1960 when the poet was forty-six years of age. Despite this very late start upon his career as a poet, Stafford's rise was rapid and steady thereafter. During a panel held at the 25th anniversary celebration of the Cleveland State University Poetry Center in October, 1986, Galway Kinnell announced that, in a poll conducted among poets by Judson Jerome for *Writer's Digest*, Stafford, a fellow panelist, had been named as the most popular poet in America — that is, popular among the poets polled, not a larger public.

The Rescued Year appeared in 1966, followed four years later by *Allegiances* (1970), and by *Someday, Maybe,* (1973); *Stories that Could Be True: New and Collected Poems* appeared in 1977. *Writing the Australian Crawl: Views on the Writer's Vocation,* Stafford's second book of nonfiction, was published in 1978.

Stafford was from the beginning a proponent of what has been called the "organic" poem, the theory of which was first enunciated — as noted earlier in these pages — by the 19th-century critic Ralph Waldo Emerson in his essay titled "The Poet." The idea of organic poetry is that the poem "chooses its own form" and grows like a plant or a conch, "naturally," in effect making itself up as it builds. The poet's job, then, according to this theory, is merely to listen, to feel his or her way into the language, to leave him or herself open to "encounters with language" so that the poet may respond when he or she feels a "nudge" toward some "larger pattern" — by which Stafford evidently meant something mythopoeic or archetypal. It then becomes the poet's job to record that pattern, though perhaps imperfectly.

Writing in Donald J. Greiner,'s *American Poets Since World War II*, Vol. 2 (1980), Steve Garrison discussed the essays in *Writing the Australian Crawl*: "For Stafford, the poet is a receiver of messages, or at least of impulses hinting at messages. He describes the act of writing as 'the successive discovery of cumulative epiphanies in the self's encounter with the world.' The poet relies totally on intuition to begin the process of composing; he is willing 'to accept the chances the moment brings.' While waiting for intuition to lead the way, he clears his mind of any obstructions, aiming for 'the exhilaration of discovery, the variety that comes as a result of being yourself.' Stafford's typical method of composing is to jot down whatever impulse comes to him...and then follow it. Sometimes it leads to meaningful associations, sometimes not. Such an open-ended thought process entails risks: most of Stafford's 'explorations' fail as poems." (293)

This was a remarkably Emersonian view and practice, particularly for a graduate of the Iowa Writers' Workshop who held two advanced degrees, one of them a doctorate. Paradoxically, Stafford long held the pedagogical opinion that teaching creative writing is impossible; all an instructor can do is encourage a student to encounter language and search for organic and mythopoeic patterns in his or her own way. In an essay, "The Minuet: Sidling Around Student Poems," written for Alberta Turner's *Poets Teaching*, Stafford said, "My first impulse, when confronted with a student's writing, is to become steadfastly evasive until some signal from the student indicates a direction where the student is ready to go. I want to become the follower in this dance, partly because of some principles about what can be truly helpful in such an interchange, and partly because I have learned that the area between us is full of booby traps: the writer may have many kinds of predispositions, hang-ups, quirks, needs, bonuses. How the student comes toward me across that area is a crucially important beginning for whatever dancing there is going to be." He continued, "The first move is the student's move, not mine." (43-44) One is reminded of the confession of John Holmes.

However, Stafford did not teach creative writing himself at Lewis and Clark; he wisely left that chore to his younger colleague and fellow Iowa alumnus Vern Rutsala. Nevertheless, Stafford spread his theories to many another graduate and undergraduate writing arts program in his travels, but despite his antiformal bias and his refusal or inability to criticize either students' or his own poems (Stafford has said publicly, "I've never met a poem of mine that I didn't like"), his work is clearly formal, as may be seen by examining an entirely typical Stafford work, the famous title poem from his award-winning book, *Traveling Through the Dark* (1962):

> Traveling through the dark I found a deer
> dead on the edge of the Wilson River road.
> It is usually best to roll them into the canyon:
> that road is narrow; to swerve might make more dead.

The speaker got out of the car to stand "by the heap, a doe" who had already begun to stiffen. He "dragged her off; she was large in the belly" because she was pregnant. "Her fawn lay there waiting, / still, never to be born." But what could be done?

> I thought hard for us all — my only swerving —,
> then pushed her over the edge into the river.

One can tell at a glance that this is a formal poem. The four quatrain stanzas with the concluding couplet coda cannot be missed. Every line is more or less iambic pentameter — "more or less" because, though all but one are certainly five-stress, there is a fair amount of metrical variation and the third line of stanza two might possibly be read as four-stress, depending on whether or not one hears an accent on the initial word "she."

Although the poem doesn't rhyme, there is a great deal going on the sonic level. Take the first stanza alone: There is alliteration (**d**ark, **d**eer, / **d**ead), consonance (*dead, edge; road, dead*), repetition (*dead, dead; road, road*) and consonantal echo, ars and dees especially.

Jonathan Holden wrote, "In this poem some of the possibilities of voice have been sacrificed for the sake of formal beauty.... The artifice, like the poem's conscious construction around the word 'swerve,' is unobtrusive yet constitutes a definite presence in our experience of the poem. The rules of the pattern leave Stafford enough flexibility to sound conversational, yet the poem manages, while sounding conversational, to remind one of poetry, one reason being that the accentual [?] prosody as deployed here by Stafford contains so many buried echoes of traditional prosody." (39-40)

All Stafford could reasonably claim is that he was not aware of what he had done; however, merely because he may not have "known" consciously what he was doing didn't mean he wasn't doing it. Certainly, Stafford's scholarly academic background made it difficult to credit such professed naiveté. Stafford also said both orally (in a Brockport "Writers' Forum" interview) and in print (in that interview published as "Keeping the Lines Wet" in *Prairie Schooner*), that he disliked figures of speech in poetry because they are too "literary," they get in the way of plain language, for writing is no more difficult than speaking, and speaking comes "naturally" to human beings. But then what does the reader do with the pun about "swerving" which is set up in the first stanza of "Traveling Through the Dark" and brought to the punch in the concluding couplet?

As to Stafford's own work, as distinguished from his theories of writing and his teaching practices, few would be likely to deny that he wrote some of the finest poems of his generation despite his "reluctance to learn a technique of poetry" if he didn't "have to." No doubt his editors had to make their own searches and appraisals and pull out of his string of more or less undifferentiated fish — caught while he was keeping his lines wet — a few finned creatures of firm flesh and full flavor.

Such, indeed, is what Thom Tammaro did for Stafford when he edited the poet's *Roving Across Fields*, subtitled "*A Conversation and* [nineteen] *Uncollected Poems, 1942-1982.*" There they lay still, those gentle iambics, beneath the "open forms" of his work; there were the sound effects still, even including rhyme, which was often internal. If Stafford's self-critical faculty was nearly non-existent, still there were the good poems among the rubble of his close encounters with the language. Unfortunately, in this volume there was primarily rubble. One wondered why his editor, on that occasion, allowed Stafford to resurrect ancient poems that no one had let him insert into volumes intervening between 1960 and 1983. No doubt the poems seemed to Stafford like old friends re-met.

David Wagoner

David Wagoner was born in 1926 in Massillon, Ohio. He attended Pennsylvania State University, where he studied under Theodore Roethke and from which he received his B. A. in 1947. Two years later he took an M.A. from Indiana University and subsequently taught at DePauw University for a year, 1949-50, then at his Alma Mater for four years, from 1950-54. In the latter year he went to the University of Washington in Seattle, which he has ever since maintained as his home base.

In David Wagoner's first book, *Dry Sun, Dry Wind* (1953), one could tell there was a promise of more than competence, though the prevalent competence of the poets of the 1950s was its main feature. The poems were well-written, structurally sound, not very experimental. Wagoner had a good ear, but one that was not better than many another. Yet even that was remarkable, perhaps, in a first collection. One thing was outstanding: In this book there was little self-conscious pose. Wagoner was at his ease; his language seemed natural — that is to say, it was truly artful — even in set pieces.

A Place to Stand (1958), Wagoner's next collection, seemed to go in two directions simultaneously. On the one hand there was greater formality of structure; on the other, a loosening up of language to the point, in certain poems, almost of jazz. One poem in particular, "'Tan Ta Ra,' Cries Mars," was a pivotal poem in the poet's development. In three sestet stanzas rhyming *abccba* there was so much sonic-level orchestration and virtuosity, yet such seeming naturalness, that the poem was a minor wonder of balance of experience (parades, wars, jazz bands), imagination (Mars as a drum-major), perception, and style. The direction in which this poem pointed was the way Wagoner took more and more often in his later books.

The Nesting Ground (1963) was one of the three or four finest books of the year in which it appeared. The thing most engaging about the poems contained in it was the music — not a lyrical kind usually, but a colloquial kind, as though the poems were rooted in the American language like oaks. Since the poems of this book were tight and formal, this seeming ease of movement was no mean indication of the degree to which Wagoner's art was developing.

That remained true of *Staying Alive* (1966), and particularly of the title poem, one of the finest georgics — versified handbooks in the arts or crafts — produced during the post-Modernist period. This poem subsequently became a standard anthology piece. Not only was it a handbook about staying alive in the real woods, it was a parable about how to stay alive as a human being and as a poet in an age increasingly antipoetic and inhumane.

The outdoors of the Pacific Northwest has been important to Wagoner, and it figures prominently in his work, both overtly and inwardly, manifesting itself at times as poems having to do with Native Americans and their lore, as in "Seven Songs for an Old Voice" which concludes his book *Sleeping in the Woods* (1974), and in *Who Shall Be the Sun* (1978) Wagoner personified natural forces and gave them Indian names in his retelling of the myths of the tribes.

Wagoner obviously followed his own advice about staying alive. Not only did he keep his voice, but he increased its strength. He did more than merely survive — his power grew from book to book, and the range of technique he came to command was impressive. The voice grew surer, subtler, more capable of nuance or oddness, of humor, irony, even controlled violence. The poems of his *First Light* (1983) were crisp and clear, the imagery evocative, the sensibility contemplative. They exhibited a keen sense of narrative, a deep insight into character, a photographer's eye for composition, and a painter's feeling for atmosphere, light, and color.

Nor did these qualities exhaust the attractions of one of the very best poets then writing in English. Wagoner developed an absolute sense of rhythm. His seemingly informal poems were expressions of a knowledge of pattern and sound so deep that one was unaware of the formalism of these pieces until one went back to reread them with critical eyes. When Wagoner chose to ignore punctuation, as in "The Bad Uncle," he did so for particular reasons — characterization, representation of situation and atmosphere, simulation of people's thought processes — and not out of a programmatic adherence to an idiosyncratic style. The subjects treated in this book were as wide-ranging as the techniques. Finally, the reason for Wagoner's not being given his due among contemporary critics has come clear: He did too many things too well to be ignored, but for the same reasons he was not easy to categorize. Although he could write plainstyle when he wanted to do so, he could also write — for example — like a drunk, as he did in "Out for a Night," from *The Nesting Ground*:

> It was No, no, no, practicing at a chair,
> And No at the wall, and one for the fireplace,
> And down the stairs it was No over the railing,
> And two for the dirt, and three Noes for the air,
>
> And four in a row rapidly over the bar,
> Becoming Maybe, Maybe, from spittoon to mirror,
> It was shrugging cheeks on one face after another,
> And Perhaps and So-So at both ends of a cigar...,

until Wagoner leaves us lying, exhausted and delighted, under the last line.

Richard Hugo

A poet who consistently gave readers a blend of personality and story was Richard Hugo who was born in 1923 in Seattle and served as a bombardier during the Second World War. He took his B. A. degree in 1948 in his home town from the University of Washington where, he wrote (in Heyen), "In the fall of '47 and winter of '48, I studied under Theodore Roethke who had just come to Washington." (123) He earned an M.A. four years later, in 1952. He was an employee of the Boeing Corporation in Seattle until 1963, but in 1964 he took his first and only academic position at the University of Montana in Missoula. He died unexpectedly in 1982. In the posthumous 1984 volume *Making Certain It Goes On* it was possible to see the whole life and life's story of one of America's more interesting contemporary poets.

Hugo's first book, *A Run of Jacks*, was published in 1961. His second, third, and fourth collections appeared subsequently at four-year intervals: *Death of the Kapowsin Tavern*, in 1965; *Good Luck in Cracked Italian* in 1969, *and The Lady in Kicking Horse Reservoir* in 1973. Others followed at frequent intervals until his death: *What Thou Lovest Well Remains American* appeared in 1975, *31 Letters and 13 Dreams* in 1977, and his two last collections, *White Center* and *The Right Madness on Skye* were issued in 1980.

Hugo had to contend with being called by some critics a "regional" poet — what would have been called a "local colorist" at the turn of this century. Perhaps one of the reasons for this type-casting is the fact that he appeared in an anthology titled *Five Poets of the Pacific Northwest* edited by Robin Skelton in 1964 — two of his bookmates were Carolyn Kizer and David Wagoner, and perhaps some of the problems they, too, have had with being accepted by their peers have the same basis. "I'm aware," Hugo wrote in his contribution to William Heyen's *American Poets in 1976*, "of the dangers of locating poems too close to home. Too much memory remains to interfere with the imagination." (126)

It is true that many if not most of Hugo's poems are set in the Pacific Northwest of the United States, where he had his roots and most of his experience. As Richard Howard wrote in his essay on "Richard Hugo" in his book of criticism titled *Alone with America* (1969), "To attach the label regional to enterprises of more ambition and moment than publicity campaigns is to qualify a man's poetry, for example, as anything but central." (232) Yet not all of Hugo's experience took place within a limited area, nor is that area all that he wrote about. As Geoff Hewitt noted (in Vinson), "Hugo's awareness of ruined civilizations is especially evident in *Good Luck in Cracked Italian,* a depressing travelogue, poems written upon his first visit to Italy since the [Second World] war, when he was a flyer. Hugo's poems in this book express guilt and the sense that since the war many cities have become ugly through both physical and spiritual ruination. Neon and greed have absorbed a finer culture. Each poem finds new human metaphors to express this theme." (753) The second stanza of "The Bridge of Sighs" is an example:

> Here we see a claw mark of despair
> ripe as those mosaic walls outside.
> We hear the sobbing of a mind gone wrong
> from years of hearing water pound
> on stone, unseen, ten feet away.

The method of this poem is that of William Stafford — loosely iambic conversation; the style is plainstyle. Very little change took place between Hugo's early and late poems — here is another example, "Gray Stone," from the section of new poems in his posthumous collected poems:

> A gray stone does not change color wet
> or dry. Baked on a scorched road or shaded
> by cedars, underground or tossed
> into a bright green sky, it's always gray.
> It is the stone of earth, of the down-to-earth
> no nonsense way of knowing life
> does not often of its own volition provide.
> A gray stone will not
> change your luck or shorten the mortgage
> or make you young again. It doesn't say
> "now" to investments — money or love.
> It doesn't say "no" when you plot wrong things
> you are sure you must do with your life
> or die from the drone. Keep one gray stone
> in a secret place, and when those you love
> are broken or gone, listen
> with a sustained, with a horrible attention
> to the nothing it has always had to say.

Jonathan Holden wrote that he finds himself calling this sort of writing "'a vernacular poetry of personal ethos,' a low mimetic mode of poetry whose tradition leads from Whitman and Wordsworth through Hardy and Frost to such contemporaries as William Stafford, Richard Hugo, and Denise Levertov." (5) Later Holden explained his concept of contemporary "form," as distinguished from traditional "fixed form," for if someone objects that "the form of most contemporary poems does not fit any known category," then his "answer to this is that our poems do fit formal categories — categories which poets are quite aware of but which, because the aesthetics of modernism has generated so much (often deliberate) mystification, have remained implicit." (16)

Dave Smith has a different way from that of Holden of classifying the work of Hugo. In his essay titled "Richard Hugo: Getting It Right," from his book *Local Assays* (1985), Smith wrote, "I had been rereading Richard Hugo's poems during the 1979 World

Series in which the all but trounced Pittsburgh Pirates made a stunning and memorable comeback to win going away. I remarked to a friend watching that last televised game that Hugo was the George Raft of poetry. I meant to imply that Hugo was a player of tough-guy roles. My friend, without blinking, said that Hugo was instead closer to the manager of the Pirates, or would be if he chewed. We were, I think, both right because Hugo as poet is the creator of scenes whose players are always constructed figures that speak with Hugo's unmistakable voice." (105)

Hugo himself had yet a third perception of the way in which he composed. In *American Poetry Observed* (1984), edited by David Bellamy, David Dillon interviewed Hugo and asked him," As you worked on the 'Letter' poems, and did more of them, did you notice any changes in the way you wrote? I sensed a greater relaxation in them not only in tone but also in structure. They seem more open." (103)

Hugo replied, "Well, I've gone back to more conventional poems now. But it is true that I'm more open than ever in the poems, though not necessarily as direct as I was in the 'Letter' poems. I still like to write a very conventional poem in stanza form like 'The Art of Poetry.' I like to make big jumps in poems and I like to hear all the little sounds rattling around. And in a rather strict framework like that, a stanza pattern, I find that my imagination loosens up a great deal, and I can move around fast. Like a worm on a hot rock, as they used to say out West."

In his essay "Poetry: Dissidents from Schools," from *The Harvard Guide to Contemporary American Writing*, which he edited, Daniel G. Hoffman wrote that the poem titled "'Degrees of Gray in Philipsburg' epitomized Hugo's obsessed concentration upon the bleak, used-up industrial towns of the American West, where the defeated and the lost summon up the consolations of reality in supple blank verse. *31 Letters and 13 Dreams...* uses this style for the dreams, a longer line for the letters addressed to other poets. These epistles are autobiographical explorations, pitched in the same gray key as the earlier work." Perhaps, then, one might sum up Hugo as a poet who might have been seen to be a confessional poet had he not also been perceived as a tough guy who wrote, in a down-to-earth plainstyle, poems that were, in effect, double-exposure word-photographs of depressed landscapes with a depressed inner landscape superimposed upon them.

CHAPTER SEVEN
Abstractionism

The great abstract poet among the Modernists was Wallace Stevens, and the great abstract poem was T. S. Eliot's *The Waste Land* as it was edited by Ezra Pound. The tradition goes farther back in American history than that, however, to the poetry of Emily Dickinson in the nineteenth century, and a clear theory of abstract syntax has existed since 1958 with the publication of the British poet and critic Donald Davie's *Articulate Energy*. Davie discussed the forms of syntax — word order in the sentence — in English language poetry.

Briefly, Davie said that there were three kinds of syntax traditionally: "subjective" syntax has the word order in a sentence following the form of a thought in the mind of the poet ("I am in love with darkness"); "objective" syntax has the word order following the form of an action ("John drew his pistol and shot the mad dog"); "dramatic" syntax has the word order following the form of a thought in the mind of a persona invented by the poet ("To be, or not to be, that is the question" Hamlet says, not Shakespeare).

Davie then spoke about other, non-traditional kinds of syntax, mainly to be found in the twentieth century, especially in such a poet as Stevens who wrote in what Davie called "musical" syntax, by analogy with music which is the most abstract of the arts (that is, there are no "meanings" attached to musical notes, yet they are arranged as "ideas" when a composer composes). However, the syntax might better be called "abstract" syntax, by analogy with nonrepresentational art, for such art dispenses with representational form in an attempt to approach the condition of music. Furthermore, the term "musical" might be confusing to the reader who may think that it refers to such elements of the sonic level of poetry as rhyme and meter. For the sake of clarity on this point the terms "egopoetic" for subjective, "narrative" for objective, and "abstract" for musical have sometimes been used.

"Abstract" syntax, then, follows the form of a thought in the mind of the poet, but without defining that thought. Thus, abstract poets paint word pictures which are not meant to be "understood" or "followed" in the ordinary sense; rather, the reader is to give himself or herself up to the poet just as an audience gives itself up to the sounds of the orchestra. Abstract poetry attempts to follow the dictum of Archibald MacLeish in his "Ars Poetica" which states that "A poem should not mean, but be." Or, to quote a couple of lines from the L=A=N=G=U=A=G=E poet Lyn Hejinian's chapbook *The Guard*, "The chronic idea turns up / a sunny day as an arresting abstract." The L=A=N=G=U=A=G=E poets constitute a nationwide extension, during the mid-to-late 1980s, of the abstract practice of the New York School, though in some of its members there is a left-wing political component added, especially among the San Francisco branch of the school, which during the period of its early expansion began feuding with Robert Duncan and the old-guard of the San Francisco-Beat school.

Wallace Stevens' poem "Not Ideas about the Thing but the Thing Itself" will serve as an example of abstract syntax. The first stanza is a statement. "At the earliest ending of winter, / In March, a scrawny cry from outside / Seemed like a sound in his mind." The poem is a narrative, then, and if it were a piece of prose fiction we would say that its narrator is the author telling a story in the third person from a single angle (one person is followed in the poem) and with subjective access — that is to say, the author knows not only what is going on in his protagonist's vicinity, but in his mind as well.

The second stanza tells the reader that the protagonist of the poem was sure, despite the sound's seeming location "in his mind," that its true origin was at dawn or just before, "In the early March wind." "The sun was rising at six, / No longer a battered panache above snow... / It would have been outside." Of course it would. The season was advancing, and the sun no longer appeared to be a bedraggled plume of feathers worn by the winterscape. But there is a suggestion — an overtone — here that the bird, the utterer of the cry, might itself be a panache, battered or otherwise; might, in fact, be the voice of the rising sun.

The protagonist could be sure that the sound he had heard was not the echo of a dream, a voice "not from the vast ventriloquism / Of sleep's faded papier-mâché..." because surely "The sun was coming from outside."

"That scrawny ['battered,' 'bedraggled'] cry — " was the utterance of "A chorister" whose note, a "c[,] preceded the choir[,]" that is to say, the full chorus of daylight. And it was, indeed, "part of the colossal sun" after all, the voice of the world of reality, not of dream or imagination, which would reach full throat in the daylight when the sun would be "surrounded by its choral rings, / Still far away." The pun on "choral rings" is evident. The sun is a volcanic atoll in the oceanic sky, surrounded by sound and living things. "It was like / A new knowledge of reality," Stevens says in a simile. The thing itself, the "scrawny cry," was like a knowledge of reality to the listener at dawn, but it was reality in and of itself. That is the thing the listener, the narrator, and the reader must understand.

Radcliffe Squires

Radcliffe Squires was born in Salt Lake City, Utah, in 1925, and he attended college, the University of Utah, in his home town, taking his B.A. there in 1940. During the war, from 1941 to 1945, he served in the U.S. Navy. Upon his discharge he attended the University of Chicago, where he took his A.M. in 1945, and Harvard University, where he was awarded a Ph.D. in 1952. His academic career began at Dartmouth College where he taught for two years, from 1946-48. In 1952 he went to the University of Michigan where he taught for the rest of his life and for part of that time edited *The Michigan Quarterly Review*. Squires self-published *Cornar*, his first book of poems — juvenilia — in 1940 at the age of fifteen. *Where the Compass Spins*, which appeared in 1951, was the first book of his mature poems; his second would not appear for another fourteen years, however, and those were years of swift change in the world of American poetry. Squires spent them developing and maturing as a poet.

The dust jacket of Squires' second collection, *Where the Compass Spins*, characterized his verse as clear and astringent. Beside *Fingers of Hermes* (1965), however, the first book seems not so much astringent as forcibly pared down. It was the work of an essentially romantic poet early in his career attempting to write in a more or less "classical" manner with few frills, few variations in diction or syntax, some annoying mannerisms, and some general awkwardness and uncertainly, rather like a would-be organist practicing the harpsichord. In *Fingers of Hermes* all that disappeared. There was a great deepening of talent. It is remarkable how many things had changed in Squires' methods of composition and ways of seeing. The jacket of the book quoted Richard Eberhart to the effect that Squires was "almost Keatsean" and sometimes "reminiscent of Hart Crane," but his work more nearly resembled that of a latter-day Shelley, not Keats, and it was reminiscent of two other American poets — the 19th-century Frederick Goddard Tuckerman and Wallace Stevens.

In Tracy Chevalier's *Contemporary Poets*, Fifth Edition, Squires is quoted as saying, "Technically my verse tends to fall into blank verse with occasional or accidental rhyme. I am not a formalist, but I should feel sheepish to turn out a poem with less metrical discipline than iambics provide. Even so, if I should have to choose between meter and metaphor, I should take metaphor, for metaphor seems to me the essence of poetry, the poem within a poem. Luckily, poetry never insists on taking one thing or the other. I believe there are colorings in my verse that come from Thomas Hardy, Robinson Jeffers, T. S. Eliot, Wallace Stevens, W. H. Auden, and C. P. Cavafy. At any rate, I have admired these poets very deeply." (950)

Thus, in his own words, Squires made the connection between Stevens and himself, and in his "Foreword" to Frederick Goddard Tuckerman's *The Complete Poems* (Oxford, 1965), Yvor Winters made the connection between Tuckerman and Stevens. (xiv) There is the same sort of relationship between Stevens and Squires who was a late exemplar of a specific abstract tradition in American poetry. This tradition has several sources, and some of them are the Romantic poetry of Shelley via New England and Tuckerman;

through Stevens, who reinforced the latent, rather French, symbolist influence in the genre — "latent, rather French" because, as Winters pointed out, Tuckerman's mystique was of the kind that motivated Rimbaud, Mallarmé, and others, though the American poet wrote in isolation from Continental influences. What this means is that Squires in his second book was concerned with abstraction and lush language. As in Stevens, the reader's interest centers on the language. As illustration, here are two poems, only one of them by Squires:

> As one turned around on some high mountain top
> Views all things as they are, but out of place,
> Reversing recognition, so I trace
> Dimly those dreams of youth and love and stop
> Blindly; for in such mood landmarks and ways
> That we have trodden all our lives and know
> We seem not to have known and cannot guess:
> Like one who told his footsteps over to me
> In the opposite world and where he wandered through
> Whilst the hot wind blew from the sultry north —
> Forests that give no shade, and bottomless
> Sands where the plummet sinks as in the sea,
> Saw the sky struck by lightning from the earth,
> Rain salt like blood, and flights of fiery snow.

And the second:

> Granite has a face of mere memory, and so insanely pure
> Is the memory that at times the world seems to humor it
> With long summer rains that swell the meadows to a dour
> Tundra. Through boreal mists, tufts of coptis float
> As a languid announcement that the ice-age is here.
>
> These storms repent as slowly as ideas. Blue starfish may
> Appear in clouds, and saffron lines of light
> Take soundings, but the rains return, and angrily.
> Even when the sky breaks and the ice-age retreats,
> Shadows of clouds brush dusk across the nervous day.
> The cloud shadows! Birds drowse and fall to wan
> Night twitters. White moths stir up from nowhere to churn
> The dusk. And you wait until you feel the day come on
> Again. Then as if you were the soldiers in Xenophon,
> Who did not gain the sea, you whisper blankly, "The Sun."

It is tempting to ask, who wrote which? — the twentieth-century Squires, or the nineteenth-century Tuckerman. Taken out of context this way, the question is unfair, and the intimation might be that Squires, who wrote "Summer Storms," the second poem, is merely imitating Tuckerman, whose "Sonnet VIII (Third Series)" appears first. But this is not the case. It is merely that both men saw and spoke in similar ways. Squires perhaps knew little or nothing of Tuckerman who has dwelt in historical obscurity for nearly a century. If one were to read all the poetry of the two men one would find differences enough. What is illustrated here is that Squires is not unique, that his beauties and graces have a tradition and a history in American letters, interesting ones.

The reader can find things both in these poems and in their tradition to which he or she might object: When and if one manages to get beneath the surface of the language there is vagueness, not merely abstraction; a cloying quality; a lack of range and depth, as in almost all of Stevens, and a humorless sincerity, as in Hart Crane.

In his later poems Squires tended to move farther away from traditional forms, even from his bedrock iambics, but he did no differently than many of his contemporaries of the period. And he tended, also, further toward abstraction, as in "A Letter from Crete to Delphi" which begins, "Three simple schemata / Three elegant models / Three configurations. // The carob trees are the form / of the wind. Like iron filings / Dusted on paper over a magnet / they translate a daimon."

The third strophe of the poem reads,

> The far hill village is a form.
> Like the absurdity of our skeletons,
> Its geometry enjoys
> Its carelessness. The whitewashed cubes
> Ascend beyond any meridian, bemusing the sun,
> Ascend and give themselves what
> No geometry can give itself: a name.

In a letter to Lewis Turco dated 8 July 1966 Squires wrote, "As to this abstract business.... I don't pretend to speak for anyone else, particularly Stevens, but in my own case, it begins oddly enough in the most concrete kind of experience. But because the experience seems alluring and suggestive I keep surrounding it with words in the hopes that something of its intrinsic mystery or difficulty will finally come through. That I don't consciously begin with abstract notions makes all this at least ironical...."

A tradition in poetry is not necessarily identical with a school of poetry; however, and in the "Preface" to their *An Anthology of New York Poets* (1970), the editors Ron Padgett and David Shapiro protested a great deal against the idea that there was an abstractionist "New York School of Poets." In the first paragraph they wrote, "We happen to know almost all the poets in this book (there is one we have still to meet), and most of these poets know each other as well. Obviously, as editors we're going on the assumption that these acquaintances and friendships, these sharings of tastes and affections, are going to go a long way toward giving this book a sense of solidarity. It would be facile as well as misleading to see these poets as forming a 'School,' to pass them off as a literary movement." (xxix) A bit later on they said, "Perhaps we do protest too much, but this is to prepare ourselves for the gruesome possibility of the 'New York School of Poets' label, one which has been spewed forth from time to time by some reviewers, critics and writers either sustained by provincial jealousy or the bent to translate everything into a manageable textbookese." (xxx) They pointed out that few of the contributors had been born in New York City, though many lived there and it "remained for all of them a fulcrum they continue to use in order to get as much leverage as possible in literature,...." The editors continued, "And, although the New York School tag is an alarmingly useless one, it does remind one that many of these poets met in schools, at Harvard, Columbia, N. Y. U. or the New School, sometimes as undergraduates taught by Delmore Schwartz or in poetry workshops taught by Kenneth Koch, Bill Berkson or Frank O'Hara. The crisscrossing of friendships is surprising and inspiring."

Rather than heading off critics and scholars at the pass, the editors of the anthology appeared to be expending words at a great rate to define categorically what a "school of poets" in fact is. Padgett and Shapiro did not blink, either, at providing a document, "Personism: A Manifesto," written by one of the pillars of the movement, Frank O'Hara. (xxxi-xxxiv) Among many personal observations and remarks, O'Hara focused on the central idea of the New York School: "Abstraction in poetry...is intriguing," he remarked. "Abstraction (in poetry, not in painting) involves personal removal by the poet. For instance, the decision involved in the choice between 'the nostalgia of the infinite' and 'the nostalgia for the infinite' defines an attitude towards degree of abstraction. The nostalgia of the infinite representing the greater degree of abstraction, removal, and negative capability (as in Keats and Mallarmé). Personism, a movement which I recently founded and which nobody yet knows about interests me a great deal, being so totally opposed to this kind of abstract removal that it is verging on a true abstraction for the first time, really, in the history of poetry. Personism is to Wallace Stevens what *la poesie pure* was to Beranger." (xxxiii)

Frank O'Hara

Frank O'Hara was born in the city of Baltimore, Maryland, in 1926, a contemporary of his fellow townsmen Karl Shapiro and Adrienne Rich. During the Second World War he served in the U. S. Navy from 1944 to 1946, and afterwards he attended Harvard where, at first, he majored in music and then switched to English studies. He was one of the founders of the Cambridge Poets' Theatre. O'Hara entered graduate studies at the University of Michigan where he won a major Hopwood Award for his poetry and a play, *Try! Try!* which was later produced, with another play, at the Poets' Theatre, together with John Ashbery's masque *Everyman*, for which O'Hara wrote the score.

When he had finished his education O'Hara moved to New York City where he joined the staff of the Museum of Modern Art in 1951. As writing became a larger part of his life, he left this position but later returned, in 1955, and five years later became an assistant curator of the collection. He not only assisted in important traveling exhibits, but organized exhibitions by major contemporary artists; he wrote books about them as well, including *Jackson Pollock* (1959) and *Robert Motherwell* (1965). Like that of his friend Ashbery, O'Hara's first book, *A City Winter, and Other Poems* (1952), was published, not by a regular literary publisher, but by the Tibor de Nagy Gallery. O'Hara collaborated with various artists in some of his books which include *Oranges* (1953), *Meditations in an Emergency* (1957), a long poem titled *Second Avenue* (1960), *Odes* (1960), *Lunch Poems* (1964), and *Love Poems (Tentative Title)* (1965). His work, together with that of other New York School poets appeared in the Donald Allen anthology *The New American Poetry 1945-1960* (1960), and these people have thus been associated with the Black Mountain, San Francisco, and Beat movements, but they are quite different. Allen edited and compiled a chronology for the posthumous *The Collected Poems*; he described the poet's death in 1966 thus:

> "In the early morning of July 24 he was struck and gravely injured by a beach-buggy on the beach of Fire Island. Taken to Bayview Hospital in Mastic Beach, L. I., he was given massive transfusions and underwent exploratory operation, but his condition deteriorated and he died at 8:50 the evening of the 25th. On the 28th he was buried in the Springs cemetery, near East Hampton. Larry Rivers, Bill Berkson, and Edwin Denby, Director of the Museum of Modern Art, delivered eulogies; John Ashbery read from his poems; and Allen Ginsberg and Peter Orlovsky chanted sutras over his grave. On his tombstone is carved 'Grace to be born & live...'." (xvi)

O'Hara had written in the Allen anthology, "I am mainly preoccupied with the world as I experience it, and at times when I would rather be dead the thought that I could never write another poem has so far stopped me. I think this is an ignoble attitude. I would rather die for love, but I haven't." (419) Ashbery, in his introduction to *The Collected Poems*, said of O'Hara that "...his poetry is anything but literary. It is part of a modern tradition which is anti-literary and anti-artistic, and which goes back to Apollinaire and the Dadaists, to the collages of Picasso and Braque with their perishable newspaper clippings, to Satie's *musique d'ameublement* which was not meant to be listened to." (vii)

Later Ashbery made even clearer the connection of O'Hara's abstract poetry with the abstract art of music and with 20th-century abstract art: "Frank O'Hara's concept of the poem as the chronicle of the creative act that produces it was strengthened by his intimate experience of Pollock's, Kline's, and de Kooning's great paintings of the late 40s and early 50s,..." (viii-ix) In her book *Frank O'Hara: Poet Among Painters* (1977) Marjorie Perloff quoted from and discussed a passage from *Second Avenue* which had to do with a description of a painting of Grace Hartigan:

> Grace destroys
> the whirling faces in their dissonant gaiety where it's anxious
>
> lifted nasally to the heavens which is a carrousel grinning
> and spasmodically obliterated with loaves of greasy white paint
> and this becomes like love to her, is what I desire
> and what you, to be able to throw something away without yawning
> "Oh Leaves of Grass! o Sylvette! oh Basket Weavers' Conference!"
> and thus make good our promise to destroy something but not us.

"Notice," Perloff wrote, "how O'Hara's heterogeneous images and syntactic dislocations 'imitate' the process of painting itself. The pronoun 'it' ('It's anxious') has no antecedent, the relative clause 'which is...' no specific referent, and yet we are told that 'this' (the 'dissonant gaiety'? the 'heavens' seen as a 'carrousel'? the 'loaves of greasy white paint'? or all these things taken together?) becomes 'like love to her' and is also 'what I [the poet] desire.' The shorthand phrase 'and what you' in line 6 again shifts perspective: 'you' is now Grace herself; her painting is all she desires it to be — a structure of 'wildly discordant images' that manages to avoid all bombast ('Oh *Leaves of Grass*! o Sylvette! oh Basket Weavers' Conference!'), that can deconstruct ('throw away without yawning') pure abstraction in favor of heterogeneity ('Images...hitherto repressed,' 'chaotic brushwork and whirling impasto,'..that is charged with personal passion ('and thus make good our promise to destroy something but not us')." (78-79) One thing that Perloff missed on the sensory level, however, was the pun between Whitman's *Leaves of Grass* and the "*loaves of greasy* white paint" [emphasis added], and that between "Grace," "Grass," and "greasy."

Ashbery continued in his introduction to the *Collected Poems*, "Frank also listened constantly to music.... We were both tremendously impressed by...John Cage's 'Music of Changes,' a piano work lasting over an hour and consisting, as I recall, entirely of isolated, autonomous tone-clusters struck seemingly at random all over the keyboard." "This climate...just about any music, in fact — encouraged Frank's poetry and provided him with a sort of reservoir of inspiration: words and colors that could be borrowed freely from everywhere to build up big, airy structures unlike anything previous in American poetry and indeed unlike poetry, more like the inspired ramblings of a mind open to the point of distraction." Here is "June 2, 1958":

> Oh sky over the graveyard, you are blue,
> you seem to be smiling! or are you sneering?
> under the captured moss a little girl
> is climbing, come closer! why it's Maude,
> or Maudie as she's sometimes called. I think
> she is looking for her turtle. Meanwhile,
> back at Patsy Southgate's, two grown men
> are falling off a swing into a vat of Bloody Marys.
> It's Sunday and the trains run on time. What
> a wonderful country it is, so black and blue
> airy green, leaning out a window
> thinking of the sea and the uncomfortable sand!

"Like Whitman," Alan Feldman wrote in his study, *Frank O'Hara* (1979), "O'Hara makes use of as broad a poetic diction as possible, incorporating the details of his experience, no matter how homely or shocking. At times, O'Hara's poetic speech is the 'queertalk' of homosexuals; when it is not, it is still, more generally, the language of a man who cares more about his feelings and his relationships than about moral or societal conventions. But while, for the most part, O'Hara's language is that of the everyday, of the interpersonal, it is also a poetic language seeking to confer heightened significance upon ordinary experience. Surreal, dreamlike images add a sense of aesthetic and psychological complexity; the poems are also infused with a sense of 'design' — an attention to verbal surface that counteracts any tendency to fall into too-easy patterns of thought and feeling." (46)

Discussing the Donald Allen and the Donald Hall-Robert Pack-Louis Simpson anthologies, Donald Barlow Stauffer in his *A Short History of American Poetry*(1974) said, "Most observers of the contemporary scene agree that there are two, or possibly three groups into which it is possible to fit the poets writing today, corresponding roughly to the Allen and Hall anthologies. These are known variously as the Academics and the Beats, the Palefaces and the Redskins, the Establishment and the Underground, or the Conservatives and the Liberals. Such obviously crude labels can only suggest rather than define the kinds of distinctions that the poets themselves and their readers tend to make.

"But they do call attention to the fact that in poetry, as in the other arts, there is an official culture, an unofficial one, and an interaction between them: one looking toward the past, the other passionately denying it; one emphasizing form and ideas, the other, freedom of form and feelings." More will be said on this subject in the 1961 WBAI-FM interview contained in the Appendix of this book, "The Sullen Art," conducted by David Ossman, a collaborator of Donald Allen.

If O'Hara was the complete iconoclast, a leader of the revolution against the old and the past and in favor of the new and the now, his friend John Ashbery was more complexly ambivalent in his approach to the composition of poetry and, in particular, to traditional form. Although he was represented in the 1960 Donald Allen "Redskin" anthology, the level of Ashbery's sophistication was high and he was also well-represented by formal poems in the 1986 Dacey-Jauss "Paleface" anthology *Strong Measures*; thus, he had a foot in the two camps and might be considered to be a unifying, rather than a schismatic, figure, one who is equally conventional and controversial to both groups.

John Ashbery

Born in Rochester, New York, in 1927, Ashbery was never an academic. He took his B. A. from Harvard in 1949 and two years later an M. A. from Columbia University where he studied French literature. He did postgraduate work briefly at New York University 1957-58, worked in publishing, then went to France from 1960-65 as an art critic for the Paris edition of the New York *Herald-Tribune* and *Art News*, of which he subsequently became an editor. He returned to New York City in 1965.

Ashbery's first book, *Turandot and Other Poems*, was published by the Tibor de Nagy Gallery in 1953; despite this previous publication, he won the first book award of the Yale Series of Younger Poets for his *Some Trees* in 1956. The judge was W. H. Auden who chose the collection over that of Ashbery's friend, Frank O'Hara. Subsequent books were *The Poems* (1960), *The Tennis Court Oath* (1962), *Rivers and Mountains* (1966), *Selected Poems*, published in London in 1967, *The Double Dream of Spring* (1970), *Three Poems* (1972), *The Vermont Journal* (1975), and *As We Know* (1979).

"At North Farm," the first poem from his *A Wave* (1984), is a good example of the level of abstraction to be found in his poems:

>Somewhere someone is traveling furiously toward you,
>
>At incredible speed, traveling day and night,
>Through blizzards and desert heat, across torrents,
>through narrow passes.
>But will he know where to find you,
>Recognize you when he sees you,
>Give you the thing he has for you?
>
>Hardly anything grows here,
>Yet the granaries are bursting with meal,
>The sacks of meal piled to the rafters.
>The streams run with sweetness, fattening fish;
>Birds darken the sky. Is it enough
>That the dish of milk is set out at night,
>That we think of him sometimes,
>Sometimes and always, with mixed feelings?

A great many critics have complained about the difficulty of Ashbery's work; indeed, of all abstract poetry. Jonathan Holden says that he admires Ashbery's work "even though Ashbery's 'use' of poetry often seems...too limited — an Olympian, noncommittal language-play that refuses engagement or to make value judgments, poetry that issues from a universe in which one never has to go outdoors or discipline a child or change a tire, from a universe consisting entirely of texts. Yet when I choose to amuse myself in the ludic, whimsical, lyric weathers of discourse, I read Ashbery." (5)

Others have criticized Ashbery for being exactly what one would have expected he would not be and, in fact, never has been: an academic poet. In his "Foreword to Kelly's Grandchild," from his book of traditionally formal poems and satires *The Ballad of the Dollar Hotel and Other Poems*, Richard Nason wrote, "The Existential poetry of William Carlos Williams, sensible enough perhaps as a reaction to the heavy metaphysical burden of the poetry of Eliot, Pound and, to a lesser degree, Yeats, has in recent decades degenerated to the grudging gibberish of Ashbery and the vacuous, verbless maundering of [A. R.] Ammons. The highly remote, almost indecipherable content of this verse has remained of interest only to those who study it so they may become initiates in the elite academia where it is taught." (Intro.) But it is not at all certain that, as Nason says, Ashbery's poetry is "almost indecipherable'; much more likely is the possibility that it is totally indecipherable, as music is "indecipherable" even as it is enjoyable to listen to.

If Nason is categorical in his rejection of Ashbery, there is an ambivalence in Holden's attitude, almost as though he were abashed to like the poetry and unable to understand why he should do so against all reason. Raymond Carney wrote, in the first volume of Donald J. Greiner's book, "Ashbery has related a wry dialogue between himself and Kenneth Koch that is very much to the point: 'He asked me, "Does your poetry have any hidden meanings" And I said: "No." "Why Not?" "Because somebody might find out what they were and then the poems would no longer be mysterious"'." (14) Ashbery does not want to attach a "program" to his language music, as composers have done to their musical compositions from time to time. He wants to achieve in language, if he can, the mysterious pleasures of music by using abstract syntax.

It is interesting to note the use of the musical term "minor key" at the end of this passage from Carney's essay: "There is no shortcut through an Ashbery text; no possibility of skimming it for key passages. It is a wonderfully democratic verse. Just as in the poetry of Elizabeth Bishop, the result of Ashbery's almost absolute renunciation of architectonic structures and rhetorical heightening is a paradoxical heightening of everything, of even the most ordinary details, in the poem. The common and mean, at moments, can become almost transcendent in Ashbery as in Bishop, who achieve their grand Romantic moments, as William Carlos Williams did, in a minor key." (14)

Echoing Archibald Macleish's poem "Ars Poetica," Marjorie Perloff wrote, "Not what one dreams but how — this is Ashbery's subject. His stories 'tell only of themselves,' presenting the reader with the challenge of what he calls 'an open field of narrative possibilities'.... For, like Rimbaud's, his are not dreams 'about' such and such characters or events; the dream structure is itself the event that haunts the poet's imagination." (252)

Ashbery's method of composition may also explain something about how his poems manage to gather "mystery" to themselves. In an interview with Sue Gangel in Joe David Bellamy's book Ashbery said, "I write down phrases and ideas on pieces of paper which I then can't keep track of. I put them in a drawer, and sometimes I can't find them, and sometimes I use ones I've already used before and then I have to do something about that. I don't keep any journal. I write down things that seem suggestive to me when they occur and I think might be usable later on. Then if I can't find them, that's all right too because meanwhile I will have already started to think about something else." (19)

If Ashbery's syntax is "abstract," and if his method of composition is at the farthest remove from the mechanical or even the rational, nevertheless one may point out that the poet's approach to versifying is neither "ludic and whimsical," as Holden suggests, nor "academic," as Nason defines it in these post-deconstructionist days, nor is it entirely without "architectonic structure," as Carney would have it. If it were so, why do some of Ashbery's poems find themselves located in the anthologies of the so-called "New Formalist" movement that was underway in the United States during the 1990s? Formalism might once have been considered academic, back in the 1950s, but formal approaches to poetry had been banned from American poetry since then. Neoformalism was considered by the later academy to be either reactionary or revolutionary, depending on whether one was defending the "tradition of Whitman," as Diane Wakoski has termed it in her apologies for the status quo, or advancing the argument that form, whether traditional or experimental, is necessary to meaning, as Dana Gioia and the other New Formalists maintained.

But this description of Ashbery's method of composition is perhaps rule of thumb rather than categorical, for he had something a bit different to say when he described "Variation on a Noel," with its epigraph from the Christmas carol, "when the snow lay round about, / deep and crisp and even...", in Lehman's *Ecstatic Occasions, Expedient Forms*. (3-4) This poem is written in the form of a pantoum. In his comment on the poem in Lehman's book Ashbery said, "I first came across the word pantoum as the title of one of the movements of Ravel's 'Trio,' and then found the term in a manual of prosody. I wrote a poem called "Pantoum" in the early '50s; it is in my book *Some Trees*. 'Variation on a Noël is the only other time I have ever used the form. "The poem was written in December of 1979." (5) This is the first stanza:

> A year away from the pigpen, and look at him.
> A thirsty unit by an upending stream,
> Man doctors, God supplies the necessary medication
> If elixir were to be found in the world's dolor, where is

A pantoum is an accentual-syllabic Malayan form. Its lines may be of any specific length, in any particular meter, and it consists of an indefinite number of quatrain stanzas with particular restrictions: lines two and four of each stanza, in their entirety, are refrains — they become lines one and three of the following stanza, and so on. The rhyme scheme is interlocking. Stanza two of Ashbery's poem reads,

> A thirsty unit by an upending stream,
> Ashamed of the moon, of everything that hides too little
>   of her nakedness —
> If elixir were to be found in the world's dolor, where is none,
> Our emancipation should be great and steady.

"I was attracted to the form in both cases," Ashbery continued, "because of its stricture, even greater than in other hobbling forms such as the sestina or canzone. These restraints seem to have a paradoxically liberating effect, for me at least. The form has the additional advantage of providing you with twice as much poem for your effort, since every line has to be repeated twice." (5) The observation about the paradoxically "liberating" effect of writing in forms had been made by many poets over the years, but increasingly in recent years as young poets rediscovered formal poetry. Here is the penultimate stanza of "Variation on a Noël":

> And I have known him cheaply.
> Agree to remove all that concern, another exodus —
> A form of ignorance, you might say. Let's leave that though.
> The mere whiteness was a blessing, taking us far.

The poem can be ended in one of two ways, either in a quatrain the refrains of which are lines one and three of the first stanza in reversed order, or in a repeton couplet consisting of lines one and three of the first stanza in reversed order. Ashbery decided to end the poem his own way: lines one and three of the first stanza became lines two and four of the last stanza, in the same, rather than reversed, order:

> Agree to remove all that concern, another exodus.
> A year away from the pigpen, and look at him.
> The mere whiteness was a blessing, taking us far.
> Man doctors, God supplies the necessary medication.

Besides Lehman's collection, Ashbery's poems also appeared in the Neoformalist anthology *Strong Measures*, edited by Dacey and Jauss. One of these, the poet's original "Pantoum" from his book *Some Trees*, was included in the text as an example of that form. Also included are "Some Trees," the title poem of that collection, which serves as an example of what the editors call "nonce couplets" and "couplet quatrains"; and "Farm Implements and Rutabagas in a Landscape," a sestina, from *The Double Dream of Spring*. The poet has always been supposed to make leaps of the imagination that surprise the reader, to make associations that others perhaps would not have made. It is evident that the difficulty readers have with Ashbery and others of the New York School is that they jump from one association to another without intervening transitions — it is a modernist technique, one that Ezra Pound discovered in the original draft of T. S. Eliot's *The Waste Land* by editing out those transitions and leaving only the fragments and abstract syntax that mirror the fragmentation and technological leaps of the twentieth century. It is a technique from which Wallace Stevens forged a career of writing poetry for himself, not for readers, but that some readers loved anyway — some, not many, for modernist and contemporary poetry left the common reader behind, just as modern music has done.

David Shapiro noted in the chapter titled "The Meaning of Meaninglessness" in his study, *John Ashbery: An Introduction to the Poetry*, that "John Ashbery once took a course of lectures in music by Henry Cowell at the New School. Ashbery recalls Cowell remarking that the intervals in music become wider as music grows more sophisticated: 'for instance, if you compare "The Volga Boatmen" and the "Love Duet" in Tristan und Isolde you see how vastly wide the intervals have become; and the ear seemingly becomes accustomed to unaccustomed intervals, "as time goes by"'.... One cannot really anticipate the next note in many serial pieces, and this suspense is a fine quality of Ashbery's own work...."(16) It is, that is, and it isn't, depending on one's point of view... on whether one is Jonathan Holden, Richard Nason, David Shapiro, or someone else. One thing is certain, however: John Ashbery writes his poems in an abstract "musical syntax," and this syntax is sometimes to be found bottled in traditional lyric verse forms. This new kind of poetry began displacing Robert Bly's "deep imagism" as the "avant garde" movement of the 1980s. It made inroads on the West Coast where most of the so-called L=A=N=G=U=A=G=E poets resided, but in 1986 signs of a further spread became evident, through chapbook publications from the "alternative press" movement, to New England and the South in work by De Villo Sloan and the late George Butterick, two members of the second generation of Black Mountaineers from the State University of New York at Buffalo.

CHAPTER EIGHT
Neoformalism

In his review "Six Poets" in the Spring 1986 issue of *The Sewanee Review*, Thomas Swiss wrote, "New poems by young writers like Molly Peacock, Baron Wormser, Mary Jo Salter, and Richard Kenney exhibit meter and rhyme. Some of these poets have been dubbed New Formalists, but how does one tell the 'new' formalists from the 'old' if all these writers are mining the same traditions, exhibiting the same manners?"

The answer lay in that qualifier, "if," for of course all those poets did not "exhibit the same manners," though they did perforce "mine the same traditions," which are the traditions of literature in English: one could tell the Neoformalists from the old by getting to know the names of the people who wrote formally twenty-five years earlier, and the names of those who were in the 1980s struggling to throw off the prevailing anti-intellectual egocentrism of the preceding two decades and more.

Donald Justice

A native Floridian, Donald Justice was born in Miami in 1925 where he took his bachelor's degree from the University of Miami in 1945, the year the Second World War ended. He took his M. A. from the University of North Carolina at Chapel Hill two years later, then attended Stanford University, where he studied under Yvor Winters, from 1947-8, then transferred to the University of Iowa where he studied under Paul Engle and other members of the Writers' Workshop; he took his Ph.D. from Iowa in 1954. He taught at a number of places beginning with Iowa, with which he has been particularly associated because of several terms of residence there, but including Syracuse University and, finally, the University of Florida in Gainesville.

As a graduate student Justice was a member of John Berryman's class which included W. D. Snodgrass, and he was a colleague of Robert Lowell—all of these were original members of the "Confessional" school; Justice, however, was never pulled into the orbit of the Confessional poets despite his proximity to the group. All of these Iowa Workshop-affiliated poets had begun as formalists; Berryman, Snodgrass and Justice remained formal. Lowell—initially the most formal of the group — turned to lineated prose poems in his *Life Studies*, but to a degree he returned to formalism in his last books.

Justice's *The Summer Anniversaries* (1960), which appeared the year following publication of Snodgrass' *Heart's Needle* and Lowell's *Life Studies*, was winner of the 1959 Lamont Award of the Academy of American Poets. It is counted his first book, although an earlier collection which he has suppressed, *The Old Bachelor and Other Poems*, appeared in 1951. A chapbook, *A Local Storm* (1963), was next, then *Night Light* (1967). A second chapbook, *Sixteen Poems*, appeared in 1970, and a hardbound volume, but really a third chapbook, *From a Notebook*, in 1972. *Departures* was published in 1973, and in 1979 the *Selected Poems* appeared. A chapbook, *Tremayne*, was issued in 1984, and *The Sunset Maker: Poems/Stories/A Memoir* was published in 1987.

In *The Summer Anniversaries* there were several fine poems in the post-Modernist traditional style that was typical of many poets writing in the 1950s. "Anniversaries," the first piece, set the tone for what followed — the diction was deceptively simple and spare, but rich in its allusiveness. This poem reached back to past anniversaries in the poet's life, evoking a nostalgic wonder as it worked up to the present, when the poet realized that the portents of his past had not kept faith with an actuality that had once been future:

>   Thirty today, I saw
>   The trees flare briefly like
>   The candles upon a cake
>   As the sun went down the sky,
>   A momentary flash,
>   Yet there was time to wish
>   Before the light could die,

> If I had known what to wish,
> As once I must have known,
> Bending above the clean,
> Candlelit tablecloth
> to blow them out with a breath.

Cathrael Kazin, writing in her entry "Donald Justice" in the *Dictionary of Literary Biography Yearbook: 1983* edited by Mary Bruccoli and Jean W. Ross (1984, p. 267), said, "Justice has long been what is sometimes known as a poet's poet. The precision of his language, his fascination with poetic technique, and the meticulous and supple quality of his diction have all had a particular appeal for other practitioners — or at least those in a position to appreciate craft. Justice seems in turn to appreciate his primary audience: "'I don't mind thinking that it's mostly poets who read what I write.... It's better, surely, because they know a bit more about what I'm actually doing.' At the University of Iowa Writers Workshop, Justice's rigorous attention to language and his emphasis on control influenced poet-students."

"Song," the second poem in *The Summer Anniversaries*, had as its main feature the fact that it was unrhymed and used instead consonance and echo in the initial syllables of the endwords. The third poem, "To a Ten-Months Child," was similar except that it was written in triplet stanzas rather than a single strophe. Unfortunately, both poems exhibited overstated sentiment. Nostalgia was one of the emotions Justice evoked often and well in such poems as "Southern Gothic," "Beyond the Hunting Woods," "On the Death of Friends in Childhood," and "Landscape with Little Figures."

Justice used the sonnet form in this collection, but some examples were tours de force of technique, as for instance "Speaking of Islands," a sonnet in which the lines of the octave consonate rather than rhyme. The "Sonnet to My Father" was the craftiest of all in that it was made of repeated endwords in the fashion of the sestina; it is the one sonnet in which Justice most obviously lost his emotional balance.

Section two of *The Summer Anniversaries* began with the poem "Thus," a statement of the author's artistic intentions, which he lived up to often in the volume. This striking piece was made up of two nine-line stanzas, each of which used the same end-words, line for line. It turned to poetry's twin, music, for its metaphor, and it ended with, "Entering quietly, let each chastened string / Repeat the lesson she must get by heart, / And without much adornment. / Thus." The single word last line was quietly climactic. Justice was enunciating the doctrine of quietism, of minimalist poetry, toward which he would turn in *Night Light*.

There were influences visible in the poems of the first collection—Weldon Kees and Yvor Winters, to name two. "Sestina on Six Words by Weldon Kees," whose *Collected Poems* Justice edited in 1960, not only used Kees' endwords for this strict form, but the poem very strongly reminded one of Kees' own sestina, "After the Trial." Justice's "The Metamorphosis" recalled John Crowe Ransom's style and diction, even Ransom's poem "Captain Carpenter," in such lines as "Then owls cried out from the woods / And terrors of that ilk / So that the bitch at heel / A little moaned and whined...." "Variations on a Theme by James" was perhaps derivative also, but aside from the title the derivation was not clear, though the poem was wordy and rather artificially "poetic," both aspects of language that ran counter to Justice's inclination in subsequent work toward ellipsis and minimal statement. "Love's Stratagem" also recalled Ransom's "Captain Carpenter," especially in the last line, "Hands cut off at the elbow." It was, however, a good poem with an original insight into the love relationship—no easy thing to come by in poems of the genre. "Sonnet about P." harked back to Ransom in "Blue Girls." When it came time to make his choices for the *Selected Poems* Justice cut many of these poems. He also dropped "Southern Gothic," a quatorzain. It was a piece with a fine last line, "Red roses within roses within roses" which, if it echoed Gertrude Stein, in context gave touching point to the quality of nostalgia.

In *The Summer Anniversaries* Justice was a fine technician, although Kazin felt the craft was overdone, for she wrote that the volume "...contains a number of ornate and potentially unwieldy forms, especially sestinas and an idiosyncratic brand of the villanelle." (268) But she admitted that in certain pieces "...he appears to be delivering the nascent life of the forms, seeming to allow them to determine the direction of the poems. His attitude toward his own poems presents a contradiction: He is at once distanced and controlling —or perhaps able to control because distanced: 'I have in my poems conscientiously effaced my self, I think, if not my personality.'"

This perspective, which used to be called "aesthetic distance"—Wordsworth's definition of poetry as "emotion recollected in tranquillity"—was at odds with what was to come during the next two decades. But Justice would not resist change in his own work; indeed, in *The Summer Anniversaries* he was something more than merely a fine technician, for he exhibited considerable variety of form and approach. He could turn an archaism or inversion without looking awkward or old-fashioned; "Ladies by Their Windows," "In Bertram's Garden," "Anthony St. Blues," "A Winter Ode," and "On a Painting by Patient B" were all successful and moving examples of what can be achieved in formal structures, but "Counting the Mad," with its imaginative ingenuity, modulated the "This Little Piggy" nursery rhyme into a minor chord of subdued horror with such lines as these:

> This one looked at the window
> As though it were a wall,
> This one saw things that were not there,
> This one things that were,
> And this one cried No No No No All day long.

There were here and there, as in this poem, hints of a dislocation of reality that would soon become, under the maestroship of Robert Bly and others, the movement toward surrealism in contemporary poetry, though Justice himself would never fall strongly under the spell of the "deep image." Justice finished this volume, after many good things, with the syllabic "To Satan in Heaven." Unrhymed syllabics, which were beginning to appear in the work of at least one member of the Iowa Workshop in 1959 where Justice was then teaching, would be the prosody Justice used in *Night Light*; thus this poem, though it is too didactic and was not included in *Selected Poems*, may be viewed as a turning point in his evolution toward something other than rhymed accentual-syllabic verse.

A Local Storm contained a dozen untitled, numbered poems (not counting "To My Mother," the dedicatory poem). All but the dedication, some of them reworked, were included in *Night Light*. In this collection Justice wrote a spare line, and he wrote by the line, painstakingly. His determination to get the perfect word in the perfect place was close to absolute, and if he didn't succeed every time, he did so often enough to make this a remarkable volume. The nostalgic lyricism of his first book was present still, but the music had been absorbed by syllabic prosody so that the songlike quality of the new poems emerged in terms of image rather than meter and traditional form. In "Early Poems," a parody of his first work, Justice wrote,

> How fashionably sad my early poems are.
> On their clipped lawns and hedges the snows fall.
> Rains beat against the tarpaulins of their porches,
> Where, Sunday mornings, the bored children sprawl,
> Reading the comics before the parents rise.
> The rhymes, the meters, how they paralyze.
>
> Who walks out through their streets tonight?
> No one. You know these small towns, how all traffic stops
> At ten; the corner streetlamps gathering moths;
> And the pale mannequins waiting in the dark shops,
> Undressed, and ready for the dreams of men.
> Now the long silence. Now the beginning again.

What was left, in the newer poems, was a sense of compassion; what was gained was a hard, clean edge and a vision to match. *Night Light* contained a number of poems that became standard anthology pieces. In "To Waken a Small Person" Justice returned to the scenes of his childhood, even to his original nostalgia, but everything was pared to the bone, making its poignancy excruciating. Punctuationless, falling down the page like rain, these triplets addressed a sleeping child, urging him (or her) to "Wake up please open yourself / Like a little umbrella / Hurry the sidewalks need you...." Nothing can move or have its significance until the child rises and goes out into the rain where "The colors of traffic lights // Are bleeding bleeding wake up / The puddles of parking lots / Cannot contain such rainbows[.]"

In a section titled "American Sketches," dedicated to William Carlos Williams, Justice wrote two imagist poems that managed to catch the stark emptiness and loneliness of

American towns in the plains in word photographs that contain multitudes more than one would have thought possible in so brief a space. The poem titled "The Thin Man" was a self-portrait that did much the same sort of thing:

> I indulge myself
> In rich refusals.
> Nothing suffices.
>
> I hone myself to
> This edge. Asleep, I
> Am a horizon.

The double meanings of "refusals," where one might have expected the word "food" had Justice been writing about a fat man, and of "Nothing suffices," give this poem the allusive qualities of two haiku—in fact, the poem looks like a set of haiku, except that all lines are five syllables long where we would expect in haiku for the second lines to be seven.

The motif of self-effacement of this poem was carried through many poems that preceded and followed it in the book, and the forms of the poems augmented and intensified the diminution of the speaker's personality. In "The Missing Person" the theme was specifically addressed. It began, "He has come to report himself / A missing person." In such knife-edge structures as these poems exhibited, every word took on great significance— the first line might be read in at least two ways: "he has come to report, himself," or as it is written, without the commas. A question of identity becomes paramount, and it is unresolved by the last line, "This last disguise, himself." If there was ambiguity in the earlier poems, there were truly no answers in these. One would have to conclude that Justice had adopted a more modern voice and sensibility in *Night Light*. Things were no longer what they had seemed earlier to be.

"The Tourist from Syracuse," according to Justice in a Brockport Writers' Forum videotaped interview, was written long before the poet knew that he would be going to that city to teach. It was a chilling poem that addressed the prevalence of accident, or fate, or mindless terrorism in our contemporary lives. Built on an epigraph by John D. MacDonald — "One of those men who can be a car salesman or a tourist from Syracuse or a hired assassin" — the poem gave substance and personality to emptiness and angst. From the perspective of the loss of thirty-five Syracuse University students and two from the nearby S.U.N.Y. College at Oswego in the terrorist bombing at Christmas, 1988, of a Pan-Am jet liner over Lockerbie, Scotland, it is difficult for one to avoid calling this poem at least foreboding if not foreshadowing.

Two pieces in this collection that exhibited some of the poet's early leaning toward nostalgia were "Girl Sitting Alone at Party" — a prose poem in couplets, and "Poem for a Survivor." "Party" was too didactic, "A Local Storm" was discursive, and two poems, "Memo from the Desk of X" and "For a Freshman Reader" were both discursive and mildly satirical. "Narcissus at Home" was a rather arch monodrama. Nevertheless, the book as a whole did show that Justice had made a new beginning after *The Summer Anniversaries*.

All of the pieces in *Sixteen Poems* were included in *Departures*. The former volume did not inexorably continue the movement toward minimal poetry that was apparent in *Night Light*, although there were poems in it that were in the Williams Imagist tradition, in particular "ABC," "Things," some of the "Portraits," "Lethargy," and "Luxury." There were a few pieces, such as the "Three Odes," that moved farther toward prose as a vehicle than most of Justice's earlier work had done, but not nearly so far as many of his academic colleagues of the period had moved. A new influence was discernible in these — the neo-surrealist movement of the late 1960s, the school of Robert Bly. Overall, the chapbook concentrated on imagery in two modern traditions, but there were fewer truly telling pieces in it — it was not an improvement over *Night Light*.

Justice's next collection *From a Notebook*, on the other hand contained nothing but twenty exceedingly minimal poems, some of them being motes of one or two lines, all of them numbered rather than titled:

> 11
> And D, they say, no longer
> Hennas her nipples.

> 13
> Sentence from a spy novel—
> 'Maybe you know Bliss by another name.'

(This previous one was no doubt a "found poem.")

> 18
> M, opening my diary, found the pages blank.

In these poems perhaps the influence of the minimalist Robert Patrick Dana may be seen. The effect of these "notes" (or, formally, motes and epigrams) was sometimes humorous, sometimes clever, sometimes arch. They added little to Justice's stature, though they did not diminish it. The chapbook, like the other pamphlets, had a very small circulation, mainly among Justice's friends, fans, and former students. The poet included some of these reverberant short subjects in *Departures* as parts of two poems that concentrated the Imagist characteristic, "After the Chinese" and "From a Notebook." The tendency of other pieces in *Sixteen Poems* to exhibit elements of neo-surrealism was continued elsewhere in *Departures*, but when it came to making selections from this book for the *Selected Poems*, Justice seems to have had second thoughts about the "deep imagism" of the Bly school, and he tended to eliminate poems that sounded like Bly but were not much more successful than most of Bly's imported pathetic fallacies. Also eliminated, however, was "Lorcaesques" which was made of two fine little Spanish-style surrealist pieces.

The last section of *Selected Poems*, titled "Uncollected Poems," led off with a "Sonnet: An Old-Fashioned Devil," dated "Summer, 1948," and the reader might well have wondered whether this poem did not originally appear in the inaccessible *The Old Bachelor*. It is a true-rhyming English sonnet that could easily have been included in *The Summer Anniversaries* as one of the better poems. "The Return of Alcestis," 1950, was an allusive five-line dialogue that gave the impression it was a fragment of a play. "Two Songs from Don Juan in Hell," 1950, was similar but more lyrical, and its parts were subtitled "Sganarelle's Song" and "Don Juan's Song." It is possible that all of these originally saw light of day in *The Old Bachelor*.

The next piece in *Selected Poems*, "The Summer Anniversaries," was not included in the book of which it had at one time evidently been the title poem. A fragment followed — "From Bad Dreams," an "Epilogue: To the Morning Light," 1959. If this was the epilogue of a drama rather than an abandoned sequence, it strengthened the impression that at some points in his life Justice was involved in writing verse plays, and he took the opportunity his *Selected Poems* offered him of saving some parts he particularly liked. "'The Furies'—for certain reviewers," dated 1962, was a muted curse, lyrical and to the point. It could only have been written on reviewers of *The Summer Anniversaries*.

The succeeding poems were undated, therefore more recent. A sequence of three titled "First Death" was beautiful in the minimalist style of *Night Light*, and "Two Blues" were something new for Justice, songs in the blues tradition of Langston Hughes: Justice, once a musician himself, said he intended to write more of these, though apparently he never did. Oddly, two poems under the title of "Tremayne" were evocative once again of Weldon Kees, elsewhere exorcised from the volume, though the prosody of these verses is syllabic as in *Night Light*, not accentual-syllabic as in Kees' work. Justice's *Tremayne: Four Poems* added two fine lyrics to the two of the same title that appeared in *Selected Poems*.

"Unflushed Urinals" was a peculiar piece in this context, a prose poem that treated a situation with what used to be called "realism," as did "Sunday Afternoon in Buffalo, Texas." "Memories of the Depression Years" was a set of three short poems that returned to the nostalgic tone of *The Summer Anniversaries*, and they were as good as anything in that early volume. The two following poems were also nostalgic, and the book ended with a long annotated poem, "Childhood," that circled back to the thirties with substance but, unfortunately, not to the early poems qualitatively.

The impression the reader received from the last section of *Selected Poems* was of ambivalence and unease. There seemed to be fits and starts in scattered directions over the years, and then suddenly the last few poems looped around to Justice's early style. The "Uncollected Poems" section was a puzzling sampler of something new and something old. No doubt there was a nice circularity about it, but it left the impression that the poet had been drifting in the years since 1973, or that he had elected to round out *Selected Poems* with pieces that would not fit into a volume of their own. The overall effect of the collection, however, was to show a fine poet's best qualities to excellent effect, those sections of the book drawn from the earlier volumes tightening and sharpening the reader's perception of the development and talent of the writer to a point in his mid-career. The volume won the Pulitzer Prize for 1979 and Donald Justice died in 2004, a victim of Parkinson's disease.

Miller Williams

Miller Williams, born in Hoxie, Arkansas, in 1930, came out of a peculiar educational background for an academic poet, for he took a B. S. in biology from Arkansas State College, Conway, in 1951 and an M. S. in zoology from the University of Arkansas, Fayetteville, in 1952. In 1961 Williams applied for and was awarded a poetry fellowship at the Bread Loaf Writers' Conference at Middlebury College. Subsequently the director, the late John Ciardi, appointed Williams a member of the staff, and in 1963 he was awarded the Amy Lowell Traveling Scholarship. Williams began his career teaching biology at McNeese State College, went to Loyola University in 1966, and after some wandering about returned to Fayetteville in 1971 where he taught in the Fayetteville English department and writing program until eventually he became a University Professor of English and, at last, director of the University of Arkansas Press, a position he used to build the Press into one of the foremost publishers of poetry and poetry criticism among the smaller university presses. Williams has also contributed to the literature of his time two important anthologies which have been widely used as textbooks, *Contemporary Poetry in America* (1973) and *Patterns of Poetry: An Encyclopedia of Forms* (1986).

In the early 1960s Williams participated in a writers' conference held at the Cleveland Poetry Center of Fenn College, now Cleveland State University, where he made a number of cogent comments, but in the course of a panel discussion on "The Poet's Masks" he said one thing in particular that is relevant to a discussion of his work: "The poet lies to tell the truth." As an illustration of this thesis the poet used an incident that involved his son. One day the boy ran into the house and said, "A lion's chasing me!" Of course, there was no lion in the yard, but out of courtesy to childhood Williams looked, and there *was* a lion in the yard...in the form of a fair sized dog. The point Williams made was that to an adult the animal was a dog, but the quality of the boy's experience was that he had been threatened by something as large and menacing to him as a lion would be to an adult, so the child had "lied" in order to convey the magnitude of the experience to an older person. Williams' poems in his first book *A Circle of Stone* (1964) were, in these terms, a pack of lies. Each of them was an exaggeration, an attempt to get a mode of seeing and thinking down on paper in such a way as to help the reader to achieve the poet's original experience, or at least its essence.

Williams was and continues to be equipped to find the right words with which to lie well, for he knows how to compose his work, not merely invent images or murk about for the sake of darkening although he is, perhaps, a "Southern Gothic" poet in the sense that he has a real feeling for the strange in mankind. He puts words down in an order that gets them into the reader's mind and makes them stay there.

Williams' second book published in the United States (*Recital*, in a bilingual edition, appeared in Chile, also in 1964) was *So Long at the Fair* (1968). *The Only World There Is* followed (1971), and then *Halfway from Hoxie* in 1973. *Why God Permits Evil* appeared four years later, in 1977, and another four years passed before *Distractions* was published in 1981. *The Boys on their Bony Mules* was published in 1983, and *Imperfect Love* in

1986. Reading through his *Living on the Surface: New and Selected Poems* (1990) was not merely a pleasurable tour through the best work of these volumes, it was a fascinating introduction to a strong personality, an interesting revelation of the development of a fine and individual literary style, and an educational experience.

One of the features of Williams' style is the tone of the Baptist preacher, a down home diction combined with a pulpit rhetoric harnessed to serve an elevated purpose as in the elegy which is also a prayer, "For Clement Long, Dead," subtitled "lines written in the dark," a poem which the poet unfortunately did not include in his most recent volume:

> Lord listen, or heaven is undone.
> He will not spell your name or take your hand,
> will hee-haw at the gate with a held breath,
> will run away to the end where death is real.
>
> Lord if you chase him like a wheatfield fire
> till hallelujahs and a choir of angels
> sing him coming and the grand gates open,
> still he will stand against your house
> where no sin ever is and no flesh fails.
>
> If even he has treasures, let the mouse
> discover the grain, take the worm to the tree.
> Give his potential pleasures to the poor,
> or watch him. And watch him well. And watching see
> how he subverts the angels, whispering this:
>
> ninety and nine returned and deserve attending;
> surely the faithful one, the unoffending
> son should have the calf; God, it's a small grace
> to be a counter of coins in the first place.

The images are organic to the poem; although they would be unusual in the mouth of a real preacher, in the lines of Williams they are unobtrusive. The contexts of his poems allow the overtones one associates with the pulpit, but literary associations are not blocked out either, and the poems can be read on two levels — the literal and the allegorical. Williams walks this fine line between rhetoric and symbolism as well as anyone has done during the past quarter century.

If we examine the first poem in *Living on the Surface*, "The Associate Professor Delivers an Exhortation to His Failing Students," we can isolate many of these elements and subsequently follow their development in the body of Williams' work. This piece combines something of the poet's characteristic oratorical quality with what is the major concern of the book, survival. At a glance, the poem appears to be "free verse" that is, line-phrased prose: each line a phrase or a clause of some kind. The typographical level also tells us that the poem is strophic rather than stanzaic; there are twenty nine irregular sections, some as small as a line in length. Here are the first two strophes; clearly, the professor is a biologist:

> Now when the frogs
> that gave their lives for nothing
> are washed from the brains and pans
> we laid them in
> I leave to you
> who most excusably misunderstand
> the margins of my talks
> which because I am wise
> and am a coward
> were not appended to the syllabus
>
> but I will fail to tell you
> what I tell you
> even before you fail to understand
> so we might in a manner of speaking
> go down together.

An examination of the poem on the sonic level, however, quickly discovers that this is no kind of prose but variable accentual syllabic prosody. The meter is variable iambics, each line ranging in length from monometer to hexameter:

> ⏑ ´ | ⏑ ´ | ⏑ ´ | ⏑ . | ⏑ ´ ⏑
> I should have told you something of importance
>
> ⏑ ´ | ⏑ ´ | ⏑ ´ | ⏑
> to give at least a meaning
>
> . | ⏑ ´ ⏑
> to the letter:
>
> how, after hope, it sometimes happens
> a girl, anonymous as beer,
> telling forgotten things in a cheap bar
>
> how she could have taught here as well as I.
> Better.

The first line of strophe three is iambic pentameter verse (see the scansion above), though it has some variations: a promotion of the central unstressed syllable, in a series of three, in the fourth foot and the substitution of an amphibrach in the fifth foot. The next line seems to consist of two iambs and an amphibrach, in that order, and the third line of strophe three would then look like two trochees. However, if one were to put lines two and three together, it would look and scan like this:

⏑ ´ | ⏑ ´ | ⏑ ´ | ⏑ . | ⏑ ´ ⏑

to give at least a meaning to the letter:

In other words, lines two and three of strophe three, taken together, are metrically a duplicate of line one. What we have here, really, is two lines of iambic pentameter verse with falling endings or, to be descriptively more accurate, iambic hendecasyllabic (eleven syllable) verse.

Taking a hint from this discovery, we may look back at the beginning of the poem and see that "lines" 1 2 are also equal to one line of iambic pentameter verse, as are "lines" 3 4. The next two combined "lines," however, equal one hexameter, so not everything is going to boil down to pentameter, but it becomes fairly clear that the line phrasing of the poem is not a strong component of the prosody; rather, it is a disguise of the fact that Williams is writing verse. Perhaps this practice was itself a poetic survival mechanism during "The Great Hiatus" of twenty years and more in American formalist poetry during the 1960s, 1970s and early 1980s when versewriting was proscribed and only "free verse composition" was allowed.

Taken at face, however, we may call Williams' prosody in this poem line phrased, variable accentual syllabics, and the meter is variable iambics, the range for the lines being from monometer to hexameter. There are great numbers of other sorts of variations in the meters; we can see some of them if we look at strophe 7. Williams substitutes other sorts of verse feet, including anapests,

⏑ ⏑ ´ | ⏑ ⏑ ´ | ⏑
The day I talked about the conduction of currents

⏑ ´ |
I meant to say

an occasional double iamb,

⏑ ⏑ ´ ´
be careful about getting hung up in the brain's things

(This line may very well be the thesis of the poem, but more about that a bit later.)

> that send you screaming like madmen through the town
> or make you like the man in front of the Safeway store
> that preaches on Saturday afternoons
> a clown.

In the beginning of the poem Williams did not do much with outright rhyme, but there are some line ending repetitions linking strophes one and two: <u>you/you/you</u> and <u>misunderstand/understand</u>; consonances between strophes two, three, and six: <u>together/letter/Better</u>, and within strophe (couplet) five: <u>beer/bar</u>. True rhyme shows up in strophe seven: <u>town/clown</u>. This rhyme continues in strophe eight:

> The day I lectured on adrenalin
> I meant to tell you
> as you were coming down
> slowly out of the hills of certainty
> empty your mind of the hopes that held you there.
> Make a catechism of all your fears
>
> and say it over:
>
> this is the most of you...who knows...the best
> where God was born
> and heaven and confession
> and half of love
> from the fear of falling
> and being flushed away
> to the gulp of the suckhole and that rusting gut
> from which no Jonah comes
>
> that there is no Jesus and no hell

This passage is the thesis of the poem stated overtly. The lecturer is delivering a sermon on the subject of religion or the lack thereof in the existential modern world — the associate professor, like Williams, is a biologist and, also like Williams, one of the lapsed and disillusioned faithful. The "failure" here is the failure of both students and teacher, each in the same and different ways. The ideational level of the poem is as important as the sonic.

Returning to a consideration of the latter, we note that from this point in the poem rhyme becomes an important consideration, and it grows as close as couplet rhyme, though more often it is still random:

> that God
> square root of something equal to all
> will not feel the imbalance when you fall

> that rotting you will lie unbelievably alone
> to be sucked up by some insignificant oak
> as a child draws milk through straws
> to be his bone.
>
> These are the gravity that holds us together
> toward our common sun
>
> every hope getting out of hand
> slings us hopelessly outward one by one
> till all that kept us common is undone.

Rhyme (*sun/one/undone*) links strophes fifteen and sixteen; the latter ends, in fact, in a heroic couplet. As the poem progresses it is pulling together, becoming more and more formal, although Williams has maintained his disguises.

The sensory level of the poem is not complex. The basic tropes are descriptions rather than similes and metaphors. There are more rhetorical tropes than images — allusion in particular:

> The day you took the test
> I would have told you this:
> that you had no time to listen for questions
> hunting out the answers in your files
> is surely the kind of irony
> poems are made of
>
> that all the answers at best are less than half
>
> and you would have remembered
> Lazarus
> who hung around with God or the devil for days
> and nobody asked him
>
> anything

The primary schemas are constructional, grammatical parallels mostly, but Williams also avoids punctuation throughout the poem: there are few marks of terminal punctuation, not many internally, either. Williams generally indicates a new sentence or paragraph, as he does in the next strophe, twenty one, simply with an initial capital letter:

> If one Sunday morning they should ask you
> the only thing that matters after all
> tell them the only thing you know is true

> tell them failing is an act of love
> because
> like sin
> it is the commonality within

Now rhyming has progressed to such an extent that the next strophe, number twenty three, becomes a heroic quatrain consisting of two couplets; Williams says to tell them that is, the students,

> how failing together we shall finally pass
> how to pomp and circumstance all of a class
> noble of eye, blind mares between our knees,
> lances ready, we ride to Hercules.

With the puns on "pass" and "class" Williams works his way into the subdued metaphor that has lain dormant throughout the poem till now. This strophe also contains the only overt metaphor of the poem: we are all knights, Don Quixotes de la Mancha, riding out to do battle with Death; we will simultaneously fail and pass on.

Another heroic couplet begins the penultimate strophe twenty four which then returns to a semblance of prose:

> The day I said this had I meant to hope
> some impossible punk on a cold slope
> stupidly alone
> would build himself a fire
> to make of me an idiot
>
> and a liar

But the last two lines are now obviously yet another disguised heroic couplet; indeed, if the word "himself" were not present, the last two "strophes" would be another heroic quatrain and might be written out like this:

> The day I said this had I meant to hope
> some impossible punk on a cold slope
> stupidly alone would build...a fire
> to make of me an idiot and a liar

The poem ends without punctuation, but Williams has asked a question, not made a statement. The mood of the poem is of disillusion; there is a touch of bitterness in it, gall brought on by a loss of faith, and perhaps of despair staved off at a great cost of will. The viewpoint is dramatic, for, though Williams clearly draws on his own background, he has created a persona who speaks a monologue to an assumed audience of his students. The level of diction is intelligent but not overly intellectual, and the style is mean, not high.

If the subject itself is the human intellect, then Williams' thesis is that, though the mind may be an untrustworthy guide through life, intellect is the only guide that mankind has.

The major genre of the poem, then, is dramatics; the specific form is the monologue, though if this were written subjectively it would be a sermon with a strong didactic element. The levels emphasized are the sonic and the ideational, though the typographical is important to Williams' disguise of his prosody, and toward the end of the poem there is heavier emphasis on the sensory.

The poem balances the conflict of intellect with mystery extremely well, especially, it seems to me, for an early poem. All, or nearly all of the elements of Williams' mature style are here, and the poem is a good one for that reason as well as for intrinsic considerations.

"Voice of America," from *The Only World There Is*, finally gives up all technical disguises and announces itself typographically as a verse mode poem written in quatrain stanzas. Sonically, it is written in normative accentual syllabics; the running foot is iambic and the line length is tetrameter, but as in the earlier poem there are many variations. The rhyme scheme is *abcb*; thus, the specific form is long measure, from the family of common measure stanzas. It is a cautionary speech in the form of a lyric utilizing the devices we have already noted including repetition and parallelism ("Do not imagine..." begins many stanzas and lines), alliteration, consonance, echo, and assonance.

The sensory level contains, again, primarily descriptions, but there is irony too, and the main image is a simile, "like a bullet hitting a head" the sperm "crashes in" upon the egg to begin the process of reproduction. It appears to be a garish image until, reading closely, we understand that the real comparison is with a rifle bullet entering the head of its victim to finish a life in the same way that life began. The mood of the poem is tense and ominous.

Eventually it will occur to the reader that the subject of the poem is not reproduction but assassination. The schemas Williams uses here are repetitional primarily, the repetitions conjuring up an obsession. The viewpoint is narrative and the syntax is objective — a cautionary tale is being told with illustrations. The level of diction is that of a parent or a teacher (or even a preacher) warning an older child by means of illustrations. The poem, then, is a didactic lyric with a strong narrative element. The levels are in balance — there is even a typographical hiatus in the penultimate line of the eleventh and last stanza to suggest the hole the bullet is making in the head of its victim. This is a poem about the death of John F. Kennedy, or Martin Luther King, or Robert Kennedy...or anyone in this world who meets a violent end.

Williams' most ambitious and longest poem, "Notes from the Agent on Earth: How to be Human," appeared in *Why God Permits Evil*. It appears at first glance to be a verse mode poem built in both long sections and short cantos and strophes; none of the cantos are titled. Scansion shows that, indeed, it is verse, normative accentual syllabic prosody, in fact: the meters are iambic pentameter, but it is not quite blank verse as in many of his other poems, there is random end rhyme which at times becomes couplet rhyme, and there are other sorts of sonic devices often taking the place of rhyme, such as consonance and repetition. Williams' jazzy variations haven't changed, either. The general form of the poem is that of the elegy, and the Southern preacher inhabits the voice of this poem, as it does in other Williams works, so that at times it partakes of the sermon.

There are seven cantos here and, though there are no titles, each of the middle five begin with a parallel: "This is about..."; the first canto is an introduction — the scene is Rome, St. Peter's Basilica. The speaker is looking at statuary: St. Gregory sits on a slab under which "the devil, winged and dog faced, cat pawed and crooked / turns in his agony and bares his teeth, / bares his broken claws, turns his nostrils / almost inside out."

The last canto is the summation, a coda. It begins, "There is much that matters. What matters most is survival." Williams' lifelong theme is thus stated in so many words. In between the prologue and the epilogue the cantos announce themselves: "This is about Love and how to tell it." "This is about Faith and how to tell it." "This is about the Will to Power, Envy, Covetousness, Ambition...." "This is about Death and how to tell it." "This is also something about Ambition. Also Love. And Faith also. And Death."

The sensory level contains, like the earlier poems, primarily descriptions that sometimes ascend to metaphor, but far outnumbering these are the rhetorical tropes; in particular, Williams here displays a real talent for coining aphorisms: "Love is Fear and Loneliness fed and sleeping; / Faith is Fear and Loneliness explained, / denied and dealt in; Ambition which is envy / is Fear and Loneliness coming up to get you; / Death is Fear and Loneliness fading out." The emotional thrust of the poem is thoughtful tranquillity shot through with neurotic disillusion.

The ideation of the poem revolves around the subject of existence. As we can see, the schemas used are repetitional and constructional, in particular the long parallels of the cantos. The voice here is only partly narrative, for Williams steps out from behind all his masks in this poem to assume the subjective viewpoint and the egopoetic stance. The syntax follows the form of his thought and only now and again the form of an action. The level of diction is slightly elevated, but the style is mean, not at all florid, though there are some gothic scenes, especially in the prologue. One might be tempted to call the form of the poem georgics, for it is a handbook on how to get through life.

Fusionally, the poem is lyrical and didactic and the levels are balanced, though clearly the ideational is most heavily weighted. For all its preacherly qualities, the poem is most readable, for Williams is ever the musician of language.

In *The Boys on Their Bony Mules* Williams wrote with a greater sense of story. His rhythms and tropes were so well grounded in meter and in the particular that the reader hardly noticed the large issue, the thought rising from its base. Williams, despite his scientific background, is one of those poets who were trained, or who trained themselves, in the basics of verse composition and built from that foundation a style of writing and an angle of vision that enabled them to range widely and plunge deeply into the world and the self.

As always in his work, the poems in *Imperfect Love* formal lyrics and short narratives considered the human condition in its myriad formations and transformations in such a way as to provide the reader with both insight and delight, as in "A Little Poem":

> *for Jack Marr*
>
> We say that some are mad. In fact
> if we have all the words and we
> make madness mean the way they act
> then they as all of us can see
>
> are surely mad. And then again
> if they have all the words and call
> madness something else, well then
> well then, they are not mad at all.

Also in 1986 Williams took a role to the forefront of the blossoming Neoformalist movement with the publication of his text/anthology, *Patterns of poetry: An Encyclopedia of Forms*, of which the late John Ciardi said, "Miller Williams has performed a brilliant service in this book.... I recommend it to everyone who dares to think he can teach anyone to be a poet." Through this volume's pages the new generation of poets began again to understand that when a poet writes formally the burden of tradition need not inhibit him or her in the treatment of the particular subject in hand. This is the true reason that many of the poets of the past two decades have shuddered at the thought of traditional forms: they feel smothered, and indeed they are, but when someone comes along, like Williams, who can understand and release the power of the old constructs in an individual and imaginative manner, the form helps the poet to say the necessary thing.

Miller Williams, then, has done contemporary poetry a singular service in that, during the indulgent decades, he maintained a level of artistry committed both to tradition and to a personal vision. This poetry of balance, of intelligence as well as feeling, serves as a benchmark to the new generation of poets who are feeling their way back to a sense of writing as literature, not merely self expression. But his commitment to the craft of poetry takes more forms than just the maintenance of high personal standards. Williams remains the teacher or, if you will, the preacher who exhorts his audience by precept and example. He uses his pulpit to spread the word and the book.

Robert Mezey

When he wrote "A Coffee-House Lecture" Robert Mezey was in 1959-60 attending the graduate Writers' Workshop of the University of Iowa. His teachers were the formalists Paul Engle and the young poet Donald Justice who had not yet published his own first book. Mezey was anticipating the coming year when he was to attend Stanford as a Fellow under the latter-day Messiah of the neoclassical poets, Yvor Winters, of whom Mezey was a professed admirer. As things were to happen, Mezey and Winters would have a falling-out even before Mezey arrived on campus, and the younger man would become one of the fringe Beats rather than the formalist poet he had been during his years at Iowa and, earlier, at Kenyon College under the Fugitive poet John Crowe Ransom.

In Iowa's Poetry Workshop one week during the academic year 1959-60 an English student-poet, Christopher Wiseman, submitted to the worksheets of the class a parody of the work of the Beat poet Allen Ginsberg. Mezey did not see the humor in it, only the threat, and he reacted by writing, and the next week submitting to the Workshop, his response, "A Coffee-House Lecture," which in fact he read publicly in a local coffee house at about that time. He later included the piece in his first book, *The Lovemaker*.

A glance at the typographical layout of the poem shows that it is written in verse mode. Its proportion in figure is stanzaic: five octaves. Every other line is indented, and the poem observes the convention of initial capitalization of each line:

> Come now, you who carry
>   Your passions on your back,
> Will insolence and envy
>   Get you the skill you lack?
> Scorning the lonely hours
>   That other men have spent,
> How can you hope to fathom
>   What made them eloquent?

An examination of the sonic level reveals that the poem's general prosody is accentual-syllabics; specifically, normative accentual-syllabics. The meter is iambic trimeter with variations:

> Blake tells you in his notebooks,
> If you could understand,
> That Style and Execution
> Are Feeling's only friend,

>   ˘   ´ | ˘ ´| ˘   ´   ˘
> That all Poetic Wisdom
>   ˘ ´ | ˘   . | ˘ ´
> Begins in the minute,
>   ˘   ´ | ˘   ´ | .   ´   ˘
> And Vision sees most clearly
>   ˘   ´| ˘ ´ | ˘   ´
> While fingering a lute.

There are only two exceptions to trimeter measures in the poem — the penultimate (next-to-last) line, and line three of stanza three, both of which are tetrameter:

> [˘] ´ | ˘   ´ | ˘   ´   ˘
> [x] Robert Burns in Ayreshire
> With meter and with gauge
>   ´   ˘ |˘   ´ |˘ ´ | ˘ ´
> Studied the strict exactitudes
> That luminate his page,
>
>   ´   ˘
> Ignored the vulgar grandeur
> That you and yours revere,
>   ´ ˘
> And labored with his body
> And his perfected ear.

Several lines are hypercatalectic: the extra unstressed syllables at the ends of the lines are caused by falling rhythms and rhymes, as in stanza one, lines three and seven; stanza two, lines one, three, five, and seven; stanza three, lines five and seven, and stanza four, lines one, three, five, and seven:

>   ´   ˘
> Paul Valéry gripped a scalpel
> And sweated at his task,
>
>   ´   ˘
> Bent over bleeding Chaos
> In spotless gown and mask;
>   ´ ˘
> And in reluctant lectures
> Spoke of the cruel art
>   ´ ˘
> And cold precise transactions
> That warm the human heart.

Stanza five, line one, begins with a spondee, and it may be hypercatalectic, depending on one's pronunciation of the last word:

´ ˘
How many that have toiled
At the hard craft of verse
Had nothing more than music
To fill their empty purse,
But found it was sufficient,
In making out a will,

˘ ´ |˘ ´ | ˘ ´ |˘.
To pay for their mortality,
And they are living still.

There are a few other metrical variations, but not many. There is substitution — some lines begin with a spondee (line one) or a trochee (line five). There is some promotion (stanza two, line one, fourth syllable and line eight, 4th syllable); demotion (same stanza, line seven, 4th syllable); some elision (stanza three, line one, last word) and counter-elision (last stanza, line one, last word).

The general form of the poem is indicated by the title — it is what it says it is, a lecture; its genre is therefore didactics, The rhyme scheme is *abcbdefe*, *ghihjklk*, and so forth, and it generally true-rhymes, though there is some consonance, as in stanza two, lines two and four (understand-friend). The rhyme scheme is that of long hymnal octave, but the meters are one foot shorter except in 3-3 and 5-7, as noted. Other sonic devices are incidental, but they include vocalic and consonantal echo particularly, as for instance the repetition of ar sounds in stanza three and the o sounds (of various kinds) in stanza one.

There is not much complication on the sensory level — the primary metaphor is that money equals music to be spent, as in stanza one. Personification is used five times in stanza two where abstractions are given human characteristics; in stanza four Chaos is a patient on an operating table. For the rest of the poem, most tropes are not descriptive, similetic, nor metaphorical, but rhetorical. The rhetorical question is used in the first and last stanzas, though in the second instance there is no querying punctuation. Mezey used sarcasm and irony heavily — the scorn he accuses Wiseman of is in effect displaced, and the author is himself guilty of micterismus — verbal sneering.

Another classical technique used in the poem is reference to authority — Blake especially, in stanza two. (It might be appropriate to note, parenthetically, that William Blake, like Mezey, wrote both verse and prose poems.) Related is the rhetorical device of *exempla* — examples: Burns; Valéry, the "doctor" in the operating room scene, his pencil a scalpel. Despite the subservience of the metaphor to rhetoric, the poem is a conceit or extended metaphor, and the poem's tradition is metaphysical. The main emotional thrust of the poem is the expression of scorn, but the reader may instead detect, and feel the effects of, pomposity.

The subject of the poem is poetry itself. Mezey has used constructional schemas — parallelism in particular, the three central stanzas being devoted to short discussions of three poets and their practice; the first stanza is introductory and the last climactic — both are rhetorical questions. The architecture of the whole is symmetrical and logical. The poet also uses prolepsis, an inclusive schema, in his expansion of a general proposition, particularizing it and giving further information regarding it.

The viewpoint of the poem is egopoetic — these are the exclusive opinions of the author, who is the speaker; its poetic syntax is subjective, the level of diction distinctly literary, and its style high. The theme of the poem is that poetry is hard work and applied craft — more perspiration than inspiration.

Fusionally, "A Coffee-House Lecture" is a didactic lyric; the level emphasized most heavily is the ideational, supported by rhetorical tropes on the sensory level, and relatively strict rhythms on the sonic level. It is technically typical of the poems in *The Lovemaker*.

Subsequently Mezey executed a turnabout in his point of view, becoming an exponent of the kind of poetry he had in this poem attacked with vehemence. He went so far as to co-edit with Stephen Berg two anthologies which were part of the avalanche of anti-formalist books that buried the Academic poets for two decades, the 1969 *Naked Poetry: Recent American Poetry in Open Forms* and *The New Naked Poetry* of 1976. In the foreword to the first volume the editors said,

> "We feel like intruders here. Two years ago, when we first decided that there was a need for a book like this, we planned to start it off with a long essay on the theory and practice of...of what? There wasn't even a satisfactory name for the kinds of poetry we were gathering and talking about, and still isn't. Some people said 'Free Verse' and others said 'Organic Poetry' (and a few old ones said, 'That's not poetry!'), and we finally came up with Open Forms, which isn't bad but isn't all that good either."

In a note appended to those of his own poems that he had included in this anthology Mezey wrote,

> "When I was quite young I came under unhealthy influences — Yvor Winters, for example, and America, and my mother, though not in that order. Yvor Winters was easy to exorcise; all I had to do was meet him. My mother and America are another story and why tell it in prose?
>
> "Once in Iowa City a friend said, 'Why do you write in rhyme and meter? Your poetry is nothing like your life.' 'What do we know of another's life,' I thought, but I had nothing to say. I no longer write in rhyme and meter, and still my life is not much like my poetry. At least, I don't think so. It is possible I'm not a poet at all. But I am a man, a Piscean, and unhappy, and therefore I make up poems."

In 1986, ten years after the publication of the second *Naked Poetry* selection, Robert Mezey was experiencing a Karl Shapiro-style change of heart. In the May-June issue of *The American Book Review* one of the younger members of the Beat generation, Diane Wakoski, had attacked formalist poetry which had dared again to rear its curly head. Mezey wrote a reply, which was published with several others in the November-December issue of the same periodical. He objected to Wakoski's calling the formalist poet John Hollander a "devil," among other things:

> "What evil thing has Mr. Hollander done, to drive her [Wakoski] into such confusion and incoherence? He has allegedly denounced free verse, which is what she writes, sort of, and perhaps she feels accused by his jokes about ill-educated and slovenly writers who pass their own illiteracy on to their students. (She may have reason to, and I doubt he was joking.) She doesn't try to refute his observation that many contemporary poets are ignorant of their art — how could she? — but in his refusal to enlist under the banners of 'the free verse revolution' and 'the Whitman heritage' she hears the voice of Satan. And, believe it or not, the voice of Reagan. Yes, children, if you won't accept Walt Whitman as your personal lord and saviour and if you harbor a secret affection for such decadent bourgeois ornaments as rhyme and meter, then you are reactionary and unAmerican and probably have an evil nature." (3)

Mezey's position in the mid-'eighties was thus very little different from his original stance back in his graduate school days at Iowa. His book *Evening Wind*, which appeared in 1987, showed the curve of his return; the poems in the early part of the volume are a restrained "free verse." The last section of the book showed that Mezey had come full circle, to the point where he could once again allow himself to write — using all of his intellect and talent — a beautiful sonnet such as "Owl":

> Nightlong waiting and listening, being schooled
> To long lying awake without thoughts,
> I hear him calling from the other world.
> A long silence, and then two flutey notes —
> The cry of nobody, but urgent, cool,
> Full of foreboding. He's in the cedar tree
> Not twenty feet beyond my window sill;
> The other world is very far away.
> When, towards morning, he ceases, the air seems
> More visible, although it's not yet light,
> The black sky drained and all our speechless dreams
> Fading into thought. Lord of the night,
> Thy kingdom in which everything is one,
> Come, speak to me, speak to me once again.

Dana Gioia

(Michael) Dana Gioia was born in Hawthorne, California, a suburb of Los Angeles, in 1950. He took his B. A. in English with honors from Stanford University in 1973, then attended Harvard University where he took an M. A. in comparative literature in 1975. Subsequently, he left the Harvard graduate program, where he was working on a Ph.D. in comparative literature, to return to Stanford where he acquired a master's degree in business administration in 1977. In the same year he took a position with General Foods Corporation, and he has remained with that firm into the 1990s, his title in 1989 being New Business Development Manager.

Despite this unorthodox early career, Gioia retained his interest in literature, poetry in particular, but he also wrote a great deal of criticism for some of the most respected journals in the United States, including *The Hudson Review*. Gioia says, "During my two years at Stanford Business School I wrote at least one literary review for *The Daily Stanford* every two weeks.... I also reviewed occasionally for other journals, such as *The San Francisco Review of Books*. In effect I taught myself to be a professional critic. That's the old fashioned way, I guess, of learning to write in public. By the time I left Stanford for New York in 1977 I was a seasoned reviewer." Gioia thus became one of those rare poets who establish reputations before ever they publish a collection of poetry.

Dana Gioia's first representative collection of poems, *Daily Horoscope*, was published in 1986, but the title poem of that book had appeared separately as a chapbook in 1982. In 1983 Gioia published another chapbook of poetry, *Summer*. With William Jay Smith, Gioia in 1985 co-edited an anthology, *Poems from Italy*, many of which he himself had translated. The poet's *Words for Music* (1987), also issued in a limited edition from a small press, contained poems that he had excluded from *Daily Horoscope* because, in his own words, he "knew critics would find them too formal." Gioia's second full-fledged collection of poems, *Night Watch*, appeared in 1989; it is dedicated to his first son who died in infancy.

Bruce Bawer wrote that, although Gioia neither looks nor acts like anybody's idea of a poet, "he is a poet, widely acknowledged as one of the finest of his generation. His [work] appears frequently in such prestigious venues as the *New Yorker*, the *Hudson Review*, the *Paris Review*, and *Poetry* and has been translated into a number of languages; in 1984 he was cited by *Esquire* in a cover story called 'The Best of the New Generation: Men and Women under Forty Who Are Changing America.'" (1) Bawer wrote further that Gioia "is also one of several younger poets — dubbed 'The New Formalists' — who are challenging the poetry-world status quo in significant, possibly even historic, ways. Some of his more vociferous critics would have one believe that he is out to eradicate free verse, repeal the modernist revolution, and inaugurate an era of philistine poetics. It is more nearly correct to say that, unlike many younger poets these days, Gioia includes [traditional] form among his options and is capable of using it very effectively."

Gioia contributed a long poem, "The Homecoming," to the special issue of *Crosscurrents: A Quarterly* titled "Expansionist Poetry: The New Formalism and the New Narrative," published early in 1989. This poem was collected in *The Gods of Winter*. An example of "the New Narrative," it tells the story of a "KILLER NABBED AT FOSTER MOTHER'S HOME," as the protagonist-narrator himself expresses it in an autobiographical headline given to his captors when they show up to take him in. It is a seamy story of abandonment and mistreatment, but not the less poignant for that, as well-written as a good short story, and just as beguiling.

While it cannot be denied that both Gioia's work and sympathies are formal, he is not hidebound. His work appears in most of the "New Formalist" anthologies, including David Lehman's *Ecstatic Occasions, Expedient Forms* (1987) which contains one poem plus an explanation by each contributor of how he or she came to use or develop the structure of the poem. Gioia's contribution, from *Daily Horoscope*, was "Lives of the Great Composers"; his comment was titled "A Tune in the Back of My Head." Far from being doctrinaire about "traditional form," Gioia wrote:

> "The musical effect I missed most in poetry was counterpoint, so it is not surprising that for years I fantasized about writing a fugue, the most fascinating of all contrapuntal forms, in verse. I say fantasize because for years it remained only that — a seductive daydream. I could imagine a poem where variations on a single theme would tumble down the page in elaborate counterpoint, but I had no practical notion of how to write it. The one example I knew of, Paul Celan's magnificent 'Todesfuge,' was too unique and lofty a model to provide any specific help, though its existence proved that the form could be approximated in verse."

Gioia was considering an experiment in prosody; he was searching for a new form, and he developed an original one for "Lives of the Great Composers" from *Daily Horoscope* where, in a note, Gioia said, "This poem is cast as a verbal fugue in a form suggested by a poem of Weldon Kees's." The Kees poem to which Gioia referred is titled "Fugue." Kees, who died in 1955, was a short story writer (whose book of fiction Gioia edited), a journalist, painter, film-maker, jazz pianist and composer and, in poetry, a formal experimentalist. The subject of Gioia's fugal "Lives of the Great Composers" is itself music:

> On rainy nights the ghost of Mendelssohn
> brought melodies for Schumann to compose.
> "Such harmony is in immortal souls....
> We cannot hear it.

Gioia's title poem, "Daily Horoscope," is an elegy to the memory of the poet and translator Robert Fitzgerald, with whom Gioia studied; it begins with an epigraph from Dante's *Inferno* praising the "master" and his beautiful style. The narrative perspective of the quotation is second person, "you," and this viewpoint is maintained throughout the poem, as is the premise of the *Inferno* — that the speaker is describing a tour of the underworld; however, unlike Dante, who accompanied the poet Virgil on his tour of Hell, Gioia does not accompany Fitzgerald except as an observer from a distance, the distance that separates the living from the dead.

Like the *Inferno*, "Daily Horoscope" is divided into cantos — six of them in this case, quite short — each titled from its first line: "Today will be...," "Nothing Is Lost...," "Do Not Expect...," "Beware of Things in Duplicate...," "The Stars Now Rearrange Themselves...," and "News Will Arrive from Far Away...." The cantos themselves are subdivided into strophes which are in fact verse paragraphs. When a paragraph begins in mid-line, it is stepped down, as in strophe three of canto one:

>   These walls, these streets,
>   this day can never be your home, and yet
>   there is no other world where you could live,
>   and so you will accept it.
>   Just as others,
>   waking to sunlight and the sound of leaves,
>   accept the morning as their own, and walk
>   without surprise, through orchards crossed by streams,
>   where swift, cold water is running over stone.

Although this is a blank verse-mode poem and there are no end-rhymes, the sonic is the most important level here, appropriately for a lyric series. The prosody is normative accentual-syllabics, and the meter is generally iambic pentameter, though a line or two is longer — hexameter — and several are tetrameter or on occasion as short as trimeter, as in the last strophe of canto three:

>   And only briefly then
>   you touch, you see, you press against
>   the surface of impenetrable things.

There is nothing monotonous about Gioia's versification, as a scansion of the first strophe of canto one will show:

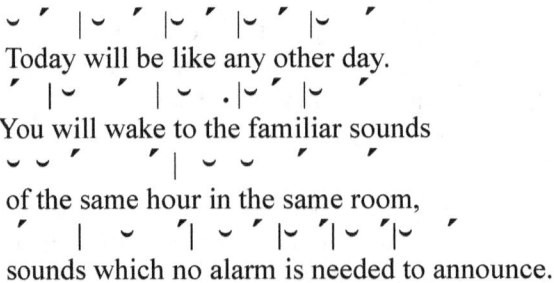

Neoformalism

> And lying in the warm half-darkness, wish
> for any of the dreams you left, convinced
> that any change would be an argosy —
> an hour's sleep, an unexpected visit.

The first line, perfect iambic pentameter verse, sets the metrical premise of the poem, but the second line immediately begins to play variations against that norm. The second line is headless, dropping the initial unstressed syllable. The stress of the third foot is a promotion because the syllable *the* is the central one in a series of three unstressed syllables. The third line begins with what Harvey Gross calls a "double iamb": two unstressed followed by two stressed syllables, which take the place of two iambs. This is followed — if one pronounces the word hour as a counter-elision containing two syllables, as Gioia seems to intend in the last line — by an iamb formed of a promoted second syllable (in), then a normal iamb, and a tailless trochee substituted for the iamb of the fifth foot. Line four is also headless, but otherwise perfect, and the only variation in line five is a demotion of *half-*, which is the central syllable in a series of three stressed syllables. Lines six and seven are perfect except for a secondary stress in each, and the strophe ends with an amphibrach substituted in the fifth foot of the last line.

While they are subtle, the verbal harmonies are as important as the meters. Though there are no refrains, nevertheless repetitions appear immediately in the first strophe: *to-day...day* in the first line, *same...same* in the third; *will...will* linking lines one and two, *sounds...sounds* linking lines two and three. There are alliterations as in the second line, *will/wake*; assonance as in the third line, *sounds/announce*; consonantal echoes, soft sounds primarily, *els* and *ars*. The sensory level does not contain complex figures of speech. The primary tropes are descriptions, but there is a subdued central metaphor: that death is the ordinary world without focus: "Beyond your window, something like a wind / is filling in the emptiness of air. / Vast, hungry, and invisible, it sweeps / the morning clean of memories, then disappears." There are rhetorical tropes that give the poem a tone of admonition, as though these descriptions own something of the nature of commands, as in the beginning of the third canto:

> Do not expect that if your book falls open
> to a certain page, that any phrase
> you read will make a difference today,
> or that the voices you might overhear
> when the wind moves through the yellow-green
> and golden tent of autumn, speak to you.

The mood throughout this portrait of the underworld is bleakly sorrowful. Of course, the subject is death. The schemas Gioia employs to depict his landscapes, including the inner weathers of the speaker, are inclusive, for as the poem progresses the poet adds increments of detail — canto three continues,

> Things ripen or go dry. Light plays on the
> dark surface of the lake. Each afternoon
> your shadow walks beside you on the wall,
> and the days stay long and heavy underneath
> the distant rumor of the harvest.

The effect of this practice is that the abstraction, death, is made extraordinarily concrete. Nevertheless, the underworld depicted here is not the religious vision of Dante; rather, it is an existential vision of both the real world and the world of the afterlife. Gioia's theme is that death is at best nothing more than the empty memory of life, and the memory resides in the minds of those who are left behind, not in that of the deceased, for it is the survivor who speaks here, not the phantom of the person who has passed beyond the portal of consciousness.

Dana Gioia's response to Diane Wakoski's attack on formal poetry was one of five published under the overall title "Picketing the Zeitgeist Picket" in the November-December 1986 number of *The American Book Review*, but Greg Kuzma attacked Gioia specifically and personally in his late 1988 *Northwest Review* essay, "Dana Gioia and the Poetry of Money." Kuzma compared Gioia's first book with that of Donald Justice, published twenty-six years earlier, and then he said, "Gioia's use of form does not seem traditional in this way," as though Justice's "way" were the only way to use traditional forms. Kuzma appeared to wish to dismiss "Neoformalism" by setting up a straw man and then setting fire to it.

But what was perhaps most disturbing to the reader was Kuzma's apparent ignorance of the subject he was discussing. Having earlier written, "Those of us who cannot write rhyme but have always respected Richard Wilbur because he cannot not write it," Kuzma continued a bit later, "It is almost as if the concealing of meter and rhyme is Gioia's singular purpose. True, at times meter and rhyme clang and scan too neatly and emphatically and what one gets is verse, such as here in the third stanza of 'Cruising with the Beachboys':

> Some nights I drove down to the beach to park
> And walk along the railings of the pier.
> The water down below was cold and dark,
> The waves monotonous against the shore.
> The darkness and the mist, the midnight sea,
> The flickering lights reflected from the city —
> A perfect setting for a boy like me,
> The Cecil B. DeMille of my self-pity.

"Tempting as it would be to label Gioia's work verse and to dismiss it as such, most of it is not. Verse accentuates rhyme and meter while at the same time expressing predictable views of sentimental postures," Kuzma concluded.

But verse has nothing in particular to do with rhyme, as a look at Ogden Nash's rhyming prose poems should tell anyone, and it has no particular relationship with "predictable views" or "sentimental postures" — Kuzma seemed to be remembering a grammar school teacher in his past making a distinction between something successful called "poetry" and something unsuccessful called "verse."

Nor does verse *accentuate* meter; verse *is* metered language. It also appeared that Kuzma did not know how to scan a poem, for if he did, he would have been able to hear the metrical variations Gioia had worked into the passage quoted above — there was nothing "neat and emphatic" about Gioia's meters; they did not "jingle," though they did scan as iambic pentameter lines.

The rules of scansion in English verse are few and simple. In every word of the English language of two or more syllables, at least one syllable will take a stress. If one cannot at first hear the stressing, then one may consult a pronouncing dictionary.

Important single-syllable words, particularly *verbs* and *nouns*, generally take strong stresses.

Unimportant single-syllable words in the sentence, such as *articles*, *prepositions*, and *pronouns* (except *demonstrative pronouns*) do not take strong stresses, though they may take *secondary stresses* through *promotion* or *demotion*, depending on their position in the sentence or the line of verse.

In any series of three unstressed syllables in a line of verse, one of them, generally the middle syllable, will take a *secondary stress* through *promotion* and will be counted as a *stressed* syllable.

In any series of three stressed syllables in a line of verse, one of them, generally the middle syllable, will take a *secondary stress* through *demotion* and will be counted as an *unstressed* syllable.

Any syllable may be rhetorically stressed by means of italics or some other typographical ploy. There really is no reason why any variety of poet shouldn't know these rules, even if they think they cannot write verse, as Kuzma admitted. Perhaps he could if he knew how to scan, for Kuzma claimed to have scanned one of Gioia's poems and thereby to have found that Gioia's verse simultaneously "clanged," and scanned "too neatly," and was otherwise too purposefully "concealed," as "in the third stanza of 'Cruising with the Beachboys.'" Here is the scansion of the poem, which Kuzma did not include in his essay:

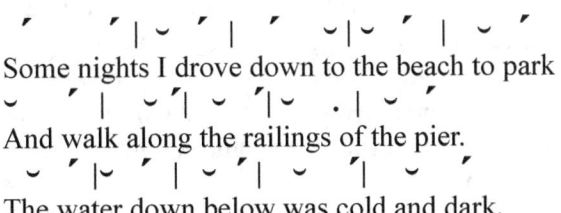
Some nights I drove down to the beach to park
And walk along the railings of the pier.
The water down below was cold and dark,

⏑ ′ | ⏑ ′| ⏑ .| ⏑ ′ | ⏑ ′
The waves monotonous against the shore.
⏑ ′ | ⏑ .| ⏑ ′ | ⏑ ′ |. ′
The darkness and the mist, the midnight sea,
⏑ ′ | ⏑ ′ | ⏑ ′| ⏑ .| ⏑ ′⏑
The flickering lights reflected from the city —
⏑ ′ |⏑ ′ |⏑ .| ⏑ ′ | ⏑ ′
A perfect setting for a boy like me,
⏑ ′ | ⏑ ′ |. ′ | ⏑ ⏑ ′ ′ ⏑
The Cecil B. DeMille of my self-pity.

The stanza was eight lines long — an octave. The mode was verse. The general prosody was accentual-syllabics, the specific prosody was normative accentual-syllabics because there was a running foot, the iamb: the meter was iambic pentameter. There was a rhyme scheme: *ababcdcd* — quatrain rhyme. Here is a diagram of the meters:

1. ′ ′   ⏑ ′   ′ ⏑   ⏑ ′   ⏑ ′
2. ⏑ ′   ⏑ ′   ⏑ ′   ⏑.   ⏑ ′
3. ⏑ ′   ⏑ ′   ⏑ ′   ⏑ ′   ⏑ ′
4. ⏑ ′   ⏑ ′   ⏑.   ⏑ ′   ⏑ ′
5. ⏑ ′   ⏑.   ⏑ ′   ⏑ ′   . ′
6. ⏑ ′   ⏑ ′   ⏑ ′   ⏑.   ⏑ ′ ⏑
7. ⏑ ′   ⏑ ′   ⏑.   ⏑ ′   ⏑ ′
8. ⏑ ′   ⏑ ′   . ′   ⏑⏑ ′   ′ ⏑

Line one had a spondee (′ ′), an iamb (⏑ ′), a trochee (′ ⏑), and two iambs, in that order — there were two variations in the line. Line two had five iambs, but the second syllable in the fourth foot was a promotion because it was the central syllable in a sequence of three unstressed syllables, and English hates three unstressed syllables in a row — this was a variation. Line three was the first line to have five iambs in it, but it didn't have the caesura (pause) after the second or third foot usually to be found in the English iambic line, (as in the first line after *drove*). This did not appear to be "jingly." Gioia was saying, "The water down below was cold and dark, / the waves *monotonous* [emphasis added] against the shore." Here, the meters were imitating the motion of the waves, a technique called onomatopoeia; even so, there was one promotion in line four, foot three — the line was not excessively monotonous.

The caesura reappeared in line five, after mist, and the variations continued in the form of a promotion in foot two, and a demotion in the fourth foot where there were three stressed syllables in a row: "midnight sea":

⌣ ´ | ⌣ .| ⌣ ´ | ⌣ |. ´
The darkness and the mist, the midnight sea,

Line six had three variations: an elision, *flick'ring*; a promotion, *from*, in the fourth foot, and an amphibrach (⌣ ´ ⌣) in the fifth: the line ended in a falling rhythm:

⌣ ´ | ⌣ ´ | ⌣ ´ | ⌣ .| ⌣ ´ ⌣
The flickering lights reflected from the city —

The next line, seven, had its subtle caesura after *setting*, which came in the middle of the third foot, just before a promotion, *for*:

⌣ ´ |⌣ ´ | ⌣ .| ⌣ ´ | ⌣ ´
A perfect setting for a boy like me,

The last line was climactic, and it was the most various line in the poem, calling attention to its self-deprecating wit:

⌣ ´ |⌣ ´ |. ´ |⌣ ⌣ ´ | ´ ⌣
The Cecil B. DeMille of my self-pity.

There was a demotion in the first syllable of the third foot; the fourth foot was an anapest (⌣⌣ ´), and the fifth was a falling foot, a trochee (´ ⌣); thus, the line ended on the downbeat.

As to the rhymes that Kuzma said "jingled" — these were the end-words with their stresses marked:

´
park
´
pier
´
dark
´
shore

> ´
> sea
> ´ ˘
> city
> ´
> me
> ´ ˘
> pity

Now, *park/dark* were true rhymes, but *pier/shore* were consonances, off-rhymes. *Sea/me* were true rhymes. To this point all rhymes had been single and rising (one-syllable, ending on the stress). But **city/pity**, though they were true rhymes, were double and falling (two-syllable, ending on the downbeat). Furthermore, *sea/me* vs. *city/pity* were consonances; taken as a group, *sea/city* and *me/pity* (or the other combination) were light-rhyming consonances (a rising ending rhyming with a falling ending).

There were many other sorts of sounds to be found in the passage as well, such as the alliterations (among the rhyme words, **p**ark-**p**ier and **s**ea-**c**ity; **w**alk, **w**ater, **w**aves; **d**rove, **d**own, **d**arkness), the assonances (n**i**ghts, **I**; w**a**lk, **a**long, w**a**ter), the repetitions (*down, down; dark, darkness*), the consonantal and vocalic echoes, like the ars in four of the rhyme words: park-pier-dark-shore.

The scene Gioia was deliberately painting with these sounds was a melodramatic movie set. His intention was to undercut it with self-irony in line eight, not only with its allusion to a movie mogul, but with all the screeching *ee* sounds of the line: "The Cecil B[ee] DeMille of my self-pity." Contrary to Kuzma's claim, perhaps Gioia is an unusual younger poet in a more important way than the press he gets in the business journals and some of the literary journals would indicate. It isn't of particular note for the long run that he is not an academic in an age of academic poets, though he has taught from time to time, co-founded the neoformalist West Chester University Poetry Conference and chaired the National Endowment for the Arts during the George W. Bush administration. Rather, Gioia is most unusual because, unlike most of those poets who teach, Gioia knows precisely what he is doing in his poetry, for he shows it in the product. He does what he does through a masterful handling of the levels of his poems. And, again unlike his academic peers, he is able to articulate his theory and practice in intelligent and constructive criticism, nearly a lost art among contemporary poets.

R. S. GWYNN

> In his *The Anatomy of Melancholy* (1628), Robert Burton says that in order to avoid melancholy — the old word for *depression* — one "may apply his mind...to Heraldry, Antiquity, invent Impresses, Emblems; make Epithalamiums, Epitaphs, Elegies, Epigrams, Palindromes, Anagrams, Chronograms, Acrosticks upon his friends' names; or write a comment on Martianus Capella, Tertullian's Cloak, the Nubian Geography, or upon Ælia Laelia Crispis, as many idle fellows have assayed; and rather than do nothing, vary a verse a thousand ways with Putean, so torturing his wits, or as Rainnarius of Luneberg, 2,150 times in his *Proteus Poeticus,* or Scaliger, Chrysolithus, Cleppisius, and others, have in like sort done."

It has seemed to me for many years that southerners tend to have an inclination toward, or at least are not generally biased against, poetry written in formal verse. Perhaps the reason for this is that they tend to be melancholics. Certainly, a case can be made that R. S. "Sam" Gwynn is one and that he has taken Burton's admonition to heart. Born in Eden, North Carolina, in 1948, Gwynn was educated at Davidson College and the University of Arkansas, and has taught at Lamar University in Beaumont, Texas, for many years. At Davidson Gwynn was already heavily involved in the beginnings of his career, for he was a member of the staff of the student-edited professional literary periodical *The Miscellany* which published as part of its contents material written by established writers.

At Bread Loaf Writers' Conference in 1968, where Gwynn enjoyed a waiter-scholarship and was a student Contributor, it seemed already apparent that he was constitutionally incapable of writing in anything but rhymed and metered verse; thus, it is not surprising that Gwynn is now known as one of the leading New Formalist poets. However, it may bemuse readers unfamiliar with his work to discover that he is also, without a doubt, a truly experimental poet, the cleverest and most daring of the new generation of poetic traditionalists.

R. S. Gwynn's two earliest publications of poetry in volume form included a chapbook, *Bearing & Distance*, published in 1977, and the hilarious tour-de-force satire of contemporary American poetry *The Narcissiad* which appeared as a chapbook in 1981. Written in heroic couplets with a concluding Alexandrine at the end of each section, Gwynn mixed classical elements with all sorts of things including slang, truisms, wisecracks, contemporary academicisms, double entendre, and this is just the beginning:

> Each age requires its gods, and this is so
> Today as much as countless years ago
> (Though in these present times of jangling nerves
> Man seems to get the gods that he deserves,
> More on that later, in its proper place),

> So let us shift the flats, move time and space
> And focus on the earliest flowering
> Of things in some archaic Grecian Spring
> When tongues of fern, lashing the winter's ices,
> Heralded the return of Dionysus,
> That god whose menstrual maidens, titties thrusting, Sprinkled
> the groves in primitive crop-dusting
> So Sophocles could tipple while he wrote
> Tetralogies to get the sacred goat
> That yet survive, sublime and oversexed,
> In every scholar's heart, each freshman's text.

Who among contemporary poets uses the vehicle of Alexander Pope with as much skill and elan? Who, except perhaps Richard Wilbur, uses it at all?

Then came *The Drive-In*, a non-prize-winner and another example to support the observation one made in a review at the time, "The Year in Poetry" (1986), that, of the year's crop of first books, those that came unlaurelled tended to be among the best. This sixty-four-page book contained thirty-eight poems, of which twenty-three are included in Gwynn's later collection, *No Word of Farewell, Selected Poems: 1970-2000*.

Gwynn's virtuosity was at once apparent the moment one began to read his work, as Dana Gioia wrote in his "Introduction" to Gwynn's selected poems: "I first encountered R. S. Gwynn's poetry through sheer serendipity," Gioia said. "In 1986 I spent an afternoon reading through the many new poetry books at Manhattan's Endicott's, a graciously and generously stocked independent bookstore now, alas, out of business. I've spent many such afternoons before and since, but I remember this day vividly because I made a genuine discovery, a little light-blue volume called *The Drive-In* by R. S. Gwynn, a poet whose name I did not recognize. I picked a poem at random and found it cleverly amusing but took no special notice until I read the opening selection, 'Among Philistines,' a singularly curious retelling of the Samson story set in suburban America.

"'Among Philistines' struck me then — and continues to impress me now — as a remarkably risky poem, one that promiscuously mixes elements that should not work together. It is simultaneously lyric and satiric — a heartfelt evocation of a fallen and doomed man wrapped inside a scathing indictment of American consumerism."

This poem opened *The Drive-In*, setting the satirical tone and the colloquial voice of an arresting new poet. It is a retelling of the Old Testament story of Samson and Delilah, the former being a rendition of someone like Tom Hanks and the latter a version of Madonna, perhaps. The satire is anything but meek and mild, and many of the poems that follow continue to refer to classical stories, but they are told as contemporary screenplays or TV scripts, and this would be Gwynn's mode throughout his career.

Gwynn is better known as a literary critic and book editor than as a poet, unjustly and unfortunately. His criticism of contemporary poetry regularly appears in the *Sewanee Review* and the *Hudson Review*. For five years in the mid-'eighties he wrote the annual essay

"The Year in Poetry" for the *Dictionary of Literary Biography Yearbook* published by Gale Research, and he is the editor of two volumes of the *Dictionary of Literary Biography* itself, covering contemporary poets; *The Advocates of Poetry: A Reader of American Poet-Critics of the Modernist Era*; the *Pocket Anthology* series of poetry and fiction from Longman/Penguin; and *New Expansive Poetry: Theory, Criticism, History*, like *No Word of Farewell*, from Story Line Press.

In a long review he wrote for the fall 1986 issue of the *New England Rreview / Bread Loaf Quarterly*, Gwynn objected to the label "New Formalist" being applied to such younger poets as Timothy Steele. He suggested that such a designation at best ought to be applied to faddists who use formal structures to write society verse, a kind of "Yuppy poetry." If that definition is to be accepted, then Gwynn himself is no neoformalist. He is certainly, however, one of the new generation of formal poets who can make the language dance and go deep. As X. J. Kennedy said in his blurb for *The Drive-In*, "Verse so strictly crafted is rare, yet Gwynn is no mere tinkering formalist: his work has equal parts of passion, energy, and outrageousness. Poem after poem reads like a tightly corked explosion. — Here is a mature, slowly perfected voice with its own distinctive power and resonance." Perhaps a brief example is in order...an example and a credo:

ARS POETICA

Sweet music makes the same old story new.
That is a lie, but it will have to do.

One poem from *The Drive-In* that was left out of the new book is "Three Views of the Young Poet," a most unusual piece in that it is written in a form that is foreign to Gwynn's nature, "free verse" (actually, prose). It may safely be taken as at least semi-autobiographical because of the universality of its situation. In the first section, subtitled "Observed," "The young poet stares into the toilet. / He sees his own reflection there / And most of last night's pink chablis. 'I greet you,' says the young poet [parodying Emerson's letter to Whitman], 'At the beginning of a grape career.'" The butt of Gwynn's satire is often himself.

In part two, "On the Movies," the writer is channel surfing through the late shows. "While the young poet feels that vampires represent / A symbolic revolt against Victorian sexual repression, / He has never said so, lest he be labeled / A smart ass by his friends." Then, "On channel 9 / Tangier, free city and teeming crosscurrent / Of international intrigue, etc., serves as the stage / For a poor comedian, played by a rich comedian / Well-known for his right-wing sympathies, / To capture a commie spy for the CIA. / With all the prophetic weight of 30 years' hindsight / The young poet says nothing, lacking an audience. / The star's last name, he notes to himself, is "Hope." The reading audience also notes the irony.

This poem should never have been left out of a selected poems if only because part three, "En Famille," is the most devastating portrait of a dysfunctional modern family one could Hope to read: "The young poet is talking to his father, / To whom he is related by blood / And a lengthy history of travail / And who is not, in any case, to be confused / With the young poet's father's wife, / Who is related to the young poet / In no way whatsoever. // The young poet's father, whose hand is inside / His shirt, is quoting Napoleon: 'Give them / History,' he declaims, 'Cornelly and Raisin knew no more / Than a good pupil in a rhetoric class. Taste / And Genius cannot be learned. Look at Geethie,' / Adds the young poet's father. 'Goothie, you mean,' / Corrects the young poet's father's wife." Alas! But then, Chicagoans have a Go-eathy Street.

One conjectures that perhaps Gwynn didn't want to include this tripartite mockery in a volume of selected poems that contains two moving elegies to his father who died in 1995, a pilot who had washed out before World War II began, as chronicled in a blank verse elegy, "Randolph Field, 1938," which Gwynn read at a memorial service:

> He'll envy [his buddies] that night when, after supper,
> He lies in bed and smokes. It isn't easy
> To think of them with girls along the River —
> Dancehalls, music, beer, all with such sweetness
> In the mild evening air he'd like to cry.
> He has missed the chance, like Aaron Rosenthal,
> To burn above Berlin; like Thomas Szulic,
> To spin in wingless somewhere over France.

Following this poem in *No Word of Farewell* is an elegy, "A Box of Ashes," with the epigraph *D. E. G., 1917-1995*, written in a highly unusual form, the French rondine — to the best of one's knowledge it is the only such poem written in English. The relationships of sons to fathers are complex and often ambivalent, and the death of a sire is unsettling to the nth degree, as the rondeau "Bone Scan" makes clear:

> Shadows surround me, building in the air
> Like clouds, were I inclined here to compare
> My kingly state to portents in the sky.
> I could say the expected: I could lie,
> Claiming our long-term forecast will be fair.
>
> So, family and friends, do not despair.
> Shadows mean nothing. There is nothing there.
> Knives will find nothing wrong. Still, I know why
>   Shadows surround me.
>
> The night my father died, I moved my chair
> Close to his bed to touch his meager hair
> While shadows gathered in his room that I
> Might gather I was not too young to die.
> Now, circuits close. A tunnel beckons where
>   Shadows surround me.

Gwynn's allusiveness can sometimes be enigmatic, as for instance in "The Hunchback with the Withered Arm," a ballade without an envoi. This is doubtless a version of Quasimodo who is misunderstood, tortured and persecuted, as in the original, but the scene is the countryside, as in *Frankenstein*, not Paris, and the locals appear to be rather passive as whatever it is that is happening happens. It is grisly enough, to be sure, but what is going on? The point of the poem seems to be not satire except in a general way, but rather a contemporary malais told in Movietone segments. The only other contemporary poet I can think of who uses movies in a similar way is Frank Polite.

But it is W. H. Auden who seems to be of most influence here in at least two ways. First, Auden and his English confreres in the pre-World War II period blended formal verse structures with an urbane conversational style, a type of writing that traveled to America and became the period style known as "academic poetry in the United States, and it persisted even into the so-called free verse "Confessional" prose poems of the 'sixties and beyond. However, those post-war poets who were best known for writing formal academic poetry were urbane, cool, blasé, not passionate or angry. Gwynn is both.

The other Auden influence comes out of a poem such as "As I Walked Out One Evening," a ballad written in ballad stanza, $a^4b^3c^4b^3$, which exhibits both ennui or *weltschmerz* (world-sickness) and regret that things and lives are so sad and tawdry. Here are a few stanzas from the Auden poem:

> ...down by the brimming river
>   I heard a lover sing
> Under an arch of the railway:
>   "Love has no ending.
>
> I'll love you, dear, I'll love you
>   Till China and Africa meet
> And the river jumps over the mountain
>   And the salmon sing in the street

and so on until,

> In the burrow of the Nightmare
>   Where Justice naked is,
> Time watches from the shadow
>   And coughs when you would kiss.
>
> In headaches and in worry
>   Vaguely life leaks away,
> And Time will have his fancy
>   Tomorrow or today.

All optimism, all romance, all hope, all glory are illusions, like the movies. The condition of man is both comical and sorry, ridiculous and regrettable or, as Gwynn put it in the last stanza of "Anacreontic,"

> It seems a pity seems a crime
> They'll get you get you every time
> It doesn't matter where you go
> Somehow they always seem to know
> You're out there but it's closing time
> Up to your nuts in drifting snow
> Up to your eyes by frosty dawn
> When you're gone you're gone.

Two further chapbooks followed *The Drive-In*: *Texas Poets in Concert: A Quartet* in 1990 and *The Area Code of God: Seven Poems* in 1993. "The Body Bags" was the title of Gwynn's contribution to *Texas Poets* — The other inhabitants of this condominium complex were Jan Epton Seale, Naomi Shihab Nye, and William Virgil Davis — and it contained ten poems plus two translations from the German of Heinrich Heine and Karl Haushofer. Works from each of these booklets (all of those from the latter — there is a good deal of overlapping among these collections) appear in the new book. *If My Song* in 1999 was a sort of dress-rehearsal for *No Word of Farewell*. It was full of many wonderful things, but because one did not know that a selected poems was in the works, it left this reader with a feeling of frustration. Among those poems from this latter chapbook that are not included in *No Word of Farewell* are "Sir Thomas More" and "Why They Love Us." It is difficult to comprehend why they are not present, but surely one day they will be a part of a Gwynn collected poems.

"My Agent Says" is a *tour-de-force* written in parallels as strict as Christopher Smart's "Of Geoffrey, My Cat," except that they are metered, they rhyme as well, and every line is an incremental refrain; the last line is a circle-back repeton of the first line. "Black Helicopters" is a pantoum, an exotic Malayan form, one of the best written in the language. "Local Initiative" is as sarcastic a diatribe as one will ever read. "The Ballad of Burton and Bobby and Bill" is a rollicking evocation of the teen years by means of a clothing store run by three home town fellers (his paternal step-grandfather, Samuel Henry Jamerson, ran such an establishment). As funny as it is, it rings absolutely true to life, as indeed it did when Gwynn was growing up.

The "Ballade of the Yale Younger Poets of Yesteryear" takes up where *The Narcissiad* left off, and of "Ellenaliv for Lew," one of "Two Villanelles," one can say nothing other than the obvious: it's a howl. Simultaneously a travesty of Dylan Thomas' "Do Not Go Gentle" and an ode, it has been elsewhere described by Gwynn as an "assbackwards Dylanic." One has never enjoyed heroic couplets more than in "Cléante to Elmire," but it's time to quote an entire poem again. "At Rose's Range" has the same quality I recall from *The Last Picture Show*. Gwynn is able to bring to life in a few words, evidently whenever he likes, a scene and a character, even a whole story. This is a sonnet:

Old Gladys, in lime polyester slacks,
Might rate a laugh until she puts her weight
Squarely behind the snubnosed .38,
Draws down and pulls. The bulldog muzzle cracks
And barks six times, and six black daisies flower
Dead in the heart of Saddam's silhouette.
She turns aside, empties, reloads, gets set
And fires again. This goes on for an hour.

Later, we pass the time at the front door
Where she sits smoking, waiting for the friend
Who drives her places after dark: *You know,
Earl's free next month. He says he wants some more
Of what she's got, and she's my daughter so
I reckon there's just one way this can end.*

Who says the sonnet form is dead? That's as clear and complete and accurate a bite of Americana as can be fitted into fourteen lines of iambic pentameter rhymed verse; it's as cogent as Edwin Arlington Robinson's sonnets from Tilbury Town.

Earlier I said that Gwynn, though a practitioner of the ancient bardic arts, was in fact a true experimentalist. No poem shows that more clearly than

CHANG   ENG

*Mount Airy, N. C.
January, 1874*

      Constant other,   *Constant brother*
     who know I think   *to lips that drink,*
    my own thoughts yet   *I would not let*
   will never part   *your sluggard heart*
  in this world from *and blood become*
the self we share — *the cross I bear,*
the ties that bind BODY AND MIND *never to find*
and fates that mesh SPIRIT AND FLESH *hopes that lie fresh*
— our blood now joins   *in our wives' loins.*
  us in one death. *Take the last breath*
   Pity the wives   *and say our lives*
    with whom we shared   *will not be spared.*
     our privacy.   *Remember me*
      Drink with me, slave,   *as one who gave*
       this unison   *warnings to one*
      toast to the grave.   *he could not save.*

The typographical level of this poem is obviously of great importance, yet it is not really a calligramme — a picture poem — although the fact is that visually it imitates the situation of Chang and Eng, the original Siamese twins who were born of Chinese parentage in Mekong, Siam, in 1811. They were exhibited in freak shows in the U.S. and Great Britain from the age of 18, became naturalized American citizens, married two sisters in 1843, and died simultaneously in 1874 — some of these events are alluded to in this pair of parallel poems that are joined at the waist, so to speak. The sonic level of the poem is as important as the typographical. The first full line is an alliterated incremental repeton: "Constant other // constant brother" which sets up the paradox of twins never fully severed one from the other; the poem begins with a burst, in effect an Anglo-Saxon stich — it is more than one can do to refrain from reading the poem the first time as though it were written in dipods separated by caesurae. The poem *almost* makes sense that way.

However, scansion reveals that, taken individually, each poem is written not in stichs but in iambic dimeter verse. The lines are not meant to be read straight across except at the jointure; however, and very strangely, in a way they are, for they rhyme as though they were couplets broken by medial spatial caesurae. Still, these are individual soliloquies spoken by the twins, as the roman type of Chang's speech and the italics of Eng's monologue clearly show. The centers of the linkage lines, seven and eight, are capitalized and are shared in common. This commonality is emphasized by internal rhymes in those two lines:

>   the ties that <u>bind</u> BODY AND <u>MIND</u> *never to <u>find</u>*
>   and fates that <u>mesh</u> SPIRIT AND <u>FLESH</u> *hopes that lie <u>fresh</u>*

The elements that comprise this center are a chiasmus (cross-parallel), for body relates to flesh as mind relates to spirit. Both the carnal and the spiritual are in shared balance between the twins. Gwynn has invented a nonce verse form that both visually and sonically shows the absolute relationship between these twins.

The poem ends with a double envelope, the last word of the first dipod of the third-to-last line rhyming, as usual, with the second dipod, but with both dipods of the last line as well:

>   Drink with me, **slave**,   *as one who **gave***
>   this unison   *warnings to one*
>   toast to the **grave**.   *he could not **save**.*

These are complicated echoics that test the perimeters laid down by Burton.

The sensory level of this poem is least important, for though there are a few descriptions (constant other, constant brother), there are no tropes other than the typographical image itself which constitutes a visual metaphor. This is one of the very few Gwynn poems that has no element of humor in it. The theme of the poem is that the life of one of these twins is the life of the other, and the death of one is likewise the death of the other. These are not two individuals, but one being in a double body.

"Audenesque: For the Late Returns" is a clear derivation from the Auden poem cited earlier, "As I Walked Out One Evening." Both poems are written in ballad stanza, both poems use rhetoric to mock the status quo, both have the same tone of *angst*:

Auden:

> O plunge your hands in water,
>   Plunge them in up to the wrist;
> Stare, stare in the basin
>   And wonder what you've missed.

Gwynn:

> O fathers, hide your daughters,
> O mothers, wash your sons.
> He leadeth by still waters
> And doth restore your guns.

This poem is obviously political in nature, but Gwynn always recalls what most contemporary poets forget when they write public poetry: that unless you wish to be dismissed out of hand as a prosy haranguer or soap-box orator, you need to *sing* your politics into the ear of the reader. After all, poetry is a form of entertainment, a fact which has been largely overlooked by the generations of passé-poets who have written from the 1960's to the present. Who reads Levertov these days, or Ferlinghetti, or even that premier self-abuser Robert Lowell? who besides her claque of feminists reads Adrienne Rich?

When our present civilization crashes and we are swept back into barbarism, perhaps poetry will resume its place at the center of culture. One needs no special equipment for it, not a computer or word-processor, nor a pencil and piece of paper, not even a cave wall. All one needs is intelligence, mnemonic devices, and a voice. Until then, if poetry is to survive as an art, poets are going to have to rediscover what Gwynn always knew: how to entertain the reader, how to "sing" without music, using only the language itself. It can be done. In 1990 Bill Baer founded *The Formalist, A Journal of Metrical Poetry*, a periodical that has been friendly to Gwynn. When he had seen it, the playwright Arthur Miller wrote Baer, "I am sure I will not be the only one who will be grateful for it. Frankly, it was a shock to realize, as I looked through the first issue, that I had very nearly given up the idea of taking pleasure from poetry." As has nearly everyone else, if they knew in the first place that language art can be entertaining and enjoyable.

The new poems of *No Word of Farewell* turn progressively sadder, but no less fine, as in "Bone Scan," "Before Prostate Surgery," "A Box of Ashes," and in "The Dark Place," but the poem that affected this reader most is "Approaching a Significant Birthday, He Peruses *The Norton Anthology of Poetry*." It's every bit as ingenious as the Dylanic villanelle, but it's also ineffably sorrowful. One had seen it before, but it must not have been read carefully enough, or perhaps its being such a tour-de-force was a distraction; in any event, it is one of the most masterful editing jobs in contemporary literature or, for that matter, in any literature. That's right — this is a true poem that was *edited*, not written. Gwynn has somehow managed to make a poem out of lines culled from the familiar poems — one might in fact say "chestnuts," of other poets; not one line is his own. Nevertheless, its effect goes far beyond the sum of its quoted parts. It is, in fact, a deeply serious poem at the same time that it is a parody of poetry. That's one of the most amazing things about Sam Gwynn's talent — he can make fun of something while simultaneously making the reader aware of how shoddily mortal he or she is. He has the ability to cut to the marrow of the human condition and show how ridiculous it is at the same time. I don't know anyone else who can do that consistently, in poem after poem. His pen is a blade with two keen edges:

> All human things are subject to decay.
> Beauty is momentary in the mind.
> The curfew [*sic*] tolls the knell of parting day.
> If winter comes, can Spring be far behind?

One has a theory that to this point Gwynn was merely fooling around, just looking for iambic tetrameter lines that rhymed and seeing if he could get them to meld. Of course, that can't be proven, but the fourth line of the first quatrain is pretty broad in its mockery, undercutting the first three lines which, taken together, may be read as a series of serious assertions.

> Forlorn! the very word is like a bell
> And somewhat of a sad perplexity.
> Here, take my picture, though I bid farewell;
> In a dark time the eye begins to see.

This stanza continues the ambiguity of the preceding one. Here it is line three that's comic, even though the stanza ends rather seriously.

> The woods decay, the woods decay and fall —
> Bare ruined choirs where late the sweet birds sang.
> What but design of darkness to appall?
> An aged man is but a paltry thing.

Who would have thought that Frost and Yeats could come together like that? But let the reader note that now there is very little comedy in these lines. The tone is somber and quiet.

> If I should die, think only this of me:
> Crass casualty obstructs the sun and rain
> When I have fears that I may cease to be,
> To cease upon the midnight with no pain

> And hear the spectral singing of the moon
> And strictly meditate the thankless muse.
> The world is too much with us, late and soon.
> It gathers to a greatness, like the ooze.

Probably the poem was becoming too heavy, too serious, and Gwyn felt it was time to bring the reader up short with the apocopated last line of stanza five. Nevertheless, it's true that feeling sorry for ourselves is ridiculous, that our fears of death are pathetic.

Then to another of Gwynn's influences, Dylan Thomas, whose nostalgic poems perhaps the younger poet wishes he could write without feeling uneasy, even foolish:

> Do not go gentle into that good night.
> Fame is no plant that grows on mortal soil.
> Again he raised the jug up to the light:
> Old age hath yet his honor and his toil.

For readers familiar with these allusions each line brings with it a load of overtone, a suitcase full of old clothes we wish we could wear again as first we wore them when they were found hanging on the rack in Untermeyer's Emporium. The third line will conjure up Edwin Arlington Robinson's old sot Eben Flood indulging in his solitary double-moonlit party while he looked down on Tilbury Town — where, one might add, one had lunch this noon at McDonald's in Gardiner, Maine. This is not a whimsical remark, for it is this type of bringing down to earth in which Gwynn specializes.

> Downward to darkness on extended wings,
> Break, break, break, on thy cold gray stones, O Sea,
> And tell sad stories of the death of kings.
> I do not think that they will sing to me.

That is a sad poem that ends, appropriately, with T. S. Eliot, the man who brought us *weltschmerz* wholesale in the twentieth century. It is also a wonderful *tour-de-force*, an experiment that went right.

Teaching is a calling, and poetry is supposed to be a fine art, but like all other callings and arts, those who are practitioners know that few will appreciate their efforts, that the vineyards are full of crabgrass, locusts, and smut, that the road to Hades is paved with the shades of good intentions misconceived, as in the case of "Our Dean of Something" in "The Classroom in the Mall" who "thought it would be good for Learning (even better for P. R.) to make the school 'accesible to all' and leased the bankrupt bookstore at the mall a few steps from Poquito's Mexican Food and Chocolate Chips Aweigh."

(The alert reader will notice a couple of things here: first, the Gwynn poem is being quoted; second, it is being written out as though it were prose rather than the rhyming iambic pentameter lines in which it appears on the pages of *No Word of Farewell*, and third, the initial letters of the lines are being decapitalized so that the verse won't appear obvious. These things are being done for several reasons, about which more later.)

"So here we are — four housewives, several solemn student nurses, Ms. Light — serious, heavy, very dark — Pete Fontenot, who teaches high-school shop and is besides a part-time private cop who leaves his holstered Glock among the purses, and I, not quite as thin as Chaucer's Clerk — met for our final class while Season's Greetings subliminally echo calls to buy whatever this year's ads deem necessary for Happiness and Joy. The Virgin Mary, set up outside to audit our last meetings, adores her infant with a glassy eye.

"Descend O Muzak! Hail to thee, World Lit! Hail, Epic ('most of which was wrote in Greek') and hail three hours deep in Dante's Hell (the occupants of which no one could spell) — as much as our tight schedule might admit of the Great Thoughts of Man — one thought per week.

"I've lectured facing towards 'the Esplanade' through plate-glass windows. Ah, what do I see? Is that the face 'that launched a thousand ships' awash with pimples?"

There's much more, but that is what teaching is like. Like every noble calling of mankind it is an everyday chore, and the uses of poetry are mundane and banal. Still, it's what teachers and poets do, and the struggle is worthwhile if one can stomach it. It is a prose exercise in a prosaic world. Gwynn never forgets, and he never lets us forget. He also knows that poetry written in verse ought to be read like prose. The late great Australian poet A. D. Hope has written that the poet's traditional job is to "harmonize" prose rhythms and verse meters. In an essay, "Free Verse: A Post Mortem," which was published in his book *The Cave and the Spring* (1970), Hope wrote that many of us confuse the terms "rhythm" and "metre." He points out that "verse employs another set of rhythmic devices in addition to...*natural* [my emphasis] rhythms.... We call this metre, or measure."

Gwynn's poems are songs, but they read as though they were stories written in prose. They are never confessions — he does not wallow around in his sadnesses and drop them into the reader's ears like molten lead, but the reader recognizes the emotion when it is heard. There are surfaces to these poems, and they are usually pretty transparent — one may read them on that level alone, but beneath the surfaces are depths and nuances, overtones and allusions. Like Arthur Miller, the reader will be rewarded beyond his or her expectations by these wonderful artifices.

APPENDIX

THE SULLEN ART
A Postmodern Radio Interview by David Ossman

David Ossman, a California poet and radio literature critic, recorded and produced several radio programs having to do with poetry in the early 1960s. This interview is one of a number Ossman conducted in 1960 and 1961 with contemporary, "new" poets, for a program entitled, "The Sullen Art," broadcast on WBAI-FM Pacifica Radio in New York City. It is archived in the Canaday Center of the University of Toledo Library, in Collection #32, Box #39, which contains cassette tapes of the WBAI interviews.

This collection, narrow in its time frame, yet comprehensive in the selection of its speakers, has two main components: a series of interviews conducted for the radio program "The Sullen Art," and the proceedings of the Berkeley Poetry Conference held in July 1965. From the interviews, Ossman edited another program, "American Poetry, 1961."

While at WBAI-Pacifica Radio in New York City, Ossman developed three types of programs devoted to poetry: readings by poets of note; a series of readings by Donald Allen of poetry both old and new; and a series of interviews with younger poets, illustrated with readings of their works. It was early in 1960 that the idea of "The Sullen Art" was born. Ossman envisioned it as a continuing series of radio programs "inquiring into the sources and future of contemporary poetry." He took the title for the program from Dylan Thomas's poem, "In My Craft or Sullen Art," since Ossman felt that poets, no matter how involved with the affairs of the world, ultimately created their work alone. He also deliberately chose to interview those younger, non-academic poets categorized as "new" or "beat," sometimes quite erroneously. Ossman set out to show that the new poets were "not a bunch of illiterate, barbaric, slightly-criminal types," as they had often been characterized in the popular press. In doing so, he interviewed over forty poets — some of whom have since achieved considerable fame. Ossman later published fourteen of the interviews in *The Sullen Art: Interviews by David Ossman with Modern American Poets*, [New York:

Corinth, 1965].

This interview with Lewis Turco was conducted by David Ossman at the New York City facilities of WBAI-FM Paciifica Foundation on September 26th, 1961, and broadcast the following October 6th at 9:30 p.m., but it has not previously been published. Turco was entering his second year as an Instructor at Fenn College (Cleveland State University since 1965). In the following spring of 1962 he would found the Cleveland Poetry Center at the College, an institution that continues to exist in the twenty-first century.

Ossman. Lewis Turco was born in Buffalo, New York, graduated from the University of Connecticut, did graduate work at the University of Iowa, the Writers' Workshop there, and his first book of poetry, titled, perhaps appropriately, *First Poems*, was published last year by the Golden Quill Press. This book contains poetry written in his early twenties, at least that's the description given in the Introduction by Donald Justice; also, poems by Lewis Turco have been published in "zillions" of magazines — that's the only word I can come up with — at least a vast number of magazines that range from *The Kenyon Review* to *Neon*.

I'd like to discuss, first of all, the University of Iowa experience, the Writers' Workshop there which has in recent years become quite a celebrated workshop, perhaps *the* most celebrated workshop in the country, as distinguished from, let's say, a summer series like Bread Loaf. It's certainly the best-known. A book recently has been released of work published there [*Midland: Twenty-Five Years of Fiction and Poetry from the Iowa Writers' Workshop*], What was your experience at the Iowa Workshop?

Turco. Well, I didn't go out to Iowa for the Workshop itself. I'd written to some people before I went out — W. D. Snodgrass being one, Stephen Berg being another — and they said the Workshop wasn't really what one went out for, it was the contacts, and I must say my experience there proved that statement. The Workshop itself isn't much; the young poets, young writers there in Iowa City are everything.

Ossman. What is the teaching technique at the Workshop? Is there a teaching technique?

Turco. No, not really. No "technique," as such. You go into the Workshop; they have mimeographed manuscripts that they pass out to everybody, poems by the students there; you sit around and criticize these poems. When Paul Engle is there, which is not very often (perhaps that's a good thing), he does most of the talking. When Don Justice has the workshop we have fairly good discussions — we had, I should say, they still have, of course. The discussions sometimes tend to be a bit vicious — there are a number of little schools, and cliques, and coteries in the Workshop. The atmosphere is not, I think, conducive to good writing; it's the after-hours gatherings that really do the work.

Ossman. Do you think that *any* workshop atmosphere is conducive to good writing?

Turco. I think, yes. I've been teaching creative writing at Fenn College in Cleveland for a year now, and I think I learned a lot about how *not* to run a workshop by attending the University of Iowa. You don't want to have the feeling in the workshop that you are God if you're in charge of it, you don't want to allow people to get vicious, you want the atmosphere to be one of constructive criticism. I think under these circumstances the workshop *can* do good work.

Ossman. During the time you were at the Workshop, who were your fellow poets? Can you name a group of people who might be known to the audience?

Turco. I'm sure I can. Of course Paul Engle is in charge of the workshop, Donald Justice is second man, and then among the students there were Vern Rutsala whose poems I'm sure you've seen — he writes mainly social criticism, he's published in quite a number of magazines. There was a chap named Edmund Skellings who had a book out in 1960; Morton Marcus, a young poet; Robert Mezey, who went out to Stanford [University] and who won the Lamont selection this year; Raeburn Miller; a number of others: James Crenner who recently had a poem in the First Appearance Issue of *Poetry* — there were quite a few people out there.

Ossman. Do you think there's a common style of writing that evolves from the experience at the Iowa Worksop?

Turco. Surprisingly, no. There are common *styles*. For instance, Robert Mezey, with Peter Everwine, another young poet, was sort of the mentor of the Neoclassical school out there. They wrote poems that at least had overtones that were similar. And Donald Justice of course wrote poems that were Romantic, and Jim Crenner was captured by Justice's poetry which I regard very highly myself. And there are little groups that get together, like Vern Rutsala and Morton Marcus who both write poetry of social criticism. I didn't belong to a group myself; I sort of played the field.

Ossman. People who are on this program almost inevitably say, "I never belonged to a 'group'." (*laughter*). And I suppose if somebody else were there he'd probably say, "Well, Lew Turco belonged to...."

Turco. Very likely, very likely.

Ossman. But that's just keeping one's own personality and individuality, which is a fine thing. The book which you published last year from Golden Quill — which is, I believe, a New Hampshire concern — was a selection of the Book Club for Poetry. It's a fairly good-sized *small* volume of poetry, and I wonder: how do you feel about it now, one year after its publication and, what, five or six years after writing the poems in it?

Turco. When my *First Poems* was published all of my friends out in Iowa City pounced on me and said, "You should never have published this book. It's not anything like your writing now." I've talked to editors who won't review my book because, they say, "We don't want to type you according to these early poems" which are, as you said earlier, I believe, formal. I'm a formal poet anyway; I'm not writing this *kind* of formal poetry anymore, but I feel that the book does stand for several years of my life that were formulative, you know? I'm not ashamed of the book. I think that I'm going to have a better book out very soon, but it's not the kind of poetry I'm writing now. I suppose you'd say it's precocious student verse. Or something like that.

Ossman. Do you think it's advisable for a poet under thirty to assemble poems which were written, let's say in round numbers, from the age of twenty to twenty-five, who is now writing differently, to publish a book of, as you say, "formulative poetry" — do you think it's advisable for him to publish, literally, his "first poems"?

Turco. Of course, you can't really make a general statement about it. It depends on the poet. Robert Mezey is I think two years younger than I am, and his first book won the Lamont Award. He was writing poetry, *real* poetry, before I was even writing verse. He was — I don't know — when he was eighteen he was a professional writer. Certainly his first book should have come out. In my case I think that the poems will stand perhaps not on the first or even the second level of poetry being written today, but as I said, I'm not ashamed of my book. Don Justice, of course, with his book two years ago was thirty-five when it came out — I don't think you can make a general statement. It depends on the poet, how far along he's gone, when he started writing, how serious he was about it for the first years.

Ossman. That reminds me of Ginsberg whose second book has appeared following — let's see — five years from *Howl*, then *Kaddish*, and now *his* first poems are going to be published, written between '45 and '55, which will be a *retrospective* volume in that sense.

Turco. Well, I'm afraid I'd have to disagree with that. I can see putting out a *first* book of first poems, but I think it's a little bit Narcissistic to go backwards in time and pull out old poems.

Ossman. It seems to me…well, I go back to the word "retrospective" — just as an exhibition might cover a showing of the work of a painter over a particular period, say 1900 to 1910, but I don't know; for a poet it's a sort of a very academic question….

Turco. Of course, in the world of publishing it's a little bit strange sometimes. You've heard of Sam Bradley, the Quaker poet?

Ossman. Yes.

Turco. Well, he had two books out, and his second book was accepted first, so his first book is going to come out second. That was accidental. I wonder if I would agree that the second book should live on the reputation of the first book. I don't know — maybe it's better than the first book.

Ossman. Let's talk about the formalism of these poems. I think there are two ways that a *real* poet starts out. One way is to begin with, let us say, formal training, feeling at home with, or at least reasonably comfortable with the writing of established verse forms: sonnets, villanelles, sestinas, and so on, or metrical forms and / or rhyme. And the other side of the coin is the poet who is unable, even at the beginning, to function within the constrictions of the form. Now eventually they all get up to a point where they're writing their own poetry, but I wonder — now you obviously come from the side that writes formally.

Turco. Umm, I'm thinking that over — I'm not sure that I agree with you about *my* starting out formally. I think you're right when you say people start writing in one of the two ways, either writing freely, which tends to be emotional kinds of verse, or in the forms, experimenting with meters, with rhyme, and so forth. In my creative writing classes I never object to a person who starts in either way. It just seems to me that a person who starts out expressing himself in "free verse" lines is going to take longer to achieve the degree of technical proficiency that the second type will — the man who sets himself specific problems to solve; who, by solving those problems learns something. I have nothing against, as I've said, the "non-formal" way of writing, but — I think, and this is only a theory — it's going to take a longer time for him to achieve this degree of mastery over the language, over the things that go into making up verse. Not necessarily "poetry," just "verse." After all, what is poetry? I don't know, you don't know. Nobody knows.

Ossman. But, Lewis, I'm wondering what your distinction is between *poetry* and *verse* because I make a distinction too.

Turco. Well, I would say that a good man who knows his craft can write competent verse — unfortunately, that's the kind of thing that's being written all over the country. Competent verse is not necessarily poetry.

Ossman. Let me stop you there. Now, it seems to me that this competent verse that *is* being written and widely published all over the country is having something of an ill effect on those poets who *are* starting *formally*. I find that the vast number of young poets that I read in magazine after magazine who have talent can't *see*, can't open up, are under the influence, whether directly or indirectly, of the poets who are content with a kind of easy verse. I think this is *very* bad, and does not bode well for the development of a really rich American verse, let's say, in the 1960s.

Turco. Well, let me say first of all that there's damn little "easy" verse being published in this country. "Easy verse" — Edgar Guest: now *that's* easy verse.

Ossman. Phyllis McGinley won the Pulitzer Prize, let's not forget that.

Turco. You have to give Phyllis McGinley a little more credit than that, though, because just to be able to say something as easily as she seems to be saying it takes a tremendous amount of craft, a tremendous amount of skill. No, if you have something beyond the craft it is bound to creep through the façade of form. If you do not, you're going to stay where you are. Certainly you need something to jar you, everybody does, but just being jarred isn't enough. The people who keep *trying* to write real poetry are very few, I will admit, but then they never would have written it anyway. Whether or not there were any influences in the country that you say are keeping them down. You've got to be honest with yourself, you've got to say, "Look, I've written this thing, is it *really* what I want to say, or is it just saying something very cleverly or very badly, or very "freely," or whatever. Poetry is actually self-examination put into solid substance, into ways of saying what you really mean, and if you don't really mean anything, you're not going to write poetry, whether you're a Beatnik or a vesifier, or a syllabicist, or a whatever.

Ossman. Well, of course the meaning has to be there and the craft has to be there, I think we all accept that, but I'd like to make mention of another thing, and that's an article you wrote called, "The House of Mirrors" that was published in the Spring 1961 issue of *The Midwest Review* in Nebraska. You make several points about new writing today, and go into the barriers against the writing of verse poetry. You say, for example, "One of the unwritten laws of contemporary verse is, "Thou shalt show no sentiment." Another is, "There is sex, perhaps even gentle descriptions of the love act from which a moral is drawn, but often the lack of emotional involvement leaves the reader with the feeling that this is a scene with which he has no connection. If one is sentimental one runs the risk of being corny." Another commandment is, "Thou shalt not be funny." Another, "Thou shalt not stray from iambic pentameter." These seem to me to be rules that are characteristic of this group of poets that I was talking about and the younger poets who are under their influence. It is *not* true of the group that you call the "Beatniks" but that I choose to call, for lack of a better term, "The New American Poets" as defined by the anthology of that title. I prefer not to call them all "Beatniks," there are only three or four "Beat" poets anyway.

Turco. When I said "Beatniks" I wasn't talking about people like Robert Duncan or Robert Creeley....

Ossman. But these rules *do* apply to the so-called "academic" poets, but they don't seem to apply to Creeley, Duncan, [Charles] Olson, and....

Turco. Nor do they apply to James Wright, or Theodore Roethke, nor do they really apply to Richard Wilbur although he's been accused of it very often. What I said in that article was that, I suppose essentially, that you can, A., either want to be a poet or B. want to be *accepted* as a poet. There is a grave and great difference between those two statements. If you really want to be a poet you're not going to remain "influenced" for very long. You're going to say, "I've learned as much as I can from these people, and now I'm going to do what *I* want to do."

Or, if you want to be *accepted* as a poet, you can say, "I'm going to write the kind of verse that everybody who *counts* is writing," and simply stay there. Now I say, further, beyond that article, that the people who stay under this influence would probably never have been able to write great poetry, *real* poetry anyway.

Ossman. But they are published anyway.

Turco. Certainly.

Ossman. Most of the magazines, most of the literary magazines in America, most of the quarterlies anyway, take these poems, and they're taken immediately.

Turco. They're not taken *immediately* — the magazines try to get the best that they can — but you know, that's another aspect of our poetic culture, the tremendous number of magazines that are being published in this country. You can, I think, get a poem published if you just keep sending it out long enough; you'll eventually find the right magazine for it. If you run down the list of magazines in the *International Guide* that *Trace* magazine puts out, eventually you're going to find a publisher for your poem — maybe not *easily*, but you don't want to get into the kind of magazines that will take that kind of verse anyway, do you, if you're a real poet? You'll try to make the big magazines, the good magazines, the ones that you *think* are good, let's put it that way.

Ossman. Yes, but I think you have to really pick and choose those magazines. Many poets who are not formal poets cannot get into "big" magazines, like *Kenyon Review*, let us say, or any number of other quarterlies and reviews. I personally would not send a poem to *Kenyon Review* because what would be the use? I would get it back.

Turco. You'd be wrong. You're talking about John Crowe Ransom's *Kenyon*.

Ossman. Yes.

Turco. Well, he's not there anymore. *Kenyon* has a new editor — Robie Macauley is open to a much wider range of poetry than Ransom was.

Ossman. Maybe I'll have to revise my practices regarding the *Kenyon Review*, but there certainly are twenty or thirty others in this category that....

Turco. Let's talk about *The Hudson Review*. Do you know Archie [A. R.] Ammons' verse? I was recently at Bread Loaf [Writers' Conference] and met Archie Ammons for the first time. He writes a long, loose free verse kind of poetry. Now *The Hudson Review* likes his work well enough to have published ten or fifteen pages of his poems in last fall's issue. He's writing poetry that's not like any other poetry in the country, I think. It doesn't approximate Creeley's work, it doesn't approximate Ginsberg's, it doesn't even approximate Carl Sandburg's. These magazines are always interested in getting what they consider to be the best poetry available. Unfortunately, there's damn little really good poetry available.

Ossman. Do you think things are breaking down into a kind of median ground now? It used to be that there were the "little" little magazines that things were published in, then there were the big ones that you didn't even care about. Do you think things are going toward a center ground? I've talked with a number of editors who are trying to put out a magazine which will publish not only Allen Ginsberg or not only Donald Justice but both Donald Justice *and* Allen Ginsberg. And then I said that this is a thing to be desired, a magazine which will publish *all* the good work that's being [written], not just one kind or another. But it seems to me majority of the magazines are devoted to just one kind of poetry or another.

Turco. Unfortunately, the reason for that is that maybe one editor runs the magazine. He has his point of view. I haven't met an honestly catholic magazine editor, though I've met a number of men who *say* they are, but whose catholicity, rather than *small* letter catholic is *large* letter Catholic. And if a magazine isn't run by one editor, it's run by a board of editors, and so a poem is run through this board and a truly outstanding poem may be liked by one of the editors, but the other four will vote against it.

I don't know what the answer is; I don't see any reason why there should be any number of magazines that are truly catholic because, if you don't like *The Kenyon Review*, if you don't like *the Hudson Review*, if you don't like *Neon*, if you don't like some of the other magazines, don't publish in them. Publish in the ones you do like, that you're able to get into. Some people publish in *The New Yorker* — I'm not one of them; some people publish in *The Saturday Evening Post* — I'm not one of them; some people publish in *The Atlantic* and in *Harper's* and *The Ladies' Home Journal* — I'm not one of any of those, nor are a number of excellent poets that I know personally.

Ossman. Well, just to conclude this so that we'll have some time to hear some of your poetry, perhaps this is advice, but the thing not to do is run down the list of magazines in *The International Guide*, but to read the magazines…

Turco. Absolutely.

Ossman. …and to say, "This is a magazine that I want to be in because I feel comfort able in this company," regardless whether it's *Hudson* or *Neon* or *Yugen* or *The Evergreen Review* or *Partisan*.

Turco. That is the attitude that I think more people ought to cultivate.

CHAPTER BIBLIOGRAPHIES

INTRODUCTION BIBLIOGRAPHY

Donald Allen, *The New American Poetry 1945-1960*, New York: Evergreen, 1961.
Philip Dacey, David Jauss, Editors, *Strong Measures,* New York: Harper and Row, 1986.
Donald Davie, *Articulate Energy*, New York: Macmillan, 1958.
Ralph Waldo Emerson, "The American Scholar," and "The Poet" in *The Complete Essays*, ed. Brooks Atkinson, New York: Modern Library, n.d. [c. 1940].
Donald Hall, Robert Pack, Louis Simpson, *The New Poets of England and America: An Anthology* [First Selection], New York: Meridian, 1957.
Donald Hall, Robert Pack, *The New Poets of England and America: An Anthology* Second Selection, Cleveland: Meridian/World, 1962.
David Lehman, *Ecstatic Occasions, Expedient Forms*, New York: Macmillan, 1987.
David Perkins, *A History of Modern Poetry*, 2 vols., Cambridge: Harvard University Press, 1987.
Donald Barlow Stauffer, *A Short History of American Poetry*, New York: E. P. Dutton, 1974.
Lewis Putnam Turco, *The Book of Forms: A Handbook of Poetics*, E. P. Dutton, 1968.
———, *The New Book of Forms: A Handbook of Poetics*, Hanover: University Press of New England, 1986.
———, *Visions and Revisions of American Poetry*, Fayetteville: University of Arkansas Press, 1986.
Various authors, "Freedom and Form: American Poets Respond," *Mississippi Review*, vi:1, 1977.
Hyatt H. Waggoner, *American Poets from the Puritans to the Present*, Boston: Houghton Mifflin, 1968; rev. ed., 1986.
———, *Emerson As Poet*, Princeton: Princeton University Press, 1974.
Miller Williams, Editor, *Patterns of Poetry*, Baton Rouge: Louisiana State University Press, 1986.

CHAPTER ONE BIBLIOGRAPHY

James Atlas, *Delmore Schwartz: The Life of an American Poet*, New York: Harcourt, Brace, 1977.
W. H. Auden, *The Double Man*, New York: Random House, 1941.
——, *Poems*, London: Faber and Faber, 1930.
Elizabeth Bishop, *Complete Poems*, New York: Farrar, Straus and Giroux, 1969.
——, *North and South*, Boston: Houghton Mifflin, 1946.
——, *Poems: North and South — A Cold Spring*, Boston: Houghton Mifflin, 1955.
Louise Bogan, *Achievement in American Poetry*, Chicago: Henry Regnery, 1951.
James E. B. Breslin, *From Modern to Contemporary*, Chicago: University of Chicago, 1984.
Cleanth Brooks and Robert Penn Warren, eds., *Conversations on the Craft of Poetry*, New York: Holt, Rinehart and Winston, 1961.
——, *Understanding Poetry*, New York: Henry Holt, 1938
J. A. Bryant, Jr., *Understanding Randall Jarrell*, Columbia: University of South Carolina Press, 1986.
Hayden Carruth, ed., *The Voice That Is Great Within Us*, New York: New York: Bantam Books, 1970.
Louis O. Coxe, *The Last Hero and Other Poems*, Nashville: Vanderbilt University Press, 1965.
——, *The Middle Passage*, Chicago: University of Chicago Press, 1960.
——, *Nikal Seyn, Decoration Day: A Poem and a Play*, Nashville: Vanderbilt University Press, 1966.
——, *The North Well*, Boston: David Godine, 1985.
——, *Passage Selected Poems 1943-1978*,Columbia: University of Missouri Press, 1979.
——, *The Sea Faring and Other Poems*, New York: Henry Holt, 1947.
——, *The Second Man and Other Poems*, Minneapolis: University of Minnesota Press, 1955.
——, *The Wilderness and Other Poems*: Minneapolis: University of Minnesota Press, 1958.
Donald Davie, *Articulate Energy*, New York: Harcourt, Brace, 1958.
John Ciardi, ed., *Mid-Century American Poets*, New York: Twayne Publishers, 1952.
Richard Eberhart, *A Bravery of Earth*, London: Cape, 1930.
——, *Poems, New and Selected*, New York: New Directions Press, 1944.
——, *Selected Poems* 1930-1965, New York: New Directions, 1965.
——, *Thirty-One Sonnets*, New York: Eakins Press, 1967.
Bernard F. Engel, ed., *The Achievement of Richard Eberhart*, Glenview, Il.: Scott, Foresman, 1968.
Paul Engle and Langland, Joseph, eds., *Poet's Choice*, New York: Dial Press, 1962.

Suzanne Ferguson, *The Poetry of Randall Jarrell*, Baton Rouge, La.: Louisiana State University, 1971.
Harvey Gross, *Sound and Form in Modern Poetry*, Ann Arbor, Mi.: University of Michigan Press, 1968.
William Heyen, ed. *Profile of Theodore Roethke*, Columbus, Oh.: Charles E. Merrill, 1971.
Donald L. Hill, *Richard Wilbur*, New York: Twayne, 1967.
Frederick J. Hoffman, ed., *The Achievement of Randall Jarrell*, Glenview, Il.: Scott, Foresman, 1970.
Randall Jarrell, *Blood for a Stranger*, New York: Harcourt, Brace & Co., 1942.
——, *Little Friend, Little Friend*, New York: Dial Press, 1945.
——, *Losses*, New York: Harcourt, Brace, 1948.
——, *The Lost World*, New York: Macmillan, 1965.
——, *Poetry and the Age*, New York: Alfred A. Knopf, 1955.
——, *Selected Poems*, New York: Alfred A. Knopf, 1955.
Walter B. Kalaidjian, *Understanding Theodore Roethke*, Columbia, S.C.: University of South Carolina Press, 1987.
Ross Labrie, *Howard Nemerov*, Boston: Twayne Publishers, 1980.
Robert Lowell, *Life Studies*, New York: Farrar, Straus, 1959.
Karl Malkoff, *Crowell's Guide to Contemporary American Poetry*,
Louis J. Martz, *The Achievement of Theodore Roethke*, Glenview, Il.: Scott, Foresman, 1966.
Ralph J. Mills, *Richard Eberhart*, Minneapolis, Mn.: University of Minnesota, 1966.
Howard Nemerov, *Collected Poems*, Chicago: University of Chicago Press, 1978.
——, *Guide to the Ruins*, New York: Random House, 1950.
——, *The Image and the Law*, New York: Holt, Rinehart, 1947.
——, *Mirrors and Windows*, Chicago: University of Chicago Press, 1958.
——, *New and Selected Poems*, Chicago: University of Chicago Press, 1960.
Oberg, Arthur, *Modern American Lyric*, New Brunswick: Rutgers University Press, 1978.
David Perkins, *A History of Modern Poetry*, Vol. II, Cambridge, Ma.: Harvard University, 1987.
Theodore Roethke, *Collected Poems*, Garden City, N.Y.: Doubleday & Co., 1968.
——, *The Lost Son and Other Poems*, Garden City, N.Y.: Doubleday & Co., 1948.
——, *Open House*, New York: Alfred A. Knopf, 1941.
——, *Praise to the End!* Garden City: Doubleday & Co., 1951.
——, *Words for the Wind*, Garden City, N.Y.: Doubleday and Co., 1958.
Delmore Schwartz, *In Dreams Begin Responsibilities*, New York: Norfolk, Ct: New Directions Press, 1938.
——, *Summer Knowledge: New and Selected Poems 1938-1958*, Garden City, N.Y.: Doubleday & Co., 1959.
Karl Shapiro, *The Bourgeois Poet*, New York: Random House, 1964.
——, *Collected Poems* 1940-1978, New York: Random House, 1978.
——, *Essay on Rime*, New York: Reynal & Hitchcock, 1945.

——, *Person, Place and Thing*, New York: Reynal & Hitchcock, 1942.
——, *Poems*, Baltimore: Waverly Press, 1935.
——, *Poems of a Jew*, New York: Random House, 1958.
——, *Trial of a Poet*, New York: Reynal & Hitchcock, 1947.
——, *V-Letter and Other Poems*, 1944.
W. D. Snodgrass, *Heart's Needle*, New York: Alfred A. Knopf, 1959.
Stephen Stepanchev, *American Poetry Since 1945*, New York: Harper and Row, 1967.
Anne Stevenson, *Elizabeth Bishop*, New York: Twayne Publishers, 1966.
Allen Tate, *The Poetry Reviews, 1924-1944*, Baton Rouge, Louisiana State University Press, 1983.
Hyatt H. Waggoner, *American Poets from the Puritans to the Present*, Boston: Houghton Mifflin, 1968.
Robert Penn Warren and Cleanth Brooks, editors, *Understanding Poetry*, New York: Henry Holt, 1938.
John Hall Wheelock, ed., *Poets of Today VII*, New York: Charles Scribner's Sons, 1960.
Richard Wilbur, *Advice to the Prophet*, New York: Harcourt, Brace & Co., 1961.
——, *Ceremony and Other Poems*, New York: Harcourt, Brace, & Co., 1950.
——, *New and Collected Poems*, San Diego, Cal.: Harcourt, Brace, Jovanovich, 1988.
, *Poems 1943-1956*, London: Faber and Faber, 1956.
, *The Poems*, New York: Harcourt, Brace, 1963.
——, *Seed Leaves*, Boston: David R. Godine, 1974.
——, *Things of This World*, New York: Harcourt, Brace, 1956.
——, *Walking To Sleep*, New York: Harcourt, Brace, 1969.
Mary J. J. Wrinn, *The Hollow Reed*, New York: Harper & Bros., 1935.

CHAPTER TWO BIBLIOGRAPHY

Donald M. Allen, ed., *The New American Poetry 1945-1960*, New York: Grove Press, 1960.
Stephen Berg, and Robert Mezey, eds., *Naked Poetry: Recent American Poetry in Open Forms*, Indianapolis, In.: Bobbs Merrill, 1969.
——, New Naked Poetry, Indianapolis, In.: Bobbs Merrill, 1976.
Robert H. Brower and Earl Miner, *Japanese Court Poetry*, Stanford: Stanford University Press, 1961.
Don Byrd, *Charles Olson's Maximus*, Urbana, Il.: University of Illinois Press, 1980.
Gregory Corso, *Long Live Man*, New York: New Directions Press, 1962.
Robert Creeley, *A Day Book*, New York: Charles Scribner's Sons, 1972.
——, *For Love: Poems 1950-1960*, New York: Charles Scribner's Sons, 1962.
——, *Le Fou*, Columbus, Oh.: Golden Goose Press, 1952.
——, *Mirrors*, New York: New Directions Press, 1983.
——, *Pieces*, Los Angeles, Ca.: Black Sparrow Press, 1968.
Stephen Cushman, "Forms of Poetry," *Sewanee Review*, xcvi:1, Winter 1988.

Robert Duncan, *Ground Work*, New York: New Directions Press, 1984.
——, *Heavenly City, Earthly City,* Berkeley, Ca.: Bern Porter, 1947.
Lawrence Ferlinghetti, *A Coney Island of the Mind*, New York: New Directions Press, 1958.
——, *Over All the Obscene Boundaries: European Poems and Translations*, New York: New Directions Press, 1986.
——, *Pictures of the Gone World*, San Francisco: City Lights Books, 1955.
Arthur Ford, *Robert Creeley*, Boston: Twayne Publishers, 1978.
Allen Ginsberg, *Collected Poems 1947-1980*, New York: Harper and Row, 1984.
——, Howl and Other Poems, San Francisco: City Lights Books, 1956.
R. Barbara Gitenstein, *Apocalyptic Messianism and Contemporary Jewish-American Poetry*, Albany, N.Y.: State University of New York Press, 1986.
Donald Hall, Robert Pack and Louis Simpson, editors, *The New Poets of England and America*, Cleveland: Meridian Books, 1957.
——, and Robert Pack, eds., *The New Poets of England and America*, Second Selection, Cleveland: Meridian Books, 1962.
Robert Hallberg, von, *Charles Olson: The Scholar's Art*, Cambridge, Ma.: Harvard University Press, 1978.
Henry Harrison, ed., The Grub Street Book of Verse, New York: Henry Harrison, 1927
Daniel G. Hoffman, ed., *Harvard Guide to Contemporary American Writing*, Cambridge, Ma.: Harvard University Press, 1979.
Yoel Hoffman, ed. & tr., *Japanese Death Poems*, Rutland and Tokyo: Charles E. Tuttle, 1986.
George S. Lensing, *Collected Poems*, New York: Knopf, 1957.
Walter Lowenfels, ed., *Poets of Today: A New American Anthology*, New York: International Publishers, 1964.
David Meltzer, *The Name Selected Poetry 1973 1983*, Santa Rosa: Black Sparrow Press, 1984.
Nolan Miller, and Judson Jerome, eds., *New Campus Writing 3*, New York: Grove Press, 1959.
Marianne Moore, Howard Nemerov, and Alan Swallow., eds., *Riverside Poetry 3*, New York: Twayne Publishers, 1958.
Charles Olson, *The Maximus Poems* [1-10 & 11-22], New York: Jargon/Corinth Books, 1960.
——, *Maximus Poems IV, V, VI*, London: Cape Goliard Press, 1968.
——, *Maximus Poems, Volume Three*, New York: Viking/Grossman, 1975.
——, *The Maximus Poems*, ed. George Butterick, Berkeley, Ca.: University of California Press, 1983.
Joel Oppenheimer, *The Dancer*, Highlands, N. C.: The Jargon Society, 1952.
——, *The Dutiful Son*, Highlands, N. C.: The Jargon Society, 1957.
——, *In Time: Poems, 1962-1968*, Indianapolis: Bobbs-Merrill, 1969.
——, *The Love Bit and Other Poems*, New York: Totem Press, 1962.

——, *New Spaces: Poems 1975-1983*, Los Angeles, Ca.: Black Sparrow Press, 1985.
Thomas Parkinson, ed., *A Casebook on the Beat*, New York: Thomas Y. Crowell, 1961.
Sherman Paul, *Olson's Push: Origin, Black Mountain, and Recent American Poetry*, Baton Rouge, La.: Louisiana State University Press, 1978.
David Perkins, *A History of Modern Poetry*, Vol. II, Cambridge, Ma.: Harvard University Press, 1987.
Kenneth Rexroth, *American Poetry in the Twentieth Century*, New York: Herder and Herder, 1971.
M. L. Rosenthal, *The New Poets: American and Pritish Poetry Since World War II*, New York: Oxford University Press, 1967.
Jerome Rothenberg, *New Selected Poems*, New York: New Directions Press, 1986.
——, *White Sun, Black Sun*, New York: Hawk's Well Press, 1960.
Robert B. Shaw, ed., *American Poetry Since 1960: Some Critical Perspectives*, Cheadle Hulme, U.K.: Carcanet, 1973.
Stephen Stepanchev, *American Poetry Since 1945*, New York: Harper and Row, 1965.
Stephen Tapscott, *American Beauty: William Carlos Williams and the Modernist Whitman*, New York: Columbia University Press, 1984.
Lewis Turco, *Poetry: An Introduction Through Writing*, Reston, VA: Reston Publishing Company, 1973.
——, *Visions and Revisions of American Poetry*, Fayetteville, University of Arkansas Press, 1986.
Hyatt H. Waggoner, *American Poets from the Puritans to the Present*, Boston: Houghton, 1968; rev. ed., Baton Rouge: Louisiana State University Press, 1984.
Diane Wakoski, "Picketing the Zeitgeist," *American Book Review*, May-June, 1986.
William Carlos Williams, *The Collected Poems*, Vol. I, 1909-1939, ed. A. Walton Litz and Christopher MacGowan, New York: New Directions, 1986.
——, *In the American Grain*, Norfolk, CT: New Directions, 1925.
——, *Paterson*, New York: New Directions, 1963.
—— *Something to Say: William Carlos Williams on Younger Poets*, ed. James E. B. Breslin, New York: New Directions, 1985.
——, *Spring and All*, Paris: n.p., 1923.

CHAPTER THREE BIBLIOGRAPHY

John Berryman, *Berryman's Sonnets*, New York: Farrar, Straus & Giroux, 1967.
——, *Delusions, Etc.*, New York: Farrar, Straus & Giroux, 1972.
——, *The Dispossessed*, New York: William Sloan Associates, 1948.
——, *The Dream Songs*, New York: Farrar, Straus & Giroux, 1969.
——, *His Toy, His Dream, His Rest*, New York: Farrar, Straus & Giroux, 1969.
——, *Homage to Mistress Bradstreet*, New York: Farrar, Straus & Giroux, 1956.
——, *Poems*, Norfolk, Ct.: New Directions Press, 1942.
——, *77 Dream Songs*, New York: Farrar, Straus & Giroux, 1964.

John Ciardi, *As If: Poems New and Selected*, New Brunswick, N.J.: Rutgers University Press, 1955.
——, *Birds of Pompeii*, Fayetteville, Ar.: University of Arkansas Press, 1985.
——, *Homeward to America*, New York: Henry Holt & Co., 1940.
——, *Live Another Day: Poems*, New York: Twayne Publishers, 1949.
——, *The Lives of X*, New Brunswick, N.J.: Rutgers University Press, 1972.
——, ed., *Mid-Century American Poets*, New York: Twayne Publishers, 1950.
——, *Other Skies*, Boston: Little, Brown & Co., 1947.
——, *Selected Poems*, Fayetteville, Ar.: University of Arkansas Press, 1984.
Vince Clemente, ed., *John Ciardi: Measure of the Man*, Fayetteville: University of Arkansas Press, 1987.
James Dickey, *From Babel to Byzantium: Poets and Poetry Now*, New York: Farrar, Straus, and Giroux, 1968.
Ed Dinger, *Seems Like Old Times*, Iowa City, Ia.: Iowa Writers' Workshop, 1986.
Donald J. Greiner, ed., *American Poets Since World War II*, Part 2, Detroit: Bruccoli Clark/Gale Research, 1980.
Emily Grosholz, editor, *Telling the Barn Swallow: Poets on the Poetry of Maxine Kumin*, Hanover: University Press of New England, 1997.
Jeffrey Helterman, "W. D. Snodgrass," in Donald J. Greiner, ed., *American Poets Since World War II*, Part 2, Detroit: Bruccoli Clark/Gale Research, 1980.
William Heyen, ed., *American Poets in 1976*, Indianapolis: Bobbs-Merrill Company, 1976.
John Holmes, *Address to the Living*, New York: Henry Holt, 1937.
——, *The Double Root*, New York: Twayne Publishers, 1950.
——, *The Fortune Teller*, New York: Harper and Brothers, 1961.
——, *Map of My Country*, New York: Duell, Sloan and Pearce.
——, *Selected Poems*, Boston: Beacon Press, 1965.
——, *The Symbols*, Iowa City IA: The Prairie Press, 1955.
——, *Writing Poetry*, Boston: The Writer, Inc., 1960.
Edward Krickel, *John Ciardi*, Boston: Twayne Publishers, 1980.
Judith Kroll, *Chapters in a Mythology, The Poetry of Sylvia Plath*, New York: Harper & Row, 1976.
Maxine Kumin, *Halfway*, New York: Holt, Rhinehart and Winston, 1961.
——, *The Long Approach*, New York: Viking, 1986.
——, *The Nightmare Factory*, New York: Harper & Row, 1970.
——, *The Privilege*, New York: Harper & Row, 1965.
——, *Selected Poems 1960-1990*, New York: W. W. Norton, 1998.
Robert Lowell, *For Lizzie and Harriet*, New York: Farrar, Straus & Giroux, 1973.
——, *The Land of Unlikeness*, Cummington, Ma.: Cummington Press, 1944.
——, *Life Studies*, New York: Farrar, Straus & Cudahy, 1959.
——, *The Mills of the Cavanaughs*, New York: Harcourt, Brace, 1951.
——, *The Old Glory*, New York: Farrar, Straus & Giroux, 1964.

Arthur Oberg, *Modern American Lyric*, New Brunswick: Rutgers University Press, 1978.
Alicia Suskin Ostriker, *Stealing the Language: The Emergence of Women's Poetry in America*, Boston: Beacon, 1986.
Robert Phillips, *The Confessional Poets*, Carbondale, Il.: Southern Illinois University Press, 1973.
Sylvia Plath, *Ariel*, New York: Harper & Row, 1966.
——, *The Bell Jar*, New York: Harper & Row, 1966.
——, *Collected Poems*, edited by Ted Hughes, New York: Harper & Row, 1981.
——, *The Colossus*, London: Heinemann, 1960.
——, *Winter Trees*, New York: Harper & Row, 1972.
Anne Sexton, *All My Pretty Ones*, Boston: Houghton Mifflin, 1962.
——, *The Book of Folly*, Boston: Houghton Mifflin, 1972.
——, *To Bedlam and Part Way Back*, Boston: Houghton Mifflin, 1960.
——, *Words for Dr. Y*, Boston: Houghton Mifflin Company, 1978.
W. D. Snodgrass, After Experience, New York: Alfred A. Knopf, 1968.
——, *The Fuhrer Bunker*, Brockport: BOA Editions, 1977 & 1995.
——, *Heart's Needle*, New York: Alfred A. Knopf, 1959.
——, *If Birds Build with Your Hair*, New York: Nadja Press, 1979.
——, *A Locked House*, Concord, N. H.: W. B. Ewert, 1986.
——, *Remains: Poems* by "S. S. Gardons," Mount Horeb, Wi.: Perishable Press, 1970.
——, *Selected Poems*, New York: Soho Press, 1987.
Stephen Spender, *Love-Hate Relations: English and American Sensibilities*, New York: Random House, 1974.
Allen Tate, *The Poetry Reviews*, 1924-1944, Baton Rouge: Louisiana State University Press, 1983.
Lewis Turco, *Poetry: An Introduction Through Writing*, Reston: Reston Publishing Co., 1973.
——, *A Sheaf of Leaves: Literary Memoirs*, Phoenix, AZ: Star Cloud Press, 2004.
Helen Vendler, *Part of Nature, Part of Us*, Cambridge: Harvard University Press, 1980.

CHAPTER FOUR BIBLIOGRAPHY

Donald M. Allen, *The New American Poetry 1945-1960*, New York: Grove Press, 1960.
Amiri Baraka, see LeRoi Jones.
Arna Bontemps and Langston Hughes, eds., *Poetry of the Negro, 1746-1949*, 1949.
Anne Bradstreet, *The Works*, ed. Jeannine Henley, Cambridge, Ma.: Belknap Press, 1967.
Cleanth Brooks and Robert Penn Warren, eds., *Understanding Poetry*, New York: Henry Holt, 1938.
Gwendonyn Brooks, *Annie Allen*, New York: Harper & Row, 1949.
——, *Beckonings*, Detroit: Broadside Press, 1975.
——, *Blacks*, Detroit: The David Company, 1987.

———, *Family Pictures*, Detroit: Broadside Press, 1970.
———, *Gottschalk and the Grande Tarantelle*, Chicago: The David Company, 1988.
———, In the Mecca: *Poems*, New York: Harper & Row, 1968.
———, *The Near-Johannesburg Boy*, Chicago: The David Company, 1986.
———, *Riot*, Detroit: Broadside Press, 1969.
———, *Selected Poems*, New York: Harper & Row, 1963.
———, *A Street in Bronzeville*, New York: Harper & Row, 1945.
———, *To Disembark*, Detroit: Broadside Press, 1981.
———, *Winnie*, Chicago: The David Company, 1988.
Mary K. DeShazer, *Inspiring Women: Reimagining the Muse*, New York: Pergamon Press, 1986.
Fred M. Feltrow, *Robert Hayden*, Boston: Twayne Publishers, 1984.
Barbara Charlesworth Gelpi, and Albert Gelpi, eds., *Adrienne Rich's Poetry*, New York: W. W. Norton & Co., 1975.
Erwin R. Glikes and Paul Schwaber, eds., *Of Poetry and Power*, New York: Basic Books, 1964.
William J. Harris, *The Poetry and Poetics of Amiri Baraka: The Jazz Aesthetic*, Columbia: University of Missouri Press, 1985.
Robert Hayden, *American Journal*, New York: Liveright, 1982.
———, *Angle of Ascent*, New York: Liveright, 1975.
———, *A Ballad of Remembrance*, London: P. Bremen, 1962.
———, *Figures of Time*, Nashville Tn.: Hemphill Press, 1955.
———, *Heart-Shape in the Dust*, Detroit, Mi.: Falcon Press, 1940.
———, with Myron O'Higgins, *The Lion and the Archer*, n.p.: Counterpoise, 1948.
———, *The Night-Blooming Cereus*, London: Paul Bremen, 1972.
———, *Selected Poems*, New York: October House, 1966.
———, *Words in the Mourning Time: Poems*, New York: October House, 1970.
Stephen Henderson, ed. *Understanding the New Black Poetry*, New York: 1973.
Theodore Hudson, *From LeRoi Jones to Amiri Baraka: The Literary Works*, Durham: Duke University Press, 1973.
Langston Hughes, ed., *New Negro Poets U.S.A.*, Bloomington: Indiana University Press, 1964.
———, *The Weary Blues*, New York: Alfred A. Knopf, 1926.
LeRoi Jones, *Black Art*, Newark, N.J.: Jihad Publications, 1966.
———, *Black Magic*: Poetry 1961-1967, Indianapolis, In.: Bobbs Merrill, 1969.
———, *The Dead Lecturer*, New York: Grove Press, 1964.
———, *It's Nation Time*, Chicago: Third World Press, 1970.
———, *Preface to a Twenty Volume Suicide Note*, New York: Totem Press, 1961.
———, *Selected Poetry*, New York: William Morrow, 1979.
———, *Spirit Reach*, Newark N.J.: Jihad Publications, 1972.
Carolyn Kizer, *Knock Upon Silence*, Garden City, N. Y.: Doubleday & Co., 1971.
———, *Mermaids in the Basement: Poems for Women*, Port Townsend: Copper Canyon,

1984.

———, *Midnight Was My Cry: New and Selected Poems*, New York: Doubleday, 1971.

———, *The Nearness of You: Poems for Men*, Port Townsend: Copper Canyon, 1986.

———, *The Ungrateful Garden*, Bloomington, In.: Indiana University Press, 1961.

———, *Yin: New & Selected Poems*, Garden City: Doubleday & Co., 1984.

Denise Levertov, *The Double Image*, London: Cresset Press, 1946.

———, *Footprints*, New York: New Directions, 1972.

———, *Here and Now*, San Francisco: City Lights Books, 1957.

———, *The Jacob's Ladder*, New York: New Directions Press, 1965.

———, *A Marigold from North Vietnam*, New York: Albondocani Press-Ampersand Books, 1968.

———, *O Taste and See: New Poems*, New York: New Directions Press, 1964.

———, ed., *Out of the War Shadow: An Anthology of Current Poetry*, New York: War Resisters League, 1967.

———, *Overland to the Islands*, Highlands, N. C.: The Jargon Society, 1958.

———, *With Eyes at the Back of Our Heads*, New York: New Directions Press, 1959.

Wendy Martin, *An American Triptych: Anne Bradsteet, Emily Dickinson, Adrienne Rich*, Chapel Hill: University of North Carolina Press, 1984.

Robert McGovern and Richard Snyder, eds., *60 on the 60's*, Ashland: Ashland Poetry Press, 1969.

Maria K. Mootry and Gary Smith, eds., *A Life Distilled: Gwendolyn Brooks, Her Poetry and Fiction*, Urbana: University of Illinois Press, 1987.

Alicia Suskin Ostriker, *Stealing the Language*: *The Emergence of Woman's Poetry in America*, Boston: Beacon Press, 1986.

Adrienne Rich, *A Change of World*, New Haven, Ct.: Yale University Press, 1951.

———, *Poems, Selected and New, 1950-1974*, New York: W. W. Norton & Company, 1975.

———, *Your Native Land, Your Life*, New York: W W. Norton, 1986.

Lewis Turco, "Angle of Ascent: The Poetry of Robert Hayden," *Michigan Quarterly Review*, Spring 1977.

———, *Poetry: An Introduction Through Writing*, Reston: Reston Publishing Company, 1973.

———, *Visions and Revisions of American Poetry*, Fayetteville: University of Arkansas Press, 1986.

Hyatt H. Waggoner, *American Poets from the Puritans to the Present*, Revised Edition, Baton Rouge: Louisiana State University Press, 1984.

Gary Youree, ed., *Poets for Peace: Poems from the Fast*, New York: Poets for Peace, 1967.

CHAPTER FIVE BIBLIOGRAPHY

David Bellamy, ed., *American Poetry Observed: Poets on their Work*, Urbana: University of Illinois Press, 1984.

Robert Bly, *Four Ramages of Robert Bly*, Daleville, In.: The Barnwood Press, 1983.
——, *The Light Around the Body*, New York: Harper & Row, 1967.
——, *Loving a Woman in Two Worlds*, Garden City, N.Y.: The Dial Press/Doubleday & Co., 1985.
——, *Silence in the Snowy Fields: Poems*, Middletown, Ct.: Wesleyan University Press, 1967.
Richard Emil Braun, *Bad Land*, Penland, N. C.: The Jargon Society, 1971.
——, *Children Passing*, Austin, Tx.: The University of Texas Press, 1962.
——, *Companions to Your Doom*, n.p.: Fresco Press, 1961.
——, *The Foreclosure*, Urbana, Il.: University of Illinois Press, 1972.
Richard J. Calhoun and Robert W. Hill, *James Dickey*, Boston: Twayne Publishers, 1963.
James Dickey, *From Babel to Byzantium*, New York: Farrar, Straus and Giroux, 1968.
——, *The Central Motion: Poems 1968-1979*, Middletown, Ct.: Wesleyan University Press, 1983.
——, *Into the Stone* in *Poets of Today VII* ed. Wheelock, New York: Charles Scribner's Sons, 1960.
——, *Night Hurdling*, Columbia, S. C.: Bruccoli Clark, 1983.
——, *Poems 1957-1967*, Middletown, Ct.: Wesleyan University Press, 1967.
——, *The Suspect in Poetry*, Madison, Mn.: The Sixties Press, 1964.
Norman Friedman, "Vern Rutsala" in *Contemporary Poets*, 2nd ed., James Vinson, ed., Chicago, Il.: St. James Press, 1975.
Donald Hall, Robert Pack and Louis Simpson, eds., *The New Poets of England and America*, Cleveland, Oh.: Meridian Books, 1957;
——, and Robert Pack, eds., *The New Poets of England and America*, Second Selection, Cleveland, Oh.: Meridian Books, 1962.
William Heyen, ed. *American Poets in 1976*, Indianapolis: Bobbs-Merrill, 1976.
Richard Jones, and Kate Daniels, eds., *Of Solitude and Silence: Writings on Robert Bly*, Boston: Beacon Press, 1981.
Weldon Kees, *Collected Poems*, ed. Donald Justice, Iowa City, Ia.: Stone Wall Press, 1960.
——, *The Fall of the Magicians*, New York: Reynal & Hitchcock, 1947.
——, *The Last Man*, San Francisco: Colt Press, 1943.
——, *Poems 1947-1954*, San Francisco: Adrian Wilson, 1954.
Arthur Koestler, *The Ghost in the Machine*, New York: Macmillan, 1968.
Vern Rutsala, *Backtracking*, Santa Cruz, Ca.: Story Line Press, 1985.
——, *The Harmful State*, Lincoln, Ne.: Best Cellar Press, 1971.
——, *The Journey Begins*, Athens. Ga.: University of Georgia Press, 1976.
——, *Laments*, New York: New Rivers Press, 1975.
——, *The Mystery of Lost Shoes*, Amherst, Ma.: Lynx House Press, 1984.
——, *The New Life*, Portland, Or.: Trask House Press, 1978.
——, *Paragraphs*, Middletown: Wesleyan University Press, 1978.
——, *Selected Poems*, Brownsville, Or.: Story Line Press, 1991.

———, *Small Songs: A Sequence of Poems*, 1969.
———, *Walking Home from the Icehouse*, Pittsburgh, Pa.: Carnegie-Mellon University Press, 1981.
———, *The Window*, Middletown, Ct.: Wesleyan University Press, 1964.
Dave Smith, *Local Assays: On Contemporary American Poetry*, Urbana: University of Illinois Press, 1985.
———, ed., *The Pure Clear Word: Essays on the Poetry of James Wright*, Urbana: University of Illinois Press, 1982.
Richard P. Sugg, *Robert Bly*, Boston: Twayne Publishers, 1986.
Lewis Turco, *First Poems*, Francestown: Golden Quill Press, 1960.
———, *The New Book of Forms: A Handbook of Poetics*, Hanover: University Press of New England, 1986.
———, *Poetry: An Introduction Through Writing*, Reston: Reston Publishing Co., 1973.
———, *Visions and Revisions of American Poetry*, Fayetteville: University of Arkansas Press, 1986.
Hyatt H. Waggoner, *American Poets from the Puritans to the Present*, Boston: Houghton Mifflin, 1968.
James Wright, *Collected Poems*, Middletown, Ct.: Wesleyan University Press, 1971.
———, *The Green Wall*, New Haven, Ct.: Yale University Press, 1957.
———, *Saint Judas*, Middletown, Ct.: Wesleyan University Press, 1959.
———, *To a Blossoming Pear Tree*, Middletown, Ct.: Wesleyan University Press, 1978.

CHAPTER SIX BIBLIOGRAPHY

Philip Dacey, and David Jauss, eds., *Strong Measures: Contemporary Poems in Traditional Forms*, New York: Harper and Row, 1986.
Jonathan Holden, *Style and Authenticity in Postmodern Poetry*, Columbia, Mo.: University of Missouri Press, 1986.
Richard Hugo, *Death of the Kapowsin Tavern*, New York: Harcourt, Brace, 1965.
———, *Good Luck in Cracked Italian*, Cleveland: World Publishing Co., 1959.
———, *The Lady in Kicking Horse Reservoir*, New York: W. W. Norton & Co., 1973.
———, *Making Certain It Goes On: The Collected Poems*, New York: W. W. Norton & Co., 1984.
———, *A Run of Jacks*, Minneapolis, Mn.: University of Minnesota Press, 1961.
Robin Skelton, ed., *Five Poets of the Pacific Northwest*, Seattle: University of Washington Press, 1964.
William Stafford, *Allegiances*, New York: Harper & Row, 1970.
———, *Down in My Heart*, Elgin, Il.: Brethren Publishing Co., 1947.
———, "Keeping the Lines Wet," *Prairie Schooner*, Summer 1977.
———, *The Rescued Year*, New York: Harper & Row, 1966.
———, *Roving Across Fields*, Daleville, In.: Barnwood Press Cooperative, 1983.
———, *Someday, Maybe*, New York: Harper & Row, 1973.

——, *Stories that Could Be True: New and Collected Poems*, New York: Harper & Row, 1977.
——, *Traveling Through the Dark*, New York: Harper & Row, 1962.
——, *West of Your City*, Los Gatos, Ca.: Talisman Press, 1960.
Lewis Turco, *Poetry: An Introduction Through Writing*, Reston: Reston Publishing Co., 1973.
——, *Visions and Revisions of American Poetry*, Fayetteville: University of Arkansas Press, 1986.
Alberta Turner, ed., *Poets Teaching: The Creative Process*, New York: Longman, 1980.
David Wagoner, *Dry Sun, Dry Wind*, Bloomington, In.: Indiana University Press, 1953.
——, *First Light*, Bloomington, In.: Indiana University Press, 1983.
——, *The Nesting Ground*, Bloomington, In.: Indiana University Press, 1963.
——, *A Place to Stand*, Bloomington, In.: Indiana University Press, 1958.
——, *Sleeping in the Woods*, Bloomington, In.: Indiana University Press, 1974.
——, *Who Shall Be the Sun*, Bloomington, In.: Indiana University Press, 1978.
——, *Staying Alive*, Bloomington, In.: Indiana University Press, 1966.
James Wright, *The Branch Will Not Break: Poems*, Middletown, Ct.: Wesleyan University Press, 1963.

CHAPTER SEVEN BIBLIOGRAPHY

Donald M. Allen, ed., *The Collected Poems of Frank O'Hara*, New York: Alfred A. Knopf, 1971.
——, ed., *The New American Poetry 1945-1960*, New York: Grove Press, (1960)
John Ashbery, *The Double Dream of Spring*, New York: E. P. Dutton Co., 1970.
——, *The Poems*, New York: Tiber Press, 1960.
——, *Rivers and Mountains*, New York: Holt, Rinehart & Winston, 1966.
——, *Selected Poems*, London: Cape, 1967.
——, *Some Trees*, New Haven, Ct.: Yale University Press, 1956.
——, *The Tennis Court Oath: A Book of Poems*, Middletown, Ct.: Wesleyan University Press, 1962.
——, *Three Poems*, New York: Viking Press, 1972.
——, *Turandot and Other Poems*, New York: Tibor de Nagy Gallery, 1953.
——, *The Vermont Journal*, Los Angeles: Black Sparrow Press, 1975.
——, *A Wave*, New York: Viking Penguin, 1984.
Raymond Carney, "John Ashbery," in Donald J. Greiner, ed., *American Poets Since World War II*, Part 1: A-K, Detroit MI: Gale Research, 1980.
Tracy Chevalier, ed., *Contemporary Poets*, Fifth Edition, Chicago: St. James Press, 1991.
Philip Dacey, and David Jauss, eds., *Strong Measures: Contemporary American Poetry in Traditional Forms*, New York: Harper & Row, 1986.
Donald Davie, *Articulate Energy*, New York: Macmillan, 1958.
Sue Gangel, "Interview with John Ashbery," in Joe David Bellamy, ed., *American Poetry*

Observed: Poets on Their Work, Urbana: University of Illinois Press, 1984.
Lyn Hejinian, *The Guard*, n.p.: Tuumba Press, 1983.
David Lehman, ed., *Ecstatic Occasions, Expedient Forms*, New York: Macmillan, 1987.
Frank O'Hara, *A City Winter, and Other Poems*, New York: Tibor de Nagy Gallery, 1952.
——, *The Collected Poems of Frank O'Hara*, New York: Alfred A. Knopf, 1971.
——, *Jackson Pollock*, New York: George Braziller, 1959.
——, *Love Poems (Tentative Title)*, New York: Tibor de Nagy, 1965.
——, *Lunch Poems*, San Francisco: City Lights Books, 1964.
——, *Meditations in an Emergency*, New York: Grove Press, 1957.
——, *Odes*, New York: Tiber Press, 1960.
——, *Oranges*, New York: Tibor de Nagy Gallery, 1953.
——, *Robert Motherwell*, New York: Museum of Modern Art, 1965.
——, *Second Avenue*, New York: Totem/Corinth Press, 1960.
Ron Padgett, and David Shapiro, eds., *An Anthology of New York Poets*, New York: Random House, 1970.
——, *The Poetics of Indeterminacy: Rimbaud to Cage*, Princeton: Princeton University Press, 1981.
Marjorie Perloff, *Frank O'Hara, Poet Among Painters*, New York: George Braziller, 1977.
David Shapiro, *John Ashbery: An Introduction to the Poetry*, New York: Columbia University Press, 1979.
Radcliffe Squires, Cornar, Philadelphia, Pa.: Dorrance, 1940.
——, *Fingers of Hermes*, Ann Arbor, Mi.: University of Michigan Press, 1965.
——, *Where the Compass Spins*, New York: Twayne Publishers, 1951.
Frederick Goddard Tuckerman, *The Complete Poems*, ed. N. Scott Momaday, New York: Oxford University Press, 1965.
Lewis Turco, *The Book of Forms: A Handbook of Poetics*, New York: E. P. Dutton & Co., 1968.
——, *The New Book of Forms*, Hanover: University Press of New England, 1986.
——, *Poetry: An Introduction Through Writing*, Reston: Reston Publishing Co., 1973.
——, *Visions and Revisions of American Poetry*, Fayetteville: University of Arkansas Press, 1986
Alberta Turner, ed., *Poets Teaching: The Creative Process*, New York: Longman, 1980.
James Vinson, ed., *Contemporary Poets*, Second Edition, New York: St. Martin's, 1975.

CHAPTER EIGHT BIBLIOGRAPHY

Anonymous, "The Best of the New Generation," *Esquire*, December 1984.
Bruce Bawer, "The Poet in the Gray Flannel Suit," *Connoisseur*, February 1989.
Darlyn Brewer, "Poets in the Corporation," *Coda: Poets & Writers Newsletter*, November / December 1985.
Philip Dacey, and David Jauss, eds., *Strong Measures: Contemporary American Poetry in*

Traditional Forms, New York: Harper & Row, 1986.

Frederick Feirstein, ed., *Essays on the New Narrative & The New Formalism*, Santa Cruz, CA: Story Line Press, 1989.

Dana Gioia, *Daily Horoscope* [chapbook], Iowa City, Ia.: Windhover Press, 1982.

——, *Daily Horoscope* [collection], St. Paul, Mn.: Graywolf Press, 1986.

——, ed., *Formal Introductions*, West Chester, Pa.: Aralia Press, 1989.

——, *Night Watch*, Chester, Pa.: Aralia Press, 1990.

——, with William Jay Smith, *Poems from Italy*, St. Paul, Mn.: New Rivers Press, 1985.

—— *Summer*, West Chester, Pa.: Aralia Press, 1983.

——, *Words for Music*, Iowa City, Ia.: Windhover Press, 1987.

Bruce Goldman, "Syllable Hill," *Stanford*, Fall 1986.

R. S. Gwynn, *The Advocates of Poetry: A Reader of American Poet-Critics of the Modernist Era*,

——, *The Area Code of God: Seven Poems*, 1993.

——, *Bearing & Distance*, 1977

——, *The Drive-In*, 1986

——, *The Narcissiad*, 1981

——, *New Expansive Poetry: Theory, Criticism, History*, like *No Word of Farewell*, from Story Line Press.

——, *No Word of Farewell, Selected Poems: 1970-2000*, 2000, Story Line Press, 199.

——, *Texas Poets in Concert: A Quartet*, 1990

Charles O. Hartman, *Free Verse*, Princeton, NJ: Princeton U. Press, 1980.

Jonathan Holden, *Style and Authenticity in Postmodern Poetry*, Columbia: University of Missouri Press, 1986.

A. D. Hope, *The Cave and the Spring*, 1970.

Donald Justice, *Departures*, New York: Atheneum Publishers, 1974.

——, *From a Notebook*, Iowa City, Ia.: Seamark Press, 1972.

——, *A Local Storm*, Iowa City, Ia.: Stone Wall Press, 1963.

——, *Night Light*, Middletown, Ct.: Wesleyan University Press, 1967.

——, *Selected Poems*, New York: Atheneum, 1979.

——, *Sixteen Poems*, Iowa City, Ia.: Stone Wall Press, 1970.

——, *The Summer Anniversaries*, Middletown, Ct.: Wesleyan University Press, 1960.

——, *The Sunset Maker*, New York: Atheneum, 1987.

——, *Tremayne*, Iowa City, Ia.: The Windhover Press, 1984.

Bernard Kaplan, ed., *Freedom and Form: American Poets Respond*, Hattiesburg MS: *Mississippi Review*, Vol. VI, No. 1, 1977.

Greg Kuzma, "Dana Gioia and the Poetry of Money," in *The Northwest Review*, November 1988.

David Lehman, ed., *Ecstatic Occasions, Expedient Forms: 65 Leading Contemporary Poets Select and Comment on their Poems*, New York: Macmillan Publishing Co., 1987.

Robert Lowell, *Life Studies*, New York: Farrar, Straus, & Cudahy, 1959.

Robert McDowell, "Poetry Chronicle," *Hudson Review*, Winter 1987.
Fleming Meeks, "Freedom To Be Creative," *Forbes*, March 1988.
Mary Anne Ostrom, "Of Rhyme and Reason," *Manhattan, Inc.*, October 1986.
Robert Richman, Review of Daily Horoscope, *The New Criterion*, February 1987.
Thomas Swiss, "Six Poets," *Sewanee Review*, Spring 1986.
Lewis Turco, *The New Book of Forms*, Hanover: University Press of New England, 1986.
——, *The Public Poet*, Ashland, OH: Ashland University Poetry Press, 1991.
——, *Visions and Revisions of American Poetry*, Fayetteville: University of Arkansas Press, 1986.
——, "The Year in Poetry," *Dictionary of Literary Biography Yearbook: 1986*, Detroit: Gale Research, 1987.
——, Gioia, *et alia*, "Picketing the Zeitgeist Picket," *The American Book Review*, November-December 1986.
Diane Wakoski, "The New Conservatism in American Poetry," *ibid.*, May-June 1986.
Miller Williams, *The Boys on Their Bony Mules*, Baton Rouge, La.: University of Louisiana Press, 1983.
——, *A Circle of Stone*, Baton Rouge, La.: Louisiana State University Press, 1964.
——, ed., *Contemporary Poetry in America*, New York: Random House, 1973.
——, *Distractions*, Baton Rouge, La.: University of Louisiana Press, 1981.
——, *Halfway from Hoxie: New and Selected Poems*, New York: E. P. Dutton, 1973.
——, *Imperfect Love*, Baton Rouge, La.: University of Louisiana Press, 1986.
——, *Living on the Surface: New and Selected Poems*, Baton Rouge LA: Louisiana State University Press, 1990.
——, *The Only World There Is*, New York: E. P. Dutton, 1971.
——, ed., *Patterns of Poetry: An Encyclopedia of Forms*, Baton Rouge LA: Louisiana State University Press, 1986.
——, *Recital*, Valparaiso, Chile: Ediciones Oceano, 1964.
——, *So Long at the Fair*, New York: E. P. Dutton, 1968.
——, *Why God Permits Evil*, Baton Rouge, La.: University of Louisiana Press, 1977.

Appendix Bibliography

Donald Allen, *The New American Poetry 1945-1960*, New York: Evergreen, 1961.
Paul Engle, Henri Coulette, and Donald Justice, editors, *Midland: Twenty-Five Years of Fiction and Poetry from the Iowa Writers' Workshop*, New York: Random House, 1961.
David Ossman, *The Sullen Art: Interviews by David Ossman with Modern American Poets*, New York: Corinth, 1965.
Lewis Putnam Turco, *First Poems*, Francistown, NH: Golden Quill Press, 1960.
———, "The House of Mirrors," *The Midwest Review*, Spring 1961; published as
———, "Considering Post Modernism" in *Visions and Revisions of American Poetry*, Fayetteville: University of Arkansas Press, 1986.

Index

"ABC," 211
abstract (musical) syntax, *Intro.*, 26, 59, 189 *ff.*, 190, 200, 202
abstraction abstractionism, 29, 30, 40-41, 74, 153, 159, 161, 189 *ff.*, 192-194
"Abulafia," 82
academic poetry, *Intro.*, 23, 114, 241
academic poets, *Intro.*, 21, 29, 34-35, 48, 50, 54-55, 159, 163, 165, 226, 236, 249
Academy of American Poets, 206
acatalectic, acatalexis, 102-103
accent, accentual, *Intro.*, 50, 51, 56, 62, 63, 65, 66, 68, 95, 102, 125, 133, 138, 163, 165, 182-183, 201, 209, 212, 215, 216, 220, 223, 230, 233-234
access, 83, 124, 126, 190, 212
The Achievement of Randall Jarrell, 45
The Achievement of Richard Eberhart, 30
The Achievement of Theodore Roethke, 48
acrostic, acrostics, 237
Address to the Living, 93
Adrienne Rich's Poetry, 147
"Adults Only," 23
Advice to a Prophet, 32
The Advocates of Poetry: A Reader of American Poet-Critics of the Modernist Era, 239
aesthetic distance, 68, 208
After Experience, 101
"After the Chinese," 211
"Afterword," 101
agnostic, agnosticism, *Intro.*, 40, 41
agonist, 61
Conrad Aiken, *Intro.*
alchemy, 71
Alexandrine, 237
Dante Alighieri, 25, 229, 230, 232, 248
  Inferno, 230
Allegiances, 181
All My Pretty Ones, 116
Donald Allen, 70, 77, 141, 195, 197-198, 249
  The New American Poetry 1945-1960 141, 195
"Allen Ginsberg and the Messianic Tradition," 89
alliteration, 24, 26, 50, 58, 66, 88, 97, 104, 105, 155, 173, 183, 220, 231, 263
allusion, 23, 27, 28, 39, 84, 96, 106, 109, 123, 132, 135, 143, 144, 218, 236, 247, 248
Alone with America, 186
alternative press movement, Introduction, 203

ambiguity, 27, 35, 40, 49, 173, 210, 246
The American Book Review, 227, 232
"American-Jewish Poetry: An Overview," 82
American Journal: Poems, 82
American Poetry Since 1945, 45, 77
American Poetry Since 1960, 79
American Poets from the Puritans to the Present, 48, 52, 114, 144
American Poets in 1976, 116, 186
American Poets Since World War II, Part 2, 181
An American Triptych, 148
amateur poet, Introduction, 61, 62
American Plainstyle, 179*ff.*
American Poetry Observed, 188, 199
American Romantic formalists, Introduction
"American Sketches," 209
"Amnesiac," 133
A. R. Ammons, 200, 256
"Among Philistines," 238
amplification, amplify, 66, 106
Amy Lowell Traveling Scholarship, 213
"Anacreontic," 241-242
anagram, anagrams, 101, 237
analogy, analogous, 68, 179, 189
analyzed rhyme, 85
anapest, 57, 155, 163, 164, 216, 235
The Anatomy of Melancholy, 237
anaphora, 22
anecdote, 64
"Angel and Stone," 41
angle, 126, 131, 190, 221
Angle of Ascent, 132, 135
Anglo-Saxon prosody, 33, 50-52, 163
anchored abstraction, 41
Anne Bradstreet, *Intro.*, 148
Annie Allen, 137
"Anniversaries," 206
antagonist, 96
An Anthology of New York Poets, 193
"Anthony St. Blues," 208
anti-academic, *Intro.*, 29, 77, 91, 160
anti-formalism, anti-formalist, 29, 54, 62, 162, 226
anti-Modernist, 52
"Aphasia," 59-60
apocalypse, apocalyptic, 82-83, 89
Apocalyptic Messianism and Contemporary Jewish-American Poetry, 83
apocopate, apocopation, 26, 134, 247

apocopated rhyme, 27
Guillaume Apollinaire, 196
Apollonian, *Intro.*
"The Applicant," 121
"Approaching a Significant Birthday, He Peruses *The Norton Anthology
 of Poetry*" 245
"April Inventory," 101-102, 106
archaism, 208
archetype, archetypal, 36, 45, 46, 49, 70, 181
The Area Code of God: Seven Poems, 242
"Are There Any Questions," 177
Ariel, 121-123, 126
Aristotle, Aristotelian, *Intro.*, 48, 61
Arna Bontemps, editor, with Langston Hughes,
 Poetry of the Negro, 1746-1949, 131
"Ars Poetica," 190, 200, 239
art for art's sake, *Intro.*
Art News, 199
art of language, 77
"The Art of Poetry," 188
art poetry, 61, 83
Articulate Energy, 189
artificial poetry — see social poetry, *Intro.*
John Ashbery, *Intro.*, 195, 199*ff.*, 203
    As We Know, 199
    "At North Farm," 199
    Double Dream of Spring, 199
    Everyman, 195
    "Farm Implements and Rutabagas in a Landscape," 202
    Introduction to the *Collected Poems of Frank O'Hara*, 196
    "Pantoum," 202
    The Poems, 199
    Rivers and Mountains, 199
    Selected Poems, 199
    Some Trees, 201, 202
    The Tennis Court Oath, 199
    Three Poems, 199
    Turandot and Other Poems, 199
    "Variation on a Noël," 201
    The Vermont Journal, 199
    A Wave, 199
Ashkenazic, 83
"As I Walked Out One Evening," 249
Richard Ashman, 175
As If: Poems New and Selected, 98
"The Aspen and the Stream," 32

"The Associate Professor Delivers an Exhortation to His Failing
 Students," 214
association, *Intro.*, 27, 28, 71, 84, 86, 97, 118, 159, 168, 181, 202, 214
assonance, 24, 28, 50, 66, 85, 123, 155, 173, 220, 231, 236
As We Know, 199
Russell Atkins, 128
The Atlantic, 35, 256
James Atlas, 25
"At Least with Good Whiskey," 99
"At Rose's Range," 242
"At the Fishhouses," 35
"At the Grave," 169
"Aubade," 25
W. H. Auden, 33, 72, 107, 147
 "As I Walked Out One Evening," 245
 The Double Man 22
 "Little Gidding," *Intro.*
 "New Year Letter," 23
 Poems, 23
 "What's the Matter?" 23
"Audenesque: For the Late Returns," 245
"Aunt Jennifer's Tigers," 147
autobiographical poem, 93, 116
"Automobile," 25
avant garde, *Intro.*, 76, 83, 141, 142, 203

From Babel to Byzantium, 118, 163
Backtracking, 172
backwoods boast, 133
Bad Land, 175
"The Bad Uncle," 185
Bill Baer, 245
Deborah Baker, 159
 "Making a Farm: A Literary Biography," 159
ballad, 131, 135, 137, 200, 242, 245
"A Ballad of Remembrance," 131, 135
"The Ballad of Burton and Bobby and Bill," 242
"The Ballad of Nat Turner, 135
A Ballad of Remembrance, 131, 135
The Ballad of the Dollar Hotel and Other Poems, 200
ballade, 242
"Ballade of the Yale Younger Poets of Yesteryear," 242

Joanna Bankier and Deirdre Lashgari, editors, 139
 Women Poets of the World, 139
ban the bomb, 127, 145

INDEX

Amiri Baraka, *Intro.*, 127, 128, 132, 137, 140 *ff.*
    Black Art, 140
    Black Magic: Poetry 1961-1967, 140
    It's Nation Time, 140
    The Dead Lecturer, 140
    "Like, This Is What I Meant!" 142
    "A New Reality Is Better Than a New Movie!" 141
    Preface to a Twenty-Volume Suicide Note, Intro., 140
    Selected Poetry, 140
    Spirit Reach, 140
Basho, 78
Bruce Bawer, 228
The Bean Eaters, 137
Bearing & Distance, 237
beat, 56, 249; also see *stress*
Beat Generation, Beatniks, Beats, *Intro.*, 53, 61, 70, 77, 79, 84, 86, 88-91, 94, 178, 195, 197, 223, 227, 249
Beatific Vision, 86
Beckonings, 137
"Before Prostate Surgery," 194
"Beginnings," 135
Pierre-Jean de Beranger, 194
Bernard W. Bell, 138
    Modern and Contemporary Afro-American Poetry, 138-139
David Bellamy, 188
    American Poetry Observed, 188
The Bell Jar, 121
"Benito Cereno" (stage adaptation from Herman Melville by Robert Lowell), 114
Beowulf, 133
Stephen Berg, editor, with Robert Mezey, 89, 116, 226-227
    Naked Poetry, 115, 231
    New Naked Poetry, 87, 231, 232
Berkeley Poetry Conference, 249
Bill Berkson, 194
Daniel Berrigan, 140
John Berryman, *Intro.*, 24, 29, 101, 107 *ff.*, 108, 109, 117-118, 206
    Berryman's Sonnets, 108
    The Dispossessed, 108
    Dream Songs, 107-109
    "Dream Song 80," 109
    "Dream Song 366," 109
    His Toy, His Dream, His Rest, 108-109
    Homage to Mistress Bradstreet, 108
    "Old Man Goes South Again Alone," 24
    "Op. posth. no. 3" ("Dream Song 80), 109

    Poems, 142
    77 Dream Songs, 109
    "Old Man Goes South Again Alone," 24
"In Bertram's Garden," 208
"Beyond the Hunting Woods," 207
Bible. *Intro.*, 33, 129
The Birds of Pompeii, 98
Elizabeth Bishop, *Intro.*, 35 *ff.*,
    "At the Fishhouses," 35
    "A Cold Spring," 35
    The Complete Poems, 33
    "The Man-Moth," 36
    "Florida," 35
    "Letter to New York," 35
    North and South, 35
    Poems: North and South — A Cold Spring, 35
    Sestina," 37
    "Song for the Rainy Season," 35
Black Art, 140
Paul Blackburn, 73
    "Shop Talk," 73
"Black Helicopters," 242
Black Magic: Poetry 1961-1967, 142
Black Mountain College, *Intro.*, 53, 62, 70, 74, 77, 81
Black Mountain II, 74
    See State University of New York at Buffalo, 70, 74, 91, 140, 203
Black Mountain Review, 70
Black Mountain School, *Intro.,* 33
R. P. Blackmur, 109
Black Muslim, 127
Black poetry, 129, 132, 135
William Blake, 22, 33, 88, 225
    "Creation," 22
    Jerusalem, 33
    "A Little Girl Lost," 22
    Milton, 33
    Songs of Experience, 22
blessing, blessings, 61, 90, 202
Blood for a Stranger, 45
blues, blues stanza, 129, 131, 135, 137, 208, 212
Robert Bly, *Intro.*, 62, 140, 158 *ff.*,
    Four Ramages of Robert Bly, 160
    Leaping Poetry, 159
    The Light Around the Body, 158
    The Lion's Tail and Eyes: Poems Written Out of Laziness and
        Silence, with William Duffy and James Wright, 167

INDEX

281

Loving a Woman in Two Worlds, 161
"March in Washington Against the Vietnam War," 140
News of the Universe: Poems of Two-Fold Consciousness, 159
Silence in the Snowy Fields, 158
"Such Different Wants," 161
"Three Kinds of Pleasures," 160

Robert Bly, 160
"The Body Bags," 242
Louise Bogan, 24
"Bone Scan," 240-241
Arna Bontemps, *Poetry of the Negro, 1746-1949,* co-editor with Langston Hughes, 131
The Book Club for Poetry, 251
The Book of Folly, 118
The Book of Forms, A Handbook of Poetics, 163
The Bourgeois Poet, 54
"A Box of Ashes," 240-242, 245
The Boys on their Bony Mules, 221
Sam Bradley, 252
Anne Bradstreet, *Intro.*, 148
The Works of Anne Bradstreet, 148
brag, braggadocio, 133, 138
The Branch Will Not Break, 167
Georges Braque, 196
Richard Emil Braun, 175 *ff.*, 177
"Are There Any Questions," 177
Bad Land, 175
Children Passing, 175
Companions to Your Doom, 175
"Flirt," 175
The Foreclosure, 175
"Goose," 175
"Harland's Hobby," 175
"Island Lore," 176
"An Unknown Friend," 178

A Bravery of Earth, 29
Bread Loaf Quarterly, 239
Bread Loaf Writers' Conference, 95, 98, 213, 237, 239, 250, 256
breath, breath length, breath pause, 63, 65, 71
James E. B. Breslin, 22
breve, 66
"The Bridge," 28
"The Bridge of Sighs," 186-187
British tradition, 33
Cleanth Brooks (and Robert Penn Warren, editors), 50, 162
Conversations on the Craft of Poetry, 50

Understanding Poetry, 162
Gwendolyn Brooks, *Intro.*, 128, 131, 137 *ff.*, 139-141
    Annie Allen, 137
    The Bean Eaters, 137
    Beckonings, 137
    Family Pictures, 137
    "Foreword" to *New Negro Poets U.S.A.*, 137
    In the Mecca, 137
    "Martin Luther King, Jr.," 140
    Riot, 137
    Selected Poems, 137
    A Street in Bronzeville, 137
    To Disembark, 137
    "We Real Cool," 138
Robert H. Brower and Earl Miner, 63
    Japanese Court Poetry, 63
Elizabeth Barrett Browning, 39
Robert Browning, 129
    "A Toccata of Galuppi's," 129
Mary Bruccoli and Jean W. Ross, editors, 207
    Dictionary of Literary Biography Yearbook: 1983, 207
J. A. Bryant, Jr., 45
    Understanding Randall Jarrell, 45
William Cullen Bryant, *Intro.*
Martin Buber, 48
Gertrude Buckman, 25, 26
    "Rejuvenation," 26
bucolics, 180
burden of tradition, *Intro.*, 39, 222
Robert Burns, 224
Robert Burton, 237
The Anatomy of Melancholy, 237
George F. Butterick, editor, 70
    The Maximus Poems of Charles Olson, 70
Byron, 164; see George Gordon, Lord Byron

caesura, 27, 51, 58, 102, 167, 234-235, 244
John Cage, 196
    "Music of Changes," 196
Richard J. Calhoun and Robert W. Hill, 163
    James Dickey, 164-165
"The Call," 163
Cambridge Poets' Theatre, 195
Canaday Center of the University of Toledo Library, 249
"The Cancer Cells," 30
canon, 29, 63, 132, 149

INDEX 283

canto, 71, 79, 111, 221, 231, 232 *ff.*
The Cantos, 71, 110
Raymond Carney, 72, 200
carol, 201
catalog, catalogue, 30, 42, 63, 88, 132, 133
cauda, coda, 37, 182, 221
C. P. Cavafy, 191
The Cave and the Spring, 248
Paul Celan, 229
    "Todesfuge," 229
The Central Motion: Poems 1968-1979, 164
Ceremony, 32
Chain 66-67
"Chang   Eng," 251
A Change of World, 147
Chapbook, *Intro.*, 101, 171, 172, 175, 190, 203, 206, 211, 228, 237,
    242
Chapters in a Mythology, The Poetry of Sylvia Plath, 122
character, characterization, 33, 67, 71, 73, 84, 87, 96, 97, 101, 106, 109,
    119, 122, 136, 141, 145-146, 171, 175, 185, 191, 200, 211, 214,
    225, 242, 249, 254
Charles Olson's Maximus, 71
Charles Olson: The Scholar's Art, 70
charm, charms, 61
Tracy Chevalier, editor, 191
    Contemporary Poets, Fifth Edition, 191
"Childhood," 212
Children Passing, 176
Chinese literature, 67
"Chinese Nightingale," 69
choka, 67
Barbara Christian, 139
    "Cultural Influences: African American," 139
John Ciardi, *Intro.*, 38, 93, 94, 95 *ff.*
    As If: Poems New and Selected, 98
    "At Least with Good Whiskey," 99
    The Birds of Pompeii, 98
    Homeward to America, 95
    How Does a Poem Mean? 97
    "A Knothole in Spent Time," 95
    Live Another Day: Poems, 95
    The Lives of X, 95
    "A Man's Voice," 94
    Mid-Century American Poets, 38, 94
    Other Skies, 95
    The Selected Poems, 98

circle-back, 106, 242
A Circle of Stone, 213
City Lights Books, 84
Civil Rights Movement, 127, 131, 139
Classical, *Intro.*, 22, 28, 32, 40, 41, 48, 61, 90, 93, 154, 180, 191, 225, 237, 238
"The Classroom in the Mall," 247
clause, 26, 88-90, 196
    dependant clause, 65
    independent clause, 65, 69, 138
    parallel clauses, 89-90
"Cléante to Elmire," 242
climactic parallel, climax, 36, 98, 174
coda, 37, 182, 221
"A Coffee-House Lecture," 226-229
"A Cold Spring," 35
Collected Poems (Creeley), 74
The Collected Poems (Kees), 154
The Collected Poems (Nemerov), 39
Collected Poems (O'Hara), 196
The Collected Poems (Plath), 121
Collected Poems (Roethke), 49
Collected Poems (William Carlos Williams), 63, 67
Collected Poems (Wright), 166
Collected Poems 1940-1978 (Shapiro), 53
Collected Poems 1947-1980 (Ginsberg), 88
College English, 53
The Colossus, 121
common measure, 56, 165, 220
"The Companions," 42-43
Companions to Your Doom, 175
compensatory caesura, 27
The Complete Poems, 191
composition by field, 71
compound sentence, 69
"Compulsory Heterosexuality and Lesbian Existence," 148
conceit, 57, 106, 225, also see extended metaphor
concrete poem, 129; also see spatial prosody
condensation, 23, 67
A Coney Island of the Mind, 84
confessional poetry, confessional poets, Confessional School, *Intro.*,
    29, 93, 101, 106-107, 109, 113, 116, 119, 121, 124, 126, 149,
    160, 169, 188, 206, 241
connotation, 168
consonance, 24, 26, 85, 97, 102, 123, 133, 155, 166, 183, 207, 217,
    220, 225, 236
consonantal echo, 28, 58, 85, 173, 183, 225, 231

Contemporary Poetry in America, 213
Contemporary Poets, Fifth Edition, 191
Contemporary Poets, Second Edition, 191
conversation, 23, 28, 32, 39, 50, 98, 153, 164, 173, 179, 183 *ff.*, 187, 241
Jane Cooper, 107
Cid Corman, 70
    Origin, 70
Cornar, 191
Gregory Corso, *Intro.*, 91
    Long Live Man, 91
    The Vestal Lady on Brattle and Other Poems, 91
Henri Coulette, 107
Counter/Measures, Intro.
counterpoint, 57, 138, 173, 229
"Counting the Mad," 208
couplet, 26, 28, 32, 39, 51, 65-68, 74, 75, 138-139, 182, 183, 202, 210, 217-220, 237, 242, 244
couplet rhyme, 26, 28, 217, 220
Roy W. Cowden, 95
Henry Cowell, 203
Louis O. Coxe, 56 *ff.*
    "Aphasia," 59
    The Last Hero and Other Poems, 56
    The Middle Passage, 56
    Nikal Seyn, Decoration Day: A Poem and a Play, 56
    The North Well, 56
    Passage Selected Poems 1943-1978, 56
    The Sea Faring and Other poems, 56
    The Second Man and Other Poems, 56
    The Wilderness and Other Poems, 56
    "Winter Night," 56 *ff.*
craft, craftsmanship, *Intro.*, 29, 31-33, 37, 43, 46, 48, 50, 53, 72, 94, 100, 102, 114, 121-122, 126, 131, 147, 164, 174, 184, 207, 208, 222, 225-226, 239, 249, 253, 254
    Hart Crane, 28
    "The Bridge," 28
"Creation," 22
"Creation Myth on a Moebius Strip," 41
creative writing, 25, 177, 182, 251, 253; also see writing arts
Robert Creeley, *Intro.*, 20, 74 *ff.*
    Collected Poems, 74
    "Greeting Card," 75
    "The Hero," 74
    Le Fou, 74
    Mirrors, 74

James Crenner, 251
Crosscurrents: A Quarterly, 228
Crossing the Water, 121
Crowell's Guide to Contemporary American Poetry, 35
"Cruising with the Beachboys," 232-233
cue, cues. cue-words, 85, 111, 136
"Cultural Influences: African American," 139
Cultural Nationalism, 139
E. E. Cummings, *Intro.*, 81, 85
Stephen Cushman, 62
    "Forms of Poetry," 62

Philip Dacey and David Jauss, *Intro.*
    Strong Measures, Intro.
dactyl, 163
Dada, Dadaism, 153, 196
"Daddy," 123
"Daily Horoscope," 228-230
Daily Horoscope, 228
Robert Dana, 107
"Dana Gioia and the Poetry of Money," 232
The Dancer, 81
Kate Daniels and Richard Jones, editors, 158
    Of Solitude and Silence: Writings on Robert Bly, 159
Dante, (Dante Alighieri), 25, 229, 230, 232, 248
    Inferno, 248
"Darkness," 25
"The Dark Place," 245
Donald Davie, 189
    Articulate Energy, 189
William Virgil Davis, 242
    Texas Poets in Concert: A Quartet, 242
The Dead Lecturer, 140
"Dear Sorrow 2," 114
"Death of a Student," 54
"The Death of the Ball Turret Gunner," 46
Death of the Kapowsin Tavern, 186
Decade of Protest, 128
deconstruct, deconstruction, 196, 201
deep image surrealism, *Intro.*, 60, 158, 159, 160, 161, 168, 169, 180, 213
Deep Imagism, Deep Imagists: See the above entry
"Degrees of Gray in Philipsburg," 188
Willem de Kooning, 196
Deliverance, 162
Democratic National Convention of 1968, 127

demoted syllable, demotion, 56, 57, 102, 156, 173, 225, 231, 233, 235
Edwin Denby, 195
Departures, 211
Eustace Deschamps, 165
Mary K. DeShazer, 147
 Inspiring Women, 147
Des Imagistes, 62, 68
dialogue, dialogues, 32, 47, 63, 145, 179, 200, 212
James Dickey, *Intro.*, 162 *ff.*, 163-165
 From Babel to Byzantium, 118
 "The Call," 163
 The Central Motion: Poems 1968-1979, 164
 Deliverance, 162
 "Falling," 164
 "The Firebombing," 160
 Into the Stone, 163
 Night Hurdling, 164
 Poems 1957-1967, 163
 "The Shark's Parlor," 164
 "The Sheep Child," 164
 "Sleeping Out at Easter," 163
 The Suspect in Poetry, 163
 "The Underground Stream," 163
William Dickey, 107
Emily Dickinson, 21, 147, 148, 189
Diction, *Intro.*, 21 *ff.*, 33, 40, 59, 72, 76, 81, 98, 108, 109, 117, 123, 138, 168, 173, 191, 197, 206-208, 214, 219, 221, 226
Dictionary of Literary Biography, 207, 239
didactic, didactic poem, 39, 71, 85, 98, 106, 138, 166, 180, 209 210, 220-221, 225, 226
David Dillon, 188
Ed Dinger, 107
 Seems Like Old Times, 107
Dionysian, Dionysus, *Intro.*, 151, 238
dipod, dipodic line, dipodic unit, 51, 244
dirge, 138
discourse, 98, 179, 200
The Dispossessed, 108
Distractions, 213
divine madman, 48
doctrine, 86, 207
documentary, 101
Don Byrd, 71
 Charles Olson's Maximus, 71
"Donald Justice," 207
dot, 66

Double Dream of Spring, 202
double iamb, 172, 216, 231
The Double Image, 144
The Double Man, 23
The Double Root, 93
Down in My Heart, 181
"'Down the Whirlwind of Good Rage': An Introduction to Gwendolyn
    Brooks," 137
dozens, 133
drama, dramatic poetry, 24, 81, 128, 212
dramatic irony, 47
dramatic syntax, 189
dramatic voice, 122
Michael Drayton, 113
    "The Virginian Voyage," 113
"The Dream," 136
dream analysis, 159
"Dream Song 80," 109
"Dream Song 366," 111
Dream Songs, 110-111
drinking song, 166
The Drive-In, 238, 239, 242
"Dry Spell Blues," 129
Dry Sun, Dry Wind, 184
duality, dualities, 59, 67, 251
William Duffy, 167
    *The Lion's Tail and Eyes: Poems Written Out of Laziness and
    Silence*, with Robert Bly and James Wright, 167
Robert Duncan, *Intro.*, 77 *ff.*, 82, 84, 86, 190, 254
    "Four Pictures of the Real Universe," 78
    "The Gate," 78
    Ground Work, 78
    Heavenly City, Earthly City, 77
    The Opening of the Field, 78-79
    "Passages," 78
    "Up Rising," 79
    "The Wall," 79
The Dutiful Son, 81

"E. A. P. — A Portrait," 25
"Early Poems," 209
Richard Eberhart, *Intro.*, 29 *ff.*, 30, 31, 108, 112, 191
    A Bravery of Earth, 29
    "The Cancer Cells," 30
    Florida Poems, 30
    "The Fury of Aerial Bombardment," 30

"The Groundhog," 30
"Opposition," 31
Poems, New and Selected, 29
Thirty-one Sonnets, 29
echo, 28, 58, 85, 97, 124, 137, 155, 173, 183, 190, 200, 207, 208, 220, 225, 231, 236, 244, 248
Ecstatic Occasions, Expedient Forms, Intro., 201, 229
"Editor's Note" to *Words for Doctor Y*, 118
Eddie House, 129
"Dry Spell Blues," 129
egocentric, 68
egopoet, egopoetic voice, *Intro.*, 30, 59, 93, 98, 102, 119, 121, 126, 145, 160, 161, 189, 221, 226
"Eighth Air Force," 46
Gunnar Ekelof, 158
elaboration, 67
elegiac, elegy, 30, 59, 110, 127, 133, 168, 174, 180, 214, 221, 229, 240
Thomas Stearns Eliot, *Intro.*, 18, 19, 23, 26, 36, 68, 73, 74, 84, 112, 137, 189, 191, 200, 202, 247
"Tradition and the Individual Talent," 73
The Waste Land, Intro., 189, 190, 202
elision, 66, 85, 102, 126, 134, 225, 231, 235
Elizabeth Bishop, 35
"Ellenaliv for Lew," 242
ellipsis, 67, 208
Ralph Waldo Emerson, *Intro.*, 48, 49, 52, 62, 71, 94, 164, 181, 182, 239
"The Poet," *Intro.*, 71, 94, 181
emotion, 52, 68, 88, 208, 248, 253, 254
emotive, emotive answer, emotive question, emotive utterance, 63-67
"The Empty House," 172
empathy, empathize, 67, 68, 145, 148, 166
emphasis, *Intro.*, 28, 62, 103, 104, 124, 162, 196, 207, 220, 234, 248
William Empson, 109, 143
"Endecott and the Red Cross," 114
end-man, 111
end-stop, 162
end-word, repeated end-word, 37, 207, 235
Bernard F. Engel, 30
The Achievement of Richard Eberhart, 30
Paul Engle and Joseph Langland, 46
Poet's Choice, 46
English ode, 180
enigma, 59, 175, 177, 178, 241
enjambment, 104

envelope, envelope stanza, 23, 244
envoi, envoy, 37, 67, 241
epigram, epigrams, 171, 211, 237
epiphany, epiphanies, 81, 95, 97, 176, 181
epistle, 188
"Essay on Man," 22, 53
Essay on Rime, 53
Essays on the Beat, 86
etymology, 101
euphuism, 52
Eureka, 34
Evening Wind, 227
The Evergreen Review, 257
Peter Everwine, 251
Everyman, 63, 81, 101, 156
Everyman, 195
exclusive, exclusiveness, 83, 226
exemplar, *Intro.*, 191
existential, 35, 40, 44, 49, 153, 170, 177
expansion, 190, 226
"Expansionist Poetry: The New Formalism and the New Narrative," 228
extended metaphor, 58, 225, see conceit

"Falling," 164
falling rhythm, see meter, 123, 163, 224, 235
Family Pictures, 137
"Farm Implements and Rutabagas in a Landscape," 202
William Faulkner, 109
Federal Writers' Project, 155
Alan Feldman, 197
    Frank O'Hara, 201
Feminist Movement, *Intro.*, 126, 147
Fenn College (Cleveland State University), 53, 213, 250, 251
Lawrence Ferlinghetti, *Intro.*, 84 *ff.*, 86, 87, 88, 144
    A Coney Island of the Mind, 84
    "Note on Poetry in San Francisco," 86
    Over All the Obscene Boundaries, 85
    "The pennycandystore beyond the El," 84-85
    Pictures of the Gone World, 84
    The Secret Meaning of Things, 86
Fred M. Fetrow, 131
    Robert Hayden, 131
fiction, 24, 39, 56, 95, 106, 120, 128, 140, 173, 181, 190, 229, 239
figurative language, figure of speech, see trope
Figures of Time, 131
fifteener, 129

The Fifties, 158
Fingers of Hermes, 191
Donald Finkel, 107
"The Firebombing," 160
"Fire Spirit," 64-65
"First Death," 212
First Light, 185
First Poems, 163, 250, 252
Robert Fitzgerald, 229
Five Poets of the Pacific Northwest, 186
fixed forms, 180
"Flirt," 176
"Florida," 35
Florida Poems, 31
"The Fly," 54
"The Fool's Song," 64, 65
Footprints, 144, 145
"For a Freshman Reader," 210
"For Clement Long, Dead," 214
Arthur L. Ford, 74
       Robert Creeley, 74
The Foreclosure, 178
"Foreword" to *Ariel*, 123
"Foreword to Kelly's Grandchild," 200
"Foreword" to *New Negro Poets U.S.A.*, 137
"Foreword" to *The Works of Anne Bradstreet*, 148
For Lizzie and Harriet, 114
The Formalist, A Journal of Metrical Poetry, 245
"Forms of Poetry," 62
form, formalism, formal poetry, *Intro.*, 21-24, 26, 28, 29, 32, 33, 35,
      37, 39, 45, 48, 49, 53, 54, 56, 59, 62, 63, 65-68, 71, 72, 74-77,
      82, 83, 85, 87-90, 95, 98, 106, 109, 112, 113, 116, 117, 119, 121,
      122, 123, 125, 128, 129, 131, 135, 137, 139, 141, 142, 147, 151,
      155, 162, 163, 165, 167, 169, 171, 175, 179-185, 187, 189,191, 193,
      197, 198, 200-203, 206-209, 243, 245, 252, 253
The Fortune Teller, 94
Four Ramages of Robert Bly, 160
fourteener, 129
Frank O'Hara: Poet Among Painters, 196
"Four Pictures of the Real Universe," 78-79
"Freedom and Form: American Poets Respond," *Intro.*
free verse, *Intro.*, 23, 24, 26, 33, 62, 75, 106, 133, 137, 139, 171,
      214, 216, 226-228, 239, 241, 253, 256
"Free Verse: A Post Mortem," 248
Fresco Chapbook Series, 175
Sigmund Freud, Freudian, 41, 46, 125

Ingegerd Friberg, 160
    Moving Inward, 160
Lewis Fried, editor, 82
    Handbook of American-Jewish Literature, 82
Norman Friedman, 167, 168, 174
"From a Notebook," 211
"From a Notebook, 211
"From Bad Dreams," 212
From LeRoi Jones to Amiri Baraka: The Literary Works, 140-141
Robert Frost, *Intro.*, 50, 93, 98
The Fuehrer Bunker: A Cycle of Poems in Progress, 101, 106
Fugitive, Fugitive Poets, *Intro.*, 23, 45, 50, 112, 162, 223
"'The Furies'—for certain reviewers," 212
"The Fury of Aerial Bombardment," 30

"S. S. Gardons," anagram pseudonym of W. D Snodgrass 101
Steve Garrison, 181
"The," 76
Albert Gelpi and Barbara Charlesworth Gelpi, 147
    Adrienne Rich's Poetry 147
genre, genres, 21, 24, 39, 98, 106, 129, 138, 179, 180, 192,
    208, 220, 225
"George Washington Bridge, December 1929," 27
georgics, 184, 221
The Ghost in the Machine, 158
Dugan Gilman, 159
Allen Ginsberg, *Intro.*, 53, 54, 61, 80, 88 *ff.*, 89, 90, 141, 195, 223, 256
    Collected Poems 1947-1980, 88
    "Howl," 89
    Howl and Other Poems, 89
    "Kaddish," 89
    "Love Forgiven," 90
    "Red cheeked boyfriends," 90
    "A very Dove," 90
Louis Ginsberg, 88
    "To My Two Sons," 88
(Michael) Dana Gioia, *Intro.*, 236, 238
    "Cruising with the Beachboys," 234-235
    "Daily Horoscope," 230
    Daily Horoscope, 229, 230
    "Expansionist Poetry: The New Formalism and the New
        Narrative," 228
    The Gods of Winter, 229
    "The Homecoming," 228
    "Introduction" to *No Word of Farewell* by R. S. Gwynn, 239
    "Lives of the Great Composers," 229

    Night Watch, 229
    Poems from Italy, editor and translator, with William Jay Smith, 228
    Summer, 228
    "A Tune in the Back of My Head," 229
    Words for Music, 228
"Girl Sitting Alone at Party," 210
R. Barbara Gitenstein, 83
    "American-Jewish Poetry: An Overview," 83
    Apocalyptic Messianism and Contemporary Jewish-American Poetry, 83
Erwin A. Glikes and Paul Schwaber, editors
    Of Poetry and Power, 127
"The Goose Fish," 44
George Gordon, Lord Byron, 164
The Gods of Winter, 229
Good Luck in Cracked Italian, 186
"Go Slow," 128
"Goose," 176
"Gray Stone," 187
The Green Wall, 167
"Greeting Card," 75
Donald J. Greiner, editor, 106, 181
    American Poets Since World War II, 72, 181
Harvey Gross, 231
"The Groundhog," 30
Ground Work, 78
"Grown Alba," 81
The Grub Street Book of Verse, 88
The Guard, 190
Edgar Guest, 254
R. S. Gwynn, *Intro.*, 237 *ff.*, 238
    The Advocates of Poetry: A Reader of American Poet-Critics of the Modernist Era, editor, 239
    "Among Philistines," 238
    "Anacreontic," 242
    "Approaching a Significant Birthday, He Peruses *The Norton Anthology of Poetry*." 245
    The Area Code of God: Seven Poems, 242
    "Ars Poetica," 238
    "At Rose's Range," 242
    "Audenesque: For the Late Returns," 245
    "The Ballad of Burton and Bobby and Bill," 242
    "Ballade of the Yale Younger Poets of Yesteryear," 242
    Bearing & Distance, 237
    "Before Prostate Surgery," 245
    "Black Helicopters," 242

"The Body Bags," 242
"Bone Scan," 240
"A Box of Ashes," 240
"Chang   Eng," 243
"The Classroom in the Mall," 247
"Cléante to Elmire," 242
"The Dark Place," 245
The Drive-In, 239
"Ellenaliv for Lew," 242
"Local Initiative," 242
If My Song, 242
"My Agent Says," 242
The Narcissiad, 242
New Expansive Poetry: Theory, Criticism, History, editor, 239
No Word of Farewell, Selected Poems: 1970-2000, 239
"Randolph Field, 1938," 240
"Sir Thomas More," 242
Texas Poets in Concert: A Quartet, with Jan Epton Seale, Naomi Shihab Nye, and William Virgil Davis, 242
"Three Views of the Young Poet," 239
"Two Villanelles," 242
"Why They Love Us," 242

Marilyn Hacker, *Intro.*,
Hades, 124, 247
haikai no renga, 67
haiku, 63, 64, 65, 67, 78, 168, 210
hemistich, 51
Halfway, 119
Halfway from Hoxie, 213
Donald Hall, 159, 197
Mac Hammond, 127
Handbook of American-Jewish Literature, 82
hanka, 66, 67
Thomas Hardy, 191
"Harland's Hobby," 175
Harlem Renaissance, 128
The Harmful State, 171
Harper's, 256
William J. Harris, 141
    The Poetry and Poetics of Amiri Baraka: The Jazz Aesthetic, 141
Henry Harrison, editor, 88
    The Grub Street Book of Verse, 88
Grace Hartigan, 196
Karl Haushofer, 242
The Harvard Guide to Contemporary American Writing, 188

Hawk's Well Press, 83
Nathaniel Hawthorne, 115
    "Endecott and the Red Cross," 115
    "My Kinsman, Major Molineux," 115
Robert Hayden, *Intro.*, 128, 131 *ff.*, 132, 137
    American Journal: Poems, 131
    Angle of Ascent, 131
    "A Ballad of Remembrance," 131, 135
    "The Ballad of Nat Turner," 135
    A Ballad of Remembrance, 131, 135
    "Beginnings," 133, 135
    "The Dream," 135
    Figures of Time, 131
    Heart-Shape in the Dust, 131
    "Homage to the Empress of the Blues," 135
    "Incense of the Lucky Virgin," 133
    The Lion and the Archer, with Myron O'Higgins, 131
    The Night-Blooming Cereus, 131
    "O Daedalus, Fly Away Home," 136
    "Runagate Runagate," 134-135
    Selected Poems, 131
    "Soledad," 136
    "Stars," 134
    "Theme and Variation," 133
    "Those Winter Sundays," 133-134
    "Witch Doctor," 133
    "Words in the Mourning Time," 135
    Words in the Mourning Time: Poems, 131
Robert Hayden, 132, 136
"Heart's Needle," 100
Heart's Needle, Intro., 30, 100, 101
Heart-Shape in the Dust, 131
Heavenly City, Earthly City, 77
Anthony Hecht, *Intro.*
Heinrich Heine, 242
Lyn Hejinian, 190
    The Guard, 190
Ernest Hemingway, 109
Hemistich, 51
Stephen Henderson, editor, 132
    Understanding the New Black Poetry, 132
Jeannine Hensley, editor, 148
    The Works of Anne Bradstreet, 148
Herald Tribune, 199
Here and Now, 144
"The Hero," 74

heroic couplet, 32, 39, 218, 219, 237, 242
Geoff Hewitt, 186
William Heyen, 116, 186
    American Poets in 1976, 116, 186
    Theodore Roethke, 48
Donald L. Hill, 33
    Richard Wilbur, 33
Robert W. Hill and Richard J. Calhoun, 163-164
    James Dickey, 164
Robert Hillyer, 93
His Toy, His Dream, His Rest, 109-110
A History of Modern Poetry, 21
Daniel G. Hoffman, 75, 188
    The Harvard Guide to Contemporary American Writing, 75, 188
    "Poetry: Dissidents from Schools," 188
    "Poetry: Schools of Dissidents," 75
Frederic J. Hoffman, 45
    The Achievement of Randall Jarrell, 45
Yoel Hoffman, 64
    Japanese Death Poems, 64
hokku 67
Jonathan Holden, 187
    Style and Authenticity in Postmodern Poetry, 187
"Hold Hard, These Ancient Minutes in the Cuckoo's Month," 24
John Hollander, *Intro.*, 83, 227
The Hollow Reed, 25, 27
John Holmes, 93 *ff.*, 95, 116, 119, 182
    Address to the Living, 93
    The Double Root, 93
    The Fortune Teller, 94
    Map of My Country, 93
    "Order Clearly Asking," 92
    Selected Poems, 94
    The Symbols, 93
    Writing Poetry, 94
Homage to Mistress Bradstreet, 108
"Homage to the Empress of the Blues," 135
The Homecoming," 228
Homeward to America, 95
A. D. Hope, 248
    The Cave and the Spring, 248
    "Free Verse: A Post Mortem," 248
Gerard Manley Hopkins, 21, 24
    "Hold Hard, These Ancient Minutes in the Cuckoo's Month," 24
    "Hurrahing in Harvest," 21
Hopwood Award, 131, 195

A Howard Nemerov Reader, 39
Richard Howard, 186
    Alone with America, 186
How Does a Poem Mean?, 97
"Howl," 89
Howl and Other Poems, 88
"How to Be Happy: Installment 1053," 157
Theodore Hudson, 140
    From LeRoi Jones to Amiri Baraka: The Literary Works, 140-141
The Hudson Review, 228, 238, 256
Langston Hughes, 127 *ff.*
    "Go Slow," 128
    "A Negro Dreams of Rivers," 128
    New Negro Poets U.S.A., editor, 137
    Poetry of the Negro, 1746-1949, co-editor with Arna Bontemps, 131
    "The Weary Blues," 129
    The Weary Blues, 129
Ted Hughes, 121, 123
    "Notes on Poems," 123
Richard Hugo, 187 *ff.*
    "The Art of Poetry," 188
    "The Bridge of Sighs," 186-187
    Death of the Kapowsin Tavern, 186
    "Degrees of Gray in Philipsburg," 188
    Good Luck in Cracked Italian, 186
    "Gray Stone," 187
    The Lady in Kicking Horse Reservoir, 186
    Making Certain It Goes On, 186
    The Right Madness on Skye, 186
    A Run of Jacks, 186
    31 Letters and 13 Dreams, 186
    What Thou Lovest Well Remains American, 186
    White Center, 186
"Human Being," 145
A Huoyhnhnm's Scrapbook, 175
"Hurrahing in Harvest." 21
"Hymn to the Supreme Being," 22
hypercatalectic, hypercatalexis, 27, 57, 224, 225

iambic, 26-28, 32, 39, 46, 50, 56, 58, 66, 85, 95, 102, 106, 129, 156, 163, 165, 167, 172-173, 182-183, 107, 191, 193, 215-216, 220, 223, 230-231, 233-234, 243, 244, 246, 247, 254
    normative iambic, 56, 95, 102, 220, 230, 233-234
    variable iambic, 27, 28, 85, 215-216
"I Cry Love!" 48

idea, ideational (thematic) level, see level, 23, 24, 27, 28, 32, 41, 48,
    52, 59, 62, 68, 75, 94, 124, 141, 147, 158, 163, 168, 181, 189,
    190, 193, 194, 197, 200, 217, 220, 221, 226, 226, 228, 245, 249
idiosyncratic style, 21, 22, 108, 185
icon, iconoclast, 63, 198
If Birds Build with Your Hair, 106
If My Song, 242
Igarashi, 65
The Image of the Law, 39
Imagism, *Intro.*, 62, 158, 159, 164, 203, 211
Imperfect Love, 213, 221
Implication, 30, 68, 71
Impressionism, impressionist, 52
incantation, incantations, *Intro.*, 23, 61
"Incense of the Lucky Virgin," 133
In Dreams Begin Responsibilities, 26
Inferno, 230
initiate, initiates, 71, 78, 79, 200
Inspiring Women, 147

International Guide to Little Magazines and Small Presses, 264
In the Mecca, 137
In Time: Poems, 1962-1968, 81
Into the Stone, 162, 163
Introduction to the *Collected Poems of Frank O'Hara*, 196
"Introduction" to *No Word of Farewell by R. S. Gwynn*, see Dana Gioia,
    238
"Island Lore," 176
It's Nation Time, 140

The Jacob's Ladder, 144
James Dickey, 164-165
Japanese poetry, 63, 65, 67
Japanese Death Poems, 64
The Jargon Society, 81
Randall Jarrell, 36, 45 *ff.*, 48
    Blood for a Stranger, 45
    "The Death of the Ball Turret Gunner," 46
    "Eighth Air Force," 46
    Little Friend, Little Friend, 45-46
    Losses, 46
    The Lost World, 46
    Poetry and the Age, 36
    "Protocols," 47
    Selected Poems, 46
David Jauss and Philip Dacey, *Intro.*

Strong Measures, Intro.
jazz, 72, 129, 130, 133, 138, 141-143, 155, 184, 229
Robinson Jeffers, *Intro.*, 191
Judson Jerome, 181
Jerusalem, 33
John Ashbery: An Introduction to the Poetry, 203
John Ciardi, 93-95
Samuel Johnson, 22
Le Roi Jones — see Amiri Baraka
Richard Jones and Kate Daniels, editors, 158
  Of Solitude and Silence: Writings on Robert Bly, 158
Jongleur, 84, 86
The Journey Begins, 171
James Joyce, 71
Karl Jung, 36
"Junk," 33
Donald Justice, 106, 107, 154, 206, 212 ff., 223
  "ABC," 211
  "After the Chinese," 211
  "American Sketches," 209
  "Anniversaries," 206
  "Anthony St. Blues," 208
  "In Bertram's Garden," 208
  "Beyond the Hunting Woods," 207
  "Childhood," 212
  "Counting the Mad," 208
  Departures, 211
  "Early Poems," 209
  "First Death," 212
  "For a Freshman Reader," 210
  "From a Notebook," 211
  From a Notebook, 206
  "From Bad Dreams," 212
  "'The Furies'—for certain reviewers," 216
  "Girl Sitting Alone at Party," 210
  "Ladies by Their Windows," 208
  "Landscape with Little Figures," 207
  "Lethargy," 211
  "A Local Storm," 210
  A Local Storm, 206, 209, 272
  "Lorcaesques," 211
  "Love's Stratagem," 208
  "Luxury" 211
  "Memo from the Desk of X," 210
  "Memories of the Depression Years," 212
  "The Metamorphosis," 207

"The Missing Person," 210
"Narcissus at Home," 210
Night Light, 212
The Old Bachelor and Other Poems, 206
"On a Painting by Patient B," 208
"On the Death of Friends in Childhood," 207
"Poem for a Survivor," 210
"Portraits," 211
"Preface" to The Collected Poems of Weldon Kees, 154
"The Return of Alcestis," 216
Selected Poems, 206
"Sestina on Six Words by Weldon Kees," 207
Sixteen Poems, 210
"Song," 207
"Sonnet about P.," 208
"Sonnet: An Old-Fashioned Devil," 211
"Sonnet to My Father," 207
"Southern Gothic," 213
"Speaking of Islands," 207
"The Summer Anniversaries," 212
The Summer Anniversaries, 207-208
"Sunday Afternoon in Buffalo, Texas," 212
The Sunset Maker: Poems/Stories/A Memoir, 206
"The Thin Man," 210
"The Tourist from Syracuse," 210
"Things," 211
"Three Odes," 211
"Thus," 209
"To a Ten-Months Child," 207
"To My Mother," 209
"To Satan in Heaven," 208
"To Waken a Small Person," 209
"Tremayne," 206
Tremayne: Four Poems, 212
"Two Blues," 212
"Two Songs from Don Juan in Hell," 212
"Uncollected Poems," 211-212
"Unflushed Urinals," 212
"Variations on a Theme by James," 208
"A Winter Ode," 208

kabbal, kabbalist, 82
"Kaddish," 89
Franz Kafka, 153
    "Metamorphosis" 153, 207
Walter D. Kalaidjian, 50

INDEX 301

    Understanding Theodore Roethke, 50
katauta, 63-65, 67
Cathrael Kazin, 207
    "Donald Justice," 207
John Keats, 27
    "Ode on a Grecian Urn," 27
"Keeping the Lines Wet," 183
Weldon Kees, 154 *ff.*,
    "After the Trial, 207
    Collected Poems, 207
    The Fall of the Magicians, 155
    "One," of "Five Villanelles," 155
    "How to Be Happy: Installment 1053," 157
    The Last Man, 155
    Non-Verbal Communication, 155
    "Subtitle," 155
    "Variations on a Theme by Joyce," 155
John F. Kennedy, 220
Robert Kennedy, 109, 220
X. J. Kennedy, *Intro.*, 246
    Counter/Measures, Intro.
Richard Kenney, *Intro.*, 205
The Kenyon Review, 45, 250, 255, 256
Jack Kerouac, *Intro.*
Søren Kierkegaard, 48
Martin Luther King, Jr., 109, 127, 135, 140, 220
Galway Kinnell, 181
Carolyn Kizer, *Intro.*, 151 *ff.*, 186
    Knock Upon Silence, 151
    Mermaids in the Basement, 152
    Midnight Was My Cry: New and Selected Poems, 151
    The Nearness of You, Poems for Men, 152
    "Pro Femina," 151
    "Semele Recycled," 151
    The Ungrateful Garden, 151
    Yin, 151
Knock Upon Silence, 151, 266
"A Knothole in Spent Time," 95
koan, 64
Kenneth Koch, 194, 200
Arthur Koestler, 158
    The Ghost in the Machine, 158
Korean War, 83, 140
Edward Krickel, 95
    John Ciardi, 95
Judith Kroll, 122

   Chapters in a Mythology, The Poetry of Sylvia Plath, 122
Maxine Kumin, *Intro.*, 119 *ff.*, 120
  Halfway, 119,
  The Long Approach, 119
  "The Moment Clearly," 119
  The Nightmare Factory, 119
  The Privilege, 119
  Selected Poems 1960-1990, 119
Greg Kuzma, 232, 233, 235, 236
  "Dana Gioia and the Poetry of Money." 232

"Ladies by Their Windows," 208
Ladies' Home Journal, 256
The Lady in Kicking Horse Reservoir, 186
Laments, 171
Lamont Award, 206, 252
The Land of Unlikeness, 111
"Landscape with Little Figures," 207
Joseph Langland, 46
  Poet's Choice, 46
The $L=A=N=G=U=A=G=E$ Poets, *Intro.*, 19, 20, 190, 203
Deirdre Lashgari and Joanna Bankier editors, 139
  Women Poets of the World, 139
The Last and Lost Poems of Delmore Schwartz, 25
The Last Hero and Other Poems, 56
The Last Man, 155
Leaping Poetry, 159
Leaves of Grass, Intro,
Le Fou, 74
David Lehman. *Intro.*, 201, 202, 229
  Ecstatic Occasions, Expedient Forms, *Intro.*, 201
Brad Leithauser, *Intro.*
George S. Lensing, 62
  "Williams after the First Quarter-Century," 62
Julius Lester, 131
"Lethargy," 211
Lethe, 124, 125, 126
"A Letter from Crete to Delphi," 193
"Letter to New York," 35
"Letters to Dr. Y," 117-118
Denise Levertov, *Intro.*, 140, 144 *ff.*, 145, 146
  The Double Image, 144
  Footprints, 144, 145
  Here and Now, 144
  "Human Being," 145
  The Jacob's Ladder, 144

A Marigold from North Vietnam, 267
O Taste and See, 267
Out of the War Shadow, editor, 127, 140, 144
"Overheard over S. E. Asia," 145
Overland to the Island, 144, 267
"A Poem at Christmas, 1972, during the Terror-Bombing of North Vietnam,"144
With Eyes at the Back of Our Heads, 144

Philip Levine, 107
C. Day Lewis, 23
libretto, libretti, 128
A Life Distilled, see Gwendolyn Brooks and Gary Smith, 267
Life Studies, 29, 106, 113, 114
The Light Around the Body, 158, 268
"Like, This Is What I Meant!" 142
"The Lilacs," 33
line, lines, *Intro.*, 21-22, 24, 26-28, 32-33, 39-40, 45-46, 49-51, 72, 74, 79, 81, 84-85, 109-110, 119, 123-125, 129-130, 137-139, 141, 145, 147, 169, 170, 172-173, 177, 179, 180, 182, 183, 185, 188, 190-192, 196, 199-202, 206-212, 217-227, 219-221, 223, 225, 229, 231, 233-236, 239-244, 246, 247, 253
lineated prose, lineation, line-phrasing, *Intro.*, 17, 33, 35, 62, 65, 75, 81, 179, 206
The Lion and the Archer, 131
The Lion's Tail and Eyes, 167
Little Friend, Little Friend, 45, 46
little magazine, 29, 70, 115, 158, 175, 256
"A Little Poem," 221
liturgic, liturgics, 180
Live Another Day: Poems, 95
"Lives of the Great Composers," 229
The Lives of X, 264
Living on the Surface: New and Selected Poems, 214, 273
Local Assays, 187, 269
local colorist, 186
"Local Initiative," 242
"A Local Storm," 210
A Local Storm, 206, 209, 272
A Locked House, 265
logic, 33, 64, 65, 106, 158, 161, 168, 231
Logos, 71
The Long Approach, 119, 264

Henry Wadsworth Longfellow, 32
long hymnal stanza, 56
Long Live Man, 91
long renga, 66
Federico Garcia Lorca, 159, 174

"Lorcaesques," 211
Losses, 45
The Lost Son and Other Poems, 48
The Lost World, 45
The Love Bit and Other Poems, 81
"Love Calls Us to the Things of This World," 32
"Love Forgiven," 90
The Lovemaker, 226
Love Poems (Tentative Title), 195
"Love's Stratagem," 208
Loving a Woman in Two Worlds, 161
Amy Lowell, *Intro.*, 213
Amy Lowell Traveling Scholarship, 213
James Russell Lowell, 112
Robert Lowell, 2, 111 *ff.*, 22, 29, 61, 106, 109, 112, 206, 213, 245
    "Benito Cereno" (stage adaptation from Herman Melville), 114
    "Dear Sorrow 2," 113
    "Endecott and the Red Cross" (stage adaptation from Nathaniel Hawthorne), 114
    "Foreword" to Ariel, 121
    For Lizzie and Harriet, 114
    The Land of Unlikeness, 112
    "R. F. K.," 140
    Life Studies, 29, 106, 113, 114
    "Memories of West Street and Lepke," 113
    The Mills of the Cavanaughs, 112
    "Mr. Edwards and the Spider," 113
    "My Kinsman, Major Molineux," (stage adaptation from Nathaniel Hawthorne), 115
    The Old Glory, 115
    "Satan's Confession," 113
lullabye, lullabies, 61
Lunch Poems, 195
"Luxury," 211
lyric, lyric poetry, *Intro.*, 59, 84, 85, 98, 100, 101, 102, 106, 114, 138, 139, 142, 159, 164, 165, 166, 168, 175, 179, 184, 200, 203, 209, 212, 220, 221, 226, 230, 236

Robie Macauley, 255
John D. MacDonald, 210
Archibald Macleish, 190, 200
    "Ars Poetica," 190, 210
madsong, 116
magical realism, *Intro.*
"Making a Farm: A Literary Biography," 159
Making Certain It Goes On, 186

Karl Malkoff, 36
    Crowell's Guide to Contemporary American Poetry, 36
Stéphane Mallarmé, 192, 194
"The Man-Moth," 36
"A Man's Voice," 94
Map of My Country, 93
"March in Washington Against the Vietnam War," 144
A Marigold from North Vietnam, 144
Publius Vergilius Maro (Virgil), 236
"Marriage," 68
"Marriage Contract," 170
Wendy Martin, 148
    An American Triptych, 148
"Martin Luther King, Jr.," 140
Willard J. Martz. 48
The Achievement of Theodore Roethke, 48
Maximus of Tyre, 71
Maximus Poems IV, V, VI, 70
Maximus Poems: Volume Three, 71
The Maximus Poems, 70
The Maximus Poems of Charles Olson, 70
"Maximus, to Gloucester, Letter 15," 71, 72
"The May Day Dancing," 40
Phyllis McGinley, 254
Robert McGovern and Richard Snyder, editors, 127
    60 on the 60's, 127
Marshall McLuhan, 129
"The Meaning of Meaninglessness," 203
Meditations in an Emergency, 195
David Meltzer, 82
    "Abulafia," 82
    The Name Selected Poetry 1973 1983, 82
    Poems, with Donald Schenker, 82
    "Tohu," 82Herman Melville, 145, 178
    "Benito Cereno," 114
"Memo from the Desk of X," 210
"Memories of the Depression Years," 212
"Memories of West Street and Lepke," 113
"A Memory of My Friend," 41
Mermaids in the Basement, 152
James Merrill, 22
W. S. Merwin, 22
Messiah, messianic, 82, 83, 89, 223
"Metamorphosis," 207
"The Metamorphosis," 207
metaphysical, 41, 59, 108, 200, 225

Robert Mezey, 89, 116, 223*ff.*, 252, 254
    "A Coffee-House Lecture," 223, 226
        Evening Wind, 227
        The Lovemaker, 223
        Naked Poetry: Recent American Poetry in Open Forms, editor,
            with Stephen Berg, 226
        The New Naked Poetry, editor, with Stephen Berg, 226
    "Owl," 227
The Michigan Quarterly Review, 132, 191
Mid-Century American Poets, 38, 91
The Middle Passage, 56
Midnight Was My Cry: New and Selected Poems, 151
military-industrial complex, 53, 55
Edna St. Vincent Millay, *Intro.*, 39
Arthur Miller, 245, 248
Henry Miller, 89
Raeburn Miller, 251
Ralph J. Mills, 29
    Richard Eberhart, 29
The Mills of the Cavanaughs, 112
Milton, 33
Earl Miner and Robert H. Brower, 63
    Japanese Court Poetry, 63
"The Minuet: Sidling Around Student Poems," 182
"Mirror," 122
Mirrors, 75
Mirrors and Windows, 39
The Miscellany, 237
"The Missing Person," 210
The Mississippi Review, Intro.
"Mr. Edwards and the Spider," 113
Modern American and Modern British Poetry, 255
Modern and Contemporary Afro-American Poetry, 138, 139
Modernism, 22, 23, 179
"The Moment Clearly," 119
mondo, 63, 64
Marianne Moore, *Intro.*, 35
Maria K. Mootry, 137
    A Life Distilled, co-edited with Gary Smith, 137
      "'Down the Whirlwind of Good Rage': An Introduction to
        Gwendolyn Brooks," 137
"Morning Song," 121
Morton Marcus, 251
Mosaic, 25
mote, motes, 69, 211
Moving Inward, 160,

"Muher," 63
"Music of Changes," 196
"My Agent Says," 242
The Mystery of Lost Shoes, 172
mysticism, 86
mythology, mythopoeia, *Intro.*, 28, 36, 41, 62, 70, 122, 149, 151, 164, 181-182, 184

Naked Angels: The Lives and Literature of the Beat Generation, 89
Naked Poetry: Recent American Poetry in Open Forms, 226
The Name Selected Poetry 1973 1983, 82
The Narcissiad, 242,
"Narcissus," 28
"Narcissus at Home," 210
narration, narrator, 44, 57, 104, 121, 124, 136, 145, 154, 181, 194, 235
narrative, narrative poetry, *Intro.*, 46, 59, 95, 98, 101, 106, 109, 119, 121, 124-126, 135, 136, 144, 145, 151, 153, 159, 164, 166, 177, 178, 179, 185, 189, 190, 200, 221,
narrative voice, 109, 121
Ogden Nash, 233
Richard Nason, 200, 203
    The Ballad of the Dollar Hotel and Other Poems, 200
    "Foreword to Kelly's Grandchild," 200
The Nation, 45
National Book Award, 32, 35, 158
National Endowment for the Arts, 236
national student strike of 1970, 127
natural poetry, *Intro.*
nature of man, 67
nature of the universe, 67
The Nearness of You, Poems for Men, 152
"The Need for Poetics: Some Thoughts on Robert Bly," 158
"A Negro Dreams of Rivers," 128
Howard Nemerov, *Intro.*, 30, 39 *ff.*,
    "Angel and Stone," 41
    The Collected Poems, 39
    "Creation Myth on a Moebius Strip," 41
    "The Companions," 43-44
    "The Goose Fish," 44
    A Howard Nemerov Reader, 39
    The Image of the Law, 39
    "The May Day Dancing," 10-41
    "A Memory of My Friend," 42
    Mirrors and Windows, 39
    "A Primer of the Daily Round," 39, 40

The Salt Garden, 39
"The View from an Attic Window," 43
neoclassical, Neoclassical period, 22, 223, 251
neo-Elizabethan, 108
neo-Emersonian, 164
Neoformalism, *Intro.*, 201, 205 *ff.*, 232
Neon, 250, 256, 257,
Pablo Neruda, 158, 174
The Nesting Ground, 185
The New American Poetry 1945-1960, 70, 77, 141, 195
New and Collected Poems, 32
The New Book of Forms, 20, 163
The New Criticism, New Critics, 46, 163
New England Review / Bread Loaf Quarterly, 239
New Expansive Poetry: Theory, Criticism, History, 239
New Formalism (neo-formalism), *Intro.*, 228
The New Life, 171
The New Naked Poetry, 89, 226
New Negro Poets, 137
The New Poets: American and British Poetry Since World War II, 74, 181
The New Poets of England and America, [First Selection], 198
The New Poets of England and America, Second Selection, see
    Bibliography
"A New Reality Is Better Than a New Movie!" 141
The New Republic, 157
News of the Universe: Poems of Two-Fold Consciousness, 159
New Spaces: Poems 1975-1983, 81
New Testament, 129
"New Year Letter," 23
The New Yorker, 56, 123, 228, 256
The New Yorker Book of Poems, 56, 123
New York School, *Intro.*, 190, 194, 202
The New York Times Book Review, 115
The Night-Blooming Cereus, 131
Night Hurdling, 164
Night Light, 212
The Nightmare Factory, 119
Night Watch, 228
Nikal Seyn, Decoration Day: A Poem and a Play, 56
nonce form, 100, 165, 202, 244
Non-Verbal Communication, 155
North and South, 35
The North Well, 56, 59
"Notes from the Agent on Earth: How to be Human," 220
"Note on Poetry in San Francisco," 86
"Notes on Poems," 123

"Not Ideas about the Thing but the Thing Itself," 69, 190
No Word of Farewell, Selected Poems: 1970-2000, 247
Naomi Shihab Nye, 242
    Texas Poets in Concert: A Quartet, 242

Joyce Carol Oates, *Intro.*,
Objectivism, Objectivists, 62
"O Daedalus, Fly Away Home," 136
"Ode: Intimations of Immortality...," 21
"Ode on a Grecian Urn," 27
Odes, 39, 195
"Of Imagery," 63
Of Poetry and Power, 127
Of Solitude and Silence: Writings on Robert Bly, 158
"Of the Sun and the Moon," 22
Frank O'Hara, 198m 199 *ff,*,
    A City Winter, and Other Poems, 195
    The Collected Poems, 195
    Oranges, 195
    Jackson Pollock, 195
    "June 2, 1958." 197
    Love Poems (Tentative Title), 195
    Lunch Poems, 195
    Meditations in an Emergency, 195
    Odes, 195
    "Personism: A Manifesto," 194
    Robert Motherwell, 195
    Second Avenue, 195
    Try! Try! 195
Frank O'Hara, 196, 198, 199, 201
Myron O'Higgins, 131
    The Lion and the Archer, with Robert Hayden, 131
"Old Apple Trees," see 106
The Old Bachelor and Other Poems, 206
The Old Glory, 114
"Old Man Goes South Again Alone," 24
Old Testament, 129, 238
Charles Olson, *Intro.*, 35, 62, 70 *ff.*, 77, 81, 141, 263
    Maximus Poems IV, V, VI, 70
    Maximus Poems: Volume Three, 70
    The Maximus Poems, 70
    The Maximus Poems of Charles Olson, 70
    "Maximus, to Gloucester, Letter 15,"
    "Projective Verse," 62, 71, 73, 74
    "A Retrospect," 73
Olson's Push: Origin, Black Mountain, and Recent American Poetry, 71,

73
"On a Painting by Patient B," 208
"On the Death of Friends in Childhood," 207
"Once More, The Round," 51
"One," of "Five Villanelles," 155
The Only World There Is, 220, 225
Open House, 48
The Opening of the Field, 78, 79
Joel Oppenheimer, 81 *ff.*
    The Dancer, 81
    The Dutiful Son, 81
    "Grown Alba," 81
    In Time: Poems, 1962-1968, 81
    The Love Bit and Other Poems, 81
    New Spaces: Poems 1975-1983, 81
Opportunity, 131
"Opposition," 31
oracle, oracular, 35, 71
Oranges, 195
"Order Clearly Asking," 94
organic form, organic poetry 89, 181
Origin, 70, 71
Gregory Orr, 158
    "The Need for Poetics: Some Thoughts on Robert Bly," 158
orthodox, orthodoxy, 22, 78, 228
David Ossman, 250 ff.
    "American Poetry," 1961, 258
    "The Sullen Art," 250 ff.
    The Sullen Art: Interviews by David Ossman with Modern American Poets, 250
Alicia Ostriker, 123, 146
    Stealing the Language: The Emergence of Women's Poetry in America, 146
O Taste and See, 144
Other Skies, 95
Ouroboros, 41
"Out for a Night," 185
Out of the War Shadow, Intro., 144
Over All the Obscene Boundaries, 85
"Overheard over S. E. Asia," 145
Overland to the Island, 144
Wilfred Owen, 45
"Owl," 227

Robert Pack, 197
    co-editor with Donald Hall and Louis Simpson, *The New Poets of*

England and America, [First Selection], 197
Ron Padgett, and David Shapiro editors, 193
    An Anthology of New York Poets, 193
pantoum, 201, 242
"Pantoum," 201, 202, 203
Paragraphs, 171
The Paris Review, 228
Thomas Parkinson, ed., 86
    Essays on the Beat, 86
parodic, parody, 67, 85, 171, 209, 223, 239, 246
Part of Nature, Part of Us, 118, 121
Partisan Review, 45
"Passages," 78
Passage Selected Poems 1943-1978, 56
Paterson, 61
pathetic fallacy, 68, 145
Patterns of Poetry, Intro., 213, 222
Sherman Paul, 73
    Olson's Push: Origin, Black Mountain, and Recent American Poetry, 71, 73
Molly Peacock, *Intro.*, 205
Thomas Love Peacock, 53
period style, Intro, 20, 21, 23, 241
David Perkins, 21
    A History of Modern Poetry, 21
Marjorie Perloff, 196
    Frank O'Hara: Poet Among Painters, 196
"Personism: A Manifesto," 194
Paul Petrie, 107
Robert Phillips, 25
    The Last and Lost Poems of Delmore Schwartz, 25
Pablo Picasso, 196
"Picketing the Zeitgeist Picket," 232
Pictures of the Gone World, see Ferlinghetti, 84
"The Pit," 48
A Place to Stand, 124
plainstyle, see American Plainstyle
Sylvia Plath, 121 *ff.*
    "Amnesiac," 123-126, 133
    "The Applicant," 121
    Ariel, 121, 123, 126
    The Bell Jar, 121
    The Collected Poems, 121, 122
    The Colossus, 121
    Crossing the Water, 121
    "Daddy," 123

"Mirror," 122
"The Princess and the Goblins," 122
"The Rival," 121
Winter Trees, 121
Plate, Platonic, *Intro.*, 48, 61, 71, 163
Edgar Allan Poe, 34
Eureka, 34
"A Poem at Christmas, 1972, during the Terror-Bombing of North Vietnam," 144
"Poem for a Survivor," 210
Poems (Auden), 23
Poems, (Berryman), 108
Poems, (Karl Shapiro), 53
Poems, (Meltzer and Schenker), 82
Poems from Italy, Dana Giois, editor and translator, with William Jay Smith, 228
Poems, New and Selected, 29
Poems 1957-1967, 163
Poems 1943-1956, 32
Poems of a Jew, 53
Poems: North and South - A Cold Spring, 35
Poems Selected and New, 1950-1974, 149
Poems, with Donald Schenker, 82
The Poems (Ashbery), 198
The Poems of Richard Wilbur, 32
"The Poet," *Intro.*, 71, 94, 142
poetic diction, 19 *ff.* 22, 108, 109, 197
poetic prose, Intro.
Poetry (Chicago magazine), 52, 54, 163, 228, 258
Poetry and the Age, 36
Poetry: An Introduction Through Writing, 63
The Poetry and Poetics of Amiri Baraka: The Jazz Aesthetic, 141
"The Poetry of Protest," 79
The Poetry Reviews, 1924-1944, 112
"Poetry: Dissidents from Schools," 188
"Poetry: Schools of Dissidents," 75
Poet's Choice, 46
"The Poet's Masks," 213
The Poet's Pack, 25
Poets for Peace, 127
Poets of Today, 162
Poets Teaching, 182
Jackson Pollock, 195
"the poor man's Pound," 71
Alexander Pope, 22, 238
"An Essay on Man," 22

"Portraits" 211
Paul Portuges, 88
    The Visionary Poetics of Allen Ginsberg, 88
Post-Modernism, *Intro.*, 25, 156
Post-Romanticism, *Intro.*
Ezra Pound, *Intro.*, 61, 62, 63, 71, 72, 73, 79, 84, 111, 143, 189, 202
    The Cantos, 71, 79
Prairie Schooner, 183
Praise to the End! 49
prayer, prayers, *Intro.*, 61, 180, 214
Preface to a Twenty-Volume Suicide Note, *Intro.*, 140
"Preface" to *The Collected Poems of Weldon Kees*, 154
pre-Modernism, *Intro.*,
pre-Romantic, *Intro.*,
"Previously Uncollected Poems," 49
priest poetry, *Intro.* 83
"A Primer of the Daily Round," 39
The Princess and the Goblins," 122
The Privilege, 119
"Pro Femina," 151
prophecy, prophet, 27, 32, 33, 61, 62, 77, 79, 80, 82, 91, 164, 239
professional poet, *Intro.*, 61
"Projective Verse," 62, 73, 74
Projectivist Movement / School, 74, 141
"Prospectus for Visitors," 173
"Protocols," 47
Proverbial Philosophy, 31, 32
pseudonym, 101
public poetry, 245
Pulitzer Prize, 32, 35, 100, 108, 138, 212, 254
The Pure Clear Word: Essays on the Poetry of James Wright, 166
Ernie Pyle, 45

quatorzain, 208
quatrain, 25, 26, 27, 32, 39, 49, 50, 51, 56, 74, 119, 125, 137, 165, 182, 201, 202, 219, 220, 234, 246
queertalk, 197
"The Quest" 168
quintet, 46, 65

"Randolph Field, 1938," 247
John Crowe Ransom, *Intro.*, 43, 48, 111, 167, 211, 212, 228, 264
    "Blue Girls," 208
    "Captain Carpenter," 207, 208
reaction against Modernism, 23
Recital, 213

"Red cheeked boyfriends" 90
Rejoice in the Lamb, 33
"Rejuvenation," 26
Remains, 106
renga, renga chain, 66, 67
The Rescued Year, 181
"A Retrospect," 73
"The Return of Alcestis," 212
Kenneth Rexroth, *Intro.*, 53, 62, 70, 71
Charles Reznikoff, 62
"R. F. K.," 140
Adrienne Rich, 151 *ff.*
    "Aunt Jennifer's Tigers," 151
    A Change of World, 151
    "Compulsory Heterosexuality and Lesbian Existence," 152
    "Foreword" to The Works of Anne Bradstreet, 152
    Poems Selected and New, 1950-1974, 153
    "Sources," 153
    Your Native Land, Your Life, 153
Richard Eberhart, 29
"Richard Hugo: Getting It Right," 187
Richard Wilbur, 33
The Right Madness on Skye, 186
Rainer Maria Rilke, 158
Arthur Rimbaud, 192, 200
Riot, 137
"The Rival" 121
Larry Rivers, 195
Robert Creeley, 74
Robert Motherwell, 195
Edwin Arlington Robinson, *Intro.*, 32, 243, 247
Theodore Roethke, *Intro.*, 24, 46, 48 *ff.*, 108, 158, 162, 163, 164, 168,
    188, 190, 263
    Collected Poems, 49
    "I Cry Love!" 48
    Open House, 48
    The Lost Son and Other Poems, 48
    "Once More, The Round," 52
    "The Pit," 48
    Praise to the End!, 49
    "Previously Uncollected Poems," 49
    "The Shape of the Fire," 51
    "The Visitant," 24
    "The Waking," 49
    "What Can I Tell My Bones?" 48
    Words for the Wind, 48

Theodore Roethke, 48
Romantic, Romanticism, Romantic style, *Intro.*, 21, 22, 30, 32, 33, 48, 61, 156, 158, 164, 191, 200, 251
rondeau, 123, 241
rondine, 240
M. L. Rosenthal, 74, 75, 90
    The New Poets: American and British Poetry Since World War II, 74, 75, 90, 144
Jerome Rothenberg, 83
    White Sun, Black Sun, 83
Roving Across Fields, 183
Ruined Cities, 173
"Runagate Runagate," 134, 135
A Run of Jacks, 186
Vern Rutsala, 170 *ff.*,
    Backtracking, 172
    "The Empty House," 172
    The Harmful State, 171
    The Journey Begins, 171
    Laments, 171
    "Marriage Contract," 170
    The Mystery of Lost Shoes, 172
    The New Life, 171
    Paragraphs, 171
    "Prospectus for Visitors," 173
    Ruined Cities, 173
    Selected Poems, 173
    Small Songs, 173
    "Sunday," 174
    Walking Home from the Icehouse, 171
    The Window, 174
    "X's Poems," 174

P. K. Saha, 127
Saint Judas, 167
The Salt Garden, 39
Carl Sandburg, *Intro.*, 256
San Francisco Poetry Center, 77
San Francisco School, *Intro.* 53, 77
The Secret Meaning of Things, 86
Percy Bysshe Shelley, 191
Siegfried Sassoon, 45
"Satan's Confession," 113
satire, satirical, satirics, 53, 170, 180, 200, 210, 241, 237, 238, 239
saturation, 132
The Saturday Evening Post, 256

The Saturday Review, 95
"Saturday's Child," 28
"The Saxophone," 25
scat, scatting, 142-143
schema, 28, 35, 50, 59, 84, 134, 218, 221, 226, 232
Donald Schenker, 82
    Poems, with David Meltzer, 82
Paul Schwaber and Erwin A. Glikes, editors,
    Of Poetry and Power, 127
Delmore Schwartz, *Intro.*, 25 *ff*, 109
    "Aubade," 25
    "Automobile," 25
    "Darkness," 25
    "E. A. P. — A Portrait," 25
    "George Washington Bridge, December 1929," 25
    In Dreams Begin Responsibilities, 26
    The Last and Lost Poems of Delmore Schwartz, 25
    "Narcissus," 28
    "Saturday's Child," 28
    "The Saxophone," 26
    Summer Knowledge: New and Selected Poems 1938-1958, 28
Gertrude Schwartz, née Buckman, 25, 26
The Sea Faring and Other poems, 56
Jan Epton Seale, 242
    Texas Poets in Concert: A Quartet, 242
seasonal element, 67
Second Avenue, 196
The Second Man and Other Poems, 56
Seed Leaves, 32
Seems Like Old Times, 107
Selected Poems (Ashbery), 199
Selected Poems (Brooks), 137
The Selected Poems (Ciardi), 98
Selected Poems (Hayden), 131
Selected Poems (Holmes), 94
Selected Poems (Jarrell), 46
Selected Poems (Justice), 206
Selected Poems 1960-1990 (Kumin), 119
Selected Poems (Rutsala), 170
Selected Poems (Snodgrass), 106
Selected Poetry (Baraka), 140
Semele, 151
"Semele Recycled," 151
senryu, 67, 69
Sephardic-American literature, 83
sestina, 37

"Sestina," 37
"Sestina on Six Words by Weldon Kees," 207
sensory level, 22, 26, 28, 50, 58, 75, 97, 125, 155, 168, 169, 196, 220, 221, 225, 226, 231, 244
sentence, sentences, 21, 22, 68, 69, 78, 81, 85, 90, 162, 170, 171, 189, 218, 231
sequence, 29, 50, 66, 70, 100, 112, 117, 126, 139, 171, 212
The Seventies, 158
77 Dream Songs, 109
The Sewanee Review, 162, 205, 238
Anne Sexton, *Intro.*, 116 *ff.*, 117, 118, 119, 160, 169
    All My Pretty Ones, 116
    The Book of Folly, 118
    "Letters to Dr. Y," 117, 118
    To Bedlam and Part Way Back, 116
    Words for Doctor Y, 117
Linda Gray Sexton, 118
    "Editor's Note," [to Words for Doctor Y by Anne Sexton], 118
Shall We Gather at the River, 168, 170
"The Shape of the Fire," 51
David Shapiro, 203
    John Ashbery: An Introduction to the Poetry, 203
    "The Meaning of Meaninglessness," 203
David Shapiro and Ron Padgett, editors, 193
    An Anthology of New York Poets, 193
Karl Shapiro, 53 *ff.*, 147, 174, 192, 227
    The Bourgeois Poet, 53
    Collected Poems 1940-1978
    "Death of a Student," 54
    Essay on Rime, 53
    "The Fly," 54
    Poems, 53
    Poems of a Jew, 53
    Trial of a Poet, 53
    V-Letter and Other Poems, 53
    White-Haired Lover, 53
"The Shark's Parlor," 164
Robert B. Shaw, 79
    American Poetry Since 1960, 79
    "The Poetry of Protest," 79
"The Sheep Child," 164
"Shop Talk," 73
A Short History of American Poetry, 197
short renga (tanrenga), 66
Silence in the Snowy Fields, 160
Leonard Silver, 127

Louis Simpson, *Intro.*, 174, 197
    co-editor with Donald Hall and Robert Pack, *New Poets of England and America*, [first selection], 197
"Sir Thomas More," 242
"Sitting in a Small Screenhouse on a Summer Morning," 168
Sixteen Poems, 211
The Sixties, 158
60 on the 60s, 127
Edmund Skellings, 251
John Skelton, 133
Robin Skelton, editor, 186
    Five Poets of the Pacific Northwest, 186
Sleeping in the Woods, 184
"Sleeping Out at Easter," 163
De Villo Sloan, 203
Small Songs, 171
Christopher Smart, 22, 242
    "Hymn to the Supreme Being," 22
    "Of Geoffrey, My Cat," 242
    "Of the Sun and the Moon," 22
    Rejoice in the Lamb, 33
Dave Smith, 187
    "Richard Hugo: Getting Right," 187
    Local Assays, 187
    The Pure Clear Word: Essays on the Poetry of James Wright, 166
Gary Smith, 137, 167
    A Life Distilled, co-edited with Maria K. Mootry, 137
W. D. Snodgrass, *Intro.*, 29, 93, 100 *ff.*, 108, 110, 114, 115, 116, 122, 206, 250
    After Experience, 106
    "Afterword," 106
    "April Inventory," 99-104
    The Fuehrer Bunker: A Cycle of Poems in Progress, 101, 106
    "Heart's Needle," 100
    Heart's Needle, 29, 100, 101, 106, 206
    If Birds Build with Your Hair, 106
    A Locked House, 106
    "*Old Apple Trees,*" 106
    Remains, 101
    Selected Poems, 106
    "Song," 100
    "These Trees Stand...," 106
Gary Snyder, 107
Richard Snyder, and Robert McGovern, editors,
    60 on the 60's, 127
social poetry, *Intro.*

"Soledad," 135
Carl Solomon, 90
So Long at the Fair, 213
Someday, Maybe, 181
Something to Say, 61
"Song," (Justice), 207
"Song," (Snodgrass), 100
"A Song for the Middle of the Night," 165-166
Songs of Experience, 22
sonic level, 22, 26, 50, 58, 102, 123, 124, 179, 183, 189, 215,
       223, 226, 244
sonnet, 25, 39, 179, 207, 211, 212, 227
       English sonnet, 39, 212
"Sonnet," 33
"Sonnet about P.", 208
"Sonnet: An Old-Fashioned Devil," 211
"Sonnet VIII (Third Series)," 193-194
"Sonnet to My Father," 207
"The Soughing Wind," 67
"Sources," 149
"Southern Gothic," 213
The Southern Review, 162
spareness, 67
"Speaking of Islands," 207
Spirit Reach, 140
split-line, 164
Spring and All, 69
Stephen Spender, 23, 107, 112
Spontaneity, 67
Radcliffe Squires, 132, 191 *ff.*
       Cornar, 191
       Fingers of Hermes, 191
       "A Letter from Crete to Delphi," 193
       "Summer Storms," 191
       Where the Compass Spins, 191
Jean Stafford, 112
William Stafford, *Intro.*, 23, 168, 179, 180, 181 *ff.*, 187
       "Adults Only," 23
       Allegiances, 181
       Down in My Heart, 183
       "Keeping the Lines Wet," 183
       "The Minuet: Sidling Around Student Poems," 182
       The Rescued Year, 181
       Roving Across Fields, 183
       Someday, Maybe, 181
       Stories that Could Be True: New and Collected Poems, 181

"Traveling Through the Dark," 182
Traveling Through the Dark, 182
West of Your City, 181
Writing the Australian Crawl: Views on the Writer's Vocation, 181
"Stars," 134
State University of New York at Buffalo, 70, 74, 140, 203
Donald Barlow Stauffer, 197
    A Short History of American Poetry, 197
"Staying Alive," 185
Staying Alive, 184
Stealing the Language: The Emergence of Women's Poetry in America, 146
Timothy Steele, 239
Gertrude Stein, *Intro.*, 208
Stephen Stepanchev, 45, 77
    American Poetry Since 1945, 45, 77
Wallace Stevens, *Intro.*, 44, 61, 69, 189, 190, 191, 194, 202
    "Not Ideas about the Thing but the Thing Itself," 69, 190
    "Thirteen Ways of Looking at a Black Bird," 69
Anne Stevenson, 35
    Elizabeth Bishop, 35
Stories that Could Be True: New and Collected Poems, 181
Mark Strand, 167
stream-of-consciousness, 124
A Street in Bronzeville, 137
street poetry, 86
Style and Authenticity in Postmodern Poetry, 179
"Subtitle," 155
"Such Different Wants," 161
Richard P. Sugg, 160
    Robert Bly, 160
"The Sullen Art," 198, 249
Summer, 228
"The Summer Anniversaries," 212
The Summer Anniversaries, 207, 208
Summer Knowledge, 28
"Summer Storms," 193
"Sunday," 174
"Sunday Afternoon in Buffalo, Texas," 212
The Sunset Maker: Poems/Stories/A Memoir, 206
surreal, surrealism, *Intro.*, 36, 45, 46, 62, 86, 124, 153 *ff.*, 154, 156, 157, 158, 159, 164, 170, 173, 174, 179, 197, 208, 211, 212
The Suspect in Poetry, 163
Sutra, 180, 195
Syllogism, 64
symbol, symbolic, *Intro.*, 22, 28, 45, 46, 49, 58, 68, 113, 157, 158, 159, 219,

239
Symbolist, *Intro.*, 22, 26, 28, 68, 69, 139, 192
The Symbols, 93
sympathetic magic, 61
syntax , *Intro.*, 21 *ff.*, 28, 40, 59, 72, 76, 113, 173, 189, 191, 201, 221, 220
    abstract (musical) syntax, *Intro.*, 26, 59, 189, 190, 200, 201, 202, 203
    dramatic syntax, 189
    objective (narrative) syntax, 98, 189, 221
    subjective (egopoetic) syntax, 59, 98, 189, 221

Thom Tammaro, 183
tanka, 65-67
tanrenga (short renga), 66
"'Tan Ta Ra,' Cries Mars," 184
Stephen Tapscott, 62
    William Carlos Williams and the Modernist Whitman, 62
Alan Tate, 112, 113
    The Poetry Reviews, 1924-1944, 112
Edward Taylor, *Intro.*
Teleuton, 37
Alfred Tennyson, 96
Texas Poets in Concert: A Quartet, see R. S. Gwynn, with Jan Epton
    Seale, Naomi Shihab Nye, and William Virgil Davis, 242
"Theme and Variation," 133
"These Trees Stand...," 101
"The Thin Man" 210
"Things," 211
Things of This World, 32
"Thirteen Ways of Looking at a Black Bird," 69
31 Letters and 13 Dreams, 186, 188
Thirty-one Sonnets, 29
Dylan Thomas, 242, 247, 249
"Do Not Go Gentle into That Good Night," 249
"In My Craft or Sullen Art," 249
"Those Winter Sundays," 133-134
"Three Kinds of Pleasures," 160
"Three Odes," 211
"Three Views of the Young Poet," 239
"Thus," see Donald Justice, 209
Tibor de Nagy Gallery, 195, 199
Philip Timberlake, 169
Time, 84, 155
To a Blossoming Pear Tree, 169
"To a Ten-Months Child," 207
To Bedlam and Part Way Back, 116

To Disembark, 137
"A Toccata of Galuppi's," 129
"Todesfuge," 229
"To My Mother," 209
"To My Two Sons," 88
"To Satan in Heaven," 208
"To Waken a Small Person," 209
"The Tourist from Syracuse," 210
"Tradition and the Individual Talent," 73
Transcendental, Transcendentalism, 52, 62, 78
"Traveling Through the Dark," 182
Traveling Through the Dark, 182
Thomas Tranströmer, 158
"Tremayne," 206
Tremayne: Four Poems, 212
Trial of a Poet, 53
triversen, triversen stanza, 63, 66, 69
Try! Try!, 195
Frederick Goddard Tuckerman, 191-193
    The Complete Poems, 191
    "Sonnet VIII (Third Series)" 193
"A Tune in the Back of My Head," 229
Martin Farquhar Tupper, 33, 88
    Proverbial Philosophy, 32
Lewis Putnam Turco, *Intro.*, 63, 163, 238-239, 250, 252
    The Book of Forms, A Handbook of Poetics, 163
    First Poems, 163, 250, 252
    The New Book of Forms, 163
    "Of Imagery," 63
    Poetry: An Introduction Through Writing, 63
    Visions and Revisions of American Poetry, Intro.
    "The Year in Poetry, (1986)," 238-239
Alberta Turner, 182
    Poets Teaching, 182
"Two Blues," 212
Two Citizens, 169
"Two Songs from Don Juan in Hell," 212
"Two Villanelles," 242
typographical level, 81, 102, 123, 138, 215, 244
John Tytell, 89
    "Allen Ginsberg and the Messianic Tradition," 89
    Naked Angels: The Lives and Literature of the Beat Generation, 89

"Uncollected Poems," 211-212
"The Underground Stream," 163

Understanding Poetry, 162
Understanding Randall Jarrell, 45
Understanding Theodore Roethke, 50
Understanding the New Black Poetry, 129
"Unflushed Urinals," 212
The Ungrateful Garden, 151
"An Unknown Friend," 178
Louis Untermeyer, editor, 247
    Modern American and Mo, 247
"Up Rising," 79
Constance Urdang, 107

Paul Valéry, 224
Cesar Vallejo, 159
Mona Van Duyn, *Intro.*
"Variations on a Theme by James," 208
vatic poetry, 61, 62, 86
Helen Vendler, 118, 121
    Part of Nature, Part of Us, 118, 121
"A very Dove" 90
The Vestal Lady on Brattle and Other Poems, 91
Vietnam War, 140, 144, 146, 159
"The View from an Attic Window," 43
villanelle, 49, 122, 137, 155, 179, 208, 242, 245
James Vinson, editor, 186
    Contemporary Poets, Second Edition, 186
Virgil, (Publius Vergilius Maro), 230
"The Virginian Voyage," 113
vision, *Intro.*, 32, 33, 36, 42, 59, 61, 72, 77, 79, 82, 84, 86, 88, 89,
    92, 94, 121, 153, 155, 159, 170, 173, 174, 175, 176, 177, 179, 180, 209,
The Visionary Poetics of Allen Ginsberg, 88
Visions and Revisions of American Poetry, *Intro.*
"The Visitant," 24
V-Letter and Other Poems, 53
"Voice of America," 220
Robert von Hallberg, 70
Charles Olson: The Scholar's Art, 70

Hyatt. H. Waggoner, *Intro.*, 48, 52, 61, 114, 144, 163
    American Poets from the Puritans to the Present, 48, 52, 114,
        144
    Emerson As Poet, *Intro.*
David Wagoner, 168, 184 ff., 186
    "The Bad Uncle," 185
    Dry Sun, Dry Wind, 184
    First Light, 185

   The Nesting Ground, 184, 185
   "Out for a Night," 185
   A Place to Stand, 184
   Sleeping in the Woods, 184
   "Staying Alive," 184
   Staying Alive, 184
   "'Tan Ta Ra,' Cries Mars," 184
   Who Shall Be the Sun, 184
waka, 65
"The Waking," 48-49
Diane Wakoski, 83, 201, 227, 232
Walking Home from the Icehouse, 171
Walking to Sleep, 32
"The Wall," 79
War Resisters League, 127, 140, 144
War of the Anthologies, *Intro.*
Robert Penn Warren (and Cleanth Brooks, editors), 50, 162
   Conversations on the Craft of Poetry, 50
   Understanding Poetry, 162
The Waste Land, Intro., 189, 202
"The Waste Land Reconsidered," *Intro.*
WBAI-FM Pacifica Radio, 249
"The Weary Blues," 129
The Weary Blues, 129
Lew Welch, 107
"We Real Cool," 138
West Chester University Poetry Conference, 236
West of Your City, 181
Philip Whalen, 107
"What Can I Tell My Bones?" 48
"What's the Matter?" 23
What Thou Lovest Well Remains American, 186
John Hall Wheelock, editor, 162
   Poets of Today, 162
Where the Compass Spins, 191
White Center, 186
White-Haired Lover, 53
White Sun, Black Sun, 83
Walt Whitman, *Intro.*, 22, 33, 34, 48, 62, 63, 82, 83, 90, 128,
  132, 149, 187, 196, 197, 201, 239,
   Leaves of Grass, 34, 88, 196
   "The Return of the Heroes," 21
John Greenleaf Whittier, 32, 145
Who Shall Be the Sun, 184
Why God Permits Evil, 220
"Why They Love Us," 242

INDEX

Richard Wilbur, *Intro.*, 23, 32 *ff.*
    Advice to a Prophet, 32
    "The Aspen and the Stream," 32
    Ceremony, 32
    "Junk," 33
    "The Lilacs," 33
    "Love Calls Us to the Things of This World," 32
    "A Miltonic Sonnet for Mr. Johnson," 140
    New and Collected Poems, 32
    Poems 1943-1956, 32
    The Poems of Richard Wilbur, 32
    Seed Leaves, 32
    "Sonnet," 33
    Things of This World, 32
    Walking to Sleep, 32
The Wilderness and Other Poems, 56
William Carlos Williams and the Modernist Whitman, 62
"Williams after the First Quarter-Century," 62
Jonathan Williams, 81
Miller Williams, *Intro.*, 222 *ff.*,
    "The Associate Professor Delivers an Exhortation to His Failing Students," 214
    The Boys on their Bony Mules, 213
    A Circle of Stone, 213
    Contemporary Poetry in America, 213
    Distractions, 213
    "For Clement Long, Dead," 214
    Halfway from Hoxie, 213
    Imperfect Love, 213, 221
    "A Little Poem," 221
    Living on the Surface: New and Selected Poems, 214
    "Notes from the Agent on Earth: How to be Human," 220
    The Only World There Is, 213, 220
    Patterns of Poetry: An Encyclopedia of Forms, *Intro.*, 213, 222
    "The Poet's Masks," 213
    Recital, 213
    So Long at the Fair, 218
    "Voice of America," 225
    Why God Permits Evil, 218
William Carlos Williams, 61 ff.,
    "Chinese Nightingale," 69
    Collected Poems, 69
    "Epitaph," 66
    "Fire Spirit," 64-65
    "The Fool's Song," 64, 65
    "The Hunter," 63

>   *In the American Grain*, 61
>   "Introduction" to Allen Ginsberg's Howl and Other Poems, 88
>   "Marriage," 68
>   "Mujer," 63
>   *Paterson*, 61
>   *Something to Say*, 61
>   *Spring and All*, 69
>   "The Soughing Wind," 67

The Window, 174
"Winter Night," 55 ff.
"A Winter Ode," 208
Winter Trees, 123
Yvor Winters, 109
"Foreword," to The Complete Poems of Frederick Goddard Tuckerman 191-193
Christopher Wiseman, 223
"Witch Doctor," see Hayden
With Eyes at the Back of Our Heads, see Levertov
Women Poets of the World, 139
word-games 61
Words for Doctor Y, 118
"Words in the Mourning Time," 135
Words in the Mourning Time: Poems, 131
Words for Music, 228
Words for the Wind, 48
William Wordsworth, 21
> "Ode: Intimations of Immortality..." 21

World War I, 18, 45, 101
World War II, *Intro.*, 23, 24, 32, 39, 45, 46, 56, 72-74, 88, 101, 112,
> 144, 149, 160, 162, 181, 240, 241

James Wright, 159, 165, 166 ff., 167, 169, 254
> "At the Grave," 169
> *The Branch Will Not Break*, 167
> *Collected Poems*, 167
> *The Green Wall*, 167
> *The Lion's Tail and Eyes: Poems Written Out of Laziness and
>   Silence*, with William Duffy and Robert Bly, 167
> "The Quest," 168
> *Saint Judas*, 167
> *Shall We Gather at the River*, 168, 170
> "Sitting in a Small Screenhouse on a Summer Morning," 168
> "A Song for the Middle of the Night," 165
> *To a Blossoming Pear Tree*, 169
> *Two Citizens*, 169

Mary J. J. Wrinn, 26, 27
> *The Hollow Reed*, 25, 27

Writer's Digest, 181

"Writers' Forum," 132, 183, 210
writing arts, 55, 182; also see creative writing
Writing the Australian Crawl: Views on the Writer's Vocation, 185
Writing Poetry, 94

"X's Poems," 174

The Yale Review, 45
Yale Series of Younger Poets Award, 147, 199
"The Year in Poetry, (1986)," 245
William Butler Yeats, 23, 36, 73, 167, 200, 246
Yin, 151
Gary Youree, editor, 127
      Poets for Peace, 127
Your Native Land, Your Life, 149
Yugen, 257

Zen Buddhism, 64, 67
Zeus, 151
Maurice Zolotow, 25
Louis Zukofsky, 61, 74

PERMISSIONS INFORMATION

"John Ashbery" includes material from an earlier version by Lewis Turco titled "John Ashbery's Handbook Forms" that appeared in *The New Orleans Review*, xix:1, Spring 1992, used by permission of the editors of *The New Orleans Review*. Other material is from the Gale Research *Dictionary of Literary Biography Yearbook* "Year in Poetry" essays by Lewis Turco, 1983-86, reprinted by permission of Bruccoli Clark Layman.

"Amiri Baraka" was published as an essay by Lewis Turco titled "Amiri Baraka's Black Mountain" in *The Hollins Critic*, xxxi:3, June 1994, re-printed by permission of the editors of *The Hollins Critic*.

"John Berryman" includes material reprinted from Lewis Turco's essay titled "Of Laureates and Lovers" in *The Saturday Review*, l:41, October 14, 1967, reprinted by permission of Omni Publications International; other material by permission of Farrar, Straus & Giroux.

"Elizabeth Bishop" includes material reprinted by permission of Farrar, Straus & Giroux, New York City.

"Robert Bly" includes material from the Gale Research *Dictionary of Literary Biography Yearbook* "Year in Poetry" essays by Lewis Turco, 1983-86, reprinted by permission of Bruccoli Clark Layman.

"Richard Emil Braun" was originally published as an essay by Lewis Turco titled "Richard Emil Braun: A Narrator of Enigma" in *Modern Poetry Studies*, vii:3, Winter 1976, reprinted by permission of the editors of *Modern Poetry Studies*.

"Gwendolyn Brooks" includes the poem titled "We Real Cool," by Gwendolyn Brooks, from Blacks, © 1987, published by The David Company, Chicago, Illinois; reprinted by permission of Gwendolyn Brooks.

"A version of John Ciardi" was published as an essay by Lewis Turco titled "Ciardi the Taler" in *John Ciardi: Measure of the Man*, edited by Vince Clemente, from the University of Arkansas Press, Fayetteville, 1987, reprinted by permission of the Press. It includes material re-printed from the Gale Research *Dictionary of Literary Biography Yearbook* "Year in Poetry" essays by Lewis Turco, 1983-86, reprinted by permission of Bruccoli Clark Layman.

"Gregory Corso" includes material from Lewis Turco's review titled "Hitting It Lucky" in Voices, 173, 1960; reprinted by permission of the author.

"Louis O. Coxe" includes material reprinted from the Gale Research *Dictionary of Literary Biography Yearbook* "Year in Poetry" essays by Lewis Turco, 1983-86, reprinted by permission of Bruccoli Clark Lay-man.

"Robert Creeley" includes material from the Gale Research *Dictionary of Literary Biography Yearbook* "Year in Poetry" essays by Lewis Turco, 1983-86, reprinted by permission of Bruccoli Clark Layman.

A version of "James Dickey" was published as an essay titled "The Suspect in Criticism" in *The Mad River Review*, i:2, Spring-Summer 1965, reprinted by permission of the author, and it includes material from Lewis Turco's review titled "Hitting It Lucky" in Voices, 173, 1960; from his memoir titled "Ideologies: The Chronicle of a Conflict" in *Escarpments*, iv:1, Autumn 1983, and from the Gale Research *Dictionary of Literary Biography Yearbook* "Year in Poetry" essays by Lewis Turco, 1983-86, reprinted by permission of Bruccoli Clark Layman.

"Robert Duncan" includes material from the Gale Research *Dictionary of Literary Biography Yearbook* "Year in Poetry" essays by Lewis Turco, 1983-86, reprinted by permission of Bruccoli Clark Layman.

"Richard Eberhart" includes material reprinted from Lewis Turco's es-say titled "Eberhart at Eighty" in *The Sewanee Review*, xciii:1, Winter 1985, reprinted by permission of the editors of *The Sewanee Review*; from Lewis Turco's essay titled "Of Laureates and Lovers" in *The Saturday Review*, l:41, October 14, 1967, by permission of Omni Publica-tions International, and from the Gale Research *Dictionary of Literary Biography Yearbook* "Year in Poetry" essays by Lewis Turco, 1983-86, reprinted by permission of Bruccoli Clark Layman.

"Lawrence Ferlinghetti" contains material reprinted by permission of New Directions Corp., New York City, and material from the Gale Research *Dictionary of Literary Biography Yearbook* "Year in Poetry" es-says by Lewis Turco, 1983-86, reprinted by permission of Bruccoli Clark Layman.

"Allen Ginsberg" includes material from the Gale Research *Dictionary of Literary Biography Yearbook* "Year in Poetry" essays by Lewis Turco, 1983-86, reprinted by permission of Bruccoli Clark Layman.

"Dana Gioia," was originally published in *American Poets Since World War II*, Third Series, edited by R. S. Gwynn, Gale Research, Detroit, Michigan, 1992, reprinted by permission of Cengage Learning. It con-tains material controlled by Dana Gioia with agreement of the Graywolf Press, reprinted by permission of Dana Gioia, and other material from the Gale Research *Dictionary of Literary Biography Yearbook* "Year in Poetry" essays by Lewis Turco, 1983-86, reprinted by permission of Bruccoli Clark Layman.

"R. S. Gwynn" was originally published as an essay by Lewis Turco ti-tled "R. S. Gwynn: A Southern Melancholic" in *The Hollins Critic*, xxxix:1, February 2002. Reprinted by permission of the editors of *The Hollins Critic*.

Versions of "Robert Hayden," were originally published as "Angle of Ascent: The Poetry of Robert Hayden" in *The Michigan Quarterly Review*, xvi:2, Spring 1977, and in ELF: *Eclectic Literary Forum* as "The Poetry of Robert Hayden." Rights reverted to the author, Lewis Turco; reprinted with his permission.

Material regarding John Holmes in the introduction to Chapter Three: The Confessional Poets includes material from a review by Lewis Turco titled "Poets, and Others," in Voices, 176, 1961; by permission of the author.

"Langston Hughes" contains material reprinted from *Poetry: An Intro-duction through Writing* by Lewis Turco, Reston Publishing Co., Reston, Virginia, 1973, copyright reversion to the author. It also contains material controlled by Alfred A. Knopf of New York City which granted permission to reprint.

"Richard Hugo" includes material from "Five Poets of the Pacific Northwest" by Lewis Turco in American Weave, xxix:1, Spring-Summer 1965, reprinted by permission of the editors of *American Weave* and from the Gale Research *Dictionary of Literary Biography Yearbook* "Year in Poetry" essays by Lewis Turco, 1983-86, reprinted by permission of Bruccoli Clark Layman.

"Donald Justice" was published as "The Progress of Donald Justice" in *The Hollins Critic*, xxix:4, October 1992, reprinted by permission of the editors of *The Hollins Critic*.

Material included in "Weldon Kees" is reprinted by permission of the University of Nebraska Press.

"Carolyn Kizer" includes material from "Five Poets of the Pacific Northwest" by Lewis Turco in *American Weave*, xxix:1, Spring-Summer 1965, reprinted by permission of the editors of *American Weave*, and from the Gale Research *Dictionary of Literary Biography Yearbook* "Year in Poetry" essays by Lewis Turco, 1983-86, reprinted by permission of Bruccoli Clark Layman.

"Maxine Kumin" contains material from an essay by Lewis Turco titled "Poets, and Others" from *Voices*, 176, 1961, reprinted by permission of the author, and from the Gale Research *Dictionary of Literary Biography Yearbook* "Year in Poetry" essays by Lewis Turco, 1983-86, re-printed by permission of Bruccoli Clark Layman.

"Denise Levertov" contains material controlled, and permission to re-print granted, by New Directions, New York City, and material from the Gale Research *Dictionary of Literary Biography Yearbook* "Year in Poetry" essays by Lewis Turco, 1983-86, reprinted by permission of Bruccoli Clark Layman.

"Robert Lowell" contains material reprinted by permission of Farrar, Straus & Giroux, New York City.

Material included in "David Meltzer" is from the Gale Research *Dictionary of Literary Biography Yearbook* "Year in Poetry" essays by Lewis Turco, 1983-86, reprinted by permission of Bruccoli Clark Layman.

"Robert Mezey" is a shorter version of an essay by Lewis Turco titled "Robert Mezey: The Curve of His Return" in *The Hollins Critic*, xlviii:2, April 2011, used by permission of the editors of *The Hollins Critic*.

"Howard Nemerov" was originally published as "Howard Nemerov's Cosmos of the Ordinary" by Lewis Turco in *ELF: Eclectic Literary Forum*, iv:2, Summer 1994, reprinted by permission of the author.

"Frank O'Hara" contains material reprinted from "The Present State of American Poetry: The Abstract Poetry Movement" by Lewis Turco in *The New York Quarterly*, No. 51, 1993, by permission of the editors of *The New York Quarterly.*

"Charles Olson" contains material from the Gale Research *Dictionary of Literary Biography Yearbook* "Year in Poetry" essays by Lewis Turco, 1983-86, reprinted by permission of Bruccoli Clark Layman. Other materials are reprinted courtesy of the University of California Press.

Materials included in "Joel Oppenheimer" are from the Gale Research *Dictionary of Literary Biography Yearbook* "Year in Poetry" essays by Lewis Turco, 1983-86, reprinted by permission of Bruccoli Clark Lay-man. Other materials are reprinted by courtesy of the University of California Press.

"Sylvia Plath" contains material from the Gale Research *Dictionary of Literary Biography Yearbook* "Year in Poetry" essays by Lewis Turco, 1983-86, reprinted by permission of Bruccoli Clark Layman.

"Adrienne Rich" contains material from the Gale Research *Dictionary of Literary Biography Yearbook* "Year in Poetry" essays by Lewis Turco, 1983-86, reprinted by permission of Bruccoli Clark Layman.

"Jerome Rothenberg" contains material from the Gale Research *Dictionary of Literary Biography Yearbook* "Year in Poetry" essays by Lewis Turco, 1983-86, reprinted by permission of Bruccoli Clark Layman.

"Vern Rutsala" was published as an essay by Lewis Turco titled "Vern Rutsala's Surreal World" in *The Hollins Critic*," xliii:4, October 2006; reprinted by permission of *The Hollins Critic.*

"Delmore Schwartz" was originally published as an essay by Lewis Turco titled "Delmore Schwartz: The Wrinn Connection" in *American Poetry*, ii:3, Spring 1985, reprinted by permission of the author.

"Karl Shapiro" contains material from an essay titled "For Poets in Search of Poetry Prose-Wise," *Shenandoah*, xv:1, Autumn1963, used by permission of the author.

"W. D. Snodgrass" was originally published as an essay by Lewis Turco titled "The Poetics of W. D. Snodgrass" in *The Hollins Critic*, xxx:3, June 1993; reprinted by permission of the editors of *The Hollins Critic.*

"Radcliffe Squires" contains material from an essay by Lewis Turco titled "Fingers of Hermes" in *The Michigan Quarterly Review*, v:3, July 1966; rights reverted to the author, Lewis Turco.

"William Stafford" contains material from an essay by Lewis Turco ti-tled "Keeping the Lines Wet" in *Prairie Schooner*, Summer 1977, used by permission of the author, and from the Gale Research *Dictionary of Literary Biography Yearbook* "Year in Poetry" essays by Lewis Turco, 1983-86, reprinted by permission of Bruccoli Clark Layman.

"The Sullen Art of Lewis Turco" was originally published on-line in the web page *Poetics and Ruminations* on April 5, 2009; reprinted by per-mission of the author and proprietor, Lewis Turco.

"David Wagoner" contains material from essays by Lewis Turco titled "Five Poets of the Pacific Northwest" in *American Weave*, xxix:1, Spring-Summer 1965, and "Occasion I: David Wagoner" in *American Weave*, xxx:2, December 1966, reprinted by permission of the editors of *American Weave*.

Material included in "Richard Wilbur" was taken from the Gale Re-search *Dictionary of Literary Biography Yearbook* "Year in Poetry" es-says by Lewis Turco, 1983-86, reprinted by permission of Bruccoli Clark Layman.

"Miller Williams" was originally published in *The Hollins Critic*, xxvi:2, April 1989, reprinted by permission of the editors of *The Hollins Critic*.

Material included here regarding William Carlos Williams was published as an essay by Lewis Turco titled "Williams' Prosody" in *The Cloverdale Review*, 1992/93, reprinted by permission of the author; other material is from the Gale Research *Dictionary of Literary Biography Yearbook* "Year in Poetry" essays by Lewis Turco, 1983-86, reprinted by permission of Bruccoli Clark Layman.

Permission to use the poems in "James Wright" was granted by Mrs. James Wright and Wesleyan University Press.

www.ingramcontent.com/pod-product-compliance
Lightning Source LLC
Chambersburg PA
CBHW051350070526
44584CB00025B/3703